BEN & JOCK

OTHER BOOKS BY GERRY FEWSTER

The Social Agency

Being in Child Care: A Journey into Self

Expanding the Circle: Mental Health and the Community

ABOUT THE AUTHOR

Gerry Fewster, is a teacher, writer, and therapist. He lives in the Cowichan Valley on Vancouver Island. In partnership with his wife Judith, he works with individuals, couples, and families on relationship issues.

Ben & Jock

A Biography

by Gerry Fewster

OOLICHAN BOOKS
LANTZVILLE, BRITISH COLUMBIA, CANADA
2001

Canadian Cataloguing in Publication Data

Main entry under title:

Fewster, Gerry

Ben & Jock

ISBN 0-88982-202-6

1. Wong, Bennet, 1930– 2. McKeen, Jock, 1946– 3. PD Seminars.

4. Psychologists—Canada—Biography. I. Title.

BF109.W66F48 2001   150'.92'271   C2001-911496-6

We gratefully acknowledge the support of the Canada Council for the Arts
for our publishing program.

The Canada Council | Le Conseil des Arts
for the Arts | du Canada

Grateful acknowledgement is also made to the BC Ministry of Tourism, Small
Business and Culture for their financial support.

BRITISH
COLUMBIA
ARTS COUNCIL
Supported by the Province of British Columbia

We acknowledge the financial support of the Government of Canada
through the Book Publishing Industry Development Program for our
publishing activities.

Canadä

Published by
Oolichan Books
P.O. Box 10, Lantzville
British Columbia, Canada
V0R 2H0

Printed in Canada

To My Father, Tom Meadley Fewster

Acknowledgements

This book could not have been written without the many people who shared their thoughts and experiences with me, usually in very personal ways and, sometimes, in very challenging circumstances. And, throughout it all, the figures of Bennet Wong and Jock McKeen remained unflinchingly at the centre as I churned their lives into my words. Such trust: I could not have expected, or asked for, more.

My thanks to Clarys Tirel and Ellery Littleton for their early readings of the manuscript and to Ardith Conlin for all her literary and technical help. In particular, I would like thank my friend Carol Matthews and my wife Judith Burrows for their encouragement and love.

PROLOGUE

When Bennet Wong and Jock McKeen agreed that I should write a book about them and their work, I had no idea what form it might take. I had no story-line in mind and there were no themes that I felt compelled to flesh out. My only inspiration was the belief that, in some way, these two men were addressing the most profound issue that confronts us all—the matter of human relatedness.

I imagined myself shuttling between the roles of writer and psychologist, teasing out a story that was there to be told. But, as I picked my way through the early interviews, I began to realize that I could not conveniently bracket off the stuff of my own life. More and more, I found myself translating their experience into my own, never being quite sure where they ended and I began. I came to the conclusion that this is something that all serious biographers and historians must ultimately acknowledge and deal with. Striving for some semblance of objectivity, I stood back to review the process. Even in the documentation of the most basic "facts," it seemed that every question reflected *my* curiosity, every answer was filtered through *my* interpretations and every picture was imbued with *my* meanings. It was clear that my story would need to be grounded in the original—the subjective world of Bennet Wong and Jock McKeen. Yet I did not want to become a mere scribe, diligently documenting and reporting whatever they, or others, told me; I wanted more ownership than that. This is a delicate equation that calls for a special kind of collaboration between the actors and the story-teller. In this, my two central characters proved themselves to be patient, understanding and trusting collaborators. Together we agreed that my methodology would be essentially phenomenological and that, whatever tapestry was to be unfolded, I would be the weaver.

The project took far longer than I had anticipated, being interrupted by personal circumstances and a series of unexpected events. Between 1992 and 1999, I spent countless hours in the company of Bennet Wong and Jock McKeen and interviewed many of their friends, associates and family members. I also met with a number of people whose observations and opinions I considered to be relevant to the story. Each, in their own way, contributed to what follows.

There are places in the book where I have described, in some detail, the personal thoughts and feelings of some of these people. While this might be considered to be a departure from the purest traditions of biographical writing, I believe it to be essential in a work that attempts to explore the perceptual and emotional underpinnings of observable behavior. I would like the reader to know that, where this occurs, the information was gleaned from the individuals themselves and not simply from my own imagination. By the same token, there are places where I have created dialogue in situations where it would have been impossible for anyone to recall accurately exactly what was said at the time. In this regard, my intention was to personalize the context and I have done my utmost to preserve the integrity of both the characters and their circumstances.

—Gerry Fewster, July, 2001

CHAPTER ONE

On October 13, 1998, I received a telephone call from Linda Nicholls, manager of Haven by the Sea on Gabriola Island, British Columbia. "I know this is short notice but can you be in court tomorrow?" she asked.

"Well, of course," I answered. I would have gone in the first place but . . . "

"Yes, I know, but it might be a good idea after all. Ben and Jock could probably use as much support as they can get."

"Really. Is there anything I should know?"

"No, I don't think so. You'll recognize a lot of the people there and they'll bring you up to date."

"Okay, thanks."

I put down the phone and eased myself into a self-righteous snit. I'd been writing about Bennet Wong and Jock McKeen for a number of years and actually had a first-draft manuscript stuffed in a cupboard, waiting for certain 'sensitive issues' to be resolved. But, despite the legitimacy of my interests, I had decided to stay away from the courtroom after the damned lawyers had said something about not wanting to turn the proceedings into a public spectacle. As it turned out, the trial was becoming a nexus for many of the threads and themes still hanging from my interrupted and incomplete story and now, with the hearing moving into its fourth day, I would have to pick up the pieces from the reflections of the idly curious who had chosen to disregard the concerns of the lawyers.

Drs. Wong and McKeen were appearing before the Supreme Court of British Columbia charged with sexual misconduct. The case for the prosecution was founded upon the complaints of a woman who maintained that, while still a 'minor,' she was drawn into a sexual encounter with Jock McKeen, aided and abetted by his partner Bennet Wong. The events were alleged to have taken place some twenty five years earlier on the remote island of Cortes, off the east coast of Vancouver Island. At that time, the accused were program leaders at the Cortes Centre for Human Development, formerly known as the Cold Mountain Institute. Founded by the radical 'humanist' Richard Weaver, this facility was an integral part of the human potential movement of the sixties and seventies, with close ties to its U.S. counterpart, the Esalen Institute at Big Sur, California.

To the initiated, the Cortes Centre was a place of pilgrimage, a Mecca for the exploration and celebration of the 'authentic' human experience. To many outsiders it was a place of mystery, a source of constant, and often wild, speculation. To some, it represented an affront to the established traditions of psychological and psychiatric practice, while others condemned it as a 'cult,' a den of iniquity that spawned the basest forms of human conduct and experimentation. Yet, in the spirit of the times, Cold Mountain and the Cortes Centre attracted many of the most notable contributors to the humanistic tradition that had its roots firmly entrenched along the west coast of North America. Virginia Satir, Ida Rolf, Alan Watts, Joseph Campbell, Will Schutz, Fritz Perls and Gregory Bateson all came to *do their thing* at this 'Esalen of the North'. Beyond my fascination with the work and lives of the accused, I wondered how such a colorful mosaic would appear on the black and white screen of the Supreme Court, some quarter of a century later.

I walked into the foyer outside the courtroom half an hour

before the daily proceedings were scheduled to begin. The place was packed with waiting spectators, some standing alone, others huddled in small groups. Linda Nichols had been right. I did recognize many of the faces but, wanting to get a feel for the occasion, I chose to keep my distance. There was a lot of eyeing-up already going on within the gathering, so I joined in. I felt hollow in my belly but I wasn't sure whether this came from the energy in the room, my own discomfort with Law Courts, or my concern for the welfare of Bennet Wong and Jock McKeen. It's impossible to spend time poking about in other people's lives without developing some sense of affinity but, in this case, the attachment probably went much deeper than I wanted to admit. I tried to convince myself that my purpose in being there was entirely investigative, yet I knew it would be a lie for me to consider myself an unbiased observer.

Peggie Merlin interrupted my deliberations. After the usual 'good to see you' chit-chat, and learning that she was in the court yesterday, I corralled her to my primary purpose. I knew that if anybody could find the words to get to the heart of the matter, it would be the astute and articulate Peggie Merlin. An urbane woman in her early fifties, Peggie was once the Executive Director of the Cold Mountain Institute, responsible for its operations in Vancouver and on Cortes. After its dissolution in 1980, she went on to become a leading figure in the Context Training organization. She had been a friend and colleague of the accused from their days on Cortes and throughout the subsequent development of their own centre at Haven-by-the-Sea, on Gabriola Island. I liked Peggie Merlin and, over the course of many years, I had come to respect her insights and trust her judgments.

"So, tell me, what's been going on in there," I asked, nodding toward the courtroom door.

"It's just horrific," she replied, shaking her head. "Whatever *did* happen twenty-odd years ago has been stripped of all its humanness. It's all so crude and undignified. The woman who made the allegations was on the stand yesterday and she was coerced into describing details of sexual acts in the most obscene way. I felt genuine empathy for her, and for the members of her family who were sitting in the front row. But, behind it all, there's so much rage. I've tried to reconnect with a few of the old Cold Mountain folks but some of those waiting to take the stand are tangled up in their own hostility. It's as if they're on a self-righteous mission of accusation and hate. It's hard to believe that these are the same people who once advocated such elegant and sensitive human values." She shook her head again.

"And how are the good doctors dealing with all of this?"

She sighed and paused for a moment. "It's really hard to tell. They sit behind their lawyers, presumably taking it all in, but they both look awful. There are times when Jock has that tight dismissive look about him, and Ben shows no emotion. Sometimes I wonder if he's even in the same room as the rest of us, though I'm sure he's very aware of all that's going on. It's like his spirit has evaporated. I remember seeing him like this after the police raid at Haven and wondered then if he would ever recover."

"Have you spoken with them since this thing started?"

"No. They're not taking any calls, and outside the courtroom, they're always surrounded by their lawyers. They seem very alone and isolated but . . . how many times have I said this? . . . 'Thank God they've got each other'."

I recalled saying the same thing myself on more than one occasion. "So what's the agenda for today?" I asked.

"I'm not sure, but I think some of the Cold Mountain brigade are to appear on the stand. I know they're angry—I just hope they can find ways to express their interpretations of events with delicacy and dignity."

Our conversation came to an abrupt end as a court usher arrived to unlock the doors to the courtroom. Engrossed in Peggie's accounts, I'd failed to notice that the crowd had already gathered around the doors, presumably in a bid to collar the best seats. We moved to join them.

Filing into the oak-paneled room, I had the distinct impression of being at a church wedding: 'Friends and family of the accusers to the left—friends and family of the accused to the right'. We shuffled our way between the pews, pausing briefly to acknowledge familiar faces along the way, and found two seats by the right-hand aisle. We sat down and I surveyed the congregation. They were clearly a divided bunch. I could see it in their faces, in their demeanor, and in the way they clumped together, some sitting quietly, others sharing confidential whispers. But the magnitude and gravity of their discord was something to be sensed rather than observed. It hung in the air, waiting to be released through whatever was about to unfold. Bennet Wong and Jock McKeen were nowhere to be seen and I hoped that they would be allowed to enter from behind the altar, or at least, well away from the aisle on the left.

Peggie leaned over. "The woman sitting in the middle of the front row, the one with the short blonde hair, wearing the brown suit, is the one who brought the charges," she whispered. "Members of her family are in the row behind."

I looked across. There were three or four women of similar age and appearance in the same grouping. "What about the other women?" I asked. "Are they all part of the family?"

"No, I don't think so. I believe they're just friends."

"My God," I murmured, "they all look so angry."

Peggie placed a hand lightly on my arm and put her lips to my ear. "Hell hath no fury . . ." she whispered.

I glanced around at the assortment of people sitting on our side of the courtroom. As far as I could tell, the call to arms had been successful. The benches were lined with Wong and McKeen supporters but they appeared remarkably subdued and oddly detached from one another. If they had any single cause it could only have been their curiosity. Unlike the grim-faced gathering on the other side, they seemed totally unprepared for combat. 'Perhaps they're waiting for *their* protagonists to appear,' I thought.

In an attempt to separate myself from the combatants and voyeurs, I pulled my notebook from my jacket pocket and scribbled a couple of irrelevant observations. It was a useless pretense. 'Drop the bullshit,' I told myself, 'let the experience speak for itself'. I closed my notebook and waited with the rest.

Now the court felt more like some mythical arena, a place where good and evil campaigned for the loyalty of their deluded warriors. I felt excitement running around in my belly. 'You're no different from the others,' I told myself. 'Why not accept your part in the charade? Facts are only negotiated fictions. Cheer when you feel like it and hiss when you feel like it. What the hell, it's only a game.' I looked down at my notebook.

Three lawyers clad in black gowns and carrying brief cases entered from rear left. They were followed closely by the accused who, in their dark suits, looked equally somber. I was momentarily stunned. For some reason, I had imagined Wong and McKeen gliding into the assembly in their old crinkled pants and T shirts, pausing to turn up the lights and turn down the music, before taking charge of the proceedings. But this was not the session room at a PD Seminar.

I watched the solemn procession make its way down the aisle and felt a heaviness in my heart. I knew these two men from a different place. There, they moved with such confidence in a world they had committed their lives to create. Now, they appeared as uncertain strangers in the world they had long since vacated. Each for his own reasons, and in his own way, had turned away from the protected place, discarded the practices and privileges of his profession and set out to delve beneath the illusions. Now the reality they had come to question was speaking back in no uncertain terms, and they would be bound by its judgments. Caught in the hostile stares and curious glances of courthouse spectators, and dependent upon their chosen representatives to maneouver them through the devious rituals of due process, their grasp on the future seemed hopelessly fragile. But this was still *their* story and it was still *my* project to write about it. It was also my place to simply be there.

They made their way down to a large polished table at the centre where the two Crown Prosecutors were already shuffling papers on the other side. Given the nature of the enterprise, I wondered why the champions of the Crown and the Accused always wear the same boring black gowns. It seemed to me that differentiating styles and colors would enhance the integrity of the affair.

The defence lawyers placed their brief cases on the table and, with cursory nods to their opposing colleagues, sat down and began their own preparations. The accused took the seats behind and, for the first time, I was able to bring them into focus. Jock, whose hard-edged charisma, good looks, and natural grace could generally be relied upon to enhance any grand or dramatic occasion, was a sadly subdued figure. While his eyes retained their characteristic vigilance, his face was pale and his skin was drawn tightly across his cheeks. Sitting next to the man who had been at his side for almost thirty years, he seemed like a fallen movie idol, relegated to some minor role and waiting for his cue. Yet it was he who was at the centre of this seething drama. It was he who was being accused of sexual impropriety by the blonde woman in the brown suit.

This was not the first time that Jock McKeen's sexual activities had been called into question. At Cold Mountain and the Cortes Centre, where any form of repression could become a target for scrutiny, sexuality constantly percolated to the surface. As it was for the participants, so it was for those who led the programs. While Wong and McKeen articulated very clear boundaries between themselves and those who came in search of authenticity, this was a highly personal residential community where relationships were not protected by carefully prescribed professional roles contained within fifty-minute consultations. In this strangely liberated place, many found themselves struggling to maintain some distinction between experience and fantasy. For some, it was simply too much.

Given these conditions, a prepossessing and sexually expressive young physician like Jock McKeen was bound to stir the pot in one way or another. Whether by design or default, he was destined to become a significant figure in the scheme of things and, as a program leader, there could be no doubt that he would be installed in a position of status and power. The question now before the court was whether he used this investiture to take advantage of a young woman who, with her family, had found her way to that eccentric island community; and whether he was, in some way, aided and abetted by the man on his left, Bennet Wong. For me, this was a question that aroused some of the most intriguing aspects of human relationships, but these were unlikely to be of interest to lawyers concerned with the 'facts' or a Supreme Court judge dedicated to upholding the Rule of Law. Truth, I concluded, is a slippery notion.

According to the teachings of Wong and McKeen, 'truth' is a relative term, firmly embedded in the experiences and beliefs of the teller. The purest form of revelation is 'honesty'—a full, non-strategic, disclosure and *ownership* of those beliefs and experiences. Through all of my dealings with Jock McKeen, I had come to regard him as a remarkably, and sometimes brutally, honest man. But, should he maintain this stance, how could such honesty possibly find its way through the strategic labyrinth of due process? Surely there had been rehearsals—what to say, what not to say, how to avoid traps, how to deliver a line and how to make the best use of opportunities. So if absolute truth is a misnomer, and honesty an impossibility, what shadows would we see of circumstances and events that took place so long ago? And yet those shadows and the judgments around them were set to determine the immediate fate of Dr. McKeen. No wonder he looked subdued.

Bennet Wong, who had once rattled the Vancouver psychiatric community by daring to treat his patients as fellow human beings, looked even more out of place, though nobody who knew him would ever doubt that his place was right there, next to his best friend, Jock. For both men, their relationship was at the very core of their work and their lives. Whether presiding over their groups at PD Seminars, or presenting themselves and their ideas to the outside world, people generally considered Ben to be the central figure in the arrangement. His presence was more substantial than dramatic. With bold oriental features that could shift easily from emotion to inscrutability, he was considered by many to be the embodiment of authenticity and wisdom. "You look like the reincarnation of Genghis Khan sitting there" an awe-struck program participant once remarked, to the delight of the audience.

But it wasn't Genghis Khan I saw on that morning, it was Bennet Wong, the Chinese kid from Strasbourg, Saskatchewan. I searched for glimpses of the man on the inside, but his face revealed little of what might be taking place. 'You're an enigma Bennet Wong,' I thought. 'You may be the most open person I've ever met, yet after many hours of observation and speculation, I still can't pin you down. How inadequate and disturbing my conclusions now sound. What if all these people who claim to love you or hate you have the same problem. Have we all colluded in some way to trap you here? No, you'd never buy that. You despise the idea of victim. Then perhaps you've been part of the conspiracy, the creator even. How absurd. You could never be responsible for the ambiguity of those around you, certainly not for mine.'

Suddenly I was ashamed. From the moment I walked into the courtroom foyer I had taken sides, condemned the opposition, ridiculed the process and urged my champions to perform on my behalf. Once in the courtroom, I reacted to the anger with my own, locking myself into a world of winners and losers. There could be no winners in this particular game. And behind all the anger, my own included, there was the pain. I had casually dismissed the anguish of the young woman sitting front row centre, along with the tormented members of her family sitting behind, turning them into the objects of my contempt. I had looked with scorn upon those Cold Mountaineers who had invested so many years in a cause that they believed would somehow make them and the world right again. The sadness finally filtered through.

On the other side, I had smeared Bennet Wong and Jock McKeen with my hurt, willing them to take it all away through their performances and, finally, through their victory over the accusers. I had created something that, deep down, my spirit reviled. Intellectually, what really stunned me was how easily the mentality I had worked so hard to establish and maintain throughout my writing of their story had dissolved in the adversarial world of courtroom justice. Somewhere, my own integrity was crying for attention.

The judge entered and we all rose to our feet. 'What, or who, are you to be the judge of?' I wondered, before checking myself. Once seated, the five men of law began to discuss fragments of yesterday's proceedings, snippets of testimony, points of law and various matters for clarification. I should have been fully attentive, taking notes and preparing myself to cover the case like a dedicated court reporter. Yet I found myself oddly detached and disinterested. My curiosity seemed to have nothing to do with the legal tussle commencing on centre stage. I was still concerned about the outcome, but the process of 'he said this and she did that' was already a bore.

This is all about relationships, I mused, or, more precisely, its about the breakdown of relationships. That's what's happening here. When we don't get what we want, or think we're entitled to, we feel hurt, become angry and call upon the ubiquitous parent to punish our siblings. When we see others who seem to have the same hurt, we gladly set aside our pain to take on the cause of *their* liberation. I've done this for much of my life, personally and professionally. But what's to be gained—a pound of flesh? A proclamation of righteousness? Vindication? Revenge? Power? Nothing is resolved and nothing of substance is gained in this way. Instead, we just push ourselves further apart and blame each other for our discontent. And, in so doing, we abandon ourselves, our humanity and our relatedness. Whatever is created in relationship can only be resolved in relationship. All it takes is commitment and courage.

In their work and their relationship, Bennet Wong and Jock McKeen had shown both courage and commitment. As I watched them sitting in the courtroom, it became painfully obvious that, like so many others, I had used them to become a spectator of my own life. When they had agreed that I should write something about their relationship, they had given me the opportunity to legitimize my voyeurism, and that's all. It was a safe place to be. Thanks to *their* openness and honesty, I had moved beyond the common speculations about their 'private' lives but my curiosity about their union continued to be insatiable. What they had learned about relationships was worth writing about yet, as they had always said, "the only real way to learn is through your own experience." What I did know was that I didn't envy or resent them for what they had; nor did I want to emulate them. My life was not like theirs, and probably never would be. I had no idea what actually happened all those years ago on Cortes Island and, in truth, the details really didn't matter that much. I firmly believed that whatever did take place could never have been intentionally abusive or degrading to another human being. What I knew for sure was that thousands of people had been touched by the lives and the work of Bennet Wong and Jock McKeen and that it was my task to write about it.

As the legal discussions continued, Wong and McKeen sat quietly side-by-side, shoulders almost touching. For a moment I thought they might be holding hands, but they weren't. Men shouldn't hold each other's hands, especially under the scrutiny of a Supreme Court Judge. But these two unusual men had challenged many of the things that men traditionally do and don't do. Their lives and their relationship often stood in sharp contrast to what was happening around them, though never more than at that particular moment, in that particular place. I took a breath and waited for the trial to continue.

CHAPTER TWO

BEN

On the morning of April 6, 1966, Anton Zivanaris was discharged from Pinehaven Community Hostel on the outskirts of San Francisco. With his arms wrapped around a fake crocodile-skin brief case, he climbed into the back of a cab and, once settled, handed the driver a voucher with the words "Airport (Air Canada)" written on it. He was delivered to his destination without a word been spoken.

"Any luggage to check?" asked the agent at the counter. Anton shook his head and tightened his grip on the brief case. "Well, have a nice flight," she said, as he turned and headed off toward the boarding area. She picked up the phone and called the flight crew.

The chief steward on Flight 217 to Vancouver arrived at the departure desk and surveyed his latest batch of passengers. He quickly picked out the solitary figure standing in the far corner of the lounge; a small man, in his mid forties, wearing a dark blue suite obviously intended for somebody much larger. His brief case was tucked tightly between his feet and he was scrutinising his boarding pass with the intensity of a child struggling with his first story book. His lips were moving. The steward watched for a few moments, let out a sigh, picked up the phone and called the aircraft.

On board, the flight attendant waited for the passengers to arrive. She smiled anxiously as Anton passed through the door and she watched him pick his way down the centre aisle, obsessively checking each row number against the stub of his boarding pass. When he vanished into slot 24, she resumed her ritual of welcoming the others on board. Anton's immediate future would be determined by the chief steward and the captain.

Shortly after take-off, the flight attendant made her way down the economy section to check on the situation in row 24. The man in the middle was sitting wide eyed and rigid. By the window sat an elderly woman reading a paperback. From the aisle seat, a middle-aged oriental man with greying shoulder-length hair, black leather vest over a claret shirt, was watching her. She remembered being oddly intrigued when he first came aboard but her curiosity had been interrupted by the call from the steward. He smiled easily as their eyes met. She smiled back with a sense of genuine relief and, without knowing why, touched him gently on the arm. Startled by her own spontaneity, she coughed nervously and continued toward the rear of the cabin.

It wasn't until the voice of the chief steward announced the beginning of their descent into Vancouver that the eruptions began in 24B. As the aircraft tilted and shuddered, a voice cried out in an unknown tongue, creating an eddy of agitation that rippled in each direction along the length of the cabin. Up in the first-class section, the flight attendant closed the door of the liquor cabinet and scurried to the centre of the disturbance. She arrived to find the man in the black leather vest with his arms wrapped securely around the trembling figure in the middle, their cheeks pressed together. On the other side, the elderly woman was desperately trying to disappear into the window recess. The flight attendant leaned forward and touched the oriental man's arm again, this time with deliberation. "Is there anything I can do?" she whispered. He turned to face her, smiled and shook his head. "Thank-you," she said with complete sincerity. She glanced at her watch. A few more minutes and they would be safely nestled in the terminal building.

"The Asian man in the black vest, did you get a good look at him?" she asked the chief steward as they pulled their seats down from the bulkhead. "Did you catch the expression on his face? How can he be that calm with a time bomb hanging around his neck?"

"He's probably a Buddhist," said the chief steward.

As the aircraft rattled along the runway, the flight attendant made her way back to row 24 with a confidence that seemed to come from nowhere. The two men sat side by side, shoulder to shoulder and hand in hand, while the woman by the window had managed to squeeze out an additional degree of separation by staring out of the window. The man in the middle remained frozen. The one by the aisle seemed remarkably at ease.

A few minutes later, the two men made their way down the aisle of a deserted 737 and headed for the front exit. The chief steward and flight attendant waited patiently at the door. The first man, desolate and battle weary, his crocodile case clasped to his belly, looked at them through empty eyes and shuffled by. As the second man approached, the fight attendant spontaneously held out her hand. He took it without hesitation.

"Thanks for your help," she said. "I'll walk with him to the terminal and make sure he finds his way from there."

"That's okay, I'll stay with him for a while," he replied softly. She nodded and allowed their hands to separate.

The chief steward squinted at the departing figure of Anton Zivanaris. "That guy could use some psychiatric help," he suggested.

The man in the black leather vest stepped out of the aircraft, paused and turned to face them again. "He just got some," he said.

Out in the arrivals area, the passengers of flight 217 gathered around the revolving luggage carousel. Still the objects of furtive glances and secret nudges, the two strangers took their place on the periphery. As the first bags began to slide down the chute, the smaller man began to shake again. Those standing closest drew back. When the crocodile case fell to the floor, the oriental man turned to face his companion, took the trembling elbows in his hands and whispered, "It's okay, just let it go and breathe. I'll stay with you." Anton responded with a series of violent convulsions and pitiful whimpers. When this fragile containment finally broke and his legs buckled, his companion wrapped his arms around his waist and drew him in even closer. "I'm here. I won't leave you . . ."

A collective murmur passed among the onlookers and many faces turned in expectation toward a police officer who had been watching it all from the doorway of the Unclaimed Baggage office. But he remained impassive. With the two figures now entwined and motionless, the crowd began to disperse. Passers-by, unaware of what the two men were up to, glanced from the corners of their eyes and walked on. Caught within the endless pedestrian stream, the fleeting terror of a human life evaporated into the transient images of Vancouver International Airport. The police officer, who had continued his vigil from his place on the edge, checked his watch and moved off.

Bennet Wong gave the address of his Vancouver office to the cab driver and settled into the back seat. The inside of the cab smelled like the public washroom where he had taken a few minutes to wash his hands and brush the crud from his clothes. He disliked public washrooms because, for the most part, they were dirty, impersonal and inhospitable places.

His brief encounter with Anton Zivanaris had slipped easily into the past and he was ready to move on. As a psychiatrist, he was no stranger to the turmoil of other lives. Time and again, he would reach out into the chaos and, when it was time to part, he would willingly let go, bid farewell and continue on his way. It was, after all, the nature of his project; he had planned it this way from the age of fourteen.

The eighth of ten children from the only Chinese family in the small town of Strasbourg, Saskatchewan, Bennet spent his early years running from the cry of "Chink," while searching the nooks and crannies of the community for a 'haven' where he might find his place. "Come To Jesus. Jesus Loves You," said the sign hanging from the sandstone blocks of the Presbyterian Church. But where was this place of love? And where could He be found in the humble streets of Strasbourg?

Bennet went to church each Sunday. Often, before going to bed, he would sit patiently before the painted figure of Christ, reading the bible, asking questions and waiting for answers. Bennet Wong and Jesus Christ, talking together, a Chink and a Jew, sharing their aloneness. He spoke openly and innocently, waiting for the Holy Father to embrace him and tell him about his place in the earthly kingdom. As the innocence of childhood dissolved into the scepticism of youth, the Heavenly Father seemed to grow more distant and judgmental.

During his first year of high school, he read Donne's "Meditation Seventeen" and wondered if he was destined to spend the rest of his life as an island. He would drift into sleep at night thinking of ways to make his island more attractive. He studied the rituals of the kids in the neighbourhood and tried to emulate them. He bought himself a sports coat, one that would make him look more like the others, and he waited. Still, nobody seemed interested. Nobody came. In his diary he wrote, "Well, today, I didn't find it, but it must be true. Maybe I won't find it before I die. Maybe that's what life is like—being an island, and knowing it so well that, when I die, I'll be able to understand that I wasn't an island after all."

By the time he reached the middle grades, he had come to see the futility of his quest. Nothing he could say or do would ever give him the passport he needed for admission into a world that continued to dance tantalisingly before him. His choices were limited, but they were choices nonetheless and they would have to be discovered among the tangled undergrowth of his own island. Here he could indulge himself in the things he liked and learn to live with the things he didn't. Somewhere, if he searched hard enough, he would find the courage he would need. In different circumstances, he might have found refuge among the downtrodden, but in the small rustic community of Strasbourg there were no deviant or disenfranchised groups looking for new members. He could have withdrawn into his own private psychosis, or led his own rebellion, but the idea of rejecting those who had rejected him offered only the prospect of self-inflicted pain in exchange for a freedom that would keep him distant and alone.

As a solitary and circumspect schoolboy, he actually thought about these things. From his reading of theology, he saw how the martyrdom of Christ was not born in the heart of the man himself, but in the minds and motives of his followers. Though Christ would remain his one and only hero, the young Bennet Wong wanted more than the shallow acceptance of the Church and the second-hand love dispensed in the name of the 'saviour.' Better to remain alone, and scared. God had placed the cards in his hand, leaving no doubt about who should play them out. There may well have been people who were interested, even some who cared, but in their failure to make themselves known, or his failure to see them, he made them irrelevant.

Within the family, however, his place was known, secure and predictable. Their corner store and small restaurant, offering locals a Chow Mein alternative to burgers and fries, gave the Wong's a legitimate, if isolated, place in the community. The structure of their daily lives, driven by pragmatic ambitions and dogged determination, provided each member with a secure niche within the enterprise and a reason to move in the outside world with dignity and self-respect. It was the Chinese way. For his part, Bennet rarely questioned or shirked his responsibilities. Whether running to the warehouse, stacking supplies, serving in the store or washing dishes, he understood that he was making his contribution and that was what really mattered.

There were many times when he wanted to know why things were the way they were, but it was not his place to ask. So he watched. He watched as his father managed the day-by-day affairs of the business and decided that it was actually his mother who ran the roost, it was she who had the power. He thought a lot about power. He could see how, even in the deprivation of Strasbourg in the dirty-thirties, powerless people turned on each other to take whatever trivial advantages were to be had. He concluded that power can only separate people. So if his mother's power kept the wheels of the family turning, did it also serve to keep them distant? Since emotions and personal feelings were rarely shared, he could only assume that somewhere woven into the routines and ambitions was the unspoken love that kept them all together.

Like all kids, Bennet wanted to know that others could see and feel what he could see and feel and that they would accept him and care for him because of these things. In times of trouble, parents and siblings would move to his side, yet they would quickly vanish again in the service of something he could never fully understand. They were all concerned with earning a living, but what was this living that had to be earned? Were they earning on the outside and living on the inside? Was it only in trouble or pain that these things could be shared? Nobody ever told him.

Perhaps other kids in other families had the same questions, but *they* weren't about to tell him either. He would have to find out for himself. He would have to go to their homes, play in their yards, listen to their stories, hear about their ancestors, soak up their tears, be giddy with their laughter. And what about their hurt? Perhaps they would reach out to him in their troubles? Perhaps they knew what living was all about but, in order to find out, he would have to pass through the barriers that others had placed in his way.

In the room he shared with his brothers above the grocery store, he sat alone with his notebook. Carefully, he wrote out the word "Chink" and read it to himself many times over, letting the anguish run its course. With each rendition, some of the pain left and he took another step toward the gate. Again, he looked at what he had written. It was an interesting word—a funny word—light and carefree, with a pleasant musical quality that actually amused him. He said it aloud and it fell harmlessly from his mouth. He shouted it out and it came back to him in innocence from the speckled flowers in the wallpaper.

Sheepishly, he began to sing it to the walls themselves. "Chink, chink, chinky-chink, chink. Here a chink, there a chink, everywhere a chink-chink." He laughed. How could such a word become the malignancy that the rest of the world could see and despise while he was supposed to shrink in humiliation? It had no capacity to hurt him—only he could do that by transforming it into a dagger and stabbing himself. If he wanted to, he could draw the blade from his chest right now, brandish it above his head and return this lilting word to its benign and carefree place in the lexicon of the language. Nobody's pronouncements offered any truth. Only he could know what Bennet Wong was all about. So he laughed again. Then he wept.

Perhaps a friend, a very special friend, would take the trouble to tell him or, at least, join him in his quest. Hughie, a boy from a nearby island, fell into the habit of dropping by, and for a while—longer than he ever dared expect—they shared the enchantment and confusion of two boys growing up together in a world that wanted them apart. Eventually, Hughie sailed away and never came back. "There'll be plenty of time for friends when you get to College," he was told.

Returning to his more reliable sources of information, he found himself deeply touched by the tales of mythology in which people discovered a deep, almost sacred, sense of connection between each other. In the Arthurian Legends and the epics of ancient Greece, he found heroic tales of men who shared a common bond and stood together in the face of adversity, a love that transcended all things, even death. By comparison, the romantic love between men and women seemed shallow and remote, more to do with rescuing and protecting than with sharing and understanding. His father loved him, perhaps his brothers loved him, but there was no communion, no confirmation of this sacred state. To *love* another is to *know* another, to share adventure, to seek the Grail, to stand side-by-side before the Trojans and feast together in the Palace of Sparta. But such a love was far removed from the world he knew, and such mythology had no place on the streets of Strasbourg. Here, whatever was given could just as easily be taken away.

In the pattern of his own life, it's possible that, had such a friend as he envisioned been available, Bennet Wong would have followed the more well-trodden trails of other adolescent boys. As it was, he forged his own pathway and the special friend who walked at his side was no more than a comforting shadow dancing on the walls of his own imagination. It wasn't even a part of him, merely an appendage with little to say about his inner place and absolutely nothing to add to his knowledge of the world outside.

By comparison, the 'real' boys did have something to offer. They could tell him what he wanted to know. So he pursued them, listening to their stories and trying to imagine what their lives might be like. But whenever they talked about their feelings, when they shared their excitement, their fears or their sadness, the mystery dissolved into the familiar, a place that could be shared. If he could see into their worlds, then surely they could also see into his; the prospect delighted him. Unfortunately, their curiosity was shallow and, for the most part, fleeting. Eventually, they would become unsettled or embarrassed, by what was taking place. Doors would close. Many would return, particularly when troubles interrupted the carefree flow of youth, but always, after the catharsis, they would disappear again. It was a lopsided arrangement, but Bennet Wong had discovered a place where he could feel a sense of purpose, a place where he was truly alive.

When he decided to become a psychiatrist he was fourteen years old. He had read his way through the Greek Mythology shelves of the public library and, moving across to the Psychology section, picked up a volume of clinical case studies. He was captivated. From unlimited possibilities, Bennet Wong decided that he was on this earth to work in the service of others. But, unlike most who choose the helping professions, he had no compelling urge to please or fix his parents; his questions were not in response to self-doubts to be resolved through the lives of others; and there was no sense of moral idealism urging him to change the face of the world. Rather, he responded to an insatiable curiosity about himself and the affairs of those who walked silently around him. Becoming a psychiatrist would be his way of exploring that elusive place where he could know and be known.

JOCK

On the 14th of June, 1964, John H.R. McKeen rose to deliver the Valedictory address at his High School Graduation ceremony. He was an academic achiever, out-performing the majority of his peers by an impressive margin. He was a local television 'personality', appearing each week on a popular panel quiz show, and his regular column in the *London Free Press* brought a responsible and respectful voice of youth to the affairs of the community. The Medical School at the University of Western Ontario had welcomed him warmly and, with two scholarships safely in the bag, he was ready to move on.

Walking past the row of smiling faculty and sombre dignitaries, he made his way to the podium and carefully placed his papers on the lectern. This was not a moment to be rushed, it was a time to build anticipation, an occasion to be savoured. There was no fear to be contained, only excitement. The rehearsals had served him well. He looked up, surveyed his audience and waited. He was ready, but *they* would take another few seconds. Somewhere out there in the haze, his mother would be watching. This was her moment too, a final public declaration of her place in the scheme of his life before he moved on. As always, his father would be beside her, quietly waiting for things to unfold. It was time to speak.

"In each of us there are certain unique abilities, born in us like mined ore. The richness of our lives is contingent upon the dedication with which we set about to mine this ore, to smelt it, refine it, shape it, and utilise it. A rich life is a continuous pursuit of goals—goals which, when attained, point the way to newer, loftier ones. Indeed, life presents a challenge to each of us to develop our talents, to equip ourselves to seek after these goals. If, like the Biblical servant, we merely bury our talent or talents, we have failed to respond to that challenge, and we have rejected our right to seek meaningful goals . . ."

How totally apt were these words to the life of the handsome young man at the lectern. How powerful and integrated the message for all who believed they knew him. How deliciously reaffirming for the collective mind and morality of middle-class Ontario where sons were urged to achieve and daughters were encouraged to seek their way into the matrimonial beds of the achievers. The audience listened in rapt admiration, unaware that behind the melody of the message and the warm sincerity of the delivery lay a secret that John H. R. McKeen had sworn never to divulge. Only he and one other human being knew that none of the words had been written by the speaker. Rather than risk the possibility that his speech might be less than impeccable, that the script might not fully enhance the stature of the actor, he had sought the collaboration of a friend and paid him for every word. It was a deception that did not sit easily but he needed to have the very best for this once-in-a-lifetime moment.

Driving home in the old two-tone Hillman, he relaxed in the knowledge that the show had gone well. By now he was able to read an audience with confidence and no longer needed the assurances of insignificant admirers. But the evaluations of the significant—sponsors, teachers and those who represented the world that beckoned him—were given an attentive ear. He knew that those who mattered would have been pleased with his performance that day. Among them, appraisals had become increasingly assimilated and consensual; Jock McKeen was going places.

As he drove by the campus of the University of Western Ontario, he considered his own ambitions and relished the prospect of becoming a physician. He thought back to the time when, as an over-weight, out-of-shape, ungainly kid, his mother had taken him to task. He was stunned by what he saw in the mirror she held before him, appalled at the prospect of being seen as a slob, a ne'er-do-well, a failure. Somehow, he had understood the agony that rejection would bring. He was repulsed by the idea that he might become a powerless figure bounced around like flotsam and jetsam in the sea of other people's projects. Now he could thank her for the hours spent in losing weight, getting fit and learning to move his body with purpose and grace. The years of study and dedication had all been worth it and their collaboration in making the right moves and the right contacts was beginning to yield a handsome return.

In the course of this transformation, he discovered the pleasures of pleasing others. He knew that their expectations would always be one step ahead of him but this always gave him something to aim for. He was also bright and perceptive and had learned to be patient. He knew that those who want to be pleased ultimately become indebted to the pleaser, at which time the delicate balance of power shifts. There was nothing malicious about his intentions, it was simply the name of the game as he had come to know it. He would have shuddered at the thought that someone might get hurt along the way.

Turning back onto the highway and heading for home, passages from his Valedictory address kept running through his head. "... hills peep over hills, and at this summit, which looked so large and imposing from below, now appears only as a stepping stone—a little rise from which we see more and greater ascents." He could see it all before him: the journey would be his now; he was ready to go it alone.

With the successes of the day carefully noted and the minor deficits critically evaluated for future reference, the one they called 'Jock' closed the door of his room, spread himself out on his bed and allowed the snapshots of his place in the musclebound world to dissolve into a blur of indistinct images. Panelled halls and podiums gave way to rowing boats and fishing reels. Caps and gowns merged into boots and rough-knit sweaters. Uncle Murray's damp, tousled old pullover filled his nostrils with the scent of childhood adventures. The tingles of anticipation and nods of admiration, along with their compelling demands, gave way to a gentle acceptance that brought a smile to his lips. There would be other times with Uncle Murray; the old man still welcomed him like a lost comrade. He reached out for the beloved anthology of poetry that lay on the bedside table and turned to the works of D.H. Lawrence.

> When strife is a thing of two
> each knows the other in struggle
> and the conflict is a communion
> a twoness.

> But when strife is a thing of one
> a single ego striving for its own ends
> and beating down resistance
> then strife is evil, because it is not strife.

He tried to weave the lines around the lingering images of Uncle Murray and the fishing trips but the accommodation was awkward and unsettling. He thought of his friend Ann and a shiver passed through his body. She had been taken away for the summer—a decision made by her parents to ease the horrors of the disease that was sapping her life away. In the face of his friend's agony, he was helpless and remote. A letter . . . perhaps if he wrote a letter he could again reach out to her suffering and into the grief that lay deep within himself. She had never been like the other girls who moved in and out of his life. They were the props, the extras, and some, for brief moments, the co-stars in his theatre of ambition. But Ann, even before her illness, had moved in a different sphere. Somehow, in confronting death, she had touched his aliveness. He didn't need to please her to make himself whole and he could do nothing to make her well. He was never in love with Ann. All he knew was the strange mingling of strength and helplessness whenever they were together. He wasn't sorry for her even though he could sense her pain, or was it his own pain? He could never be sure.

He turned out the light by his bed and sent a message out into the darkness. In the absurd and unfathomable scheme, Ann was going to die and he was going to be a doctor.

BEN

The sanctity of the human spirit is a matter of faith; an unquestioned knowing that, in some way, every life is related to every other life and that, together, all lives belong to an eternity that is the universe, that is God. If this is so, then the mysteries of the cosmos, and our place within it, will be re-solved when finally we see the whole reflected in the part that is us. For this, we can cast aside the one-way instruments of science. What we seek is not discovery, but recognition. And what we need is not a scope, but a mirror—one that will take our eyes out into the heavens and back into ourselves, without impediment.

From a very early age, Bennet Wong came to see himself as being different but the mirror was clouded and rejecting. Carrying the legacy of Chinese parents and a North American Indian great-grandmother, what made him different was obvious and unchangeable. If acceptability is born of conformity, then he would have to work harder, much harder, than those who bore the unmistakable trademarks of desirability.

Certainly, he was a conformist. In fact, his apparent dismissal of all but the noblest of pursuits, earned him the reputation of a 'snob' among his younger siblings. He listened carefully to what others had to say and, within the family, he deferred to the opinions and wishes of his elders. From the younger ones he expected the same for himself and was quick to distance himself, even admonish them, should they falter in the execution of their obligations. In this way, he was an integral part of a family held together in a totem of ritualized interdependence. Love and caring were implicit in their commitments to the family as a whole but rarely expressed in their personal dealings with one another. His mother reserved a special place for Ben, although, in the daily routines of running the restaurant and store, many of his infant and early childhood needs were attended to by his elder sister, Effie. Reflecting upon the experiences of his own childhood, he could not remember ever having been touched or spoken to in a manner that affirmed their love, or his own lovability. Once, his father massaged his cheek to ease the pain of an aching tooth but this physical union of a son with his father was never repeated . . . or forgotten.

Little wonder he felt at home in the ordered and impersonal hierarchy of the classroom. Here again, his conformity and dedication drew the approval of his teachers, along with a certain quality of respect from the other students. Yet, with his place assured and his desk assigned, he had no interest in setting himself apart through academic performance. What he wanted was to be a part of whatever was going on and, by corralling twenty other restless young lives around him for six hours each day, the school created a condition that he could never have established on his own behalf. He did not know how or when it would happen but, even into the early years of high school, he clung to the notion that, whatever the teacher taught, they all would somehow learn together. But, apart from unpredictable bursts of energy around certain tasks or topics, he and his fellow students remained as separate as their ink-stained desks. In fact, most of his classmates seemed to regard time in the classroom as an unwarranted intrusion in their affairs and he wondered how they could manage to drift off for such long periods of time; where did they go? Meanwhile, those who listened and went to the library afterwards, seemed distant and self-involved. If they approached him at all it would be to discuss and compare achievements. Then, at precisely 4 p.m. they would all disappear; the non-contenders rushing off excitedly to resume their secret lives elsewhere and the achievers quietly gathering up and taking home the spoils of the day.

36

Generally he walked home alone, but always with lots to think about. How were the lives of kids in Tonga different from his own life in Saskatchewan? Did Mary and Joseph work together in the carpentry business? If mathematics really was a language, then maybe the universe had its own voice and its own ears. Certainly music was a language he was learning to speak and hear. Chopin spoke to him; he tried to speak back through his piano practice and sometimes Effie would eavesdrop on their conversation. Sarah Newfeldt, soft and mysterious, sat at her desk in the corner and didn't listen to anybody. Perhaps she dreamed of making daisy chains and chasing white rabbits through Pemberton's fields.

No thought was ever far away from any other thought. On occasion he would find himself joined by stragglers who were temporarily separated, or ejected, from the pack. He would listen intently to their stories, asking questions, pushing for more, waiting for the moment when some part of his own life might touch theirs and they could laugh or cry together. But they always stopped short, switching from topic to topic, leaving him to speculate about the connections, about the untold threads that wove the pieces together. Perhaps some other language would help unlock the door.

The chances are that by the time he entered High School, his outside differences blended into the grain of teenage life and there really was no conspiracy to exclude him. What set him apart now was as much his own doing as theirs. He could not, or would not, reveal his place without mutuality and they could not, or would not, join him there. To break the deadlock, he could have abandoned his island sanctuary and settled for a place on the adolescent mainland, but it was too late. On both sides, the conditions had become unacceptable. The difference was that he continued to feel excluded and devoutly curious while they rushed over to Turgeon's place with little interest in anything that he might bring to the party. So he turned the other way and went home.

From the outside, the Wong family was solid and unknown.

On the inside, it was highly organized, disciplined and determined. And the same could be said about each individual member, including Ben. When Mother issued her exhortation that being a Wong "really meant something," her children carried the banner out into the world and returned to tell the story. Thus prepared, they all went on to pursue professional careers with great distinction. But Ben remained convinced that somewhere behind the rituals and ambitions was the love that brought and held them together without any condition, and this he wanted, for its own sake. But how could they love him unless they *knew* him? And how could they receive what was in his own heart unless *their* hearts were open?

He had seen, heard and read enough to know that there were families, somewhere out there, where the daily obligations were punctuated by moments of unearned recognition—a special look, a hand reaching out to touch, gentle knowing words of one acknowledging another. If he couldn't find his way beneath the crust of his own family then where in the world would he find another opening? If it was that important to know what it meant to be a Wong, then why wasn't it just as important to know what it meant to be Bennet Wong? And if he couldn't know what it was like to be Effie Wong, then how could he possibly find out what it might be like to be Ronnie Turgeon?

Occasionally he would have glimpses of what happened inside and between other people and he savoured each revelation as a voyeur might savour the momentary parting of a bedroom curtain. Yet, once revealed, he rarely understood the purpose of the secrecy—unless, of course, it was kept for the sheer joy of letting it go. He became fascinated with the things that most people chose to hide away. For him, a personal revelation was like an unexpected Christmas gift and, though it would have been both ungracious and ungrateful to ask, he always wanted more. But, should the gift turn out to be a deception, he would slink away feeling cheated and devastated. If his own gift was abused or tossed carelessly aside, he would feel hurt and humiliated. If it was taken with only a perfunctory nod, he would feel locked out and abandoned. Perhaps they were all trapped in the fear of being different and all they had to do was let it out—what a gift. Either way, there was much to learn and little to lose. So he would listen respectfully, always looking for the unaffected gift, yet always reminding himself that other opinions belonged to other lives; they didn't know him, so what they said didn't have to fit for him. He could look at his own reflection without falling into the mirror.

"You should always tell the truth," his parents said. "Don't ever lie to me," the teacher once told them. "The truth shall set ye free," the Minister promised, opening his arms to his congregation. But what was this truth? It wasn't about facts. He had read enough history to dispel this illusion. It wasn't about sincerity. He had listened to so many people who had told different versions of the same story with equal sincerity. And, if the truth was so good for everybody, why was it so often wrapped up in discreet packages and squeezed out in whispers? Was it truthful to say nothing, or leave some things unsaid? The only truth he knew was that he didn't know the real truth about anything. Whatever happened could only take place within his own experience and, in this, there was no end to the deliberations, no point where something absolute emerged to sound the irrefutable bell of certainty. Honesty was something he could live with and, while he wasn't about to tell all to anyone who would listen, he saw no value in deliberately deceiving anyone, particularly himself.

So, in a society that exhorts children to tell the "truth" while teaching them the arts of deception, Ben managed to spring himself loose from the moral predicament and make a tangible commitment to something called "honesty." Given that the rest of world was not about to embrace his resolution, he made up his mind that, should he ever fulfil his dream of having a "best friend," this would be the one fundamental criterion for their continued association.

Meanwhile, he was his own keeper, moving in his own orbit. There was always just enough 'out there' to keep him on the edge. Since he had no idea how the world *should* be, what he found was always acceptable, even when the suffering of other lives touched his own. He had come to know his pain, to acknowledge its place and respect its integrity. It was not for him to wish away the things he didn't like in other lives. But he felt it nonetheless.

Whatever western psychology might say about the importance of role models for children, by the time Bennet Wong was poking and prodding his way through high school, it is doubtful that anybody could have come along to show him where he wanted to go. There was no one with whom he could identify and, beyond the most basic behavioural rituals, there was nobody he cared to imitate. So, he found the audacity to look past the models of the mortal world to keep Jesus Christ his one and only hero; not the Christ who gathered followers, performed miracles and offered salvation, but the Christ who refused to abandon the integrity of his own knowing and continued to care about the world, even through the agony of His crucifixion.

But he never directed himself to follow in the footsteps of the stained-glass figure impaled on the cross and imprisoned on the chapel wall. His dreams were more of emulation than imitation and the quality he sought was more of love than of performance. He knew about this love; it came from the inside and, like laughter, he could let it out, wait for an echo, make his skin tingle. For it was out there too. He also knew about the false echoes, the seductive beckoning of those who would use his love to deceive or control him. Even though they might take away all he had to offer and condemn him with their pronouncements, they could not—they must not—take away what he discovered and so carefully nurtured on the inside. Christ found his place by refusing a place in the temple. He shared Himself because He cherished His inside place. He understood because He too was a man. He served because His substance was eternal. He rose above the indignity and torment by resisting the terrible temptations of helplessness. And, given the cards of His destiny, He fashioned His own life through His own labours.

So Bennet Wong worked hard. He remained fascinated by

those who held a totally different place in the world—the powerful, the beautiful and the favoured. He wanted to know what it was like to move in the world as a man, to experience fully the prerogatives and the price of the masculine ideal. For this, he would need to approach each 'successful' male as a connoisseur might experience a work of art for the first time, with appreciation for its uniqueness and without judgment for its value. He invested much of his time in hanging around the heroes of his high school, questioning them, appreciating them and, in his own way, thanking them for whatever gifts they unwittingly offered. Over time they grew to like him and willingly accepted his uncommitted presence around them and their activities.

Not all of the boys welcomed the attentions of young Benny Wong, but those who did were drawn to the intensity of his interest in them and their experiences. He listened to them as no one had ever listened to them before, participating in their joy, their anguish and their confusion, directly and without judgment. Always patient and respectful, he earned their trust and, walking home from the ball game or sipping on a Coke at Greerson's Cafe, they told him things they would never dare tell their parents or share with their 'real' friends. He didn't have to push. If the conditions were right, they just talked and he listened. They never told him everything he wanted to know, but he had his own way of searching behind the words, fleshing out possible connections and testing them in the run of the conversation. Sometimes, if they seemed open and receptive, he would offer his speculations for their consideration and they would wonder how he could see such things. It wasn't difficult. He had discovered most of the elements in his own life and was beginning to see how they were woven into the patterns of other lives.

While none of them seemed particularly curious about *his* life, he had found a way to prise the door to their lives open. While listening he could allow his own thoughts and feelings to rise to the surface. Even if they weren't seen or acknowledged, they were alive, awake and out there, moving with the pulse of another human being. He began to notice subtle changes taking place on his own insides that seemed to correspond with shifts in the mood of the other person. Was there some other form of communication at work? Would it still work if he closed his eyes and covered his ears?

For the most part, girls remained outside his field of enquiry. They didn't have the stories he was looking for and seemed quite determined to keep whatever they did have to themselves. When he did eavesdrop on the tearful tragedies of Claudette Marchand, the tinkling excitement of Rosie Cross, or the softly murmured philosophy of Suzanne Tucker, he ended up feeling even more ignorant and isolated. How could they ever reveal themselves or understand *him* from such a distance? Whatever questions his body was beginning to ask, the answers always seemed lost in the dreamy world that comes before sleep and dissolves as soon as mind wakes up. The thought that some day one of these mysterious creatures would sit by his side, hold his hand, and tell him the secrets of the dream world sent shivers deep into his belly, but the prospects seemed remote.

Jennifer Brigham, a demure princess who moved in the world with the delicacy of a dragonfly caught in a summer breeze, once opened her strawberry heart and told him of the Prince she would one day find. "He'll be warm and sensitive. He'll be interested in me as a person and not just in . . . well, you know. He'll be gentle and loving and not bothered with all that silly stuff that guys get into when they're together. And he'll be loyal and faithful for all of our lives together." Her round green eyes looked up at him through the glaze of a heart-warmed tear and he knew that *he* was the Prince she was looking for. He also knew that, should he reveal his royal identity, she would be off pursuing the corpus of "Brock" Peterson, the high-flying quarterback with the dismissive sneer and the sensitivity of a charging Bull Moose. He could understand why she might search for her Prince and why she might fail to see the glass slipper in his hand. But the appeal and the power of the leather-skinned football player was beyond his comprehension. This he could find out only from his friend "Brock."

JOCK

When we educate children, we give them our version of how the world works. When we train children, we show them how to use this information to keep that world intact. The good students stand as a testimony to our efforts. They measure themselves against our yardsticks and dedicate their medals to our glory. Then, as they take their place and their power in the labyrinth, we hand over the banner of 'truth', appoint them as the new protectors and disappear into our portraits. The creative ones may search beyond the walls, but their new horizons will be ground into more bricks and mortar for the stronghold. The rebellious ones may hurl themselves against the buttresses, but their crazy ways can only serve to increase our vigilance and strengthen our resolve. We are all part of the conspiracy, warding off the images and nightmares from other realms; protecting our slender truth and fragile sanity from foreign invaders.

Even to this day, Jock McKeen is afraid of vampires. There was a time when he was afraid of people, even the other kids who lived in the war-time housing district of Owen Sound, Ontario. A seven year old Teddy Mills knelt on his chest and pounded him in a frenzy of rage and rejection. The 'real' boys—those who didn't like pink and hated poetry but could catch a baseball and say "fuck" without having to take a breath first—waited for him in the alley, and he shrank away in terror. But the more he ran away from the boys and their bats and toward the girls and their giggles, the worse it became. Occasionally he would find some other reject and befriend him but, generally, the solace was temporary and short-lived. For a time, Bob was his friend, but when they were both apprehended by a group of desperate alley-way marauders, the eight year old McKeen was invited to leave while they beat up on the ill-fated Bob. He accepted the invitation without hesitation. Much as it hurt, he was always alone.

His pain was shared by his parents. He was given a quarter

for every stand he took against other kids and offered assurances of future success in individual sports and 'grown-up' pursuits. But such potentials were remote and obscure. In the early grades, his school performances were mediocre and his athletic achievements were even worse. He was lonely, inadequate, under-stimulated, overweight and scared. And, furthermore, he was inclined to like the things the girls liked. In his isolation, he created his own private world of musings, music and masturbation, but these things served to divert him even further from his own dream of acceptance and the parental dream of success.

When the family moved to London, Ontario, the futures of Jock and his younger sister Cathy, were central considerations in the decision. The timing was perfect. The family was ready to invest in creating a 'new life' and the infelicitous son desperately wanted his own circumstances to be different.

By the end of grade ten he was still considered to be a 'schmuck' by many of his peers but now, at least, he was a 'brainy schmuck.' To four hours of study each day, he added an hour of callisthenics and weight-lifting, committing mind and body to the same level of elegance and agility. He won prizes, first for academics and then, the most satisfying of all, for physical education. His parents complained to the Principal about the practice of awarding prizes to students of lesser ability but their concern was unfounded; their protégé continued to shine.

And the more he shone, the more confident he became. He enjoyed the approval of his parents, the attention of his teachers and the respect, however begrudging, of his fellow students. But the eyes that were always upon him seemed distant, full of expectation, and he longed for the softer understanding eyes that would welcome him and ask for nothing in return. Grandma and Uncle Murray were still out there, and he thanked God.

Along with his weekly television quiz show appearances, he was an active member of the student council. He had many insightful things to say about educational issues. When his friend Bill announced his intention to stand for President of the Student Council, Jock decided he should offer support in the role of

Vice President. He entered the election uncontested and his posters were distributed and displayed liberally throughout the school. Then, as he prepared himself for the rewards and responsibilities of office, a new eleventh-hour candidate was thrust into the fray. Jock's immediate response was to withdraw from the competition and avoid the indignity of a public popularity contest. But, on reflection, there was little to be concerned about. Rick O. was an unknown, a nobody put forward by the football crowd in an attempt to unsettle those they called the 'brain brigade.'

True to the nature of the opposition, McKeen posters were systematically defaced or destroyed and vulgar "Pick Rick" placards were plastered all over the pastel walls of Oakridge High. While the serious students went quietly about their electoral business, the opposition worked feverishly to turn the contest into a scrimmage. As the energy shifted and the day of reckoning drew near, it became increasingly apparent that Jock McKeen was about to face the rejection of his peers. Immediately following the counting of the ballots, the news that 'McKeen was Creamed' was written into the solemn faces of the faithful in their campaign room while the 'Pick Rick' crowd filled the halls with chants of victory.

Jock McKeen withdrew. He was hurting to the depths of his being and the anger welled up within him. He expressed it cruelly to those who had chosen to stand by him, particularly his girl friend and campaign workers. A concerned Principal called him to the office and counselled him to ignore the puerile judgments of the 'mob.' "Your destiny is too great to be handed over to the common herd," he told him. He suggested that politics was an inelegant pursuit and invited him to consider the editorship of the school newspaper as a far more appropriate vehicle for his talents. Jock was pleased and a deal was struck.

But the pain ran deep and, with the counsel of Mother and other selected advisors, he established a new resolve. The hurt that had given rise to his anger was replaced by a simple determination that his destiny would never again be left to chance.

Having accepted the editorship of the school newspaper, he assigned himself diligently to the pursuit of academic excellence. He refused the position of Prefect along with other offers of status within the school community. Five or six hours of study each evening was the price he was prepared to pay for his ambition.

Nobody ever doubted that Jock McKeen was the top student at Oakridge High—at least not until Ernie McFarland arrived from Toronto. When the final grades were announced at the end of the year, Jock McKeen registered an unprecedented 88.8%. Ernie McPharland attained an average of 88.9%, the second highest grade point average in the City of London. By any standards, third place in a school system the size of London, Ontario, would be a remarkable achievement—but not for Jock McKeen. Once again he had been foiled at the eleventh-hour but, this time, there were no villains to be held responsible and he was left with a sense of personal failure. It was a devastating experience. Along with the self-doubts came yet another insight—academic achievement alone would offer no guarantee that a star would shine.

When finally he graduated from Oakridge High, he took his career and his scholarships to the University of Western Ontario. Zealous scouts representing many of the major clubs, committees and fraternities offered tempting invitations but he was determined to steer his own course. He turned down approaches from the Young Liberals, remembering what the Principal had said and believing that his future would be better protected in the hands of people of influence, who could, themselves, be influenced.

His pre-med work was exemplary and the faculty of the School of Medicine welcomed him warmly to their student body. He toyed briefly with the idea of studying literature but concluded that medicine would open many more doors. As a young medical student, he served as a member of the Student Advisory Council and became fascinated with the patterns of power among the various faculty members and groups. He enjoyed mingling with them, learning the game from the inside out. His intentions and techniques did not go unnoticed, but he gave little credibility to those who questioned his motives.

At a cocktail party hosted by the Faculty, he saw an elderly, white-haired gentlemen who stood alone, though not unnoticed. He could tell from the poorly disguised glances and clumsy whispers of the 'in-groups' that this man meant something within the status-conscious world of his academic masters. But there was something strange and incongruent about his place in the gathering. His hair was long, though immaculately groomed, with light curls that fell about the collar of his finely tailored cashmere jacket. The lines of his face were etched with the utmost precision but, by contrast, his mouth was loose and his eyes shone with the mischief of a young boy contemplating the sabotage of his sister's pyjama party.

Jock excused himself from his conversation, walked over to the man, and held out a hand. "Good evening sir, my name's Jock McKeen."

"And mine is Albert Trueman," said the white-haired gentleman extending his own hand in return.

"I'm here representing the student council," Jock explained. "Events like this give us a chance to meet with our Faculty on a less formal basis. I'm afraid most of my fellow students prefer to stick to their own groups so nothing much happens. I'm pushing against the river I suppose."

"Well keep pushing Jock. I'm a stranger in this group myself so I can't serve your cause too well. But let me buy you a drink anyway."

They made their way to the bar and, true to his word, the stranger signed the chit. "I'm here at the invitation of the Senate," he said, after they had shuffled to a respectable distance from the Bar. "They want me to be the Dean of University College although I'm not really sure what that means or what the job entails."

Nor did Jock McKeen but he was sufficiently impressed to leave his glass at his lips for an additional second or so. He had always had an attraction toward older men who stood out from the crowd; they seemed to offer a glimmer of hope for his own future. When they left the reception, the two men stood in the parking lot and chatted about their respective ambitions. On parting, they agreed to stay in touch.

Albert Trueman did become the Dean of University College. He also taught a course on Shakespearean Tragedies which Jock McKeen took as an 'elective.' Jock's own neglected love of literature was re-kindled and set afire by this ex-opera singer who breathed a new magic, and bellowed a new magnificence, into the works of the Bard. He proudly walked the line between the enthusiastic student and friend. When the Dean needed his car to be driven from London to Ottawa, it was Jock McKeen at the wheel. They spent evenings together in animated literary discussions and frequently wrote lengthy epistles to each other. Jock treasured these letters, signed by 'Bud.' and stashed them away in the drawer by his bedside.

Throughout his medical school years, people speculated about his relationship with Albert Trueman and some openly aired their suspicions that Jock McKeen might have some power over the older man. Their friendship continued, sometimes close, sometimes remote but always appropriate. In a strange way, Jock sensed that the eyes of the Dean were always upon him, just as Uncle Murray's had been in the years before. Most people could see that Albert Trueman served his young friend's interests in some way and a few would begrudgingly admit that Jock earned, and deserved, the older man's attention. What everybody missed, however, was that, in his own way, the young medical student adored his older friend.

Dean Albert Trueman always promised that, come what may, he would be there to see his favourite student receive his degree. In the packed Convocation Hall, the newly anointed doctors filed past the congratulatory smiles of the academic elite, while families and friends sat in silent admiration. Then, to the surprise of all who had attended the rehearsal on the previous day, the Chancellor of the University of Western Ontario rose from his central place on the podium and walked majestically down the line of graduates. He stopped before one of the fledgling physicians and, with a smile that came directly from the heart, took him by the hand. Just like Uncle Murray, 'Bud' had kept his promise.

During the latter part of his medical school career, Jock McKeen conducted his own 'safe' rebellion. He wanted to shine, to stand out from the crowd, and academic excellence was not enough. He let his hair grow long, talked excitedly about psychology, and advocated for the bedraggled kids who found their way to the old trailer in central London that served as a makeshift drug treatment centre. He presented them personally at seminars and accused the medical establishment of abandoning the very people it purported to serve. So, even before he had fully earned the privileges of membership, he was preparing to steer a professional course that would be his own, that would be different. Certainly he was anxious to service his own ego but there was more to it than that. He was passionate about his readings in psychology and fully committed in his desire to ease human suffering. And he really cared for the street kids who lined up to see him every Tuesday and Thursday evening.

Had Jock McKeen been assured in his own sense of significance, he may never have driven himself to such levels of academic achievement. Had he decided to turn his ambitions inward, he may never have chosen the medical profession as his formal niche in the world. Had he noticed that beneath the surface of his accomplishments, there was still the little kid who could be beaten into submission by the flailing fists of Teddy Mills, he may never have challenged the voice of authority. And had he not been all that he was at that moment in time, Bennet Wong may never have found the friend he had been seeking for so many years.

BEN

When the kid pulled out a gun and announced his intention to kill him, Bennet Wong was afraid. It wasn't the mindless terror of death—more the mindful transparency of life—that froze him to the moment. It was his business to listen while desperate souls screamed so loud to be heard that the assurances they sought could never rise above the din. Yet always his own Soul would urge him forward, pushing this way and that to find a way through, for its own sake. But now this young man, with his staring eyes and shaking gun, seemed poised to take it all away.

He knew this kid. The would-be assassin was also a patient who, through countless hours, had wept, whispered and screamed his troubles into their weekly sessions. It made no sense that now he would want to kill his friend Ben. Whoever it was he wanted to kill, it would not be the off-beat psychiatrist who had listened to him, held him, wept with him and shared the 'truth' with him. Behind the delicately balanced charade, they both knew that the object of the anger was not in that room at that time. To draw this young man back into the reality of the moment, Ben would need to unstitch himself from the shadow of his patient's hostility. Whatever the nature of the threats against him, this transformation would have to be *personal*—the recognition of a man called Bennet Wong. People who see each other in their human-ness don't kill each other.

The kid was standing only a few feet away. "I hate this goddammed office," he said, glancing nervously around and allowing the gun to stray from its target.

"Right now it's not my favourite spot either," Ben admitted.

"So neither of us will have to come here any more, right?" The kid turned back but avoided Ben's eyes.

"Then my sadness will have to be for both of us Gordie. What we've shared over the past few months has meant a lot . . . to me anyway. You've done some courageous work but nobody can take away your pain or your anger. Only you can see this thing through."

Gordon Proctor shifted from one foot to the other and forced his face into a sneer. "Hey Doctor Smartass. You know the meaning of everything, so what d'ya think this means eh?" He raised the gun in front of his face and closed one eye, as if to take aim.

Ben pushed himself to breathe. "It means you've closed me out again Gordie. You've done that before. That's the easy way for you."

"Easy . . . yea . . . it's goin' to be easy. Why should you care? Keep talking and when I've had enough therapy . . . bang . . . end of session . . . right?" He lowered the weapon and, for the first time, looked directly at the man in the old leather chair.

He was a good-looking young man, and Bennet Wong was intrigued by good looking young men. They were different from him. They aroused his curiosity. He had envied them in a way, but, more and more, he could sometimes see the hurt in their eyes. It was no less than his own hurt; only different. He looked beyond the gun, through the tension and back into his own sadness. "Like you, I'm not sure if anybody else cares, or even understands. I used to spend a lot of time wanting people to care and trying to get them to understand, but I don't think that's what it's about any more."

"So, who gives a shit what you think?"

"Maybe nobody."

"So I might as well pull this fricking trigger, right?"

Ben leaned forward in his chair, his eyes drawn and heavy. "I think it's possible Gordie. I care about me and I care about other people. So it makes sense that someone would care about me. But, just like you, I've never really known for sure."

Bent on maintaining a precise distance, Gordon James Proctor took a step back and stumbled into a chair. On the verge of panic, he grabbed at the gun as it fell loose in his hand and jerked it in the direction of Ben's face. The locus of control shifted to the unknown authority. For an instant they became as one, a terrified unity of life staring at nothing and preparing to cut out from the lunacy once and for all.

Struggling to retrieve his lost delusions, Proctor sat on the arm of the chair and concentrated on keeping the weapon thrust forward. But there was nothing delusionary in the tears that welled up in his eyes. He coughed and blinked at the same time, trying to squeeze out the haze. "You're a goddammed shrink and you know nothin'." His voice was throaty and tired. "All you got is power man. All you got is fucking power." His body sagged over the chair arm. "Well you're not going to change me man." He waggled the gun aimlessly and began to shout. "No motherfucker's going to tell me what to do, not any more, man, not any more." His voice trailed off.

Ben took a breath, slow and steady. "As a friend, I don't want you to be anybody other than who you are Gordie, not even when you've got a gun in your hand. It's just hard to keep friendship alive this way."

Even with the prospect of death before him, the option of throwing himself at the mercy of a gunslinger was unthinkable. He hated helplessness. Nor did he harbour hopes of a third party intervention, divine or otherwise. For him, hope was just another form of helplessness, a refusal to deal with what *is*. So he made the choice to remain in the moment.

They both heard the door of the outer office open and close. There were voices outside. "That's my secretary and a guy with a nine-o'clock appointment," Ben said. "I don't want Margaret walking in here and finding us like this. I'm just going to let her know that we're still working in here. I'll be right back." He got up from his chair and walked toward the door.

Caught off guard by the sudden shift of events, the young gunman tried to pivot on the arm of the chair and lost his balance. By the time he found himself facing the door, it was firmly closed. Once outside, Bennet Wong walked over to the reception desk and whispered to the woman at the typewriter. "Listen, Gordie Proctor is in my office with a loaded gun." She looked up, her fingers hovering above the keys. "First, call the police and get them over here. Then call Corinne and tell her what's going on here. I don't want my wife picking this up on some radio station. I'm going back in there and I want you to call me on the phone when the police get here." Then, with a smile for his nine-o-clock appointment sitting quietly on the sofa, he disappeared back into his office.

Gordon's desperate attempt to reclaim life through the death of his father had run its course. When the phone rang and Margaret confirmed that the police had taken up positions in the outer office and around the building, Ben calmly passed the information on to his patient He stood up, took the gun from a limp hand, walked over to the door and tossed it casually on the reception desk beside his secretary.

"Did you know there was no safety catch on that gun Dr. Wong?" asked one of the police officers after Gordon had been led from the reception office.

"I'm afraid not. I don't know anything about guns."

Following the incident, Bennet Wong continued with his morning appointments, doing what he loved best, still in the moment. In the break before the afternoon sessions he sat in his office, nibbled on his corned beef sandwich and thought about Gordon Proctor. He had been deeply moved by the young man's story but, even in his sadness, Ben did not feel sorry for him. Just like all the other patients who felt abused and downtrodden, Gordon had no inherent right to believe that anything should be different, even with a gun in his hand. In Ben's experience, helplessness and hope were insidious collaborators and Gordon had blended them into a cannon against a world that would always fire back. All the psychiatric help in the world would not break the cycle unless this young man came to understand that his discontent was now being created by his own day-by-day decisions. Even at that moment, as he sat in a police cell waiting for the next cruel blow to strike, Gordon Proctor's life was in his own hands. But who would be there to support him, if not his friend Ben?

The psychiatrist leaned back in his chair and sighed. He knew something about living in a world that didn't seem to care. He remembered the doors being politely, but precisely, closed in his face when he was a student looking for accommodation in

Saskatoon. Then, when he stood on the 25th Street Bridge intending to take his own life, there was the passing student who inquired about his intentions, agreed with his decision, and walked on. But, as he looked down into the frigid waters beneath, it occurred to him that such a death would serve only to confirm his own worthlessness. As long as he was alive, there were still options to explore and choices to make, however dismal the prospects might appear.

In preparing to become a psychiatrist, Bennet Wong found his own way into the heart of human affairs. Most people who knew him came to like him because he believed in them, just as he believed in himself. A lover of the performing arts, he took particular delight in encouraging others to delve into their creativity, to cast off the harness of self-doubt and let the inside out. Immediately following his sombre encounter with the waters of the North Saskatchewan river, he organized a prize-winning float for the university Home Coming Parade. With the assistance of his younger brother Ernie, he designed and built a representation of Mount Olympus and invited his fellow students to rise above their humble station in life, to become Gods for a day, which they did, in spite of the snow. Later, as a medical student at the University of Alberta, he spent his summers working at the Ponoka Psychiatric Hospital and, for both staff and patients, the annual appearance of the unassuming Psychiatric Attendant heralded the beginning of their "Summer Festival." During this short season, the spirit of this fringe community came alive as people danced, sang, read their words and applauded each other. He organized them, encouraged them and, at times, gently pushed them forward. As his own spirit rose to meet them, they rediscovered the spontaneous joy of simply being alive; and they loved him.

His performance in medical school was of the highest order and, to his delight, he finally found himself in a community that was ready to open the doors and bestow its privileges upon him. After completing his M.D., he went on to do his psychiatric training at the prestigious Menniger's Institute in Topeka, Kansas. As always, he dedicated himself to the task at hand, being recognized for both his talents and his commitment. And it wasn't that he set out to impress his teachers. Some even questioned his commitment to the psychiatric sacraments. During one of his final orals, the chairman of the examining committee appeared frustrated with Ben's insistence that a patient's own experience was more relevant than the practitioner's theories. The old man stared at him over his rimless spectacles.

"Have you any idea what Freud would have said about this particular patient's pathology?" he asked.

"Of course," Ben answered truthfully.

"Then what is your response, Dr. Wong?"

"I suppose my response is 'so what?'" Ben told him.

Throughout his training, Bennet was widely respected by his teachers and popular with his peers. He was constantly invited to formal and informal social events and he made use of these opportunities to explore the hitherto forbidden territory. But it was his work with patients that he most enjoyed. Here he could look behind the masks and explore the 'real' world. Somewhere, within the undisguised chaos of their lives, he found what he most sought, connection. He liked women and, occasionally, went on dates but, for the most part, these encounters only served to satisfy his romantic and sentimental indulgences. Deep down, he never really believed that any woman would actually find him desirable as a lover, as a man.

Yet, despite his doubts, he met Ruth, a vibrant Filipino girl and she agreed to marry him. He was entranced by her beauty and delighted in her quiet sensuality. She was a classical musician and, indeed, there was a rich and gentle harmony that resonated between them. There was the unmistakable romantic fog that drifted around them but, with the touch of her skin upon his, the wild and wishful inventions of the mind tumbled into a thoughtless ecstasy, another new domain waiting to be explored. What happened on the outside seemed of little consequence.

Marriage had a central place in the world he had set out to know and, as such, it was something to be tried, to be lived in, at least once. Also, the timing seemed to be right. He was soon to conclude his psychiatric training in Topeka, Kansas, and marriage would provide the vehicle through which to transport their relationship, with all of its possibilities, back to Canada.

When his family declared the union to be illegitimate, he was confused and distressed. Within the culture of the Wong family this would be viewed as a mixed marriage and the unfortunate consequences of such a union would contaminate the integrity of future generations. For the last time in his life he deferred to the wishes of his mother and returned to Topeka to explain his decision to the woman who was waiting to become his wife. Predictably, she was stunned and devastated but the decision had been made and there could be no turning back. He sank into a deep and lasting sadness. The man who feared abandonment above all things had, himself, abandoned.

When he returned to Vancouver to set up his practice in Adolescent Psychiatry, he met and married Corinne Quan and the family approved. Corinne was bright, articulate, attractive and loyal. She had some of his mother's strength, but without the insatiable appetite for control. The world left little room for doubt, Corinne would make a wonderful wife, and she did.

In the years they spent together, Bennet continued to reap the benefits accorded to a Chinese husband surrounded by the affluent circumstances of upper middle class North American life. Professionally he was well remunerated and respected, despite his reputation as a radical practitioner. His comfortable home in fashionable West Vancouver was blessed with the presence of his two sons; and, along with his wife, he had easy access to both the Chinese and Caucasian communities. The only serious question raised by those who observed him and his activities was why he seemed to spend so little time at home.

For anybody who knew him, the answer was relatively simple. More than most roles, 'doing husband' seemed to carry expectations that kept him from what had now become a very clear and articulated design for his life's work. He wanted to explore the nature of relationships beyond the patterns and prescriptions of the social order. Ironically it was one of his former projects, that of finding a place of acceptability within the predominant culture, that now stood in his way. 'Doing wife,' on the other hand, was central to the well-schooled cause of Corinne Quan, and she was exquisitely proficient in the art. But her dutiful place required the presence of an equally dutiful husband and, in the coercive process of such reciprocity, Bennet found his spirit fading.

The time spent with his patients often stretched well into the night. With them he was significant, and he found a quality of relating that was missing in the shallow waters of domesticity and in the pretentious doings of his professional colleagues. Somehow the distorted outpourings and stifled whimpers of his clientele offered a refreshing level of honesty to which his own soul could relate. Although he continued to work within the psychoanalytic traditions of his training, he had become convinced that healing requires an interpersonal context in which the self of the practitioner is fully engaged. He would openly express his own thoughts and feelings through the course of the sessions, although he would never allow his own issues to impose, or determine, the direction of the work. He loved the kids, particularly those who refused to have their adolescent energy quashed by the collective authority. Even he could only stretch the doctor-patient relationship so far, however, and he continued to yearn for a level of sharing, or intimacy, through which his own being could know and be known. For this, the prescription of marriage seemed hopelessly inadequate.

Fortunately, the spirit of the times spoke back supportively. The emerging 'love' generation of the early 1960's carried with it a surge of humanistic psychology that was to have a fundamental impact, especially along the west coast of North America. It was not particularly pronounced in the conventional practice of psychiatry but it was enough to offer Bennet a convenient context for some of his less conventional ideas and aspirations. Through his work, he began to attract the attention of like-minded professionals from a variety of disciplines, along with a number of other individuals collecting under the flag of the "human potential movement." With them he could step beyond the protocols of practice, engaging them as colleagues and, he hoped, as friends. But, for the most part, they preferred to maintain a respectful distance and nobody came forward to meet him at the place where his spirit cried out for contact.

In his search for those who might share his perspective, he came across Richard Weaver who, along with his wife, Jean, operated an organization known as The Cold Mountain Institute. Located on Cortes Island, off the north east coast of Vancouver Island, Cold Mountain was generally considered to be the northern outpost of a west coast version of humanistic psychology that stretched down to its Mecca, the Esalen Institute in Big Sur, California. These were the achromatic days of 'Encounter' and many of the leading proponents of the movement participated in the Cold Mountain experience. But the Cortes community, offering residential programs for all who sought the grail of self-actualization, had its own unique characteristics, many of them directly attributable to its founder and Director, Richard Weaver.

An ex U.S. Marine, Weaver had found personal meaning and strength through the horrors of the war in the Pacific and from this grew a passion for eastern philosophy and mysticism. When he returned to civilian life, he used his military compensation to become a student of eastern studies and, on completion of his Master's degree, he took up a teaching position at the University of Alberta in Edmonton. A forceful and dogmatic man, he was often inclined to polarise students and alienate faculty by vociferously condemning the beliefs and practices of contemporary education. Recognizing that he was actually advocating a way of being, he decided that the university was a hostile environment and, with his wife, Jean, established Cold Mountain as an alternative place where people could learn about different things in a different way. Naturally, it attracted many adherents from the helping professions, and a particular therapeutic orientation quickly emerged. For many, this took the form of heavy-duty Encounter directed toward the stripping away of artificial pretences and defences and the revealing of the inner self.

Bennet Wong accepted a faculty position with the Institute and began to lead short-term residential programs and workshops while maintaining his practice in Vancouver. His less confrontational style attracted a growing number of participants, though some of the faithful were unsure about the odd-looking shrink who brought music, laughter and fantasy into the serious business of self-analysis. He and Richard Weaver were very different in both presence and style, but both men shared enough commonality of purpose to acknowledge and tolerate their differences. For Bennet, the remote Cold Mountain environment offered a God-sent opportunity for him to explore and practice his own way of being. He was able to investigate levels of honesty and disclosure that were generally unacceptable in the world of traffic lights, garden parties and appointment books.

At Cold Mountain, he found himself in the company of people who seemed determined to live beyond the pragmatics and illusions of everyday cultural prescriptions. Some, like Paul Reps and Alan Watts, were contributors to the growing popularity of eastern philosophy while others, like Will Schutz and Virginia Satir, were making names for themselves in the areas of Encounter and Personal Growth. Although he resisted buying into any predetermined ideology, these people provided support for his own belief in personal authenticity as the central pathway to the experience of 'being.' On the other hand, none of them seemed to share his conviction that such a journey could only take place through full and unrestrained interpersonal revelation, through a relationship with another being, whether mortal or god. In speculating about these alternatives, however, he concluded that they were essentially equivalent.

Corinne showed little interest in participating in her husband's project. The more he talked about the kind of relationship he wanted, the more she became convinced that he was intent upon turning her world upside down, and she withdrew even further. For Bennet, the possibility of pursuing an intimate relationship with some other woman was unthinkable. But there were other possibilities. His work at Cold Mountain had attracted an expanding group of followers, mostly males, enthusiastically committed to the cause of Self-Awareness and Personal Growth. For the most part, however, they saw Bennet Wong as their teacher, and their need to create such a division restricted their ability to meet him as equals.

Some, like architect Jerry Glock, were also struggling to find their own place in the world in spite of (or because of) their mantles of acceptability. With a broken marriage and serious questions about his own ability to maintain relationships, Jerry was cautiously feeling his way through a Cold Mountain program when he discovered Bennet Wong talking with another group of participants. Hanging around on the periphery of the session, he was surprised when Bennet paused and waved for him to join the discussion. He was even more surprised when it dawned on him that this particular group leader was more interested in what others had to say than in teaching or doing therapy. As the session moved along, he found himself examining his own experience while listening to the experiences of those around him. When he took the risk of sharing some of his own thoughts and feelings, the others listened respectfully and shared their own stories. In contrast to the Encounter group he had participated in earlier that week, it was all so gentle and self-affirming. And, in all of this, Bennet Wong seemed to understand. Only on reflection did it occur to him that Bennet was teaching and doing therapy, albeit as a full participant in the process.

On his return to Vancouver, Jerry developed the habit of dropping into Bennet's office where he was often invited to participate in sessions with individual patients or groups of kids. Sometimes there would be discussion groups involving seasoned practitioners and others, like himself, with no formal training in counselling or psychotherapy. Here he would pick up bits and pieces about the profession that continued to fascinate him but they were never quite what he expected. Apart from the odd exchange of jargon, the language was simple and the interaction personal. As mental health practitioners, they showed little regard for the revered ethic of confidentiality and talked more about energy and breathing than about psychopathology and treatment. They seemed to make little or no distinction between the body and mind and, in his naiveté, he assumed that this was a common psychiatric perspective. Only when he embarked upon his own formal training in the field did he discover that this was not, in fact, the case.

He began to regard Ben as a friend, although for much of the time he felt and acted more like a son or a student. He became a frequent visitor to the Wong home in West Vancouver and developed comfortable relationships with Corinne and the two boys, Kevin and Randy. He enjoyed meeting the wide variety of guests who also dropped in at Ben's invitation. It all seemed so together, so integrated and so complete. There were times when Ben would talk openly about his own quest for "intimacy" but Jerry could never fathom why a man with so many relationships would feel so alone. Of course he would never ask. He was not *that* much of a friend.

Nobody else asked, so nobody really knew, why Bennet Wong seemed to be dancing to a different tune. Some talked among themselves about it while others speculated privately, but, for the man himself, the answer was ridiculously simple; it was the only tune he had heard, at least with any clarity. Where other young men had been taught to tune into the social symphony, he had found himself straining his ears to the strange discordant sounds flowing from the concert hall. When those same young men were learning how to outshine each other in the orchestra, he was struggling with his minor-key solo in his room above the store. Ironically, his determination to experience the rhythm of the world took him further and further out of harmony.

Encouraging others to dig beneath the crust of respectable discourse, he prompted many to reject him through their fear of whatever demons might be awakened. Alternatively, those who chose to draw close saw, in him, the hidden and empty parts of themselves and stood in awe. They saw the healer, the mystic, the teacher, the leader and, for many, the father they had always hoped for. But they did not see the young boy who sat alone on the scorched streets of Strasbourg Saskatchewan and tried to bring the shadows to life. They did not see the young man who struggled to find a place for himself in a world of strangers. And they did not see the soul that now cried out to touch and be touched.

So the man who backed away from turning people into objects had, himself, become an object to those he most wanted to reach. The man who searched for intimacy had somehow drawn the curtain between himself and the rest of the world. Those who said they loved him, did so from a distance and, in a cruel irony, they were strangling him.

JOCK

By the time he entered the internship phase of his training, Jock McKeen was already pushing against the parameters of the medical profession. In particular, he was convinced that there was something about illness and healing that involves both the body and the mind. While spending a few weeks studying in the West Indies, he had watched a local surgeon running a sixty-bed hospital single-handed, under pressures that no Canadian physician would tolerate, in conditions that would have appalled even the most negligent and slovenly hospital. With fourteen nurses providing the back-up care, the surgeon performed all of the essential procedures by himself. To make matters worse, the man persistently broke many of the most sacrosanct rules in his manner of practice and in the way he used and maintained his meagre equipment. In a fly infested surgery, he never sterilized swabbing or bandages and seemed unconcerned that open wounds were often left exposed to the squalor of the patient's own domestic surroundings. From all that Jock had learned and believed, these people should not have healed and many should have perished from the infections initiated by the surgical procedures.

But, in most cases, the procedures appeared to work and the patients did get better. With no laboratory tests to assist in his diagnoses, this cavalier physician had an uncanny way of reading the problems and dispensing solutions with little or no regard for the standard practices of his profession. Casting aside his thoughts of Voodoo, or some other version of the black arts, Jock came to the conclusion that the healing process must be independent of the observable procedures. Whatever was taking place within the patient, or between the patient and the physician, was having a profound influence on treatment outcomes but, other than a couple of lectures on psychosomatic medicine, there was nothing in Jock's training that might unlock the secret. From his extra-curricular reading, he believed that the key was more likely to be found in the 'new psychology' than in the more formal teachings of the old psychiatry.

When he returned home, he shared his thoughts with his girlfriend Cathy Barbour. A practising nurse, she had taken a particular interest in non-traditional psychiatric approaches and had spent some time in New York City training in group therapy methods. She had brought these skills, along with many of her own ideas, to the out-patient trailer in London, Ontario where she and Jock counselled drug-crazed kids.

"Physical symptoms are only the tip of the iceberg," he told her as they drove back to her apartment after a particularly hectic evening at the trailer. "I don't care if we're dealing with drug addictions, cancer, or broken bones, healing involves the patient and, somehow, that man brought his patients into the process."

"So we're back to the mind-body thing," she said, "What else is new?"

"That's easy to say, but what does it mean? What actually happens, and how can it be induced?"

"Perhaps it has something to do with his relationships with his patients," she suggested.

"What relationships? The man hardly said a word to his patients. His bedside manner was non-existent."

"Well, words are just words, sometimes they can get in the

way. Think about the times when you and I are really *involved*—who needs words?" She placed a hand on his knee and gave it a squeeze.

"Yes," he said, with more enthusiasm for the idea than the gesture. "Some form of mutuality, but how can we define it? How can we make it observable?"

She ran her hand up the inside of his thigh. "So how can you define and observe what happens between us?"

He took the question seriously. "Well there are visible cues and measurable physiological parameters. It's not that obscure."

"Spoken like a physician," she said, taking her hand away. "The only way to really know what's possible is to experience it, to participate."

"That's exactly what I'm getting at," he said. "To maximise the healing potential, the patient must participate, but how?"

He brought the car to a halt outside the apartment building, switched off the motor and continued to stare out of the windshield. "But, if they participate in the healing, they must also participate in the disease. Now what the hell does that involve?"

"Well, we're obviously in for a participatory night," she said. "So what about the physician? How does *she* participate?"

"I don't know. Let me think about it."

"Oh God, let's go in and read a good book."

Jock had no doubt that Cathy Barbour was good for him, though he did his best to avoid the issue of marriage. Unlike the other women who had auditioned for the role of Doctor's Wife, she had a mind of her own, a foot in the door of psychiatry and a habit of thumbing her nose at middle-class values and conventions. She shared his interest in troubled kids and, when they worked together at the drug centre, things happened. She challenged him intellectually and he delighted in the sparks that often flew around their recurrent debates. He also knew that his mother regarded Cathy as a hippie from the wrong side of the tracks; an opportunist who would no nothing to enhance a potentially brilliant medical career. For his part, marriage to any woman simply meant a savage intrusion in an infinity of options.

So, when Cathy announced that it was marriage or nothing, Jock decided to play for time. Knowing that she was being given the run-around, she cut off their relationship abruptly and turned her attention to other things.

In the weeks following her decision, he felt strangely alone, despite his frenetic schedule of medical, social and sexual encounters. He missed the silliness of being 'in love' but, above all, he missed where his head went on those long evening rambles beyond medicine's borders. His career ambitions were changing. He was now a doctor, but the prospect of plodding his way through years of white coats and clip boards for recognition in a profession that he was coming to regard as an anachronism, did little to excite him. Cathy stirred his excitement. The ideas they shared opened up new possibilities, new directions for his aspirations. She had been his friend, his lover and, above all, his partner. So, despite the horror expressed by his mother and others who had invested in his medical future, he called Cathy and agreed to her proposition.

Shortly after their reunion, Cathy brought the name of Bennet Wong into one of their discussions. She had learned about this avant-garde psychiatrist from some of her more adventurous colleagues and concluded that he was someone they should get to know. So, together, they devised a plan to make it happen.

Fortuitously, Jock was already destined to complete his internship on the West Coast and had been pushing for a psychiatric component to be incorporated into the internship program. If he could convince the authorities to let him test the waters, he would achieve his own ambitions, while bestowing his own distinctive parting gift upon the Medical School at the University of Western Ontario. It was a brilliant move that would enable him to slip by the old guard of the Ontario medical establishment, even receive their blessings, and move directly to the leading edge of adolescent psychiatry. He called Dr.

Wong and asked if he would supervise a special "rotation" within the internship. Bennet agreed. The School and the hospital agreed also.

Dr. and Mrs. McKeen loved Vancouver from the moment of their arrival. A far cry from the obdurate world of western Ontario, the city invited them to join in its irrepressible celebration of the Sixties. 'Love and Freedom,' that was the promise, and that was what they both wanted. Like most who came to the party, however, they had no idea how much it takes to create such an elusive combination.

A few days after their arrival, Jock McKeen walked into Bennet Wong's waiting room. Hoping to impress the man whose reputation he already envied, Jock had chosen to wear his trendy new doctor's suit for the occasion. Now, walking over to the reception desk, he felt strangely out of place. By contrast, two street-stained kids lounging on the sofa looked remarkable at ease with themselves, and each other. The receptionist, a dark-eyed, auburn-haired woman wearing a wedding ring smiled as he approached her desk.

"You must be Dr. McKeen," she said in a voice that had none of the hushed confidentiality usually contrived in mortuaries and psychiatrist's offices. He nodded his head and admired the smoothness of her skin.

"Ben said you should go right in when you arrive."

"Well I think I've arrived. Is he alone?" He waited for their eyes to meet again.

"No, Peter Lambert is with him, but that's okay, you'll like Peter." The smile on her face lingered for a moment. Then the telephone rang.

There were two chairs at the centre of the room. Bennet Wong was leaning forward from one, his face no more than a few inches from that of the young man in the other. Peter Lambert was a craggy youth with long grease-matted hair, a graffiti-smeared combat jacket, threadbare jeans, no socks and open-toed sandals. He was sitting upright with his shoulders hunched and his head tilted toward his psychiatrist. They spoke in whispers paying no attention to Jock. Feeling like an intruder, he closed the door quietly and perched himself on a stool by the wall.

The whispering stopped and, for a few moments, Peter and Ben looked at each other in silence. Then, without warning, the talking resumed but this time the words were clearly audible. "That's gotta be Jock McKeen who just walked in. He's the doctor from Ontario I told you about. He's going to be working with me for a time. I'm going to go over and say Hi."

Bennet Wong rose from his chair and turned to face Jock. In response, Jock slipped down from his perch and, for the first time, scrutinized the man behind the name. Bennet Wong looked to be in his mid or late thirties. His greying hair was long, almost down to his shoulders, and cut in the contemporary 'Beatle' style. He wore an olive shirt, black leather vest, dark maroon slacks, white socks and soft crinkled shoes. Dark eyes looked through the lenses of wire-rimmed spectacles and offered little information. His mouth, full and slightly pouted, was suspended across the high angles of his cheeks and his smile was open and easy. He glided effortlessly across the space between them and held out a hand.

For a moment the two men stood face to face, studying each other with their hands still firmly clasped. "Welcome Jock," Ben's voice was soft and inviting.

"It's good to be here at last," Jock replied. They exchanged smiles and Ben turned back toward his patient.

"This is my friend Peter. We've been working together for about two months and we've just discovered that we both get scared by the same things. Actually, we made the discovery just before you walked into the room."

Jock walked over and shook the young man's hand.

"How be if we bring Dr. McKeen in on our discussion? He knows a lot of kids out in Ontario and they've been looking at the effects of all kinds of drugs. He may have some interesting ideas."

Peter Lambert thought for a moment and studied the new doctor. Jock was in no doubt that he was being evaluated. "Fine," the young man said at last. Dr. McKeen was relieved. He was also flattered that his new mentor had presented him as a colleague with something to offer. "Then let's get another chair in here," Ben suggested. Jock dragged one in from beside the desk and sat down.

"I don't really think of myself as providing treatment for mental illness," Ben explained as they sat in the Casa d'Italia sampling some of Vancouver's finest home-made pastas. "I find it more helpful to think of myself working with people who are different. This way I don't fall into the medical trap of turning people into objects or classified abstractions."

Jock McKeen had been watching and listening carefully for almost an hour, tossing in the odd question to keep the information flowing in his direction. Some of it he recognized from his own understanding of humanistic psychology, but he wanted to explore the limits of Ben's radicalism and this he could do best by taking a reactionary position. He used medical words. "But the kids you see here, there must be some generalizations you can make, some etiology, or even symptom clusters, that can be classified in a way that at least enhances our understanding."

Ben took a forkful of tortellini to his mouth, dabbed his lips with his napkin and thought for a moment. "Sure," he said, "but it depends on what you mean by the word 'understanding.' I can't begin to understand the story of Peter Lambert by reading a textbook or a case history. If I believe I can, and I impose this on his life, the Peter I know will disappear into his symptoms. Then, if I resurrect him as a clinical object, I will have lost what most interests me, what I most care about and what most needs to be healed." He broke off a piece of bread and delicately mopped the sauce from this plate.

With the next question already in mind, another thought entered Jock's head. While he was pushing to uncover some esoteric form of psychiatric practice, Bennet Wong kept putting himself at the centre of whatever topic happened to hold their attention. The questions remained general and abstract but the responses were always specific and often personal. Whenever the discussion moved toward theory or philosophy, Ben would gently but firmly turn it back to his own experience. It was an interesting stance, egocentric without being egotistical. In fact, there was nothing pretentious about the man, but he expressed himself with articulate assurance. He ate, drank, spoke, paused, pondered, invited responses and listened as though each was a vital and integral part of the encounter. Jock reformulated his question. "So you leave Peter to be himself, unfettered by diagnosis, and this provides a basis for making contact?"

Ben placed his napkin on the table and sat back in his chair. "The Peter I want to make contact with is very elusive. Most of the time he's so wrapped up in the symptoms he imposes on himself that he splits off and slams the door. What he feels is his anger and what he sees is a state-sponsored shrink trying to pick away at the lock. He won't reach out to me and he refuses to see me reaching out to him. So if I sit there with my head full of speculations and clinical possibilities, then neither of us is available. The chances are that, between 'Hi' and 'Goodbye,' we will have been totally inaccessible to one another. What good could possibly come of that?"

Though the question was rhetorical, the look benevolent and the topic remote, Jock felt defensive. He could think of nothing to say. For some reason he held the defences back, allowing himself rise to the surface without breaking through the skin. The silence was almost unbearable, yet exciting, intimate, the kind of candle-lit tension he felt with women at that pivotal moment when small talk gives way to a sudden speechless unpredictability. Only this time, the excitement was not centred in his groin, more in his head and upper body, and this time he was in the company of another man, a man who probably could see beyond the flush of his face and into the secret stirring. He had pushed to the limits of his toleration and was just about to close down with some otherwise irrelevant gesture when the waiter arrived with their cappuccinos.

"So, if you were describing Peter's problem to a colleague, how would you define it?" he asked after carefully removing the froth with his spoon and sipping it noisily.

"I just did."

"So, in your analysis, psychiatry seems to be part of the problem."

"Well that's possible, depending on what you mean by the term 'psychiatry.'"

Ben seemed to know the questions before they were asked and Jock found himself letting go of his agenda. After a brief silence, Ben continued. "Usually kids like Peter are sent to me because they're considered to be a threat to others or Society. Yet many of them are more in touch with themselves than those who make the referrals. In some cases, they have moved beyond conformity to experience what I call the implosive level of being. Their real feelings are there and potentially available, but, because they remain unexpressed, they eat away on the inside— and that's the disease. For me, conformity and normality aren't the issues."

Jock understood the real issue, or at least one of them. He had often thought that the medical ideal of normality painted a very narrow picture of health. Now he was beginning to see how it might actually undermine the healing process. Could it be that a physical illness might also have its own inherent value; potentials that could be lost through swift and effective eradication? He shuddered at the idea of disease being an integral part of healing. And what of the physician who would take such a perspective? How would such a practitioner, a professional healer, maintain any accountability to the patient, the profession or society? The more he thought about it, the more complex it seemed. Yet, somewhere at the back of his mind, was the idea that, if he could move through the complexity, he would find something remarkably simple. "So where do you go with that?" he asked.

Ben had waited patiently through the ponderous silence. "The question is, where do *they* go with that? Jock, if I had a pill that would remove their pain, I might be tempted to use it. But, since I'd really be seeking to remove my own pain, I'd fight that temptation with all my heart, for both of us. But, if they're ready to move through the pain and into the explosive state of being, where the self is experienced through its own expression in the world, then I will be there with them. Here the inner and the outer experience are brought together, instead of each standing apart and judging the other. Now non-conformity and abnormality become choices. At this point we are no longer trapped."

Jock by-passed the implications and latched on to the hidden theory. "Ah, kind of like Karen Horney's notion of the authentic self being masked by the presented self and judged by the idealized self."

"Well, yes, if that's what Horney said. I believe that this kind of conflict produces a pervasive form of self hate. In other words, the unexpressed self becomes an offensive object and the authentic feelings are transformed into anger that may be turned either inwards or outwards. This won't change if people simply adjust to the expectations and demands of others. On the surface they may seem to get better, even report feeling better about themselves at some superficial level of esteem. But the pain will just go deeper and, ultimately, the anger will become even more destructive."

Jock's mind was bursting. He searched desperately for some framework in which his thoughts could at least be contained for future consideration. "Some people might argue that these kids *have* been expressing their feelings. That's why they end up in your office. From that perspective people like Glasser, the Reality Therapy man, would say that the real problem is in their refusal to accept responsibility for the way they express themselves in the world."

Ben looked back at his young colleague and smiled. "Well, that being the case, I'd probably end up disagreeing with Bill Glasser. Whatever feelings these kids express, they are rarely real or authentic. Usually they're distorted and confused reactions to what's actually going on inside. The inner experience, the real feelings, may be masked through aggression or depression, or hidden behind their own versions of what the world expects. It's in the release of these inner resources that the process of healing begins to take shape."

"You're talking about catharsis then?"

"No. In and of itself, catharsis is simply an undifferentiated upsurge of emotion. It might open a door but the contents have to be known, brought under control and integrated before they can become effective resources of the self. As it is, many of the kids I see cathart on drugs, but it's a poor substitute for the real inner experience. Like most of us, they're actually afraid of their own insides. Only when we can explore the full range and depth of our true feelings can we come to know that we won't fall apart or disintegrate in their expression. Then we can be at one with ourselves. We can take charge of our lives, make choices and, back to Bill Glasser, become responsible . . . able to respond."

"I like that definition of responsibility, the ability to respond," said Jock spontaneously. "That takes it out of the realm of other people's agendas."

"Yes, I agree," Ben whispered, leaning forward as if to divulge a confidence. "And that includes the agenda of the therapist."

"Are you talking about treatment?" asked Jock.

Ben pushed his cup to one side and leaned back in his chair. "I'm talking about our ideas of normality. I'm talking about our need to provide cures. I'm talking about our obsession with clinical procedures and protocols. I'm talking about anything that in any way imposes itself on the process. I'm suggesting that, through many of our most revered methods, we may not only miss the boat, we can also pollute the waters. The simple idea is that the patient is the one who does the healing, not us."

Thoughts of the West Indies flooded back. "Does this also apply to treating physical injury or illness?" Jock asked.

"Yes. I believe that mind and body share the same essence, the same resources, the same energy and that the movement toward physical and mental well being, the treatment if you like, involves the same common denominator."

"And that is . . . . ? "

Ben leaned forward again. "Relationship," he said quietly. "Relationship with self, relationship with others and relationship with the world." He paused for a moment, then continued. "From this perspective, health is a state of relatedness and what we call illness is really a breakdown in relationships at one level or another. Even injuries that we attribute to accidental causes can be viewed as a momentary fracture in our relationship with the outside world."

Jock had been right all along. The key was remarkably simple and the implications monumentally complex. It was as if he already knew these things and was using Ben to pry them loose from the bedrock of his own beliefs. Now he wanted to be alone, to dig deeper and draw out the conclusions. Then he would return for more. Meanwhile he struggled to conceal his excitement. "So what does it take for your patients to create these relationships?" he asked. "What determines the prognosis?"

"Honesty and courage," Ben replied.

"And if we can't do it for them, what can we offer?"

"Honesty and courage," Ben repeated firmly.

For some reason Jock suddenly found himself floundering like a boy dragged from his hiding place and admonished for some undisclosed misdemeanour. Once again he could think of no response, but this time the silence was filled with agitation rather than excitement. He glanced at his watch, brushed imaginary crumbs from his lapels and waited for Ben to make the next move.

Finally it came. "Well Jock, are you joining me for my afternoon appointments?"

"That would be great."

They divided the bill down the middle and left together.

BEN

In 1966, Bennet Wong was offered power. Three representatives
of the West Vancouver Social Credit organization, the
well-established ruling party in the province of British Columbia, turned up at his office and invited him to consider running
as a candidate in the up-coming Provincial election. The Attorney General telephoned the next day to pledge his support for
the idea. Nobody seemed concerned that Ben had never been a
member, or even a supporter, of the Social Credit Party.

Most political commentators were predicting that the Social
Credit Party, under the leadership of W.A.C. Bennet, would win
a Provincial election but an energized New Democratic Party,
brandishing its left-wing alternatives, was beginning to air some
serious concerns and people were listening. Many British
Columbians were willing to believe that "Wacky" Bennet and
his 'boys' had no social conscience and that their patriarchal organization was committed to promoting and protecting the interests of the powerful at the expense of the 'common man.' At
that time, the problems of rebellious youth were high on the
political agenda and there was legitimate fear that the type of
reactionary confrontation, typically employed by Social Credit
Governments, would turn alienation to open warfare.

Whatever he had in mind, it would certainly make sense for
the wily Premier to corral a high profile professional, widely
respected as a humanitarian, who would not be charged with
naiveté or right-wing fundamentalism. It would also make sense
for him to have such a Minister operating from one of the human service portfolios in a new Social Credit Government. The
only problem would be in finding a person with such qualifications who was not already dedicated to opposing the policy and
the philosophy of the Social Credit Party.

By this time, the reputation of Bennet Wong and his work
with kids had spread throughout the lower mainland and across
Canada. Apart from his private practice, he was involved with
the Department of Corrections and ancillary organisations such

as the Central City Mission in downtown Vancouver. Social Workers, psychologists and probation officers who needed psychiatric services for their clients, were referring their clients to him in ever increasing numbers. Prior to meeting him, many of these practitioners had come to consider psychiatry as the authority, used by society and the medical profession, to facilitate the disposition of 'deviants.' They were intrigued by this long-haired oriental shrink who actually related to kids; who was more concerned with his patient's personal experiences than with the hackneyed diagnostic clichés of his profession, and more committed to their well-being than to the norms of society or the retributive demands of the system.

His reputation was not restricted to the clients and colleagues who experienced his work. An accomplished speaker, possessing a rare ability to be 'personal' with large audiences, he was very much in demand at gatherings throughout the lower mainland. Through radio programs and newspaper articles, he and his views became part of the local tableau. And his views were controversial. In the face of those who dreamed of unbridled freedom, he talked about personal responsibility. To those who demanded a return to the discipline of the "good old days," he talked about respect and personal choice. To those with 'the plan,' he offered 'the personal' and to those with fanciful visions of a new tomorrow he offered the simple reality of what *is*. In matters of politics he dispensed with the right-left continuum, making no value distinction between the winners who fought to protect their power or wealth and the losers who demanded third party intervention with their own versions of justice and equality. To him, both were collaborators in a senseless game. While he might empathise with his disenchanted clientele, he refused to accept them as victims and, though he was known to be critical of the power-brokers, he respected most forms of mastery and accomplishment.

With his enigmatic presentation, he could never be captured by any movement or cause since there was no package to be purchased or delivered. He viewed all forms of idealism as banners carried by the right and the righteous in the service of their own immortality, and he despised the politics of inclusion and exclusion that emerged from such noble intentions. On the other hand, he constantly touched those whose minds remained open; people whose senses had not been dulled by repression or the opiates of fabricated ideologies. Above all, he touched those who encountered him personally—a phenomenon that was witnessed across the nation through a CBC television series in which he would sit and talk with groups of adolescents about their issues, both personal and general.

So there was a certain naïve wisdom in the Social Credit plan. Dr. Wong would elicit the support of many voters who would otherwise dismiss the Social Credit Party and, taken out of context, some of his views did seem to fit with their traditional platform. The naiveté was inherent in their belief that the man himself was contained within a selective smattering of his opinions and that, given the responsibilities of office, he would be compelled to toe the party line because of his own principles. The more enlightened prediction would have been to the contrary; that he would have challenged the party line as soon as it was drawn—if for no other reason than his own principles.

Nevertheless, for at least a few minutes, he did toy with the offer. He knew the health system from experience and was horrified by the insensitivity of its administration and the indignities of its practices. Once, as the Acting Clinical Director of a mental hospital for the chronically ill in Kansas, he had seen naked human beings herded together and left to wallow in the stench of their own bodily functions until hosed down at regular intervals by uniformed orderlies. In the face of powerful resistance, he set about the task of changing the practices within the hospital and within the State mental health network. In the health system generally, he saw how people could be classified, stripped of their human-ness, and treated as objects in the name of 'care' or 'treatment.' In particular, he saw the need for a wide range of services that would support the growth and development of children and young people.

But none of these impressions were inspired by a bleeding heart or a left-wing, victim-oriented, mentality. On the contrary, he talked of a critical connection between personal health and personal responsibility; a notion that has a certain right-wing appeal, and someone in the Social Credit Party must have been listening.

Bennet Wong, however, rejected their offer. As the Minister of Health for the Province of British Columbia, it might have been possible for him to address some of the issues that were close to his heart. He was not well-versed in the ways of bureaucracy, however, and the territorial rigidity and closed mindedness of a government department would have created insurmountable obstacles, even for him. He had no interest in the personal power of the position and, in rejecting this motive, he would have turned his back on the very force that drives the political machine. In the bureaucracy, where the mechanisms of change are typically regressive and self-regulatory, he would have daily encounters with pathological duplicity and this, above all, he would have found intolerable. In the final analysis, he never would have accommodated a pre-existing ideology and, given his repulsion of political motives, he would have been a liability to them from the outset. Without an untenable sacrifice of Self, his term of office would have been stormy, and short.

The interesting aspect of his brief flirtation with political power is that it demonstrated society's readiness to embrace him because of what he presented on the outside. Whether or not he chose to accept the evidence, the doors that had once slammed in his face had been thrown open and the red carpet laid out in welcome. Ironically, had he accepted the invitation, in all likelihood the forces of rejection would have returned to reaffirm what he had always known but, this time, because of what they found on the inside.

Then, and in the years that followed, few people came to see and understand the unpretentiousness in his style or the simplicity of his aspirations. Attributions of power, brilliance, intellectualism, radical humanism and nihilism were, and continue to be, used to classify the nature and motivation of the man. But behind such attributions, Bennet Wong was not seeking anything, at least not in the traditional sense. Instead, the kid who always thought himself to be unacceptable to others, was cautiously inviting the world to pull the curtain aside and risk the prospect of mutual revelation. For his part, he was prepared to risk the terrifying possibilities of exclusion and abandonment. His life was *that* important.

Yet, one by one, Ben passed the tests of acceptability that others placed before him. And with each accomplishment, he was handed yet another vestige of impersonal respectability, along with some of the most coveted decorations our culture bestows upon those who are truly welcome within its ranks. In 1975, *Who's Who in Canada* listed: "Bennet Randall Wong, B.A., M.D., C.R.C.P., F.R.C.P. Self employed psychiatrist in Vancouver since 1961; Director: Moffat Communications, Winnipeg 1972; Faculty, Cold Mountain Institute, 1970 and Director, 1973. Member: B.C. Medical Association; Canadian Psychiatric Association; Canadian Society of Youth Psychiatrists; American Psychiatric Association; Menninger's Alumni Association. Author of scientific papers in `The Canadian Doctor', `Child Welfare' and Journals of the B.C. Corrections Association and the B.C. Nurses Association. Married Corinne Quan, daughter of Wah Quan, July 7th, 1972; has two sons (Kevin and Randall). Clubs: Big Brothers of B.C. (Advisory Board). Society: Phi Kappa Pi. Residence: 1165, Chartwell Crescent, West Vancouver, B.C." The legitimate life! A life still young enough to be strangled by the inertia of words yet unwritten, a splendid biography, a grand obituary.

But not even *Who's Who* could tuck Bennet into a known and safe place. Judy LeMarsh said it very clearly. "You're a very dangerous man Bennet Wong. You're a threat to the values that maintain the balance of power in this society. There will come a time when someone will decide that you're too dangerous to have around." The Federal Minister of Health and Welfare took his hand and held it. As a politician, broadcaster and writer, she knew what it meant to push the limits she had experienced the horror of being hailed as a hero and despised. Her concern for Ben was from the heart.

They were sitting together in a hotel coffee shop, with writer and broadcaster Laurier Lapierre, after their panel presentation to a conference of British Columbia school teachers in Nanaimo. Ben had painted his picture of an arrogant, coercive and authoritarian school system that taught kids *what* to think rather than *how* to think. In response to questions about how to help or discipline non-compliant students, he had suggested that the system was more concerned with its own inherent need to punish. He described how these punishing strategies are more likely to express the hidden fears of the adults than address the alleged transgressions of the kids. He referred to the educational regime as "a system of unconscious self-control through which kids become the pawns in adult purges of the conscience." But those supporters of the popular liberal laissez-faire movement who applauded and cheered in celebration of their cause quickly muffled their ecstasy when he went on to talk about the teaching of personal responsibility and the type of instruction that would be necessary for all people, including students, to make self-satisfying and responsible choices. Then it was time for the 'back to basics' reactionaries to applaud.

As a public speaker, Ben was not propelled by images of his own performance. Nor was he inclined to cast himself in the role of 'expert' in order to hurl professional dogma down on those who had come looking for the answers. But he had acquired his own innate sense of choreography and timing, and his words came easily from the inside. Even when his thoughts pushed solidly against the grain, those who listened knew that they were being credited with the ability to think for themselves and, in the uncluttered honesty and spontaneity of the man, many listeners would find reasons to challenge their own beliefs. Others would turn their confusion into anger.

Judy LeMarsh's concern was not founded upon some fleeting impressions formed through the course of the evening. As a politician and a 'mediaphile,' she had been fascinated with the public persona of Bennet Wong for some time and made no secret of her respect for the ubiquitous psychiatrist who stood unflinchingly in the turmoil between a society and its children. She was drawn by his habit of taking well publicised contrary stances whenever the conventional voices of authority spoke out on the problems of an undisciplined and rebellious youth population. But this was no gentle mediation in the tedious saga of the generation gap. These were not issues that appeared as human interest stories in the special weekend sections of the local newspapers. This was the time of Rock Concerts, Protest Songs, Love-ins, the Vietnam War, Campus uprisings, smoking grass, dropping acid, the sexual revolution and the psychedelic counter-culture. It was a time when the behaviour of young people across North America, and particularly on the West Coast, was striking at the very heart of the social order. The word "anarchy" scrawled across the walls and buildings of downtown Vancouver expressed the futility of the rebels and aroused the fear of the reactionaries. From the anxiety of widespread *anomie*, kids had become the most accessible objects of fear. And for many observers, Bennet Wong appeared to be using his power to support the cause of the anarchists.

"While establishing our efficient, orderly and legal society, we have sacrificed our souls," he told a High School Graduating Class in 1968. "It is no wonder that so many of your numbers have dropped out, some doomed to lives of uselessness and despair, some struggling to discover those qualities of love and caring which our society abandoned a long time ago. We have raised you by authoritarian means to fit into a democratic society . . . "

In the trendy *Vancouver Life* magazine the 'hip headshrinker' offered a clue to his own view of the future. "Something I share with my teenagers is a sense of doom, although not in the way they do. I think we're doomed in a temporal and local way, local meaning Western Society as a whole . . ."

Unfettered by the values and beliefs of the old order, it was the young people who could smell the fear, the dissonance, the resistance and the hypocrisy. Socialized and educated in systems that continued to reflect the ideals of absolutism, however, they were totally ill-prepared to respond to their frustrations in a constructive, caring and responsible manner. Bennet Wong's lament, "We have taught them what to think, not how to think," haunted him continually. He sensed that participants in the 'me generation,' in detaching themselves from the formal structures and institutions, would lack the internal resources for creating a context in which the 'me' could become known and expressed. Realizing that the freedom of the sixties was a shallow phenomenon that could not be sustained, he committed himself to the task of sharing these speculations with those who chose to listen.

In a monumental schedule of interviews, lectures and public addresses, he offered his views on the struggles of adolescence. He talked about the drug culture, morality, delinquency, education, sexuality, family life, discipline and a myriad of related issues. He posed questions rather than solutions. He challenged his audiences to consider their own experience and their own beliefs rather than accept the beliefs of the experts or the demands of the authorities. Behind all of his comments and observations was a pervasive view of a society desperately in need of discovering its own human-ness while lacking the courage to face itself. With an elegance that few could detect or appreciate, he challenged arrogance with penetrating humility and intolerance with poetic confrontation.

"Our shaky identities are threatened by our kids so we retreat to greater authority. . . 'God is dead, do we have the courage to be?' Without God, we become mere cogs in the wheel unless we discover the essential nature of our individuality." He believed that the quest for identity, commonly associated with adolescence, had become the core anxiety of society at large and that, through their alienation and anger, the young people had actually become the expression of a deeply rooted existential fear that belonged to us all. By understanding the experience of these kids, we might come to understand the nature of our own dilemma. His greatest concern was that the authorities would shrug off their own anxieties by punishing the kids; and, invariably, they did.

He invited people to listen to kids. He organized and participated in public forums where young people, caught up in the systems of education, corrections, mental health and social services, could speak back openly to attentive audiences. He believed that if they were acknowledged for who they were—young people with their own experiences, thoughts and feelings—they would be heard without fear. This was the theme of a series that aired on the national CBC Television Network.

In 1968, he created a road show designed to provide adults with glimpses into the inner experience of adolescence. With himself in the role of narrator, the show featured a number of popular performers offering musical delicacies on the sitar, the tabla and the like. *Psychedelia for Straights* played primarily to adult audiences at the 'Retinal Circus' in Vancouver and throughout the lower mainland of British Columbia to mixed reactions and reviews. As one local newspaper critic put it, "Nobody seemed to go away with a neutral opinion." For those young people who did see the performance, it was overwhelmingly embraced as an authentic representation of the contemporary adolescent struggle.

For many people, Bennet Wong was some form of 'populist.' For others, he simply fell into the trap of over-identification with his patients and, indeed, he did nothing to hide his respect and admiration for the kids who refused to buy into the system. In an address to the students of Magee High School he said: "I am a shameless, unabashed admirer of youth, of your generation. You have swept me up with your idealism, your humanism, your care for one another, your concern for our surroundings. You have helped me see my own inadequacies, my ambiguities, my dishonesty and, in so doing, you have helped me become a better person. I have been excited by your peace marches, your love-ins, your Woodstocks, your paint-ins, your participation in volunteer programs and your insistence on changes in all our institutions.

"On the other hand, we have also been witness to a long series of confrontations and violence. After having little or no voice in the affairs of state, your generation, by sheer mass and physical strength, occupied and controlled institution after institution (the activists), then proceeded to ensure that those in opposition had little or no voice in the affairs of state, justified on the basis that they are the 'Establishment.' At one university, following a 'liberation,' a 'freedom mike' was set up for anybody to talk to the crowd. When one young man stood up to support the Vietnam War, the mike was taken from his hand and thrown to the floor. Freedom? Loving? Surely that seems to be the action of a warring rather than a loving faction?

"Make love not war! What happened? It seems that the slogan in theory has become in fact, 'Make war for love.' Immediately I am reminded of the bloody wars of the Crusades, all in the name of love, in the name of Christ. The number of atrocities committed in the name of 'love' would appear to have been superseded only by the great number committed in the name of 'right.' Your generation now seems well on its way to reproducing the violence in the name of 'love' and 'right.'"

In this, and many other presentations, he took the most universal symbol of the youthful 'revolution' and turned it back in the only way that made sense to him. He talked of a 'love' that could not be given by one person and taken away by another, but as a quality that could only be created by people invested in the process of coming to know themselves and each other. "When I hold a baby, I'm filled by the baby's love—an equal sharing. Perhaps my greatest contribution to that baby is not my love for him, as the mother myth would have us believe, but rather, it is my offering him the object and the means through which he can share his love with me."

Under the heading "Love is Junk" he articulated the possibility that the contemporary concept of love was no more than an opiate or addiction, much like heroin, through which people became dependent upon one another. "Only through the other can they become whole or complete." From this perspective it was a perpetuation of the love-dependency relationship—a deliberately created and unresolved need for 'mother.' "Did you know that junkies refer to their pushers as 'Mothers'?" he asked a middle-class audience at a Unity Church of Vancouver Conference.

His essential belief was that the term 'love' had become a euphemism to mask a system of social control in which people contrived and colluded to meet their needs through each other: "People who need people are the luckiest people in the world," exhorted the popular song. But the basic and underlying theme is that 'without me you can never be whole,' and this message was being wilfully, skilfully and surreptitiously peddled as 'love,' between parents and children, men and women, clergy and congregation, leaders and followers, hippies and flower-children, doctors and patients.

He was particularly concerned with the practices of the 'helping' professions. At a time when probation officers were reacting against the authoritarian order by becoming more humane and therapeutic in their practices, he told them that they were in no position to become therapists. As representatives of that authority, they might be able to humanize their roles but they would never be in a position to move with their clients in an open and non-judgmental manner. To attempt this would be irresponsible and potentially disastrous for both the client and the practitioner. When he expressed these views in an article published by the British Columbia Corrections Association, there were people who actually left the probation service to pursue alternative careers.

To the Institute of Psychiatric Nursing he said: "When we stand before our patients honestly and unafraid, prepared to relate genuinely as ourselves, no longer hidden behind our own defences, surely then, and only then, can real communication occur. It must be a communication between persons, not between doctor and patient or nurse and patient. What you relate must be yourself, not your role."

And, in an address at a conference of physicians in British Columbia he listed the characteristics that generally rendered them "impotent" in helping adolescents to deal with their real problems. He suggested that their role was usually "isolated, aloof, objective, and uninvolved"; their character was generally "compulsive, judgmental, achieving and authoritarian"; their time was typically "limited, resulting in hurried and anxious encounters with patients"; their minds were commonly "intellectualizing, defensive and full of expectations for others"; their morals were frequently "self-righteous and hypocritical"; their training was "too scientific, not humanistic enough and limited in terms of empathic skills"; and their narcissism "created a constant need to be considered important, right and needed."

No wonder Judy LeMarsh was afraid . . . and fascinated. As they walked out into the damp night air of Nanaimo, Laurier Lapierre had a compelling notion that he had met Bennet Wong before, but he could recall no time or locality for such an encounter. Later he wrote: "What he was about I did not fully comprehend until a few weeks, months even, later. Then it dawned on me that 'what he was about' I was in many ways seeking. The discovery of Ben Wong accelerated the decision to search for Laurier Lapierre buried somewhere under the rubble . . ."

Much of what Bennet Wong was 'about' arose from his work with his young patients—kids like Peter Lambert. Through their experiences, he developed his understanding of how the world worked and, with an innocence bordering on naiveté, he offered his views in the belief that self-responsible people would be equally thoughtful and purposeful in coming to their own conclusions and making their own decisions. Many of his patients were in trouble because they had relinquished such authority over their lives and, beyond circumstance or pathology, this was the nature of the problem to be addressed. It was simply illogical for him to play the role of expert in someone else's life. His task was to rekindle their curiosity, invite them to consider their options, and encourage them to make the decisions that best fit for *them*.

Peter Lambert ran desperately short of options when he was only twelve. That was when the glaze slid across his eyes and the craziness began. Then, as the world tried to punch him back into shape, first his father, then the school, and finally the juvenile justice system, he set out to destroy the only thing he had left—himself. After his suicide attempt came the shrinks with their diagnostic strait jackets and the care brigade with their bleeding hearts. The world was now ready to let him off the hook, to transform him from villain into victim. All he had to do was accept their offers of 'help' and hand over the last remaining vestiges of control. He refused, but his heart was weary and he directed whatever resources he had left into passive resistance. They called him "untreatable," "unresponsive," and "unreachable." They put drugs into his body, stuck electrodes to his temples and he began to disappear. He wrapped his aloneness in fantasy but the pain of his loneliness was often unbearable. It was only a matter of time.

Dr. Wong liked his fantasies. They were the rich and innocent fairy stories of a little boy, unfettered by the rules and unadorned by the pretences of the ego. They were gentle and cruel, hopeful and despairing, joyful and demonic. They wove life into death and death back into life, often obliterating this terrifying dichotomy altogether. Breaking through the heavy layers of drugs and judgments, the stories and images began to tumble out before the fascinated and appreciative audience of Bennet Wong.

Dr. Wong did not prescribe drugs. Nor did he impose judgments, professional or otherwise, although he did offer his impressions. Dr. Wong didn't let him off the hook. On the contrary, he held Peter Lambert responsible for the stewardship of his own life, past, present and future. And when it came to behaviour, there was never any doubt about who was making the decisions. While this sometimes left Peter angry and resentful, he also understood that his new shrink was carefully nudging him toward the helm of a ship he had tried so hard to abandon.

When Jock McKeen arrived on the scene, Peter's session was

almost over. A figure hesitated for a moment at the doorway and then, closing the door quietly behind him, glided over to a tall three-legged stool in the corner. Ben and Peter remained in their chairs at the centre and continued to talk as the intruder adjusted his position on the stool. He shifted two or three times before settling into quiet anonymity. It was Peter who finally acknowledged the stranger's presence, raising himself up to peer over Ben's shoulder and sinking back down again to make his whispered enquiry.

When he turned to welcome Jock McKeen to his office, Ben was immediately taken by the elegance, and the absurdity, of the dark-suited statue perched on the stool by the door. The face was finely carved and evenly textured, black curls springing loosely around the temples and falling casually about the collar of a bleached white shirt. The eyes were dark and intense and the mouth bold. He was beautiful. Not the blonde Adonis type of beauty that Ben most admired, more a dark and slender elegance. But sitting there, in his immaculate suit complemented by a flowered tie and square toed moccasins, it seemed to Ben that he looked like a hippie at a masquerade party. "You've got to be kidding," Ben thought.

The young intern smiled, slipped off his stool and stood with his hand outstretched. Ben took it and smiled back. "Hello Jock," he said, "this is my friend Peter Lambert."

For a few minutes the three chatted together, Ben participating and observing within the frame of each moment, Peter and Jock shuttling backward and forward in the dance of becoming acquainted. Peter was clearly impressed with the visitor's style and Ben amused himself with the odd similarity between the two young men. He liked the deferential attitude of the physician toward his patient. He liked his obvious respect for the kid's experience and, from the outset, he liked working with Jock McKeen.

JOCK

The clarion of freedom rang from the mountains and echoed through the hot tubs and field-stone lounges of the Whistler Ski Resort north of Vancouver. He had taken well to the sport and he swept over the light powder of the lower slopes allowing his body to make all the decisions. His hips swung easily and rhythmically above the gliding boards, while the sharp morning air bit into his cheeks.

Dr. Jock McKeen, aged twenty-three, was now an Emergency Physician at the Royal Columbian Hospital. The internship had gone well and he had been invited to join the practicing elite, intense, sharp-eyed young men dancing through the heady dramas of the emergency room and the carnal releases of the ski-slopes. When they asked him to be a member of their team and offered him part ownership of their ski-chalet, he wrote to the Dean of Family Medicine at the University of Western Ontario to say that he would remain on the west coast. His ideas about entering family practice and his dream about a speciality in psychiatry were laid to rest for the time being. It was time to feel the ground beneath his feet and take what he had earned.

They all liked this good looking, long-haired newcomer with his blue MGB and his far-out ideas about medicine and psychology. They also liked his wife Cathy, a zesty psychiatric nurse with an inclination to call a spade a shovel. She was bright, outgoing and outspoken, challenging the traditions of medicine and the world, without threatening the security of their place in either. In Vancouver, while the Beatles sang their visions of Lucy and her diamonds and the flower children shared their insatiable love in Stanley Park, Jock and Cathy where creating the new mould for doctors and doctor's wives. Back in London, Ontario, this relationship was viewed very differently, however. Seen through the eyes of his former supporters, Jock, the man who had captured so many lives, had himself been captured, lured into the uncompromising web of a woman who would draw him away from his calling.

But he was free of the old order and a new one was taking shape. He slipped the bindings of his 'Head' skis and locked them into the racks at the Lodge door. He glanced back at the figures trickling down the slope and decided not to wait for them. Clarys, the one with the irresistible breasts and 'come-to-bed' eyes, would be in the lounge and he was already fifteen minutes late. He had met her briefly at a West End party and had no doubt that she would be waiting for him in the lounge. Within the hour, the others would have left for the city and the chalet would be theirs alone. Later, they would consummate their union and drink a toast to their youth, their freedom and to his future.

Within a year, Jock McKeen was a member of the Cardiac Arrest Team at the Hospital and a standard bearer for a new genre of young doctors. He collected highs from 'code nine' emergencies, Lysergic Acid Diethylamide, sexual conquests and his growing mastery of the ski slopes. As an emergency physician, he was confident in his role and skilled in this speciality. Building from his brief rotational internship with Dr. Wong, he continued to explore the potential for the integration of psychiatry and general medicine, although there were few opportunities to apply this notion in the daily bustle of the emergency room. He personified the prevailing philosophies of youth; advocating the proliferation of love and expounding the principles of humanistic psychology.

Cathy did not share his enthusiasm for this brand of freedom. They had moved to a house in the Kitsilano area of Vancouver and, despite appearances, she sensed that they were drifting apart. Their visions for the future were no longer shared and her own career offered little stimulation. She became pregnant and, for a time, had hopes that a family would bring a new cohesion into their lives. But, as she prepared herself for motherhood, her husband seemed committed to a career and a lifestyle that excluded her even more.

Behind his preoccupation, Jock was well aware of his wife's discontent. There was no doubt that she had helped him get this far, but her mind and body now regurgitated ideas and experiences of the past and he felt the need to move on. In a way he felt sorry for her but he also knew that their ambitions had become separate and irreconcilable. He knew that, one way or another, things would have to be different although he wasn't sure what that might look like.

Working only three days a week at the Hospital, he had time for more reflective pursuits. He read Nietzsche, D.H. Lawrence and discovered the *I Ching*. He bought a flute and found a new expression of sensuality in the notes that flowed from somewhere inside. He liked to sit cross-legged on the beaches, letting his sounds mingle with those of the birds and the ocean. In the idioms of the popular philosophy he was able to use the 'idea' of love to protect himself from the experience of love. "Two branches reaching out and touching . . ." allowed each tree to remain solidly and eternally apart.

Beneath the demands of his ego, Jock McKeen, like most physicians, had the heart of a savior. Having internalized the expectations of medical principles and protocols, however, he was thorough and cautious, calling upon consultants whenever he sensed the possibility of an unpredictable outcome. In the throes of one cardiac arrest, with the drugs and electronics failing and the paddles ready for use, he was relieved when the consultant finally walked into the room.

"Let him go," said the consultant immediately, "this man is a patient and a very dear friend of mine. We've known each other for years. He's seventy-nine years old and he's tired . . . very tired." He came over to the table and took the old man's hand, gesturing to a nurse to bring him a chair.

Jock McKeen and his two breathless colleagues stood back and gave the consultant command of the emergency room. The tensions dissipated as they watched the two friends acknowledge each other with their eyes. The face of the old man relaxed visibly and, for a moment, the light returned. The consultant smiled at him and nodded a gentle affirmation. As the spirit of love passed between them, the old man silently said good-bye and closed his eyes. Time came to an end.

Jock McKeen had no program for the tears that ran down his cheeks. He had glimpsed a power far beyond himself. He had witnessed a dignity and grace that could never be scored and choreographed. He was overwhelmed by what he had seen; a love between two men that was different from anything he could remember. And yet it wasn't new. The whole experience had a familiarity that taunted him but it remained suspended in the mists of his childhood. There was something here that he wanted above all things.

CHAPTER THREE

Bennet Wong was a different kind of psychiatrist. He was insatiably curious, but it was not the kind of curiosity that sets off in search of symptoms and diseases. He wanted to know about other lives and how they related to his own. He was profoundly caring, but not in the way most doctors talk about 'patient care.' He cared about them, rather than for them. He was committed, but his was not the dedication of a saviour, it was a wholehearted desire to be involved in life. Those who attempted to learn his ways quickly discovered that his secrets were not so much in his methods but in the man himself. Some tried to be like him and lost themselves along the way.

Apart from his own private practice, he worked with the Central City Mission in Vancouver, where he provided training for the staff of that agency's group-living homes for 'disturbed' and 'delinquent' kids. Rather than relying upon externally induced discipline and control, he encouraged the staff to establish highly personal relationships with the kids in their care. He asked them to look at behaviour as a form of foreign language that needed to be decoded and understood rather than something to be classified and manipulated. "Behavior should spark your curiosity rather than your wish to reward, deprive or punish," he told them. "So if young Mike goes out and steals a car, you might assume that he needs more understanding and move closer. You may want to keep him at home for this very purpose. But don't separate yourself from him with some detached consequence."

Well versed in playing the time-tested game of predictable punishments and rewards, some of the kids complained that the system was 'unfair,' and the agency Board agreed. They demanded that specific punishments be prescribed for specific transgressions. This, they argued, is the way things work in the 'real' world. The group home staff rose in opposition to the stance taken by their Board but, rather than spearhead a mutiny, Ben resigned.

With the encouragement of the Superintendent of Child Welfare for British Columbia and the direct involvement of many Central City Mission staff, he established the Youth Resources Society, a private foundation operating group living homes for children. This time he carefully set up his own Community Board, choosing people who cared about children and could be relied upon to support his methods and beliefs.

In an inexplicable turn of events, two members of that Board began to agitate in favour of a punishment-deprivation approach for kids who were 'defying authority' even though, at that time, there was very little acting-out behaviour to contend with. He wondered what possible motives might lie behind such demands but could only speculate. Again, he found himself caught up in the politics of morality and decided to dissolve the Youth Resources Society. By this time, however, his work and his ideas had attracted considerable interest and support in the field and, wherever he spoke, he could be relied upon to draw in the crowds.

He accepted an invitation to deliver the keynote address and conduct a workshop at a conference in Minnesota sponsored by the Child Welfare League of America. Two days before the event the organizers phoned to say that there would be two thousand people at the address and that five hundred had registered for the one-day workshop. He was horrified. Rather than create a last-minute crisis, however, he suggested that it might be possible to maintain his original commitment if they would agree to him bringing a colleague along at their expense. They agreed without hesitation.

By that time, Jock was working as an emergency physician in New Westminster and was in the habit of spending a few hours each week hovering around the person and the practice of Bennet Wong. Together, they had taken courses in 'Reichian' breathing techniques and were sharing the dubious pleasures of being 'Rolfed' by a local masseur. For Jock, these were opportunities to explore the body-mind connection that might someday rock the foundations of medical science. For Ben, they were simply interesting experiences. Through their association, Jock could learn what he wanted to know while reaping the many benefits of being favoured by of one of the leading figures in the humanistic movement. Ben loved having a colleague at his side and he left the door of friendship wide open.

It never occurred to Ben that Jock might not accept the invitation to join him in Minnesota and the prospect of them working together delighted him. From the very beginning Jock had shown a natural ability to understand the kids who came to the office and they related back to him, not as a distant expert or surrogate father, but as someone who seemed to know and feel their issues. Whenever they saw patients together, a whole new dynamic came into play, a relational network that seemed to contain infinite possibilities. Working in partnership gave the kids more opportunities to be seen, Jock was able to experience psychiatric practice and Ben was no longer alone. It was an arrangement that Ben was ready to explore further but he would wait patiently for the young physician to make his own decisions.

At that time there where were other possible partners, like Jerry Glock and Jim Sellner, a young City Planner who had embarked upon his own personal journey. There was Lee Pulos, a clinical psychologist, who worked in the same building and was establishing himself as a pioneer in humanistic practice. But Jock stood out from the crowd. He wasn't blonde and his eyes weren't blue, but he had the macho presence to arouse Ben's curiosity. He had the determination and assertiveness to take life by the collar, the intelligence and tenacity to explore experience and, somewhere, hidden beneath all the preening and the posturing, beat a very gentle and caring human heart. On the pragmatic side, he was a physician and this would make a professional partnership easy to establish and maintain.

Jock accepted the invitation to go to Minnesota without question. It just seemed that everything was falling into place, with little effort on his part. He had tried to conceal his amazement when, after their first meeting at the session with Peter Lambert, Ben had come up with the idea of them working together. At first, he took it as a rather patronizing compliment. Then, as Ben began to create more opportunities for his participation, Jock could only assume that destiny had taken over. After all, he had done nothing to earn the respect of Bennet Wong. It was time for him to write his poems, play his flute and 'go with the flow.'

When they arrived at the hotel in Minneapolis, Jock again congratulated himself on his choice of mentor. They were greeted in the lobby by senior officials of the Child Welfare League and shown to the Penthouse suite, with its vast spaces and lavish Chinese decor. These were the standards to which he wanted to become accustomed. Without the gentle hand of destiny, it might have taken years. He smiled to himself as he eyed the glossy posters by the elevators doors; white stickers over blue notices announced to the world that Dr. Bennet Wong would be joined in his presentations by Dr. Jock McKeen. It was all happening so quickly, but who was he to question the cosmos?

Even as he anticipated their appearance at the conference, there seemed little for him to be concerned about. Ben would be delivering the key-note address and leading the workshop. His task would be to follow Ben and contribute according to changing circumstances and events. "If you stay with whatever's going on, you'll know what to do," Ben told him. On the flight from Vancouver they had discussed some experiential exercises to get the workshop rolling but, from that point on, Ben would take the lead and he would pitch in as the inclination arose. He was staggered by how little preparation Ben had made for either event, and how unconcerned he seemed to be; Jock simply assumed that this was the *modus operandi* for those who light up the conference circuits of North America. Personally, he would have needed notes, citations and rehearsals but this was not *his* show, thank God. His only commitment was to stay close and move with Ben as the workshop unfolded. Ben had said something about the need to "read each other." He would do his best to learn the language that would enable him to follow the instructions. He was a good student, he didn't have to prove that to anybody. Meanwhile, he was free to enjoy the privileges of celebrity.

Ben was his teacher. Even though the style was different and the evaluation methods obscure, there was a known framework for their association and a predictable future for their relationship. The teacher would give whatever he had to offer; the student would take whatever he needed to learn and, eventually, the student would move on to eclipse the teacher. But this time it was a struggle to keep everything in place. Whenever he was around Ben, he felt like a puppy-dog trying to please its master. Whenever they saw patients together, Ben was brilliant and he was lousy and he took Ben's parting appreciations with a blank smile and a perfunctory nod. Yet, whenever he stepped back into this familiar place, Ben would turn it all around again by treating him as an equal, a colleague. Even worse, and quite unpredictably, Ben would blow the whole game off the board by embracing him as an intimate friend with some startling personal revelation.

Jock needed to find new ways to deal with the enigmatic Dr. Wong. Meanwhile, all he could do was live with his inadequacy, learn what he needed to know and trust that the rest of the world wouldn't notice. He was convinced that Ben noticed but was too gracious to unmask the obvious. While he was drawn to Ben for many reasons, known and unknown, whenever they were alone together he never felt completely at ease. He was thankful that their beds were at opposite sides of the Oriental penthouse suite.

On the night of their arrival, Ben stretched out in his bed and slipped into an easy sleep. There had been many conferences before but, this time, he would not be operating alone. There was nothing to plan, only the anticipation of something to be shared. There was nothing to understand, other than the simple commitment of two men to a single purpose. But Bennet Wong did not fully understand the ambitions of the young physician who drifted off into his fantasies. And Jock McKeen did not really understand the young boy still roaming the streets in search of a best friend.

When Jock finally fell asleep, he had no idea that Miss Ferguson would be waiting for him. She was wearing the same black skirt she had worn at the museum. For the most part, she had taught him well, had let him know that he was her special student, but she could also be cold and retaliatory. Now it was his turn to teach her a thing or two before moving on. All year he had gazed at the forbidden undulations of her silken blouses and hip-tight skirts. Once, while leaning over the desk of the boy in front, she had turned suddenly and caught him at it, spilling his silent fantasies before the sniggering mob. Later, when he wanted so much to be a man, she had placed her arm around his shoulders, allowing the softness of her skin to touch that special place on his neck while her delicate aroma scuttled his senses. But now the others were gone and they were alone. Now it was just Jock McKeen and Miss Ferguson . . . Jock and Margaret . . . Margaret and Jock. She was sitting at her desk pretending not to notice him but he could see the slight trembling of her hands as she flicked through the pages of her lesson plans. She looked soft and vulnerable. As he approached, she looked up and their eyes met. There could be no doubt about his intentions and her complicity. With the tenuously contained passion of a skilled artist he reached out to touch her. Then, without warning, everything went black and a voice screamed down from the heavens.

"WHAT THE HELL ARE YOU DOING? HOW CAN YOU DO THIS NOW?"

Jock McKeen was torn from his classroom of carnality back into the darkness of some God-forsaken hotel room in Minnesota. The misty figure of Bennet Wong was standing over his bed screaming fury into the night. If he moved quickly, kept his eyes closed and denied all access to the intruder, he might be able to get back and finish what he set out to do.

"Leave me alone. Get lost," he muttered. He turned over, gathered the covers around him, buried his head in the pillow and concentrated. But the invasion persisted.

"You've already left ME alone. This wasn't our agreement. If you're going to go away like this, the deal is off." Ben's voice tore into his cocoon without mercy.

He passed the point of no return and the dream faded into its lost reality. Reluctantly, he let it go, unfurled himself, and stared into the trespassing face that hovered above him. "What the hell do you want?" he demanded.

"I want you to keep your commitment to be here, to stay present. Without that, we can't do what we came here to do. We can't stand in front of five hundred people tomorrow and work in partnership if you can't be bothered to stay around. There will be no partnership."

Ben's eyes continued to bore down on him, his voice tight and accusatory.

"But I was sleeping for God's sake. When I sleep, I drift off—I go away, just like everybody else."

The dialogue seemed absurd.

"Sleep isn't an act of escape, it's a state of rest."

"But I was dreaming. I don't control my bloody dreams," he protested.

"Your decision came well before the dream," Ben insisted.

"What decision? What the hell are you talking about?"

"Your decision to leave, to disappear." Ben's voice had calmed but his face was still inflamed. "Last night we agreed to stay present for each other and I took you at your word."

"This is nuts. How do you know this? How can you tell what's happening when I'm asleep? How do you know whether I'm here, or there, or anywhere?"

Ben's demeanour shifted from outrage to dejection. "I missed you," he said, sinking down onto the bed. "Suddenly you weren't there."

"Oh, for Christ's sake Ben. Why weren't you asleep?"

"I was."

"Then how in God's name could you have known what I was up to?"

"How do you know when anything happens? I just woke up and you weren't there. You may just as well have left town." He seemed sad now, like a little boy grieving for his *own* lost dream.

Jock sat up. "How could you tell?"

"The same way I can see, hear and smell."

Ben returned to his own bed and sat down. He knew what his anger was all about. The partnership that had been so clearly articulated and agreed upon had been dissolved without notice. He had been abandoned. He was familiar with the way his patients came and went in their struggle for survival and could even appreciate why Corinne might want to keep her distance. But it never occurred to him that Jock would not understand their commitment. Even if their friendship meant nothing, there was a conference to be addressed and it was their joint responsibility to 'be there.' Throughout his years of working on his own, he had simply assumed that all helping professionals would be there for their clients and Jock's decision to disappear was an outrageous act of disrespect. Leaving his bed to demand accountability and explanation was the only thing that made sense.

But Jock had misunderstood his new instructor. He had learned about the importance of being 'present' and was fully prepared to bring himself fully into their work together. He was always 'there' when there was something to be learned, or gained but it was his prerogative to return to his private retreats when the action was over. Who, other than God Himself, could expect otherwise?

So, when Jock blinked into the angry face above his bed, he had no real understanding of the nature of his transgression and the explanations he was offered seemed to flow from a world far more remote than the classroom from which he had been unceremoniously dragged. But, good student that he was, he always listened to his teachers in the end and, with sleep a forgone possibility, he began to reconsider his position. With the night-raider safely back in the confines of his own bed and the unsteady light of the downtown glitter playing upon the plaster dragons above his head, he carefully reviewed the bizarre new expectations. All he knew for sure was that he had let Ben down and this, alone, was cause for concern.

In the other bed there was no call for a review. The picture was abundantly clear and it was time to move on. But, in the heat of the battle, a new piece of information had been temporarily skimmed over. Until that moment Bennet Wong, with his carefully honed awareness, had never sensed the loss of another person from the sanctuary of his own slumbers. "I suppose it's never been this important before," he concluded before wrapping the night around him again. At that point there was no way for him to fully appreciate the importance of this event in the evolution of his relationship with Jock McKeen.

From the moment of their first meeting the seed for some type of relationship had begun to germinate. When Ben began to talk about some form of professional liaison, Jock was flattered, but he continued to quiver at the prospect of trying to establish what he called 'equivalency' with such a man. And whenever Ben shared his dream of working in a highly personal partnership, Jock nodded enthusiastically and recoiled in private horror. For good reasons, nobody had been allowed to penetrate the inner world of Jock McKeen, but if anyone was capable of launching such an assault, it would probably be Bennet Wong: for Jock, the prospect was unthinkable.

Yet Ben persisted in talking about 'self-revelation' and kept pushing and ferreting away at the edges of their personal boundaries. At only their second meeting, pressured by his own shaky marital relationship, Jock asked a seemingly abstract and impersonal question about potential conflicts between matrimony and medical practice. Moving swiftly to an intimidating level of personal disclosure Ben talked of his own marriage. He described a union that, in spite of his commitment to openness, was in the process of becoming a conspiracy of silence. It was not so much the content of the disclosures that had Jock on the run as the intensity and complexity of the feelings. Not realizing, at that time, that there was absolutely nothing for him to do, he sat as a passive and helpless listener. In his fear, he became even more convinced that self-revelation was about exposure and that exposure was the enemy of power.

When he became established with the emergency team at the Royal Columbian Hospital, he became more confident in dealing with the overtures of his mentor. They even discussed the possibility of a joint living arrangement in which Ben, Corinne and the two boys would share a house with he and Cathy and their young son, Justin. By that time, however, he knew that such a plan could never come to pass. As his relationship with Cathy slowly slipped away, he was offering only the most perfunctory matrimonial gestures and resisted anything that might curtail his professional, sexual and recreational activities.

Basking in the new consciousness of West Coast radicalism, he danced joyfully around his role as a quintessential man of the times. When he moved to the house on York Street, he instituted divorce proceedings and declared to himself and the world that his separation from the state of matrimony was final and complete. It was a relief; finally a decision that even his mother would accept. His work at the hospital took only three days out of his week and, with an annual income in excess of fifty thousand dollars, he had all the time and resources to create the life he wanted. A full professional association with Bennet Wong would serve him well but, unless he could find a distinctive place for himself, establish that elusive sense of equivalency, he would forever be the junior partner.

He decided to seek psychiatric training through the Faculty of Medicine at the University of British Columbia. If he were to unlock the secrets of the physician in the West Indies and assimilate the wisdom of Bennet Wong, his gift to medical science would need the ribbons of legitimacy. If he was to share, or perhaps eclipse, the accomplishments of his new mentor he would have to produce his own ticket when the inspectors called. While others might have noted the opportunism in his ambition, his planning was independent and pragmatic. His mission was of his own making and he was prepared to work hard, damned hard, to make his mark. While his mother might have questioned the form, she could hardly condemn the objective.

But the gatekeepers of the Department of Psychiatry did not rush to embrace the young man with the pig-tail and the impeccable academic record. At his first interview they made it very clear that he would be granted no special consideration, either for his work with young people or for his association with Dr. Wong. As far as they were concerned, he was an applicant with no psychiatric experience. He felt humbled but took their stance to be essentially political. The real shock came when, after a suspiciously lengthy delay, he was called back for another interview to address 'certain questions.' On this occasion he was seen by a number of faculty members, each seeming to questioning his suitability for psychiatric training and practice. A few weeks later he was called for yet another interview.

He was stunned by the treatment. It was so completely different from anything he had received in all his years of education and training. Surely they had contacted the School of Medicine at Western and were aware of his performance and potential. Despite their claims to the contrary, they must have respected his close working association with one of the most renowned adolescent psychiatrists in the country. He wanted to show them, to punish them in some way, but they held all the cards.

Ben noticed his young friend's frustration. "I really don't know why you want to take psychiatric training anyway," he said. "It didn't do very much for me, other than provide a high-priced passport from medicine. If we work together, you don't need to do it at all." But Jock wanted that passport, and he wanted it for himself. Beyond the pragmatics, he was seething about the apparent rejection by the Fathers of his chosen profession.

The discomfort of yet another delay did little to deflect him from his ambitions in the field of humanistic psychology, however. At Ben's suggestion, he had already taken one of Richard Weaver's workshops at Cold Mountain and, as a committed student of eastern philosophy, he studied hard and wanted more. Moreover, Richard seemed to like him and this was particularly gratifying since Ben had become a central figure within the community on Cortes Island. So, when Ben invited him to share the leadership of a seven day program entitled "Sex and Identity," Jock accepted without question. This would take him straight to the heart of the action, not as a mere participant but as a bona fide leader. And not just any leader, he would be working among the initiated, sharing the spotlight with the man who appeared to be carrying the brightest new torch of all.

When Richard Weaver objected to the arrangement, Jock McKeen reacted with horror and disbelief. Since Weaver had offered him money to study eastern philosophy in India, it seemed inconceivable that he would now object to him working under the auspices of Cold Mountain. Either he was losing his ability to read his sponsors or Weaver was skilfully deceptive.

Ben was not at all surprised by what Richard had to say as they took an early afternoon stroll along the beach. Richard had wanted a close relationship with Ben, he had made that clear, and Ben had been open to the possibility, but neither had taken the initiative. Now the issue was Jock McKeen. "The man's a phoney," Weaver said. "It's obvious he's after your power and he'll take it and use it any way he can. I believe he's toxic to people and potentially dangerous." He stopped, took Ben by the arm and fixed him with his eyes. "And I worry for you Ben.

He's preparing to eat you up and spit you out. If I thought it would change anything I'd just ban him from this property but I know you'd never accept that. I don't want to lose you as well."

Ben nodded thoughtfully as Weaver released the grip on his arm and they continued to walk. "I agree with your observations Richard, but I don't share your fears. I wouldn't want a relationship with Jock if he wasn't like that. I'm not about to be possessed by Jock, or by anybody else for that matter. I don't have the power thing, perhaps it's my weakness, but I don't want it either. And since I can only be scared by what I want, I've no need to fear someone taking it away from me." He turned and faced Weaver squarely. "Listen Richard, you created Cold Mountain as a place where people can come and look at themselves and I believe that's what Jock wants to do. Why would you want to prevent him?"

They stopped again. "I didn't set this place up for people to play their pathological power games. That kind of stuff doesn't help anybody and it can shoot the hell out of the integrity of the community before you even smell it." Weaver continued to dig himself in.

Ben drew a breath and exhaled slowly. "Playing for power is part of how most people operate in the world, whether you like it or not. And it's going to take place here, whether you like it or not. It just so happens that Jock's pretty good at it, better than most. The trouble is he's dying behind his own defences and, at some level, he realises this. But, like everybody else who comes here, he has to experience the fear of pushing those defences to one side. To ban him from the property is to make the statement that only particular kinds of people with particular kinds of issues are welcome here. If you're going to do that, then you'd better be clear about the rules."

Realising that his primary objective was lost, Weaver shifted to a more conciliatory position. "Oh come on Ben. This isn't a psychiatric hospital dealing with cocked-up disorders and phoney diagnoses. My comments are based upon my experience and my sense about particular people."

"Well, based on my experience with Jock, I believe he wants to take a close look at himself and, for my part, I'd like to participate. You see, my sense is that, behind the strategies, there lives a bright and loving soul. And of course you're absolutely right, if there's no place for Jock here, then there's no place for me either."

"But you're asking for him to be a leader," Weaver protested mildly, "not just a program participant. Hell, I've already accepted him as a participant in my own workshops."

"That's right. But he'll be a leader with me. That's the arrangement you'll need to have faith in."

Richard Weaver, the seasoned warrior, sought to negotiate a truce. He turned and looked back down the beach toward the fortress he was building to challenge the foundations of the western world. He wanted Bennet Wong on his side.

They reached the uneasy compromise that four people would lead the "Sex and Identity" program. Ben and Jock would be joined by Margaret Woods, an established leader, and Lynne Vogel who was training to be a group facilitator. While this arrangement effectively brought Jock to where he wanted to be, some ground had been lost along the way.

When Ben told him of the concerns and allegations, Jock was suitably aggrieved and indignant. But when he learned that Ben had actually agreed with Weaver's 'diagnosis,' he was devastated.

"Why would you agree with something like that?" he asked.

"Because that's the way I see it too," Ben told him.

"Then why hang around with someone like me?"

"Because there's much more to you than that Jock."

"So you're interested in other parts of me."

"No I'm interested in *all* of you. There are no separate parts."

"But you want me to change in some way, right?"

"No, I just want you to be who you are."

"So who am I then?"

The question was out before he could check himself and he wanted to crawl away. He tried to smother it with words and

105

qualifications but it was too late, the smile was already etched into Ben's face. He permitted a social smile, just to keep Ben happy, and wondered why his belly ached. Ben continued to grin.

Beyond his embarrassment, Jock's mind battled the logic of Ben's reproach but, in that secret place where he and Uncle Murray had once played, a young boy stood alone, watching the dawn and waiting for the fish to rise. Of course it could have been Bennet Wong's own brand of psychiatric power-playing, skilfully exposing the pathology with one hand while extending the other in a gesture of unconditional acceptance. Then, with the victim dependent and defenceless, the most crippling contingencies could be imposed without fear of resistance or retaliation. It didn't feel right, but the possibility had to be considered.

"You always seem to be scrutinizing me," he complained as they drove back across the Island to catch the Quadra ferry from Whaletown. "It's like you get some kind of pleasure by catching me out." He was still simmering from the 'who am I?' incident.

"Sure I'm curious about you," Ben admitted, glancing at his watch and stepping down on the accelerator. "But there's no game here, at least not for me. Even if there was such a game, and I understood the rules, I'd have no interest in playing cat and mouse with you."

For a while they were silent. Jock lowered the window and let the night air blow into his face until his eyes watered. There was more to it than curiosity for God's sake. Ben was holding out on him, keeping something back. If he agreed with Weaver, then why hadn't he said something before? At least the chill on his face was real and the wind cut into him without judgment. He could switch it on and off by just turning the handle. He raised the window again and rubbed his cheeks. "You seem to know what's going on inside me when I don't. I find that really disturbing," he said.

"That's probably because you really do know what's going on inside but rather than use your own voice, you use mine.

That way you only have to deal with me." The car trundled down the wooden boards of the dock and came to a stop on the deck of the ferry.

"So what's your part in all of this? What's in it for you?" His words came out harsher than he'd intended.

Ben turned to face him. "It's the process of revelation Jock, I already told you that. You share things with me, I make my assumptions or judgments and I offer them back to you for your consideration. You may chose to agree or disagree. That's all."

"So once you get to know everything about me, then what? What do you do with that information?" He lowered the window again to assure himself that the world was still there.

"In the first place, I'd never get to know everything. In fact, I'm not sure that I can actually know *anything* about you. I can only make guesses based upon what you tell me and what I know about my own life. They are simply my imaginings, separate from you. I share them in case you're interested. If they don't make any sense to you then accept them for what they are, reflections of my life, feelings from my own insides, creations of my imagination. If they do make sense, then maybe some aspect of me is searching to find to some aspect of you. I'd like to know what makes us similar and what makes us different. I'm curious about what brings us together. It's really quite simple. If we explore these things together, the only real commitment we make is to be honest with each other. That's it. So for you to try to be anything other than who you are just makes a mockery of the whole thing."

Simple indeed. Hardly the position of a trained psychoanalyst.

"So you're prepared to share any judgments you might have?" Jock asked.

"Yes."

Jock finally turned his face toward Ben. "And you have no agenda for me at all?"

"None."

"Why do I find that hard to believe?"

107

"Perhaps we can begin to answer that by looking at you rather than me?"

The ferry shuddered away from the jetty.

News from the Department of Psychiatry at U.B.C. came to Jock as another humiliating blow from a hostile world. Ben had decided to conduct his own search for the inside story on his friend's application and, in conversations with members of the Selection Committee, it was revealed that Dr. McKeen was considered by some to possess a 'sociopathic personality' and, as a consequence, 'might be dangerous.' While Ben could accept the former, he could not accept the latter. He entertained the possibility that there might have been political forces at play and that he, himself, could have been one of the ingredients in the political stew, but the evidence was entirely circumstantial. Predictably, he relayed the information to an incredulous and dejected Jock McKeen.

The following week Professor Jack Worsley, from Oxford, England, was scheduled to present a lecture at Kingsly Hall on "Acupuncture and Traditional Chinese Medicine." Jock learned of the event from a colleague at the Royal Columbian Hospital and, given his current interest in the integration of eastern mysticism and western humanism, he went along looking for a new angle. Shortly after the flamboyant Worsley had commenced his address, Jock was convinced that he had found one. He listened with growing excitement as the self-styled doctor of Chinese medicine wove his cockney charm around a spellbound audience. As the words danced about his ears, the ideas in his head began to fall into place: the mystery of the West Indies; the elusive integration of body and mind; the never ending exchanges of Yin and Yang, sickness and health, good and evil, life and death, Wong and McKeen. And in the expression of these things came the music of metaphor to challenge the uncompromising face of science. Caught up in the web of western empiricism, he knew that his steps would have to be small and his achievements incremental but from the Tao he could create a medicine that was different, total and complete. Finally, he could throw off the shackles imposed by the repressive establishment and point the way to a new order.

At the end of the presentation he introduced himself to Jack Worsley and spilled his excitement. The western father of eastern medicine was delighted and, placing a paternal arm around Jock's shoulders, invited him to come to Oxford for a three month period of study and training. It was the familiar and receptive arm of a teacher who would accept him for his ability to perform and his mind sprang forward to meet the challenge. He was weary of introspection and tired of rejection.

Ben liked the idea. He knew very little about Traditional Chinese Medicine but it seemed to fit well. Of course he would miss Jock. Yet he understood the young man's desire to find a place for himself. It was a decision that had to be made quickly since the special training program was due to begin in a matter of weeks. Then, as Jock waited for his visa to arrive, came the final summons from the Department of Psychiatry at the University of British Columbia.

The Chairman of the Admissions Committee was pleased that the wrangling about Jock McKeen's application was finally over, but he shared the concerns of some of his colleagues that they were taking a definite risk in this case. In the interests of the profession, and the Department, he wanted to convey an austere message to the young radical sitting on the other side of the desk. "We have considered your application very carefully Doctor McKeen," he said slowly, with appropriate reverence for the significance of the occasion. "Many questions arose from your interviews with members of this faculty and I want to assure you that the delays in reaching a decision cannot be attributed to the red tape of academia. In the final analysis, however, we have decided to accept you into the psychiatric program at this university." Without rising from his chair, he held out a hand of welcome across the desk.

Jock paused to relish the excitement of the moment and attune his timing. It was one of those rare exquisite occasions that are all too often rushed in the moment and embellished on reflection; a moment when the balance of power shifts, when the servant becomes the master. He ignored the outstretched hand. "So I can now take it that you are formally accepting me?" he asked with slow deliberation.

"Yes, this is official Dr. McKeen. Congratulations." The hand pushed out another six inches.

"Well, that's really too bad, because it's too late and I'm rejecting you." Again, timing was critical. Then, at the moment when the energy could no longer be contained, Jock delivered the blow. "I've just accepted a personal invitation from Dr. Jack Worsley to study Traditional Chinese Medicine and Acupuncture with him in England. You may have heard of him. I'll be leaving for Oxford in a couple of weeks." He smiled graciously.

"So you won't be entering our program then?" With the rhetorical question, the frozen arm was slowly retracted and the transaction died.

"No," Jock replied unnecessarily.

Still looking besieged and bewildered, the Director of Admissions rose from his desk with a grimace and reached for his walking cane that was propped upright in the wastepaper basket. "I think we should just pop next door and let the Dean know of your decision." Pressing down heavily on the cane, he pushed himself awkwardly into vertical posture and grimaced for the second time. "Damn this back," he said through tightly clenched teeth, "I slipped off a damned ladder this weekend."

Jock sprang from his chair. "Accidents may not be accidental you know," he said, placing a supportive hand under the man's elbow, "but I don't have to tell *you* about such things." The patient grunted and allowed himself to be eased out of his office.

Jerry Glock was delighted to take over Jock McKeen's house while the aspiring student of Chinese Medicine went off to study with Professor Worsley in Oxford. Gradually his interest in architecture was being overshadowed by a curiosity about people . . . particularly himself. While he had no formal training or credentials in psychology, Jerry was impressed that Ben had not only encouraged him to consider a career in counselling but had actually invited him to participate in sessions with some of his patients. So, on most Fridays, and many Saturdays, he would go down to the office on Broadway and become involved in whatever was happening. He knew very little about traditional psychiatric practice and had come to believe that most psychiatrists held themselves and their activities in secret. He was flattered by the invitation, curious about the work, and scared to death.

Even in his ignorance, there was no doubt in Jerry's mind that Ben's style of practice deviated from the time-tested traditions of mainstream psychiatry. He had assumed that something called "treatment" would be based upon something called "diagnosis," but Dr. Wong made little reference to such things. He had expected to learn something about neurological processes, unconscious motivation, and the significance of past events in the life of the patient but such matters, if they arose at all, seemed to be peripheral. The focus was upon whatever the person was experiencing in the moment and, as one moment flowed into another, a story would begin to unfold, unprompted by questions, uncensored by judgments and, as far as he could tell, uncluttered by psychiatry.

So often, as he listened and watched, Jerry could see what was happening and he struggled to contain his insights. But Ben, who must have seen even more, generally remained passive. Sometimes, if the person's words were empty, or frozen, he would have them breathe into the chest and the belly and the feelings would come back, bringing tears, anger or laughter.

"The present is always more accessible than the past," Ben once told him. "In fact, that's all there is really."

"Is the past irrelevant then?" he asked.

"Not when we bring it into the present," he was told. It made sense but it was far too simple for him to grasp the full complexity of the implications

There were times when Ben would intervene and the course of the session would be irrevocably altered. It was as if he had reached into the other person and pulled something out, holding up the detached fragment and inviting the 'patient' to reclaim it. The effects often were profound and transformational. Was this the miracle of psychiatry at work, or was this the magic of Bennet Wong, the mystery that had drawn Jerry in, while cautioning him to keep his distance?

There were also times, rare and unpredictable, when such caution seemed justified; times when Ben would spring from his non-judgmental and supportive stance to confront a patient with undisguised, though brilliantly articulated, anger. On such occasions Jerry would find himself reeling from the impact, wanting to jump in and protect the hapless recipient but fearing that he might also become the object of Ben's disdain.

"Were you really that pissed off?" he asked after one such event.

"Yes," Ben said without hesitation. "I wanted Brian to hear my judgments and know about my anger. I wanted him to know that I care that much."

"So you're not as non-judgmental as we all think," Jerry observed.

"We all make judgments," Ben said, "but if you're interested in a relationship, the important thing is to have the courage to know them, share them, and *own* them. But, in a professional relationship, the key is to make sure that such sharing is always in the other person's best interests."

At the end of each session, it was usually the 'patient' who did the analysis, while Ben listened. Once, when Jerry jumped in to share his own observations, Ben cut him off sharply. "If you want to say something, talk about yourself and not about Ivan," he said. Later, he explained that the only insights that mattered belonged to the person who was doing the work.

Whatever was taking place in these sessions, it wasn't the psychiatry that Jerry had always imagined. It wasn't about the diagnostic investigation of psychic phenomena or the realignment of emotional states through the precise manipulations of a mental surgeon. To his untutored eye, it was about spontaneity, telling the truth, and unencumbered awareness, the stuff of Cold Mountain. In Ben's own terms, it was about being 'vulnerable.' It really was the patient doing most of the work while the 'therapist' stayed in touch, fully present, vigilant, caring and connected. It was all so personal and he found himself totally caught up in the process. As he had discovered through the Resident Fellow Program on Cortes, the more he allowed himself to experience his own feelings and thoughts, the more *the* process became *his* process.

Then he would feel guilty about having feelings at the patient's expense and wondered how Ben, whose own feelings were so available, could maintain the true objectivity of the doctor/patient relationship. Ben was always in charge, his presence constantly supporting the patient and his timely responses lubricating the proceedings. Sometimes he would seem to sense Jerry's guilt and invite him to talk about his feelings while the patient listened.

"You know something about struggling in relationships Jerry," he said, after one patient's grief around the loss of his girlfriend turned to anger. Jerry talked about his own relational difficulties and the sadness he now felt. "Mike, what's happening for you as you listen to Jerry's story?" And so it would go on.

With such practices, it was impossible for Jerry to take up a comfortable position as a curious, though uncommitted, spectator. Then, when he felt himself being drawn out in this way, he experienced an odd blend of fear and excitement. But this was not Cold Mountain and there were rules to be understood and respected. Yet, invariably, he came forward, resisting the nagging thought that he had suddenly become the 'patient.' Once he had taken the first step, however, he trusted Ben to see him through. Ben knew the territory. Ben knew the rules. Ben was responsible.

Ben was the open, accepting and available father he had always longed for. Whenever he took the risk to come forward, Ben was there to welcome him, accept him and reassure him. But he was never quite sure what part of him would seep through to water his eyes, tingle his cheeks or moisten his hands, so how could he possibly know how the world, including Ben, would speak back to him? Each week, he returned to find out; moving through the pain and pleasure of each session and gaining more and more confidence in his relationship with himself.

Jerry Glock was smart enough to realize that his distance from Bennet Wong was the same distance he kept from himself. Why else would he worry about being discovered? He also had the courage to recognise that his fear was not about Ben. When he drew back from Ben's invitation to come forward from his well worn shell of protection, there was no hint of condemnation or rejection. Even Ben's anger could be taken as a gift from a friend. Why, then, should he be afraid?

He often spoke of Ben as a 'friend' but the word was one of convenience, for he could never really see the reciprocity or symmetry of such a friendship. He considered himself to be part of the inner circle of associates, but he was never sure about his own qualifications for membership. He wasn't a doctor, psychologist or social worker. He had no compelling charisma that would attract the admiration of audiences in the way Jock McKeen drew in the crowds. He was good looking and he had come to expect a satisfying level of interest from women but this could hardly account for Bennet Wong's willingness to keep him around. And what about the other young men who continued to gravitate around the renegade psychiatrist? What about Jock McKeen? Were they all part of something beyond their comprehension? Was there some overall design known only to Bennet Wong, or was it all random and spontaneous? Was destiny enfolded in some pre-existing order that consumed all their lives? He had so many questions and Ben seemed to hang on to so many of the answers.

It was Ben who first introduced Jerry to Jock McKeen as "... an interesting person you should get to know." Jock had arrived to visit Ben on Cortes Island at the time when Jerry was completing the Resident Fellow program. But Jock seemed quite disinterested in Jerry. It appeared that the young physician's mind was preoccupied with things other than the quiet young man from New Brunswick who held out a tentative hand in greeting. It was Ben who suggested that Jerry might like to take care of the house while Jock was in England and it was with Ben's encouragement that he stayed on in the back room when the newly qualified acupuncturist finally returned.

After three months of amicable co-habitation, Jock and Jerry acquired a new house on Arbutus Street in Vancouver and officially moved in together. By that time there was a growing connection between them although, without Ben as the common point of interest, they would have made unlikely companions. As it was, the hard-edged, self-promoting physician and the hesitant introverted young architect moved in concert around the man they admired and feared. They spent time with him in his practice; they travelled with him on the 'circuit' and became frequent visitors to his home in West Vancouver. Corinne and the two boys, Kevin and Randy, accepted their weekend appearances as an on-going aspect of family life. Yet, behind the games of football and the trips down the road for burgers and milkshakes, there was an emerging dynamic among the three men that could find no place in the scotch and sherry world of West Vancouver.

Bennet Wong had yet to experience the relationship in which his own sense of Self could exist in the simple acknowledgement of an Other. On Cortes Island, he had found fertile ground. In the group that gathered around his work, he had access to people who seemed interested in the project, and, in McKeen and Glock, he found the energy to sustain his purpose.

They met frequently, usually at the house on Arbutus and often until late into the night. Moving on from their experiences with patients, and within the informal 'training' sessions of the larger circle, they continued the task of exploring themselves and their relationships. In this, Ben led the way. His confidence called out their courage; his personal revelations provided a bridge for their risk-taking; and his curiosity offered an invitation for them to cross over and meet him.

Jerry was characteristically cautious and went through lengthy phases of free-floating anxiety in which he began to question the substance of his own being. The more he looked behind his fears, the more convinced he became there was nothing there, no self, nothing of substance to be revealed. To assure himself of his place in the world, he created a set of habituated behaviors, like humming tunelessly, tapping his fingers or clicking his tongue. True to the cause, even these nervous mannerisms were noted and the flimsy veil of protection often confronted by the others. Then, he would look to Ben as his anchor.

Inevitably, Ben would destroy the illusion. He might begin with a humorous comment about Jerry's inane whistling around the house. Whatever the intention, the experience was one of being assailed and abandoned by the protector himself. Jerry would try to turn away but the assault on his tenuous foothold often seemed relentless. He could turn his fear into anger but this would only provide more ammunition for the forces against him. There were times when he came close to hitting back physically, even though he knew the price would be the loss of the man whose presence he most sought. Some years later, he said, "I've seen many people fall by the wayside with Ben but all you have to do is be honest and stay close. I'm still jealous because he doesn't include me. In some crazy way, I think I might have been included but I've been under his scrutiny for a long time now. I've been in agony when he's been on my case, usually because of my withdrawal, or non-presence, but he never let go. Then I'd get mad. Even Jock came close to hitting him. There were times when I thought he was using me to feel better about himself but I know better now. I still don't really understand Ben."

For most of the time, Jerry wanted to stay close and connected. He was beginning to understand how his restricted and tentative way of being in the world was all wrapped up in a set of personal beliefs that had never been explored. The seeds of his general discontent, his inability to sustain relationships, and his fears about his own significance were slowly rising to the surface. Through Ben, he found the father and he could see how the unresolved resentments and dependencies of childhood continued to fuel his beliefs about power, masculinity and sexuality. Through Jock, he discovered many of the ideals and expectations that urged him to question his own competence and acceptability. And he realized how, despite these insights, his old patterns of behavior continued to maintain his familiar place in the world. He still sought the elusive father and competed with his surrogate brother for attention and affection, even though he believed that this brother had all the aces. He questioned why two doctors would decide to include him in their projects and he was completely at a loss to explain how Ben could possibly believe in him as a counsellor or therapist. At the same time, he was preparing himself to challenge for a more substantial place in the "family."

While Jerry wondered what might happen next, Jock continued to work through the pieces of his own plan. Not only was he going to be a practitioner of humanistic psychology, but he was going to be the best or, at least, the most famous. With the principles of Chinese Medicine in his head, the art of acupuncture at his finger tips and the reputation of Bennet Wong at his side, his resources were abundant. Self-revelation enhanced his confidence and he had learned how to achieve an 'acceptable' level of personal openness and vulnerability. Having studied the behavior of 'Humanists' in Vancouver and on Cortes Island, he had even created his own distinctive style of relating. And he took pleasure from this, just as he had taken pleasure from creating his own distinctive style on the ski slopes.

As in most things, this aspect of Jock's life was a mesmerising dance between the demands of the ego and the strategies necessary for its satisfaction. He moved skilfully and gracefully, drawing his audience in and dismissing them whenever they stood between him and his next objective. For Ben, the choreography had an aesthetic fascination, but it was always a solo performance and never a *pas de deux*. So he watched and wondered what new forms might be created should their relationship continue. Perhaps some day his friend would let go of his secrets and they would find a way to dance together.

Sexuality was a central issue for Jock. It lay at the source of his power and provided constant affirmation of his existence. In the convoluted game of sex, he moved with the guile of a master strategist and the confidence of a seasoned performer. In this role, he was able to cast aside his fear of a woman's strength and his own impotence. In the spotlight of a woman's admiration, the fat little kid from Owen Sound basked in his own significance. But the game called for a carefully managed distance between himself and his partner, one in which the tensions could be seductively cultivated and sustained. There could be no assurances, no commitments. Above all, there could be no love. Experience had taught him that pronouncements of love carried contingencies that where unacceptable.

Sometimes the three of them would talk openly about sexuality; not in the usual manner of men and their exploits, but in a personal way, about feelings, fantasies and fears. Jock would disguise his fear and embarrassment behind a few carefully chosen 'disclosures.' Then there were times when the matter of homosexuality would be raised and, bringing the issue into the present, they would discuss their attraction toward each other. This would bring Jock to the brink of panic but he was determined keep the lid on. He had never been at ease with the physicality of Cortes Island, and the hugging of another man still aroused an unexplored discomfort, particularly if there had been the slightest hint of sexual attraction. Although their definition of 'sexuality' was broad enough to encompass the simple pleasure of bodily contact, Jock lived with the fear that, at some point, their personal explorations might break lose into a frenzy of homosexual experimentation.

If Bennet Wong was working from some vision or blue-print, it was never clear to either Jerry Glock or Jock McKeen. Nevertheless, they were both conscious of being involved in some enterprise that stretched far beyond the walls of the house on Arbutus and it seemed to be drawing them in deeper and deeper. Jerry began graduate work in psychology and Jock finally gave up emergency medicine to open a full-time practice, using his own blend of western medicine and acupuncture. On his return from England, he had converted a waiting room next to Ben's office where he practiced the art of acupuncture for five days each week. He had little difficulty in attracting patients and soon began to exceed the daily quota prescribed by the British college. As a physician, he was able to bill for each visit but the procedure of acupuncture was not recognized for payment under the Provincial Health Plan. Nevertheless, he was anxious to unleash his new weapons against the unyielding citadel of Western Medicine and he walked away from his lucrative position at the Royal Columbian Hospital. He also rejected Jack Worsley's offer of training for the Doctorate in Acupuncture and the possibility of heading up a new school in the United States. His pathway was becoming clear and his purpose was becoming intense.

The new arrangement brought Ben and Jock into daily contact. Each morning they met in one of the offices to talk about themselves, their work and, of course, their relationship. At these times, Jock would learn more about Ben's practice but, in a new spirit of reciprocity, there were times when an inscrutable Chinese psychiatrist would listen intently while an animated Caucasian physician talked about the Tao, Qi (Chi) and the Law of Five Elements. While Ben had never studied Traditional Chinese Medicine, he was no stranger to bioenergetics and was exploring massage therapy as a relaxation technique. But it took a third party to bring the connection to life.

Larry Swanson was Ben's patient. Stricken with a severe speech impediment that accompanied even his earliest childhood utterances, Larry had been subjected to all available diagnostics and procedures in an attempt to solve, or at least identify, the problem. Finally, at the age of fourteen, he had been referred to Ben with the vague suggestion that the disorder might be related to some form of infant trauma. Every week for five months Ben had seen Larry and, while they had worked hard and become close, there was no noticeable change in the boy's speech. It was time for Ben to formally acknowledge what they both already knew.

The youngster, obviously saddened by the prospect of not seeing his friend Ben every Thursday morning, accepted the rationale that such sessions could no longer be justified on medical grounds. As they talked together about present issues and future prospects, Ben mentioned the massage course he was taking and pointed to the new padded table in the corner of the office. Larry asked a number of questions about massage and went over to inspect the table. Seeing the youngster's curiosity was genuine, Ben offered him a facial and upper body massage as a parting gift. Larry accepted immediately.

Concentrating on the touch and the motions, Ben began to move his hands over Larry's face, pausing to reach into areas around the jaw and the neck. Since this had not been part of the formal course, he allowed himself to go wherever his senses took him. Meticulous as ever, he noted the places where his fingers sensed the need for stimulation in order to check these out with the instructor later in the week.

"How does that feel to you?" he asked, moving down to the lower neck and shoulders.

"Fine, it feels good," was the effortless reply.

"What was that? What did you say?"

"I said it feels good. It feels really good."

In less than a minute, Ben was across the waiting room and standing in the open doorway of Jock's office. Ignoring the patient who had just taken a seat, Ben motioned for the acupuncturist to abandon the task at hand and follow him back across the waiting room.

"Larry, this is Doctor McKeen. He has the office on the other side. Could you tell him what you just told me about the massage." Ben waited, his eyes wide in anticipation.

For a moment the boy looked stunned. His mouth trembled and his eyes became fixed. It was as if his face had divided across the middle, detaching the jaw from the rest.

"Well, Ben started to massage my face and I just started to talk. I mean like this . . . like I'm talking now."

Jock was not particularly impressed but he could see from the boy's demeanour and from Ben's excitement that something unusual had taken place. He prepared himself for the story.

"Show me the places where you did the deep massage," Jock asked after the reason for the excitement had been explained.

With Larry's permission, Ben took a felt pen from the desk and marked the six places on the cheek bones, the jaw and lower neck. He then looked at Jock for a reaction.

Jock's normally resolute jaw dropped limply. "My God!" he gasped. "I want you to come with me, right now."

Leaving Larry to play with some more words, they shuttled back across the waiting room and into Jock's office. Four patients in the waiting room strained their necks to see what all the fuss was about while the lady in the consultation chair contented herself with a tattered *Reader's Digest.*

Jock took a rolled-up chart from the desk draw and spread it across the examination table. He beckoned for Ben to join him. "These are the meridians we're concerned with, here, here, and here," Jock whispered, "and here are the points you were using. For God's sake Wong, I spend all that money and take all that time to learn this stuff and you extrapolate from some rinky-dink Mickey Mouse massage course to come up with a treatment that would send Jack Worsley into ecstasy."

Ben put his arm around his friend's shoulders and whispered, "Seems like there might be something to this Chinese Medicine stuff after all." He turned, smiled warmly at the lady in the chair, and went back to celebrate the occasion with young Larry Swanson.

Jock continued to speculate about "The Case of Larry Swanson" for many weeks. How did Ben manage to find the exact position of the points? How did he know which points to use in the treatment of a speech disorder? Was such information lying somewhere in the collective unconscious of the Chinese people? Was such knowledge universal? Had Ben actually seen and memorized an acupuncture chart without realizing what he was doing? Ben, on the other hand, accepted the incident as part of experience and moved on with few questions. The more fascinating issue was that they had established a foundation for integrating their work; this was an idea that could be actively pursued.

In the months that followed, they took courses and attended sessions, offered by itinerant practitioners, dealing with Bioenergetics and Integrative Body-Work. They concluded that the energy models, and the general principles of eastern philosophy, were more suited to the cause of healing and humanistic psychology than the more restrictive analytic and mechanistic paradigms of western medicine and psychiatry. More specifically, the notions of health as free-flowing energy and disease as blockages in that energy stream was consistent with their own assumptions and experiences.

As time went on, they became increasingly convinced that this basic idea could be applied to all aspects of individual health and even extended into the arenas of relationships and human group behavior. Within the same framework, they began to consider the more spiritual dimensions of life as their speculations on psychology moved beyond the symbiosis of mind and body to incorporate the possibility of universal wholeness and relatedness. By the same token, the energy they generated between them through the hours of discourse pumped a giddy excitement into their relationship and they played like two boys with a new construction kit. But into this project they also brought the minds of two highly trained physicians who developed their ideas with all due caution, discipline and rigor. Whatever their individual motives and aspirations happened to be, they were beginning to act more and more like two friends sharing a common set of interests. In this, at least, they related as equals.

CHAPTER FOUR

While Ben and Jock's professional association created an unavoidable degree of exclusivity, they made serious and persistent efforts to involve Jerry as much as possible. He always had a special place in their training groups and, whenever circumstances allowed, they would find ways for him to participate in their out-of-town conferences and workshops. Their sessions at the house continued and invitations to the Wong residence were always extended to both roommates. Ben continued to encourage them in their relationship with each other and, at one point, he even suggested that Jerry might be the person with whom Jock could work through his much postulated fear of intimacy. Both of them knew, however, that the only common bond holding them together was their mutual interest in staying close to Ben. They also knew that the names of Wong and McKeen were becoming a popular single billing on the professional circuit.

To this end, Jerry realized that he was losing ground and his resentment of Jock deepened, though he struggled to keep these feelings from seeping out into their evening sessions. At some level, he had concluded that Ben's search for intimacy was becoming focused upon Jock but it was also apparent that the freewheeling physician was afraid to make such a commitment. Even when Ben actually announced that he was available should Jock decide to accept the invitation of intimacy, Jerry continued to hope for some resolution that would, at least, maintain a three-way balance. He was convinced that his roommate would continue to run from the prospect of intimacy and that Ben would never force the issue. Of course, there was always the possibility that Jock might give up someday but, meanwhile, he held the power. In a dream, Jerry murdered and butchered his elusive competitor, placing the pieces in plastic bags and leaving them out to rot on the side walk. This dream he shared with the others, and each in their own way understood.

On reflection, the situation seemed quite childish and trivial although at the time it was all very serious and substantial. Their differences might have made more sense in the esoteric shadows of Jungian psychology or the crystal lights of Cortes Island but in the 'real' world of doctors and architects there was no legitimate place for openly addressing these fundamental issues of Being. Who else filled their offices with deep interpersonal disclosures and pushed their speculations out into the cosmos? Yet here they were, three mature professional men, sharing their infantile fantasies and petty jealousies, talking unashamedly about things that others fought so hard to avoid. Yet for them, this *was* the 'real' world; the world of selves and relationships. The rest was an elaborate pretence in which doctors and architects create distortions and illusions in the hope of protecting themselves from the horrifying prospect of simply being. And they had every reason to be afraid since they could not expect to find a Bennet Wong waiting to take them by the hand and show them the way.

More and more Jerry found himself hanging around on the edge, questioning the reality he had always known while peeking anxiously and excitedly at the new terrain. He was scared, but he had found the courage to keep pushing, to follow his mentor into the unknown. It was unthinkable that he should be abandoned now. Why should he be left to scramble through the undergrowth while the 'chosen one' continued to play around on the periphery like a stray wolf? It was all so childish, so unreal, so unfair.

From his own place in the bushes, Jock was also scared. His play was not that of a child hovering between fantasy and ecstasy but that of a man trapped between patience and fear. Yoga, Tai Chi and the flute at sunrise were mere symbols, relics stolen from a journey that he was not prepared to take. But he worshipped them, for they had been consecrated in that secure world of doctors and architects. They were part of a world where he had already established his place while juggling the illusions of the mystics and glimpses of a realm beyond. Through them, he might find his way without ever having to leave home.

By contrast, Ben's offer was an invitation to risk it all with fear as the only imaginable consequence. Ben had defined intimacy as "the revelation of one self to an other through the direct, uncensored sharing of experience." In this, there would be no place for abstractions or selective truths; only immediate revelation and reflection. And in the meeting of two selves so engaged, all that 'is' would unfold and all that was ever meant to be would ultimately find its way into that sacred hollow. But this could never be a project, a state to be pursued with guile and tenacity. Rather it would be an act of grace, a meeting that could never be convened, only *allowed*.

For Jock, this was an invitation to draw the veil back from a self he hardly knew that protected a soul he might not have. Around this empty grail, he had constructed a stronghold of concepts, theories and ideas about himself and the world, and he was still 'learning.' He had even taken Ben's thoughts on intimacy and abstracted them into the familiar categories of his own belief system. He was still pushing to secure his foothold and elevate his presence within the coveted relationship. Everything he knew urged him on but all that he didn't know screamed for him to stop.

In the impasse that seemed to settle upon them, Jerry made his move to realign the balance of forces. At the beginning of an evening session at the house, he made his pitch for a three-way relationship based upon equal participation, equal sharing and equal commitment. What he was really asking for was that Ben be as interested in him as he was in Jock. He was in no doubt that it should be that way, given all that had happened. He had earned the right to equality, having worked to stay in with the 'process' without all of the advantages bestowed upon his rival. Even so, he was still the inferior member, the second class participant, the odd man out. The existing circumstances were unbalanced, and unjust.

Ben listened in sadness. He sensed the young man's pain and understood the morality to which he was appealing. But this was not the time or place for pain killers and he had no intention of embracing a morality that created arbitrary 'shoulds' in the face of what was.

Without hesitation he made it clear that his primary interest was in Jock and that this was not something that could be changed like the reallocation of a salary budget. He pointed out that this interest had everything to do with him and absolutely nothing to do with the relative worth of his two friends. To believe otherwise was an act of attempted robbery. From his heart, he spoke of how he felt when he was offered the power of attorney over the self-attributions of others. In being held responsible for their pleasure and their pain he could not be seen in his naked humanity but only as an object—father, teacher, or guru—vested with a power that could never be his, and he never wanted. But the greatest tragedy came with his own reluctance to reveal himself for fear that others might attribute their own responses to him. As the stored up tears of this perennial issue welled up in his eyes, he acknowledged his own fear that he might choose to close-off from others rather than face their projections. This was why he practised psychiatry as he did, why he found freedom in the community of Cold Mountain, and why he continued to spend so much time at the house on Arbutus.

But there is more to change than insight. Following this session Jerry understood what Ben had said, yet continued to feel inferior, jealous and abused. Jock continued to enjoy his position as the chosen one and lived with the fear that the expectations of this status would catch up with him someday.

It was Thursday evening and the fading light of the Pacific sun filtered across the city, gently blushing the basement room where Jock McKeen sat on a carpet, cross-legged, transfixed and transcended. A pair of candles burned on either side of a brick and board 'altar' set before him. He was naked but for a beloved pair of drooping under shorts purchased at the Eastern Emporium some months before.

He heard voices upstairs and knew that Ben had arrived. Jerry and Ryan, a patient of Ben's who had taken up residence in the house, were sitting in the living room and the three of them had obviously decided to use the moment of Ben's appearance as an excuse to clown about. First they shouted and laughed. Then came the racket of feet stomping around on the thinly matted floor. This bedlam was interspersed with thuds, as though large and heavy objects were being thrown to the ground. Each thud was followed by yet another howl of raucous laughter.

He gritted his teeth and cursed them for their stupidity and their insensitivity. Surely they knew about his serene presence below them. Then the door of his sacred room was opened and, without notice or apology, Ben entered, trod lightly down the basement steps and stood behind him. Jock refused to turn around but could tell from the muffled sniggers that the other two were watching from the stairs. The Philistines were truly upon him. He remained in a tenuously held half-lotus, refusing to give them the satisfaction of his attention for their cretinous behaviour.

He felt a gentle moist sensation at the base of his spine, just above the waist of his drooping undergarment. Then the same sensation in the middle of his back; then between his shoulder blades. And with each delicate touch there was a warm waft of air upon his skin—someone's breath—he was being kissed along the ridge of his spine. He recoiled in horror from what was taking place and, with his own breath caught in his throat and his body stiffening by the second, he tried to sit through the ordeal, dignity in the face of indecency. Unfortunately Ben was not about to restrict himself to a token celebration of barbaric vulgarity. Across the shoulder blades and into the nape of the neck, the lips continued on their hideous journey. Finally, they landed delicately and sickeningly at that well stimulated spot behind the left ear. That was enough!

"Oh for Christ's sake! This is so bloody infantile . . . and you talk to me about respect and maturity. Well I've got some things to teach you about growing up . . . so . . . so . . . just fuck off, okay?"

He sprang to his feet and turned, only to confront the unbelievable horror of his droopy undergarment imposing the final indignity by gliding down his thighs and locking around his knees like the fetlocks of a mutated farm horse.

This was more than the wide-eyed gallery could handle and an outburst of heinous guffaws destroyed the last hopes for dignity. There could be no transcendence, not now. He glared toward the stairs, hoping that his eyes, or perhaps his genitals, would convey the appropriate message. By now the incense smelled like manure and the sitar sounded like a broken bed spring in a Bangkok brothel. In their unforgivable ignorance, they had desecrated the sacred and the serene. Even as they were caught in the consummation of their own version of transcendental ecstasy, the others knew that the chances of forgiveness would be remote, very remote.

Many years passed before Jock could actually bring himself to acknowledge that it was Ben who had 'cured' him of his self-indulgent transcendental ambitions. Even then, the memory of the incident carried an unmistakable sting of antipathy.

Some weeks later, Jerry left the house sensing that, whatever was happening, he had no part in the unfolding action. For almost a week, Jock had been withdrawn, pensive and preoccupied. He seemed tired and listless, preferring the seclusion of his room to either the company of the household or the doting attentions of his girlfriends. On this particular evening, he had arrived home from work early and maintained his distance with only the most essential and perfunctory gestures of communal life. "I'd like to spend some time with Ben before our session tonight," he said without elaboration. Jerry felt sick but was afraid to ask for more.

When Ben arrived, his consideration was clearly for Jock. As they sat in closed conversation on the living room floor, they seemed oblivious to Jerry's awkward display of nonchalance around the periphery of their meeting. Suddenly *he* was the lone wolf. Finally he made his way out into the hallway, closing the front door gently behind him with just a passing hope that, in some way, Ben would be aware of his absence.

The troubles of Jock McKeen ran deep. His mind had eagerly embraced Ben's ideas of intimacy and self-disclosure and he had declared himself willing to participate in collegial collaborative experimentation. Each morning, before their respective patients arrived, they would invest an hour in the 'process' and then, after the last stragglers had taken their lives back into the ano-nymity of Vancouver, they would meet again to share their experiences of the day, and of each other. On occasion these exchanges would roll in and out of their sessions with patients and three, or even four, lives would come together in a spontaneous laboratory of searching souls. For the most part, Jock pushed himself into the fray but, stifled by a sense that there was something to lose and something to prove, his defended self continued to seek new ways of holding back without being discovered.

In his practice of Traditional Chinese Medicine there were times, always unplanned and unexpected, when physician and patient, treatment and symptom, seemed to melt into a single transaction, an involuntary shift from ritual to purpose. What-ever 'it' was, the Tao perhaps, brushed past the ego of the healer and swept across the boundary where techniques ended and *he* began. It was so direct and personal that unsolicited tears would come to his eyes.

He suspected that Ben might have the answer but he didn't want to talk about it directly for fear of bringing yet another expectation into their relationship. But, on occasion, he actually tried to make it happen between them by deliberately dropping his guard, pushing himself beyond his carefully imposed limits and daring the universe to take over. Invariably, however, he would scramble back from the brink of embarrassment with assorted explanations and deceptions. Meanwhile, the inside watched as the outside conducted its business through the currency of fear. At stake was nothing less than his manhood and Ben was relentless in this area. Jock had shared more than he would ever repeat to another soul and was running out of material, yet the inquisitor asked for more. He was obsessed with the thought of crossing some unspecified sexual boundary. He was afraid of what Ben might ask and what he might find within himself.

But the outer journey was going nowhere. He was ready to champion the cause of acupuncture but the medical establishment was not about to hail him as a saviour. "We'll get back to you," they all said, but they never did. Now he was standing at Ben's side before an attentive public but, for much of the time, he felt alone, inadequate and disconnected. He would never make his mark on the humanistic movement by playing second fiddle to the Maestro. On the other hand, he would never be able to take, or even share, the spotlight unless the secrets of the Maestro were passed on and woven into his own performance. And this the Maestro seemed prepared to offer—for a staggering price.

It was an odd conundrum. While the torch of his ambitions grew even brighter, the small portion of the world actually available to him seemed to be diminishing with time. Meanwhile, he was being urged to give it all up, to drop through the trap door and wander thorough the sealed-off catacombs that had driven him away in search of the shimmering lights of stardom. During his deliberations, it had dawned on him that, while this was the price that Ben was demanding, the urging also came from somewhere deep within his fear. Through some strange inversion of the universe, the god-forsaken hell-hole now stood between him and his dreams. If he continued to dance around it, he would be condemned to a life of meaningless repeat performances. Retracing his steps to cross burned bridges and recover lost faces was out of the question. Yet, if he took the plunge without Ben to guide him, he would surely perish. He was trapped. Had he chosen to make his mark in any arena other than the humanistic movement, he would never have been so unwittingly snared by the forces of his own ambition.

It was unlikely that Ben would wait much longer. It was clear that he would pursue his quest for intimacy and, if not with Jock, then there would be other people, Jerry maybe. For whatever reason, it was not going to happen in his marriage to Corinne, and Jock was certain that there was no other woman in Ben's life. But intimacy must embrace sexuality and God only knew where *that* might lead. While he could learn to tolerate the ritualistic greetings and departing hugs of the inner-circle, he still closed himself off from fully experiencing the bodily contact of another male. And Ben had a perverse habit of thrusting his pelvis forward, thereby violating the most sacrosanct physical boundary of them all. It was very possible that Ben was looking to find acceptable expression for a homosexuality currently contained by a perverse curiosity and a compulsive need for aesthetic stimulation. All of which meant that he, Jock, was really an object of *desire*.

The thought shuddered through him. By this time, he knew enough to realize that his fears were concealed beneath the stage. The repetitive affirmations and re-affirmations of his sexual prowess with women could be mere disguises. This thought had occurred to him on more than one occasion. So, if he was to become sexually involved with a Chinese male psychiatrist, everything he had so skilfully presented as Jock McKeen would become part of the charade and the persona of John H. R. McKeen and would fall apart at the seams. And what other realities would be lost to illusion? How would the pieces ever be brought back together? What new forms would they take? Where would he find the mirror? Would he have the courage to look? What new demons would be there to spring out and consume him? When he left his room to ask Jerry for some private time with Ben, he knew he had to find out.

On the other side, Ben had no idea what an intimate relationship would look or feel like. He just believed that this would take him to another level of experience in the risky business of meeting life. His options were limited, however. A close personal relationship with one of his patients was completely out of the question. With the possible exception of Richard Weaver, those who surrounded him at Cold Mountain regarded themselves as his students, hanging onto his words and deferring to his wisdom. Those who gathered in his office each week saw him as their leader and, with the exception of Jock McKeen, nobody was going to challenge, or even question, this arrangement. In the terms of his own profession, Dr. Wong was trapped in 'transference;' he had become an object for the projections of those around him. Their ideas and their feelings were not about him, but about their own unfinished business. It was more a formula for therapy than intimacy. It was possible that someone would come along and meet him on equal terms but the chances seemed slim.

By this time, it was clear that he would not find what he was looking for in his marriage. Corinne wanted a normal relationship in which his version of intimacy made little sense. She wanted a full-time husband and a full time father and resented the colleagues and patients who kept appearing at the door. His sexual appetite was hardly that of a man pursuing intimacy, at least in the traditional sense, and his interest in young men disturbed her. But, for Bennet Wong, sexuality had never been the source of his attraction to others. He was drawn to physical beauty in both males and females and enjoyed the eroticism of close physical contact. He was at ease with his own body and would move into shameless contact without hesitation. But the intoxicating tensions, penetrations and orgasmic releases of sexual encounter brought limited pleasure. The sexuality that wove intrigue and deception into receptive themes of domination and submission were oppositional to the intimacy he sought. He remained uncertain about the responses of women toward him and no woman had ever demonstrated any serious interest in his brand of intimacy.

He understood his wife's distress and made sporadic attempts to draw a line down the middle of his life. Each time, however, the experience was one of self-abandonment. On one occasion, they consulted a marriage counsellor. When he was asked what additional compromises he was willing to make, his answer was clear and unequivocal—"None." For him, compromise was a negotiated peace in which both parties agree to reduce themselves, and each other, to the lowest possible common denominator. In this, he could see no possibility for a relationship. But this clarity did little to ease the pain. "So many men would love the attention you shower on me and would thank God for a wife so committed to the kids and the home," he told Corinne. He realized that she wanted only what other people seemed to be seeking—the security of a home, family and community. It was *he* who was deviant, not her.

All things considered, Jock McKeen seemed like the best bet, despite his games of hide and seek and relentless quest for power. There were other possibilities, but none drew the same curiosity or promised the same challenge. He realized that it would take considerable drive and ambition to stand up in the face of his expectations and that most of his friends, including Jerry, would run out of steam. He shared Jock's expressed desire for "equivalency" but not, perhaps, in the way that Jock intended. For Ben, it wasn't about power, it was about strength. Sometimes, he wondered how things might have been had he turned away from the demands of his family and married Ruth. She seemed to have the heart to meet him, and the female experience was certainly a mystery to be explored. But there were no regrets. All decisions, whatever the outcomes, were simply a way of exploring life.

When he arrived at the house on Arbutus that evening he suspected that there would be new information to deal with. Jock had been either evasive or vacant for most of the week and had begged-off from three of their daily meetings. Ben had some sense of his friend's dilemma, although the particulars were being hidden behind a prosaic façade of courteous and routinized behaviours. When they sat together on the floor the strain was clearly visible. He was aware of Jerry's awkward presence in the background and, as Jock began to talk, the click of the door latch confirmed the creation of a new order.

Ben wanted to share experience. And if that shared experience happened to be Tai Chi on the beach as the early morning sun shimmered across English Bay to drench the deserted sands of Kitsilano, so be it.

Clad in their white robes, the solitary figures of Bennet Wong and Jock McKeen moved through "embrace-the-tiger-return-to-the-mountain" and "white-crane-spreading-wings." As the ocean swayed to the symphony of the spheres, Jock abandoned himself to the symmetry of the motion and the harmony of their souls. His body moved with grace and precision and, with Ben at his side, he sensed that everything was just as it should be.

Then, from the corner of his eye, he caught sight of the dilapidated figure of an old drifter bearing down on them from the direction of the public washrooms. "Not now!" he protested to himself, forcing his face into an expression of transcendental determination. As he "grasped-the-sparrow's-tail," he glanced over toward Olympus and pleaded for the protection of the gods. "Please keep this mangy old bugger away . . . just for a few more minutes."

But the figure was upon them, staring at them, walking around them, inspecting them as a street urchin might inspect the guards at the palace gates. They moved into "golden-pheasant-on-one-leg" passing over the ignoble presence by staring fixedly out across the tranquility of the ocean. Then the intruder pulled a battered cigarette stub from his pocket.

"Gotta light?"

Jock's grounded leg stiffened in resistance. Ben's wavered slightly but he managed to retain his balance as a ripple of mirth ran through his body. Seeing the determination in his friend's posture, however, he continued to move slowly and meticulously in concert.

Their spectator maintained his anticipatory stare, the stub hanging limply from his unshaven jaw. As he entered "snake-creeps-down" Jock's face was no more than two feet from the malefactor's mid-section. In a brilliant reciprocal move, the drifter dropped to his knees and their eyes were in contact. Then he was down on all fours barking like a dog and sniffing enthusiastically at their ankles. When he delicately raised a 'hind' leg to Jock's white flannel trousers it was time to abandon the enterprise. "Oh for Christ's sake . . . what's the use?" It was all so familiar.

He carved his body into "man-ready-to-strike-disgusting-derelict" and spoke from the heart. "No! We don't have any matches, okay . . . OKAY?"

The man nodded, rose to his feet and walked away. After six or seven paces, he turned and looked back at the motionless figures.

"Don't watch your own creation," the drifter suggested and continued his solitary journey down the beach.

Over a thousand people crammed the conference hall. Jock was nervous, but with Ben at his side he could afford to savour the occasion. One thousand pairs of eyes cast upon the spot where he and his inscrutable partner stood and prepared to deliver. As usual, there was no script for the presentation, just a loose collection of ideas and options discussed the night before and on the short flight to Edmonton. Ben was to focus on the topic of 'love,' and Jock was to blend in the eastern concept of 'energy.' Jock would stay fully present, moving with Ben as the themes unfolded and his knowledge permitted. They had made a number of joint presentations over the previous weeks and Jock was becoming increasingly confident in allowing the exchanges to evolve. Already there were two or three recurring sequences that seemed to fit together well, and they were always there to be used as appropriate. Since these had been created through their spontaneous interactions, they could be put forward legitimately as products of their relationship, and he felt good about that.

Jock had never confronted this many people before in his life, however, and he rose to meet them by reminding himself of the anonymous weekly television audience that had watched him back in London, Ontario. But this time Bennet Wong was the star, the one they had all come to see and hear. His own legitimacy was borrowed, and even that would quickly vanish unless he could rise to the occasion, establish his own presence, and match the performance of the Master. He cast his eyes across the sea of blended faces as the introduction came to an end and the applause of welcome set his ears afire. But, as he tried to check in with himself, he discovered to his horror that his mind was nowhere to be found. When it came to his turn there would be no words, no ideas, nothing to say. It was too late to take any remedial action. Ben touched him lightly on the shoulder and, taking the microphone from its stand, moved out to engage the audience.

Ben's opening remarks were extemporaneous, though the theme was familiar and comforting. Jock pulled away from the terrifying lure of the crowd to challenge the paralysis that was threatening to take his body as well. He knew that his task was to become finely centred and fully present for his friend. This was the cornerstone of their contract and he was determined to work his craft with the discipline and loyalty of a bonded apprentice. He pumped his breath into the pit of fear until the energy started to percolate through the inertia. The spirit of Jock McKeen came forward, bringing with it the familiar sense of confidence and optimism that had always served him so well. Then, with a brief testing glance at the audience, he released himself and rejoined his colleague.

He watched the easy flow of Ben's movements, and his own body seemed to pick up and resonate with the same pulse. Urging himself to move with whatever was taking place, he found himself repeating, predicting and elaborating upon the words as if their minds were being blended within the same mold. He sensed the feelings behind each of Ben's expressions, and his own emotions echoed to the call. And deep inside, rising from the calm that had replaced the terror, he felt excited, alive and connected. This was a 'high,' a self-propelled 'trip,' surpassing anything induced by Pot or wrung out from Acid. He had pushed himself to the brink and now the bounty was there for the taking. All that he had hoped might be, was true.

He moved in and out of reflection, participating in the mystery that he had come all this way to unravel. Now, before the eyes of a thousand witnesses, the puzzle that he had forced into ice-cold concepts was dissolving into his own lived-in reality. And there was more, much more.

His focus returned to Ben and the connections were firing from the torrent in his head to the calm at his centre. This partnership was the fortuitous combination that could change the course of medical science; challenge the Western mind to re-form its structures of reality. His decision to study with Worsley had been preordained and he could see that the road ahead was wide enough for them both, even if he must walk a step or two behind for the time being. Even as the thought occurred, Ben was casting the light of wisdom, preparing the way for them to walk together, side-by-side. What was happening at that very moment, on that very stage, was a metaphor for the destiny of Bennet Wong and Jock McKeen.

It was almost time for him to make his move. He could tell from the words, from the flow of the thoughts, and the excitement arose within him. The balance between them shifted as the melody of Ben's voice gently urged him to respond. His hand reached out for the microphone and they consummated the exchange. Over a thousand minds moved in concert and he was there, at the centre of it all. There was so much to say, so much they needed to know. Having stumbled thus far through the tangle of his life, it was time to throw off the shackles. The voice that had been silenced by the oppression of the times and the suppression of Jock McKeen trembled, waiting for the precise moment and the right words.

And the words came. Love and energy, East and West, body and mind, healing and being, light and dark, Yin and Yang, Ben and Jock, a rich juxtaposition of insights skilfully designed to challenge a world fragmented by the ego-bound images of the medical mind. And the audience moved with him; he could see it in their faces and feel it in the intensity of their silence—connection.

Ben was contained in his abandonment. He watched his intoxicated partner and wondered if relationships could ever really be created and sustained beyond the ego. When, finally, the microphone was returned to his hands there was a sadness that remained with him until the applause of an enthusiastic audience died away.

As they sipped their hot chocolate silently in the deserted hotel coffee shop, Jock waited for the inevitable evaluation. There was no doubt that the presentation had gone well. He had confronted his anxiety with commitment and courage, finally bringing himself fully forward into the task. He had walked to the edge and discovered a new realm of relatedness. He had picked up the threads left by Ben and blended in his own thoughts and experiences. Furthermore, he had done this in such a way that Ben had been able to re-employ these in the amplification of their chosen themes. The recording they had used in closing, "In a Simple Way I Love You," seemed to take their words into the hearts of the assembly. And, of course, the audience had loved them. But, Ben always had his own unique perspective, so Jock waited.

Ben was aware of the expectation hanging heavily in the silence but he allowed the feelings to continue to stir within him. In his hurt was yet another experience of being abandoned. In his sadness, yet another opportunity for relatedness was lost forever. And in his anger he wanted to let the world know; he wanted Jock to feel some of the pain too. He waited for the anger to rise and then he pounced.

"Why did you leave me in search of power?" he snapped. The question was rhetorical, but, for a moment, he let Jock struggle to come up with a response. Predictably, the only reaction was a blank and dumbfounded expression. "Instead of standing with me," he continued, "you took everything you could and used it in the service of your insatiable ego. I've been alone for much of my life and I can live with that but what you did was a blatant violation of our commitment. I want you to know that I will never be a pawn in your narcissistic indulgences. At whatever level you decide to capture and use people before spitting them out I want you to hear me very clearly . . . I AM NOT FODDER FOR YOUR VANITY!"

Jock continued to stare back in silent disbelief, his entire body straining in protest. This man's judgments were totally unexpected, clearly undeserved and grossly unfair. Not one person in that hall would have supported the charges now being laid. *They* would have noticed his communion with Ben; it was there for all to see. *They* would have acknowledged his skill in weaving their words into a single message. *They* would have felt his human-ness and appreciated his humility.

He looked across the table into the impenetrable eyes of his teacher. The anger, now softened by the hurt, hung loosely on Ben's face. Jock understood. His own planned remonstrations lost their charge and stayed inside. "I'm sorry if I hurt you," he said sincerely. "It wasn't my intention to do that."

"You'll never have the power to hurt me, only I can do that," Ben replied, his eyes still firmly fixed upon his repentant partner, "and I never suggested that your intention was to hurt me. But I *do* hurt, and I want you to know about it. What you decide to do about your ego is up to you."

They pushed back their cups in unison and rose from the table. Together they walked across the empty foyer and through the doors of an open elevator. Ben pressed the button. Jock held onto his tears.

There were times when Jock became obsessed with his own guilt. Ben's negative judgments were all that was needed to spark off an autonomic sequence of self-deprecating ideations and gestures of remorse designed to make things 'right' between them. But the apologies, promises and rationalizations elicited only more anger and, seemingly, more punishment.

"Your guilt is nothing more than a cop-out," he was told one day in Ben's office. "It's a pretence that comes from your own self-deception. Rather than face yourself, you create some external notion of right and wrong, make me its guardian and then use me as the assailant in your own self-flagellation. Well, I'm not interested in that stuff, not from anybody, and particularly not from you."

Ben was right, but Jock felt trapped. "I'm only trying to tell you my feelings for Christ's sake," he protested. "Why can't you just accept them at face value?"

They continued to stare at each other across the desk.

"Because the face you show has no value for me, and the feelings are no more than your own insecurity in not having me on a string." Ben's own face was sad; he was black in his eyes. He sighed. "And now you're angry because your attempts to bring me into line with your postured remorse aren't working. When you do this you abandon me, just as you did on the stage in Edmonton."

"Oh God, haven't I paid enough for that one?" Jock looked away. If he couldn't be forgiven for his acknowledged transgressions, then how could he ever be free of them? "A thousand apologies wouldn't be good enough for you," he mumbled.

"Nothing has to be good enough because I don't want anything. And one apology is as stupid as a million. Can't you see that?"

"Well, if an apology is no good for you, what will you accept?"

"Honesty."

There was that damned word again. It meant a million different things. "And where the hell is honesty, or at least the honesty you seem to want?" His thoughts began to drift out of the window and dissipate in the rumble of the traffic below.

"If you're going to disappear, there's no point in asking questions," Ben said, with a familiar mixture of resignation and contempt.

He came back quickly. "I'm listening, for God's sake. I am listening."

Ben waited for the light to come back on and continued. "The honesty is somewhere behind the duplicity that seems to get you what you want. But if what you want now is a relationship with me, that old stuff won't work. Whatever you do is a statement about you . . . about what you want and who you are. There are no convenient lapses, mistakes, oversights, or unfortunate products of circumstance that temporarily disrupt your designs. It's all *you*. You can't avoid the responsibility with a quick apology, a gesture to appease some higher authority, whether your mother, father, me or God, and blindly move on. The reality is in your behaviour and the honesty is locked away somewhere in your own heart, if you have the courage to look."

Jock's courage continued to drift limply out of the window, carried away on half-thoughts waiting to be completed elsewhere and recalled as needed. He felt tired. "I guess I don't know what honesty means." It was all his mind could muster.

"In my definition, honesty is always about you, not about the world, or the imagined world, outside." Ben noted his friend's flimsy state of presence but decided to continue with the lecture, for his own sake. "If you end up feeling bad about something you've done, it's because you let yourself down, not me, or anybody else. What's left to reveal is not your *guilt* but your *shame*. Shame calls for no apology and demands no forgiveness. And, Jock, I'll listen to your shame any time, but please don't objectify and patronize me with your wretched guilt."

It was the intellectual challenge that brought him back. He

had heard Ben make this distinction between guilt and shame before but he had never really thought about his own guilt as a form of dishonesty. It was an interesting notion. "Well I do try to be honest with you," he said.

"Honesty without awareness belongs to well-meaning politicians."

The statement was curt, and clearly derisive, but Jock was too caught up in the idea to depreciate himself again. "Okay, so my dishonesty is not so much with you as with myself. Now that's a thought." He waited for Ben to provide more fuel. It came quickly.

"I really don't know how much you're aware of and how much of your cheating is actually blind self-deception. I'm always curious about this." Ben took a candy from the jar on his desk and eyed it thoughtfully.

There was something about the word "cheating" that chilled him, though Jock fought to ignore it. He wanted to talk now, to remove the curtain that had fallen between them.

"I'm not sure myself," Jock said, "so I'll spend some time with that one. Meanwhile, just know that it's not my intention to deceive you." It was a conciliatory statement but he considered it to be honest.

Ben stared down at the candy jar and then looked up. "Oh no . . . then what about the missing jujubes?"

It didn't sink in at first.

"The what? Now what are you talking about?" Jock thought it might be some kind of joke.

"The candies you've been taking from this jar when I'm not looking."

Ben's eyes were upon him with an intensity of a courtroom prosecutor. It was no joke. Now he was to be cast as a felon, a delinquent with his hand caught in the proverbial candy jar. It was almost unbelievable that an experiment so noble and profound would be reduced to this level of banality with such infantile accusations. Now it was his turn to show *his* disdain, to make it clear that *he*, at least, was an adult, living in an adult world, facing adult issues in an adult way. "Oh go to Hell," he said.

Ben said nothing. Rather than follow whatever advice he had just been offered, he delicately unravelled a candy from its wrapper, popped it carelessly into his mouth and continued to stare.

Jock was outside himself again. He let out a perfunctory gasp of resentment to terminate the engagement and, brandishing his well-worn mask of outrage, stormed out, pausing with dramatic deliberation to take one of the last remaining jujubes from the jar. He crossed the waiting room and disappeared into his office, slamming the door and thrusting himself into the wicker patient's chair like a grounded schoolboy. "That petty self-righteous prick," he muttered to himself. "They're not even his jujubes ... I'm sure I paid for them. Yes I did, I remember now. So here I am again, colleague one minute, Casanova the next, candy thief the next. Who needs this childish crap? I don't want some surrogate mother telling me what I can and can't do. Jujubes, for God's sake."

Slowly, as his fury lost its bite and melted into a comfortable sulk, he began the tedious work of digging himself out. It was an odd habit, almost like sending one part of himself into a corner while the other took up the trowel and carefully sifted through the dross for clues. It was a lonely task. Caught up in the battle, he was far too concerned with defending himself from the ploys and judgments of those around him to weaken himself with such a division. But, in the aftermath, while one part continued to dig and search, the other watched gloomily from the corner, knowing that there could be no escape from the intense and painful *ex-post-facto* analysis of Ben's virtue and his own corruption.

On this particular occasion, his anger had been embarrassingly disproportionate to the triviality of the incident and the gentleness of the confrontation. More likely his reaction sprang from his many raids, on many other candy jars, that he felt sure had gone unnoticed. Why now, when he was making every effort to clean up his life, did the whistle have to be blown on such a minor infraction? Why now did he choose to drown himself in feelings of being judged and paternalized when a simple acknowledgment would have kept him afloat? He despised the sulking figure lurking in the corner, protecting his hurt; he turned away in disgust.

He sank back into the chair and told himself to breathe. Slowly, as his body eased and his mind gave up the contest, his belly filled with memories of a long and arduous battle. Images, dreamy and formless, drifted from the heart of the infant. Then the light that shone in his eyes could be doused without warning, the warmth that oozed over his tender flesh could turn to ice, and the comfort that filled his infant belly could seep from him, never to return, never to be replaced. But there was something 'out there,' sometimes distant, sometimes close, always hovering, holding his life in the balance. It could never be allowed to go away. It must never desert him. Whatever he had to do, whatever the sacrifice, he had to keep it by him, nourishing him, comforting him, serving him. When the boy reached out from the heart of the infant to push his massive cot across the bedroom floor, his grasp on life had seemed more assured, more under his control. Yet that same terror, tucked away somewhere in his watchful mind and woven into ever fibre of his straining body, continued to fuel his determination. It rose and grew stronger whenever the deficient or recalcitrant child was rebuked or cut off and left to die. But he learned how to bend the will of the mother and he didn't die. He committed himself to serving the servant. Then came the father, the one who took his tiny hand, squeezed it gently and left. He learned to call out their names; they belonged to him. But still, she was the one with the power, the one who could turn out the light, the one who had to be pleased. He, the father, could have stopped her, turned the light back on, but he always let her do it. However much the small boy dreamed, there was nothing he could do to restore the balance, to extend his options for survival. But, as time became his mentor, there would be other 'she's' and he could take the power from them. And there would be other 'he's' who would accept that power and hold it for his protection. Such 'he's' would have to be *chosen,* and handled, very carefully.

His coddled mind moved to resume its rightful position at the helm. Now he was a physician, this was *his* office, those were *his* drapes. It didn't take much to figure out that he still wrapped the tattered remnants of Mommy and Daddy around the selected others, that he continued to serve the servant. Hell, who didn't? Sure there was a time when pleasing Mother was his sole ambition, but there was no reason to release her now. Of course he resented his father's reluctance to get involved and take a stand but that was then, and this was now. Now he could make his own way, in whatever direction he chose. Hadn't he proven that already? Proven? What was there to prove and to whom? Could he ever be sure where the expectations of others ended and his own ideals began? Personal growth and self-awareness were big issues, but were they really his, or had he taken them from Ben? And what about his current dedication to celibacy? Was this just another attempt to align himself more closely with Ben and Jerry, or could this be his own way of cleaning his window on the world? Perhaps he had no agenda of his own.

He remembered their reactions when he made his infamous 'exception' in his seven months of celibacy. The three of them were sharing a hotel room on a long-anticipated pleasure trip to San Francisco. He had first met Caroline in England, a sultry, melancholy creature and, by chance, she had chosen the same time to visit with friends in the Bay area. It was only natural that they would want to see each other, and, after seven months in storage, sex seemed like a perfectly normal and timely gift . . . i n the name of friendship. When he returned to the hotel and told them, they colluded against him with cries of "abandonment" and "irresponsibility." And, of course, there was Ben, self-righteous as ever and vociferous in his condemnation, while enjoying whatever pleasures he might choose to draw from his own bona-fide marital relationship. They had been relentless, Ben using his formidable analytic skills to open the wounds and

Jerry pouring in the salt. How convenient. Again, he had sacrificed himself on the altar of his own guilt, apologizing for his misdemeanour, appeasing them with his remorse and appealing to them for forgiveness. How stupid.

Criticism lies in the heart of the critic, not in the actions of the criticized. It had been his choice to explore the spiritual path by reading esoteric literature and spending many hours alone in contemplated serenity. Ben and Jerry's mockery was about them. Their ridicule was born of ignorance. His quest for inner harmony was sincere, yet Ben continued to be more interested in his sexual exploits, constantly annotating them with attributions, or accusations, of dominance and power. What happened to the non-judgmental acceptance they all talked about? Where in the handbook of personal growth was it written that the price of awareness could be this high? "A master does not have to be perfect," said Suzuki, "just a perfect mirror." But Ben only reflected himself. It was *his* apprehension about power and *his* fear of abandonment. They were just part of Ben's experience and had little to do with Jock McKeen.

So why the hurt and why the anger? "The Master does not give you knowledge," said Rajneesh, "and the disciple is not in search of knowledge, he is in search of being." Yet Jock's 'being' was burning on the inside and, while he could accept the principle of being fully responsible for only his own experience, it still seemed that his teacher was often the instrument of his torture.

Within the safety of his own private musings, he was beginning to discover that it was possible for him to play with differential perspectives without losing himself in the chaos. Yes, there were times when he was evasive around his commitment to openness, or intimacy. Of course he had a tendency to be 'selective' in his review and the sharing of information, but he was no malicious liar. He was being completely honest in his commitment to explore his experience and overcome his fear of disclosure. And Bennet Wong offered him the opportunity of a lifetime. Maybe he could rekindle the innocence lost somewhere in his infancy, to explore the unknown under the protection of the father's eye. Perhaps he would then be able to destroy the illusions, be with Ben, alone together, man-to-man. He didn't want to die without having tried.

If there was punishment and pain involved, it had to be self-imposed. Perhaps it really was something inside that made him hurt so much. His behaviour on the stage in Edmonton had been fashioned by his own ego and this was not what he wanted. Not because it was wrong, but because such behaviour stood in the way of what he truly wanted. He wanted to move further along on the journey he had shared so briefly with Uncle Murray. Once, while in high school, he had placed his head affectionately on the shoulder of his friend Brad Chisholm only to draw back in disgust and embarrassment as the shoulder was snatched away with a grunt of revulsion. Now he wanted a shoulder that would accept him without discomfort and without condition.

But his ego and fear conspired against him. It was clear now that his anger over the jujubes had more to do with his own pervasive sense of guilt than any response to Ben's pettiness . . . although it *really* was petty. For Jock's part, he had been secretive and defensive because he had something to hide, other than the stupid candy.

He was ready to go back into Ben's office and clear the tensions between them. There could be no apology, just an acknowledgment of his own thoughts and his own feelings. But if Ben remained distance, Jock knew that his empty belly would cry out for help and he would want to fill the void with useless words and desperate postures. Then Ben would move still further away. It was always like that. And with each evasion, each moment of deception, something was destroyed and lost forever. In the treachery that his fears and ego wreaked upon the world, the face that Ben wanted to see, the face that could illuminate their relationship, was painstakingly hidden. In his duplicity, he was incrementally destroying the very thing he wanted most in the world.

Then there was Ben, the boy who had looked out from his

own isolation and wondered where he stood in the world, and the man who, if he could find his special friend, was ready to reveal all. For many reasons, known and unknown, Jock wanted to be that friend but he couldn't seem to make it happen. The truth was that he had never been able to make it happen, not with Ben, not with anybody. The Jock McKeen that hid behind the mask of ambition was cold, alone and helpless. He knew how to please, how to serve, how to make demands and how to walk away, but he didn't know how to be a friend.

Ben had watched Jock's dramatic departure with heartfelt resignation. It was as predictable and tedious as Charlie Brown playing football with Lucy. Just as the game started to take shape, the ball was taken away and he was left standing alone on the forty-yard line. He was ready to move on but he was also prepared for the possibility that he would be moving on alone. There was no doubt in his mind that Jock had the strength to stay with him but he remained elusive, there one minute and gone the next. Yet, even if they were to go no further than this, he still had a best friend and they still could continue to share experience together.

Perhaps that would be all. Perhaps he always would be cast as a shadow on the wall of other people's lives, the itinerant teacher, triggering their curiosity and disappearing at the end of each semester. It wasn't what he wanted but that's what they seemed to want of him, to dance as silent silhouettes on his wall, watching, listening and anxiously waiting for their test results before moving on to the next class down the hall. It was never his intention to impart knowledge, to provide answers, to draw conclusions from some unknown truth, but he did speak and others did listen. Unlike many of the others, however, Jock McKeen had shown himself capable of stepping out into the light, to be his own instructor. Clearly the more seasoned 'researcher,' Ben was ready to offer whatever experience had shown him, bring himself fully into the dialogue, even take the risk of confrontation. But so often when this happened, Jock would leave and blend into other shadows, waiting to be educated with selective praise and retribution. Unless they could stand together, their project was futile. Whatever was there to be learned would have to be co-taught.

Then, behind the role of teacher, lurked the more sinister shadow of the father. He really was a father and made no secret of his occasional paternalistic indulgences with some of his adolescent patients, though they were always with a particular purpose in mind. He would also don the garb of psychiatrist, collaborator, facilitator, or just plain voyeur, depending on the circumstances, his sense of the patient's issues, and his own inclinations. These empty identities defined a place for him in the personal lives of others and he filled them with a life that was completely and unmistakably that of Bennet Wong.

But, with Jock McKeen, he wanted such illusions to be recognized for what they were, to peer into their forms and examine their functions. He wanted a relationship in which neither of them would use such objectifications to separate themselves from each other. It was sufficient that their inherent human differences would serve to affirm their individuality.

However hurt and angry he might become, Bennet Wong could honestly say that he had no interest in changing anything about Jock McKeen anymore than he wanted to change his patients. Whether in his office, sitting in a circle at Cold Mountain, or locked into his seat in a theatre, he would stare unabashedly into any spirit that took the risk to throw off the shackles and, for one moment, allow the brilliance of the person to shine through. It wasn't about performance, it was about innocence. And it wasn't about change, it was about transformation. At such times he would stand in awe and humility, knowing that what was taking place was far beyond his ambition and that what he saw was within him also.

In the psychedelic Sixties, when many of his contemporaries set off in search of their own version of the 'peak experience,' Bennet had found what he was looking for through the simplest of designs. He never set out to make it happen, for he alone was not God. Nor would he wait in hope, since this would have rendered all else insignificant. What he wanted was enfolded in each and every moment, the essence of a life unburdened by such fanciful devices of intrigue, guilt and remorse. Whatever fears the moralists might choose to invoke, he was firmly convinced that, behind all of these deflections, the essence of every human being is essentially innocent and that, in this innocence, all are connected.

Contrary to conventional wisdom, Ben had come to believe that lost innocence is more readily reclaimed in men than in women. In his mind, men had simply locked away their vulnerability for fear of showing weakness in a world that demanded confidence and power. The door was there to be opened. Women, on the other hand, had transformed their innocence into guile. Facing the repressive structures of what future feminists would refer to as the 'patriarchy,' they had created illusions of innocence as strategies for power and control. He had seen this as he watched his own father forge ahead with the family business while his mother, from a place of apparent servitude, moved delicately and deftly to maintain both hands firmly on the wheel. He had seen it again in the girls who claimed to be seeking sensitivity, caring and love, while planning their next move in capturing the most insensitive, but powerful, prize. And in marriage, he saw how the pretence of innocence could be used to maintain the prison of co-dependence.

From his own experience, Ben was able to understand why women might be attracted to men who moved powerfully and purposefully in the world. There, after all, was the charismatic force of Jock McKeen with all the developing attributes of Nietzsche's "superman," and there was Bennet Wong, riddled with curiosity, wondering why such a man would chose to spend time in his company. When it came to the matter of power, however, there was no doubt in the mind of either man, that it was Ben's for the taking.

But Ben's interest was in exploring the Self and meeting the Other, rather than adorning the Self by exploiting the Other. He had looked and failed to find this theme in male-female relationships and wondered if the power-plays of sexuality were a cause or a consequence of the problem. This question could not be addressed in the placid arena of his own sexual experience, but the incendiary world of Jock McKeen had all of the ingredients necessary to illuminate the issue. Meanwhile, the broader question of whether intimacy is even possible in a sexually charged relationship continued to draw his curiosity.

"I don't want to argue about the goddamned jujubes," Jock insisted. He had planned and rehearsed the line before leaving his room, hoping it might dispense with any further need for defence. True to form, he had swept back into Ben's office ready to lay down the fruits of his own soul-searching. Conscious of occupying the chair normally reserved for patients, he was determined to make his own analysis carry the day. Ben remained at his desk and continued to flick through the pages of a loose-leafed binder. He had that sandstone look on his face. It wasn't going to be easy. "Okay, so I know I've been evasive and self-involved," he began, "I'm creating the barrier between us. My apologies were designed to smooth over the issues, to get you off my back and to move away from looking at myself. I've done a lot of thinking and this isn't what I want."

Ben looked up for an instant. "Well, it was what you wanted at the time." He went back to flicking pages.

"But, on reflection, it isn't what I want," Jock continued, as the anticipation of further punishment tugged at his belly. "At least, it's not what I want now."

"Oh." Ben didn't bother to look up this time. It wasn't even interrogative, just a perfunctory "Oh" casually sacrificed to convention. Jock had paused deliberately, waiting to be asked the question that would release what he had to say, but it never came. The empty consulting chair in front mocked his isolation. This was the punishment he'd been expecting. It was time to take ownership of this part of his life, to call upon his own resources, to re-assure the fearful child. "You know that I'm scared," he said, trying to ignore the indifference of Ben and the empty chair.

"Yes," Ben said, closing the binder on his desk and looking up to eye the figure of young Jock McKeen still sitting there, still hanging in, still pushing forward.

"It's like a constant case of anxiety looking for somewhere to land," Jock mused, still staring at the wall. "And it seems like the closer we get, the more it lands on you . . . no that's not right . . . the more I land it all on you." He turned in his chair and faced Ben, his eyes wide and deep, demanding a renewal of the contract.

Ben looked back but said nothing. There was no doubt that Jock had taken the ball away but nobody had ever brought it back with this degree of predictability, or intensity. Ben admired such grim determination and the pleasure of the return began to eclipse the grief of the loss. He pushed the binder aside, stood up, walked around the desk and settled down into the familiarity of his old leather chair. Jock shuffled his own chair an inch or two closer.

For a few moments, the two men looked at each other in silence. They did it openly, not as two adversaries might size up the opposition while planning the next move, but as two men simply living the experience of being together. For Jock, this frequently evoked ritual was not without its inner tensions and he had to remind himself to "stay inside and breathe." However awkward or objectionable such behaviour might seem within the normal babble of social discourse, he knew how empty words carry their own momentum, freezing the senses rather than responding to them. While authentic spontaneity might be the voice of the self, there's little point in throwing out gestures of expression without first exploring what's actually there to be expressed. But exploring personal experience, while shuttling between self and other, calls for considerable discipline and determination. For Ben, it already was a well practised art. For Jock, it was still a stumbling adventure.

He checked Ben's eyes for contact before ending the silence. "I feel ashamed," he said. "I feel ashamed because I see how I constantly dump my stuff on you right after I've decided to own it all myself. When you see through it, I feel caught, my guilt shoots through and I come back fighting . . . fighting *you* for God's sake. Then, when I see what I judge to be your hurt, I smear on another layer of guilt and try to make amends. Then, when that doesn't work, I turn it all into defensive anger, dump the whole package at your door and run. It's quite a game and it goes back a long way, well before I met you. But it doesn't fit for me anymore and, whatever it takes, I really do want to kick the habit. I just don't want to lose you in the process." He paused for a response but nothing came. "My struggle has nothing to do with you really," he added.

He saw the sadness still in Ben's face. It hung over his brows, pulling down on his cheeks and the corners of his mouth, forcing his chin to recede under the strain. But this was not the sadness of a man helpless and victimized by forces beyond his control. This was the sadness of a man full of himself, full of his own substance and unafraid to let the world know. For Jock McKeen to believe that he might be in some way the puppeteer of this man's emotions, whether in joy or despair, would have been a delusion born of psychosis. When Ben finally spoke, it was as if the voice was coming from somewhere deep down in his belly.

"Well it does have *something* to do with me but I think you're telling me that I'm not responsible and I certainly agree with that. And, sure, you don't cause me to hurt and, yes, I do choose to distance myself when you go away. But if you're also telling me that the finger should be pointed at someone else, like your mother or your father, then we're back to square one."

Jock flinched to ward off another dagger of guilt. How the hell did Ben know about his private deliberations? And now that he did know, why the sudden involuntary firing of his defence system? He thought for a moment before attempting a response. "No, I'm not putting them up as the cause of my distress, only as the original objects behind all the subsequent stand-ins."

"Including me?"

"Including you."

"So, Jock, if I go away, what will you want then? Will you go off in search of another substitute for the unavailable original?" They were Ben's words but the question was already in Jock's head.

"I might. But I might also see myself doing it and step in. It's like the times when I think I'm doing all this personal awareness stuff to please you but then I find that it's something I want anyway, for myself. Then I can move on a bit further each time."

Suddenly Ben was smiling. "So your real enemy isn't me, or your mother, or your father. As you do your life your way, you have made an enemy of the universe itself and your real struggle is with eternity."

Why was Ben smiling? Perhaps he was tired of the confessions, sick of the tedious redundancy and was looking for a way to step out lightly. Was it his way of saying that he was about to disappear into the eternal and join the others? Who could blame him? Jock's spirit ran dry. He had nothing to say.

"You know that we can work on that one together Jock. I can be the object in your life if you're prepared to stay with yourself and let me see what you see, however it might look." Ben's voice was soft.

The assurance was clear, even if the metaphor was vague and ambiguous. "The price for my deceptions and evasions just keeps getting higher," said Jock wearily. "I don't want to scam my way around the human potential movement exhorting authenticity for the masses while my own guts are burning up in protest. But the more I say it and don't do it, the harder it becomes. I watch myself being phoney, incompetent and unacceptable, not only through your eyes, but through my own. That's what I'm seeing right now, and it certainly doesn't look very good does it?"

"Good or bad, you see yourself presenting a false image to the world," Ben said. "and you pay the price with your feelings of self-contempt, along with fears that I'll reject you, just as you reject yourself."

Jock listened and watched. At first he wanted to walk out of his misery, to do something that might put the smile back on Ben's face, but he knew better than that. Then he wanted to absorb Ben into his own desolation, to create a single experience, but the idea quickly snarled in his gut. So he left things to be as they were, looking at Ben and nodding.

Ben nodded back and continued. "The faces of honesty and shame are real, Jock, and when you offer these to me, I feel close, privileged and cared about. Through them I can know my own love and the love that I believe flows between us. This doesn't depend upon you being a particular way, saying or doing the right things. But unless you are there, in all that you are, you can't express your love and there's nobody there to receive my love."

Jock had no more words. Something had opened up inside and brought tears instead. Here was a man who would be his friend, his brother, father, teacher, even Jesus Christ if need be. All he had to do was to be there and, in that moment, he was. The warmth that streamed through him was moving in all directions, almost impossible to contain. It was in his belly, in his heart, in his eyes and in his tears. He wanted to express it, to send it out on well-chosen words, but he was speechless. Whatever it was, belonged to a different realm.

They rose in unison from their chairs and embraced until their bellies moved to the same pulse. Then, in parting, they stood hand-in-hand, each peering out at the other through his own tears. Within the vast oceanic mass of humanity that surrounded them, what measure of significance could be attached to the momentary experience of two solitary figures, men of medicine, caught up in their histories, captured by their cultures, standing together and holding hands in an otherwise deserted office building somewhere on the west coast of North America?

It was Ben's idea to use acupuncture in conjunction with Reichian breathing and body-work. It just seemed to make good sense, given their combined skills and interests, and recognizing that all three 'techniques' were concerned with releasing blockages in the same energy flow. Certainly it was a package that would fit well with the current trends in humanistic psychology, bringing together the best of East and West. On the other hand, none of these methods had achieved respectability in mainstream psychiatric practice and, by embracing them, Ben was stepping even further out of the professional mould. Not that he used them at random with his regular patients. He still worked with the more traditional 'talk' therapies, although the fundamentals of encounter, gestalt, non-verbal and cathartic techniques had become increasingly assimilated into all of his work.

More and more, his interest was in working with groups, both in his regular practice and the 'workshops' he was beginning to co-lead with Jock. While his early training in group psychotherapy at Menningers had been distinctly psychoanalytic, the new elements were gradually finding a place in all aspects of his work. This rare blend of forms was also creating the foundation for a unique style of practice in which the relationship between the two men was becoming increasingly evident.

Strangely enough, it was Jock who resisted the integration of acupuncture with the new methodologies of the humanistic movement. Much as he was interested in finding a path to professional equivalence with Ben, he was still tied to Jack Worsley's notion that the only legitimate context for the practice of acupuncture was Traditional Chinese Medicine (TCM). In this, as in all of his serious pursuits, he wanted to do things the right way, the prescribed way. Encouraged to "at least try," he discovered that the integration was both harmonious and effective.

With all new innovations, they used themselves as the experimental subjects. Their own bodies, their own minds, and increasingly their own relationship, became the crucible in the alchemy of their ideas. The concepts and the practices were then introduced to the familiar group of friends and practitioners who continued to gather around homes and offices to pursue their own personal and professional growth. "Take risks," "follow your bliss," "let it all hang out," "see and be seen," were some of the contemporary clichés that, for the first time in history, encouraged people to throw off the masks of convention and work through their armour of defence and inhibition. And these were men, traditionally armoured and protected from each other, edging closer to the terrors from which they had always been protected—incompetence, fathers, exclusion, sexuality, mothers, impotence, failure, punishment, death and damnation. At a time when the pop culture cried for 'Love' and 'Freedom' they, at least, understood that such ideals demanded profound personal growth and not merely changes in ideology or social convention.

The more Ben and Jock worked with the body, the more they became convinced that the issues of the psyche are mirrored in the musculature, and that working with one is bound to working with the other. Time and time again, they noticed that the release of an energy block at the somatic level would have its reciprocal effect at the psychic level, and vice-versa. So a release from a particular area of the body would trigger the catharsis of a particular set of memories and experiences. As physicians, they were fascinated with the idea of a body-brain.

Since the body is the outer reflection of inner experience, it is a storehouse of information for whoever is able to 'read' its wisdom. Such diagnostic techniques are essentially sensory. The topography of the body, nuances of movement, and particularly breathing, combine to chronicle each individual human journey. The traumas of the past and the fears of the future, manifested in rigidly constructed defence systems that block energy and inhibit personal growth, are written in a language that will not deceive with words. "The body doesn't lie." To nobody's surprise, Ben showed himself to be remarkably adept at this particular diagnostic art. Using direct 'hands-on' manipulation of the musculature, along with techniques of breathing and, of course, acupuncture, they developed their own unique style for stimulating the passage of 'Chi' through the body. In private sessions, workshops and meetings with their friends, they began to lay the foundation for an extraordinary professional partnership. Within a matter of months they had developed a reputation in the personal growth community where they were known as "Needles and the Shrink."

Taken in isolation there was nothing fundamentally new in any of their methods. Wilhelm Reich, Alexander Lowen, Moshe Feldenkrais and Ida Rolf were just some of the notable contributors to the body-mind therapy movement of the Sixties and Seventies. At that time, the growing popularity of Eastern philosophy among Western humanists offered practitioners an unprecedented opportunity to break from the Cartesian notion of the separation of body and mind and share a common ground. In the new freedom, many radical and bizarre therapies were being tested and advocated, particularly along the west coast of North America. While Abraham Maslow, Carl Rogers and Fritz Perls were placing the person at the centre of the psychotherapeutic process, others, like Michael Murphy, George Leonard and Will Shultz were pushing the limits out to encompass the likes of Nude Encounter and Anal Rolfing, an excruciatingly painful version of a particularly painful process. However history might judge this era of experimentation, these pioneers were serious in examining the threshold of human experience and potential.

While they were prepared to participate in the spirit of the times, the emerging partnership of Wong and McKeen steered its own course from the outset. From their earliest experiences together they worked toward an openness between each other and among their patients and participants that allowed their uncensored thoughts and ideas to flow immediately and directly from personal experience. While they were not bound by the limitations of theories or methodologies, they were not content to just splash around in the waters of the new freedom. Their vast and relatively untapped data base was nothing less than the depth and immediacy of human experience and, beginning with themselves, they scrutinized data with the passion and rigor of dedicated scientists.

Very early on in their analyses they began to entertain a possibility that, even today, stretches the credulity of many notable advocates of the mind-body paradigm. Having witnessed, and experienced, the contiguity of the movement of energy through the body with the mobilization of thoughts and emotions, they invited friends and colleagues to consider the notion that the body and the mind were one and the same, a single entity. From this perspective, the search for some connection between soma and psyche is redundant.

Certainly, their particular blend of traditional and non-traditional approaches was new. Their emphasis upon the quality of relationships as the central ingredient in the process of healing was a stance that, to this day, remains largely unexplored. Even more remarkable was the fact that they were both physicians, well versed and respected in the conventional domain of western medicine. To put this into perspective, it is necessary only to recall the exclamations of amazement, euphoria and outrage that followed the publication of Bernie Siegel's book, "Love, Medicine and Miracles" in which he, a physician, had the temerity to suggest that the creation and cure of cancer may have something to do with the person as well as the disease. This book was published in 1987, some sixteen years after the early formulations of Wong and McKeen.

But what was really different had little to do with philosophy, concepts or practices. In 1973, in Vancouver, British Columbia, two highly intelligent, highly trained Doctors of Medicine were preparing to live and work from a radical and unique frame of reference . . . a committed relationship of openness, according to their definition of the term "intimacy." They were preparing to 'be,' in themselves, precisely what they were about to offer to others through their practice.

From Ben's perspective at least, there were no grandiose schemes to revolutionize the worlds of medicine or psychiatry. Even the integration of the 'new therapies' was a gradual and systematic process, generated around the periphery of their day-to-day practices. The first major step forward occurred through a process that was taking place, almost imperceptibly, among their respective patients.

As they continued to work from opposite sides of the same waiting room, the psychiatrist and the acupuncturist explored the potentials of their association. Through their regular morning meetings, they began to notice how the issues they discussed were often raised by their own patients in the afternoon. It was as if there was some unseen connection between them and their patients.

Bob Wilkie, a physician who had followed Jock in completing an internship rotation with Ben, attended many of the morning sessions and made the same observations. Whatever was taking place, it was not within the patient alone, but within the configuration of relationships. Jock's thoughts went back to his experience in the West Indies, although the critical role of the doctor-patient relationship in the process of healing was also central to the philosophy of Traditional Chinese Medicine. But it was never spelled out, other than in the most general terms. Yet now, having taken but a small step beyond the confines of their training, this relational issue was crying out to be explored.

Through their awkward and, at times, hilarious attempts at non-intrusive observation, they discovered that their waiting room contained an ever-emerging culture that varied in tone and content on a day-by-day basis. As far as they could determine, it began when some of Ben's 'delinquents' would wait for each other to finish their individual session. While waiting, they would meet the youngster with the next appointment and, invariably, a conversation would begin. Then there might be a commitment to 'stick around' while *that* person 'saw the shrink,' and so the build-up of bodies would occur. Meanwhile the patients of Dr. McKeen, would move tentatively and painfully in and out of the adolescent parade, each making his or her own contribution to the collective mill.

It became clear that whatever was happening in the early morning sessions the energy was being group-processed in this space of convenience between the two offices. Once aware of this, they began to ask patients about their waiting room experiences and discovered that many of the issues were more thoroughly explicated and explored than in the sessions sponsored by the correctional and health care systems.

"Oh great," Jock said, as they sorted through their findings and speculations, "we both may as well move out into the waiting room, there's obviously more good stuff going on out there."

"Or better still," Ben suggested, "let's give all our patients a day instead of an hour and bus the whole days' roster out into the country. Then we'll give each person their individual hour while the rest watch and listen. They can learn from each other. Later we can be part of the group experience and whatever is going on will be to everybody's benefit."

"Confidentiality Dr. Wong," Jock interjected in his own special version of an Oxford accent, "the most sacred trust between the patient and the physician would be totally violated by your insidious, deviant and highly unprofessional proposal."

"I'm serious," Ben continued. "So what the hell, they're doing it anyway? There can be just as much respect for confidentiality in a group. Anyway, I'm tired of the rampant paranoia that plays on the myth of confidentiality. Secrets . . . that's what this stuff's all about, secrets. It's not the isolated pathology in their lives that brings people here, it's the damned secrecy in their lives. At least those kids out there seem to understand that. If only people would come clean, half their illnesses would disappear overnight. It's so obvious to me that your issues help me to understand my issues. Why do we keep ignoring the obvious? Why haven't we just taken the plunge?"

Jock considered the questions until the realities of his chosen profession caught up with him. "Because the College wouldn't like it. Nor would some of my little old ladies who've been keeping their little old secrets behind their little old symptoms for as long as they can remember. What you're talking about sounds more like a workshop than a practice."

On certain nights, whoever remained in the waiting room after the last patient had been seen, was invited into Ben's office. Most were adolescents and most accepted. In principle, this was no different from the way other groups had sprung up around the practice and these gatherings quickly developed their own distinctive style and purpose. They paved the way for other groups, some planned, some spontaneous. At the end of each day Jock would join, sometimes contributing a patient of his own. And others would appear mysteriously; Jerry Glock and Bob Wilkie along with probation officers for some of the kids, street workers, parents, friends and itinerant professionals.

While there methods were radical, their reasoning was sound, grounded not so much in theory as in experience. They concluded that if the body and the mind are one then the energy that gives life and health to the organism can be only one energy. If the process of healing occurs within and between people, then it follows that the group contains the greatest potential for individual growth and change. By comparison, talk-group therapies generally isolate individual issues and revolve around the particular theoretical orientation of the particular therapist; Ben himself relied upon the psychoanalytic scripts drawn from his formal psychiatric training. But there were no documented and replicable models directed toward working with individual and group energy. The encounter group movement generated through the Esalen Institute in California and the T-Group designs of the National Training Laboratories in New York probably came the closest. Both embraced 'body-mind' and 'energy' principles and employed techniques ranging from the psychodrama of J. L. Moreno to the Gestalt Therapy of Fritz Perls to the body methods of Alexander Lowen and Ida Rolf. Yet Ben and Jock made no conscious effort to emulate the work of any particular individual or to compile a preferred package of contemporary approaches. Where most aspiring therapists struggle to match themselves to the criteria of their methods, the partnership of Wong and McKeen struggled to discover and develop methods that would best reflect their own combined experience and purpose. It was bound to be unique.

At the very centre of it all was their relationship and, to this,

Jock dedicated himself. He was even prepared to delve into the cauldron of sexuality if need be. His commitment to celibacy had been a personal purge, a purification, though he was never quite sure about the nature of the toxin that was to be purged, or why such a cleansing was even necessary. He understood how the excitement of the chase, culminating in the final orgasmic thrusts of each encounter, enhanced his sense of power, but the idea of an insatiable demand for domination seemed shallow and he searched for something beyond, something more complex, more satisfying. It was as if his ego were seeking some explanation beyond itself.

Certainly, his objectification of women provided no foundation for intimacy, but intimacy was never the object of the exercise. So, beyond the lust for power, what was really being satisfied and, beyond immediate sense gratification, what did these women contribute to his sense of being? If they were dissatisfied with the arrangement, why did they accept his obvious objectification of them? Why did they not come back to wreak punishment and revenge? As it was, apart from their thwarted attempts to capture him, most gave up without so much as a retaliatory jab.

Somewhere he had the idea that there were answers to be found in his relationship with Ben, but he would never allow the thought to settle long enough for consideration. They were becoming closer, much closer; in fact, there were times when it seemed that they might be merging at the edges. Each was no longer a stranger to the other's body, or even nakedness, having probed the most resilient and the most sensitive regions in their quest for knowledge and connections. He had seen beyond Ben the mother and Ben the father, recognizing at times the absurdity of his ambitions to capture and harness this man's learning and power. He had seen the wisdom in innocence and the strength in vulnerability—not the vulnerability of a fearful man staring into the eyes of the enemy but the vulnerability of a feeling man with the courage to be seen.

But there were also times when he wondered what the hell was going on and what this strange man wanted of him. If it included sex, would he have the power or the strength to say no, or was this to be part of the journey? Was their physical closeness, the holding and the stroking, a protracted foreplay leading to the inevitable humiliating submission of his body? Now, having experienced celibacy, he knew that he could maintain his place in the world without the physical exchange of sexuality. Perhaps that would be the only fare to be paid for the journey.

They had ordered a double room, but hotel clerks sometimes make assumptions. It was already late when they arrived at the Banff Springs Hotel. Had there been only one bed, it would have been difficult to make alternative arrangements without alerting Ben to the fear that never went away. They had talked about sexuality on the two hour drive from Calgary but it had been contained in theory, illuminated with vignettes from Jock's heroic days of conquest. Jock had made a conscious effort to avoid any images that might stir the groin and had steered attention toward their anticipation of the Hypnosis Convention that had brought them to Alberta and to the resort town of Banff.

"Hey what a great room," said Jock enthusiastically, on seeing the two beds and the six feet of floor between them. With the lightness of relief in his body and confident that he was now protected from a fate worse than failure, he taunted the world with his bravado. "I still don't know if it's possible to have a really close relationship and keep the sexual charge alive," he said, continuing their conversation from the car. "Look at all the popular literature designed to lift couples out of sexual boredom. It all seems to emphasize role-playing, or some contrived form of objectification. Deception disguised as technique. It's like the people have to hide to make it work."

He peeled off his silk shirt and glanced at his upper body in the angled mirror of the dresser. He noticed how the muscles of his back were accentuated by shadows cast in the diffused glow of the bedside light. He discovered that he could move them, imperceptibly, with a subtle rotation of the shoulders. His black, almost skin-tight, pants clung from the sharp indentation of his waist to stretch out over his hips, profiling the lineation of his thighs and buttocks. He smiled to himself and snapped the buckle of his belt, forcing his thumbs between his skin and the waistband to manoeuvre the material over his legs.

"I don't believe I've ever actually loved a woman, at least not in the sense that we've talked about love, as a state of being. But there's definitely been an element of romance around my desire."

He was standing in his black bikini shorts and, again, the mirror confirmed what he already knew. His genitals, substantial, hidden and supported, projected him forward, giving his body a sense of balance, power and purpose. He sat down on the bed and pulled off his shorts, tossing them carelessly onto a vacant chair. Then, like Narcissus by the pool, he stood up and took a final glance at his own impeccable reflection; and like Narcissus, he died in the experience. There, in the mirror, was the face of Ben, watching him with the intensity of a dedicated voyeur.

"Why did you turn off the light?" Ben asked when plunged suddenly into darkness through Jock's life-saving lunge at the bedside lamp, "I wasn't ready."

"I was self-conscious, embarrassed."

"About what?"

"Me preening myself and you watching me."

"I find you very beautiful, I like to watch you. Are you afraid of my intentions?"

The time had come and he was surprisingly calm, actually relieved. "I wonder where sexuality fits into our relationship," Jock asked from the darkness. "It's got to be there in one form or another. You like to look at my body and I'm scared out of my wits. What's the message in all of that?"

"Is it the idea of sex between men?"

"Yeah, that's the gut part of it. But there's also the relationship between sex and love. Can sexuality come from loving someone, or is it always there in some repressed or unfulfilled form, even beyond Freud?" He thought about Ann who died, about his music teacher, who listened, and the unmistakable touch of Uncle Murray's old fishing sweater that felt so warm against his skin. He thought about his growing love for Ben and wondered how close they would, or could, become.

"Do you really want to explore sexuality within our relationship?" Ben's disembodied voice seemed to drift in from all four corners of the room.

"Yes," he said, without thought, and he waited for the aftershock.

"Can I come over there and be with you?"

"Yes."

Lying naked on their backs, on top of the covers, they remained still, each taking in the presence of the other. Ben invited his body to speak while Jock committed his to a paralysed catatonic silence. Ben's hand reached out and Jock took it instantly, like a child clutching a parent from the terror of the dentist's chair. The unquiet silence revealed nothing.

"You might get more from the experience by breathing," Ben suggested.

"Oh yeah, right!"

They dissolved again into the empty darkness, their hips now touching lightly. The distant sounds of the normal world drifted down the carpeted hallways as they maintained their vigil, their pelvises frozen to the bed cover. Jock broke the silence

"Anything happening for you?" he asked.

"No, nothing, how about you?"

"No, nothing at all."

The silence returned but there was a clear non-verbal agreement that the experiment was over, at least for the time being. Jock gestured a yawn. "Well I'm ready to sleep now, how about you?" There was no doubt that this implied a return to the celebration of *his* celibacy and *their* double room.

"Phew," said Jock to the darkness as he pulled the covers up over his aching shoulders.

Some months later they walked together down Government Street in Victoria. It was early January and the muffled-up sidewalk crowds stirred with the myopic madness of the post-Christmas sales. But the immediate objectives of Wong and McKeen were far removed from the retail rituals and year-end extravaganzas of the local merchants. They glided through the unconnected multitudes with light faces and fragile feet, dancing past the weary windows toward the inner harbour and the parking lot of the Empress Hotel.

One other person stood apart from the frenzy of the bargain hunt, a bright-eyed young woman looking out from a coffee shop window on a world that passed her by. She saw the two figures approaching on the other side of the street and, in an attitude of fixation, she allowed her cappuccino cup to hover between the saucer and her lips. As she watched them go by, a smile eased across her face and, within a moment of returning the cup to the saucer, she was outside the café and searching for a breach in the traffic. Once on the other side of the street, she moved quickly through the parade until she was alongside her quarry. Then, in the moment when Bennet Wong suddenly became aware of her presence, she threw her arms around his neck. "You're beautiful," she said, without further elaboration. Jock McKeen stood and gaped in wonder until the arms wrapped themselves around his neck also. "You're beautiful," she repeated. "You're both so beautiful." Then, as they met her eyes, her confidence seemed to falter and a self-conscious hesitation flashed across her face. The next moment she was gone, lost forever in the tired glitter of once-in-a lifetime opportunities.

Ben had a wife, two children and a reality where Jock was little more than a peripheral figure. There were no tensions around this arrangement. When Ben attended to his 'other' life, Jock slipped quietly into the pressure-free world of his own musings and celebrated this tenuous connection with the normal world. He always maintained a romantic commitment to the institution of the nuclear family and felt comfortably grounded in his visits to the home in West Vancouver. But Corinne was becoming less visible. She would either go out or simply disappear on the evenings when he, Jerry, or the others, would show up, and would not return until after they left. At weekends there were opportunities to play with the two boys but, again, Corinne was notably absent.

Ben shared Jock's attachment to the sanctity of the family. His relationship with Corinne had ground into an irreconcilable impasse, but he continued to search for accommodations that might preserve the family, at least in response to the needs of Kevin and Randy. He could see no reason why they should disband the home, even if the marital relationship could no longer be the pivotal force. There was still space for a mother, a father and two children to be together. Corinne was not prepared to entertain such a mockery of family life, however, although she was tolerating Ben's alternative sleeping arrangements in the spare room. On the other hand, she was becoming increasingly intolerant of his continued use of the home as a venue for extended professional and extracurricular activities. Her resentment of the visitors increased in proportion to her diminishing involvement in her husband's life.

By contrast, the partnership of the two men continued to glow and its existence in the world was increasingly affirmed. When they entered the session room as participants at a 'Reichian' workshop, a woman explained away her boldfaced stare with the remark that there was "something shimmering" between them. Later at a pool-side party, a group of people discussed the "arch" that appeared to connect the two doctors. Now at ease with the notion of energy systems, they had no reason to challenge the experiences of the observers "Perhaps we're becoming single-minded," Ben suggested at one of their morning meetings.

The impasse broke with an urgent message from Richard Weaver of the Cold Mountain Institute. Given his own ailing health, he was desperate for someone to lead a three month

Resident Fellow Program. The institute was having significant financial difficulties and Ben's workshops had proven to be the most popular and profitable of their offerings over the past year. If he would agree to taking the leadership role, the Resident Fellow Program could not only be saved but virtually assured of bringing in additional revenues.

By this time, Jock McKeen was an acceptable commodity at Cold Mountain. "Either you've changed or I've changed," Richard Weaver told him one day after a program leader's meeting at the Cortes Lodge. Nobody really understood what was behind his dramatic change of heart, but Jock accepted the sentiment graciously and gratefully.

Ben gave very little thought to Weaver's proposition. Assured that Jock could, and would, join him as a co-leader, he accepted both the concept and the conditions. Immediately they set about putting their practices in storage for the three month period and attending to the many practical matters of establishing residency on Cortes Island. Richard Weaver had offered them his own house since he, and his wife Jean, would be spending that time in Vancouver where Richard's health, and the Vancouver branch of the Cold Mountain organization, could receive the nurturance they needed.

For Bennet Wong and Jock McKeen it was a time to examine carefully the direction of their lives and to formulate some general pictures of the future.

CHAPTER FIVE

For the romantic traveller in search of mists and mysticism, Cortes Island is a cryptic place. A two hour excursion from the Vancouver Island community of Campbell River, involving two ferries set apart by a lengthy trek across Quadra Island, it rises from the ocean like an indelible shadow. Those who came to seek enlightenment at the place they called the "Cold Mountain" discovered their destination on the eastern shore—an old Lodge surrounded by several rustic residential buildings and a large round wooden structure that served as the main session room.

Waiting to welcome them were those who had chosen to live within the dream of the Institute's Founder and President, Richard Weaver. They considered their mission to be essentially educational. As a lecturer in English Literature at the University of Alberta, Weaver had made no attempt to hide his disdain for a system that was obsessed with the trivia of the external world, while ignoring the fundamental realities of inner truth. An enthusiastic participant in the Encounter programs at Big Sur, California, he collaborated with his friend Gary Snyder, a poet and scholar, to establish an "Esalen of the North." They planned to turn the process of education inside out, producing a completely new generation of graduates—people who would move in the world from their own inner sense of Being. From the outset, Richard Weaver, along with his wife Jean and Executive Director Sterling Scott, began negotiations with Antioch University, a registered non-resident institution, for accreditation in Baccalaureate and Masters degree programs. There was nothing cautious or tentative about the enterprise. With spirited enthusiasm, Cold Mountain quickly became a reality with offshoot programs in Vancouver, Edmonton and Lethbridge. In all of this, they were actively supported by some of the most notable contributors to the personal growth movement in North America.

The location of Cold Mountain presented its own unique challenges to those who chose to participate. Alan Watts and Bennet Wong were in a small single-engined Cessna turning to settle on the calm waters off Manson's Landing when the passenger door fell off. The warm evening wind tore into the cabin, pinning them back into their seats. The pilot, realizing the futility of delay, signalled his intention to complete the landing manoeuvre as the aircraft buffeted in protest against the forty-five degree bank.

Ben, who was unfortunate enough to be sitting in the front passenger seat, found himself slipping to the side with nothing but a straining lap belt between his body and the racing ocean below. In the seat behind, Alan Watts pressed forward, his hair and beard uniting in a streaming circle about his face. He called out against the terrible noise, but the words were ripped apart. Ben leaned back to listen and Alan's voice rose above the din.

"Here we are on the brink of death. Isn't it marvellous?"

Ben managed to turn around and look into the face of the ecstatic philosopher. The man had come to life.

Some months before, Alan had stood on the dilapidated wooden dock at Manson's awaiting Ben's arrival in the same aircraft. A lone figure cast against the swell of the water, his orange ceremonial robes flowing in the wind, he had captured ocean and mountains in the momentary majesty of his presence. Even the un-mystical fishermen had stared in silence. But behind the illusion, the brilliance was fading. The mind that had fired the imagination of Henry Miller and devotees of Zen Buddhism throughout the Western World was beginning to close its own eyes on the universe it had sought to grasp. The wind-borne figure at Manson's Landing was preparing to discover the truth behind his own words:

This is all there is;
the path comes to an end
among the parsley.

Ben had always felt sadness around Alan's fading spirit but had no wish to join him in the final expressions of life, however 'marvellous' they might be. They both had commitments at Cold Mountain the next day and Ben's unequivocal preference was that they would be fulfilled. When the floats finally touched the ocean and the tail-feathered spray fanned out behind them, the destinies of Bennet Wong and Alan Watts went their separate ways.

Jock McKeen's status as co-leader of the three month Resident Fellow Program was a contentious issue among the faithful. Richard Weaver with his "either you've changed or I've changed" speech had officially opened the doors but this was the price he felt he had to pay for the participation of Bennet Wong. The unofficial reactions ranged from the benign disinterest of Alan Watts to the smouldering hostility of seasoned participants and workshop leaders. Even Jock's old friend Jerry Glock was inclined to stir the pot, questioning motives while jealously eyeing the growing partnership that increasingly excluded him. Less involved observers like Moffat Director Jim Pryor, who was becoming increasingly enamoured with Richard Weaver and the

Cold Mountain community, continued to regard the impostor as an "opportunistic ass" hanging onto the coat tails of his teacher.

Such opinions were also expressed among friends and family back on the lower mainland. Ernie Wong, Ben's brother and a psychiatrist practising in Vancouver, had become convinced that Ben had been "captured," and was saddened by this further dissolution of family ties. As a single man, Ernie maintained his attachments within the constellation of the Wong family and, since early childhood, had questioned Ben's apparent indifference to family matters. Now, he felt sorry for Corinne and the two boys and undertook to strengthen his own relationship with them. Whatever the motives of Jock McKeen, it seemed to the younger Dr. Wong that his brother would always act in accordance with his own ever changing interests, regardless of the consequences to himself or those around him.

Ben was aware of the judgments being directed toward him, Jock, and their relationship, but his concerns were elsewhere. His decision to take on the Resident Fellow program had more to do with separating from Corinne than being with Jock. While the role of husband had been discarded, his love for his sons and his sense of duty toward the family lived on. The three months on Cortes Island might, in some way, realign his sense of Being with his style of life.

In some ways, Jock's anticipation of the three month commitment would have confirmed the most severe judgments of his harshest critics. He would enjoy playing a lead on the stage of other people's lives and felt confident that his own secrets could be contained behind the protection of Ben and the choreography of his own performance. On the other hand, he *did* care, he *did* want to help others and he *did* want to make a difference in the world. But he was scared as never before. As they loaded the car for the trip from Vancouver, sulphurous fumes began to curdle up from his belly. "The curing of Souls," suggested the anthropologist Hocart, "derives from the cravings of the stomach." He glanced at the brochure: "Leaders: Bennet

Wong and Jock McKeen"; equal billing (and equal pay) in a practice that was ready to challenge the weed-infested fields of health care, education, psychotherapy and psychology. But first, he must stake out that place of equality; if only he could rid himself of the fearful apprentice within his belly.

As they drove along the east coast of Vancouver Island, their conversation rarely delved beyond the pragmatics of wrapping up their commitments in Vancouver and making plans for their new living arrangements on Cortes. By the time they reached Campbell River, Jock could feel the pressure building up in his body and was grateful for the prolonged silences that left a space between them. Sitting behind the wheel of the borrowed truck, his mind returned to the obsessive task of impression management. But this time, there was more to consider than the usual deliberations about control and power. Unless he took decisive and persistent action, he was about to be branded as a homosexual in an environment where personal information was passed around as common property.

It was a matter of privacy. For three months he and Ben would be working together and living together without the usual avenues of escape. They had rented Richard and Jean Weaver's house on the Cold Mountain property, their workshops would be jointly facilitated and all uncommitted time would be in each other's company. Given this opportunity, Ben's expectations would be unfettered and uncompromising. At first he thought his fear was about Ben being able to scrutinize his round-the-clock behavior, but digging deeper he discovered that he was equally apprehensive about observing Ben under the same conditions. Against the backdrop of personal and domestic routines, any Magus could lose his magic. Then, once the spell had gone, what would be left for the committed and ambitious apprentice? The word 'marriage' came up from nowhere and he pushed it away in revulsion.

As they drove across Quadra in silence, the sheer incongruence of their relationship urged him to find some category or mold that might make sense of it to the outside world. Since nothing seemed to fit for him, how could it be explained to others? Obviously, some information was missing, but who had the secret? He glanced at Ben and felt strange. It was true that he had wanted to dominate, take over, possess and eclipse the Master, but this man was no furtive female, brandishing the guile of innocence. Lady Macbeth maybe? But no, it was abundantly clear that this man had no heart for intrigue and illusion. Was he father, or mother maybe? He had looked at that one often enough. What twisted theme of his own fearful child might be weaving itself into the enfolded fabric of their relationship? If Ben had the answers he would have made them known unless, of course, he had decided that Jock was simply not ready.

There was only one upper story bedroom in the Weaver residence. But there was a basement cubby-hole masquerading as a sleeping space for unexpected, and presumably unwanted, guests.

"I'll take this," Jock said, with an air of magnanimous relief. "It reminds me of my old meditation room. Remember?" He threw his jacket down on the crumpled Hudson's Bay blanket, laying claim to the territory in the name of John H. R. McKeen.

"There's a large bedroom upstairs, Jock. There's lots of space up there if you want to share."

"No, that's fine. I really like it down here. I can read late into the night without disturbing you . . . even play my flute when the urge takes me. I'll go up and get my things." If he could keep the issue out of his own head it might never be picked up by Ben.

"Okay, if that's what you really want." Ben said.

Even with the sheets washed and his own things carefully arranged around the tilting bed, it was a most unsavoury sleeping arrangement; no more than a roughly partitioned storage compartment stuffed between the furnace and the rusting pipes of the plumbing system. The light came from a bulb, precariously suspended from a cross-beam and activated by yanking on a frayed length of string. There was one well-worn braided mat, just large enough to protect the first bare-footed step of the morning from the cold concrete of the floor. Rough plywood walls mocked the few personal adornments that he had carefully selected as statements appropriate to the persona of a leader of the Resident Fellow Program at the Cold Mountain Institute.

He sat on the bed and picked up his anthology from the small pile of books on the floor. It fell open at Byron's *Prisoner of Chillon*. Once again the universe had spoken back. He looked around his cell wondering how this place would seem in three months time. It was late afternoon and gentle shadows of Cortes Island beckoned.

Ben, who also had spent the last two hours settling into the upper story, was quiet now. In less than an hour they would stroll over to the old Lodge, the heart of the estate, and have supper with the other members of the resident community; the new leaders would officially be in place and Wong and McKeen would initiate a new episode in the life of Cold Mountain. Tomorrow, the program participants would start to arrive and the new order would begin to take shape. Impressions would be offered, judgments would be made and memories would live on. Excitement and fear mingled.

Jock climbed from his basement, crossed the kitchen and went up the stairs. The bedroom door was open and Ben welcomed him from a well worn armchair. He closed the book that rested on his knees. "Come and join me for a few minutes," he said. "I was hoping we could spend time together before supper."

Jock sat on the closest of the two beds and looked around. Illusions of 'partnership' began to melt down, first to 'assistant,' then to 'apprentice' and finally to his old and familiar status of 'student.' This was the room of a program leader, spacious and well furnished with windows that brought in the sunlight and framed images of the ocean and mountains. In his own inimitable style, Ben had created an orderly and personal space; the touches were subtle but the impact was transformational. As with the man himself, the room offered a simple invitation, while providing thinly disguised clues to suggest that any acceptance of another soul here would not be unconditional. Casting aside a fleeting temptation to reconsider Ben's invitation, Jock concluded that such conditions would never be made explicit; they would have to be discovered through perform-or-perish intuition. Then, of course, there was the other matter—it was critical for the world to know that they slept in separate rooms.

"Okay," Jock replied finally, "let's walk around the property before supper. A visit to the old Chicken Coop might help me deal with a few of the old ghosts that still hang around this place."

It wasn't really a chicken coop but rather an old wooden building situated between the Lodge and the session room that was used for a variety of purposes. The ghosts that continued to linger in Jock's mind dated back to a meeting held there earlier in the year.

Richard Weaver had called the meeting. Despite the tireless enthusiasm of the devotees, The Cold Mountain Institute was beginning to falter. Jean Weaver had reported an increasing cash-flow problem that was threatening the financial base of the operation. Many workshops were operating at less than full capacity, though many of the leaders continued to maintain that it was the responsibility of the Institute to attract people and that the remuneration to the professional staff should not be contingent upon the number of participants. Their commitment to the philosophy and the work of the Institute did not extend to the fiscal well-being of the organization. It was Richard's company, with all four corporate shares held by the Weavers, and it was the responsibility of the organization to support and protect its leaders, the pioneers of a new humanity.

At a deeper and more pervasive level was the problem of Richard's failing health. Physically, mentally and spiritually it seemed that he was slowly losing heart. But those who knew him well also knew that his vision for Cold Mountain extended beyond his own direct involvement. He wanted the Esalen of the North to be an enduring symbol of the 'other way.' Most specifically, he saw the degree programs as the foundation for a revolution in post-secondary education and, if all else failed, this initiative would carry his dream to future generations.

A nihilist who stared out at the world from his own philosophy, he seemed to understand that his beloved Cold Mountain would always need the collective spirit to support his radical and rampant individualism. But now, having exhorted so many others to peer into existential blackness, he seemed to be juggling his personal dreams with his own growing despair.

Jean was there, along with current leaders. They sat in a circle on the floor waiting for Richard to set the direction. He began by inviting them to consider their own purposes and the ways in which Cold Mountain might provide a context for their personal aspirations. They talked about autonomy, authenticity, personal space and carving out their own unique pathways toward enlightenment, while encouraging others to cast aside the masks and delusions of the material world. Ben talked about love and relationships and they were indifferent. Jock offered a few words about his own personal journey and they sat in silence.

Richard then declared the meeting to be about personal and professional sharing. This, he told them, was the true spirit of Cold Mountain. He wanted them to know how wonderful they were and how they had already exemplified that spirit through the authenticity of everything they had just said. His confidence and faith in each of them was such that he would never hesitate to do his own personal work with any member of the assembly. This was intended, and generally received, as a gracious compliment. There was a silence.

"Well I wouldn't choose to do my personal work with many of you. In fact, I probably wouldn't do it with any of you. And furthermore Richard, I don't believe that you would either." Ben's voice rose challengingly from the silence.

"And what the Hell is that supposed to mean?" asked an angry voice from the circle.

"Probably what you think it means, "said Ben. "In your case, Richard, I know you always go down to California to do your work. I don't understand why you would decide to make such a statement at this time."

Richard Weaver recoiled and waited for the tensions to draw tightly around him. Finally, another voice came from the circle. "You're destroying the spirit of Cold Mountain with your bitterness. If this is your way of making a pitch for power when the leader is vulnerable, then you'd better make your intentions clear. I don't believe that you have any chance in this group." The speaker offered Richard a supportive nod and a ripple of agreement passed among them.

"I'm not the least bit interested in making a pitch for anything, except honesty," Ben proclaimed.

"Okay, then let's have honesty on the table," suggested another voice. "Let's go around the group and say who we would work with and who we wouldn't . . . and why. And let's talk about our own process in terms of what we're really after." While many held their breath, they all agreed to the process.

With few reservations, they validated one another and gave Richard a consensus of confidence and support. When Ben offered his observations to each member of the group, the tensions mounted. "You're just being objectionably hostile," protested one leader after receiving Ben's feedback. Others preferred to remain silent and express their resentment through their refusal to select Ben as an acceptable working partner. When he spoke of his own search for 'relatedness' he was dismissed, along with the concept.

Jock, Jerry Glock and Margaret Woods, who had co-led a number of workshops with Ben, understood his intentions and could sense his pain. But the others held firm to the tacit agenda of their leader in a silent and indignant coalition. On the surface, their resolve offered Richard some brief assurance that his dream was being protected but, beneath the shallow comfort, Cold Mountain, as a living and purposeful organism, was tearing itself apart in an orgy of self-deception. However desperate he might have been, Richard Weaver was no fool and it is unlikely that he was ready to deceive himself.

Ben listened carefully to it all, his face impassive, as the group became increasingly committed to its stance of opposition and resentment. Finally he said, "Richard, I don't believe you. You're all so busy covering things up. I see no point in sitting around here sharing lies." And, with those few words, he quietly rose to his feet and left the room. Jock followed without hesitation. Jerry Glock watched for a moment, looked around at the faces in the circle and, calling upon the full resources of his courage, rose to join his friends outside.

Now, as Ben and Jock stood in that same doorway, some eleven months later, the Chicken Coop seemed like a benign and dishevelled place, though Jock could still sense the bitterness from the group that had long since departed. He still smouldered from the injustices that had been committed on that day. On the other hand, he had learned much from the incident. Richard's aspirations had become clear to him early in the meeting and, one by one, he was able to see through the masks of deference and authenticity worn by the disciples. Some had revealed themselves through the nature and intensity of their attack upon Ben, while others were revealed through their silence. None had stepped forward to challenge Weaver's authority but Jock could sense their ambitions. In this particular arena, they were the neophytes and Richard was unquestionably their master. He could see how the tensions they created around Ben's position served to release the hidden tensions of different agenda. Jock smiled to himself when Jean Weaver, the astute business mind behind the Cold Mountain operation, came up later to express her support for Ben and acknowledge his contribution to the Institute. "You may have enemies here," she said, "but please don't include me among them." She, of all people, must have understood how Ben's stance had challenged Richard's attempt to push his dreams beyond the approaching edges of his own mortality.

In Jock's mind there was little doubt that Ben, in his artless challenge, had been used by the self-interests of the others. He had seen the phenomenon many times before in the exchanges between Ben and his patients. But this was different. These were professionals, humanists, shamelessly cloaking themselves in honesty and authenticity to conceal their guile. And Ben, who must have seen through the deception, again chose not to defend himself against the assault upon his intentions. It was almost unbelievable.

Without setting foot in the room, Jock closed the door on the Chicken Coop and on his own reflections. "Let's go and eat," he suggested, though his mind was far from dinner. Unthinkingly he reached out and took his friend's hand. There really was a place for him at Ben's side.

The three month Resident Fellow Program had been designed to offer a broad and continuous learning experience, while generating a steady flow of 'graduates' capable of furthering the cause. To this end, it encompassed a series of seminars and workshops, each bringing in additional participants for relatively short periods of time. For celebrity leaders like Alan Watts, Joseph Campbell, Virginia Satir, Will Schutz, Paul Reps and Gregory Bateson, these sessions were no more than stopovers in hectic international schedules. Most local faculty members, however, relied upon their leadership of program sections to generate income and establish more modest reputations. While they drew in fewer additional participants, they could always be assured of the Resident Fellow Group and, since their fees were never based upon numbers, their income was predictable and guaranteed. As the financial pressures mounted, the efficacy of this arrangement came under the critical eye of Mrs. Weaver.

Bennet Wong and Jock McKeen had nothing to fear. In fact, the decision to invite them to direct a Resident Fellow Program was primarily based upon economic considerations. Ben already had established himself as one of those rare leaders capable of generating local enthusiasm while creating a reputation across the continent. Now, as "Needles and the Shrink," the partnership was becoming known, respected, and highly marketable.

When their directorship of the program was announced, over

thirty people signed up for the three month experience. At that time, even Richard Weaver himself could only draw between seven and fifteen participants. In all likelihood, the unacknowledged reality that only Wong and McKeen could pay the bills and subsidize faculty salaries fuelled the resentment. Jean Weaver's notion that salaries should be based upon participant fees invited the disenchanted to shift their anxiety into criticism of Wong and McKeen's success, rather than examine the nature of their own shortcomings. Philosophical indignation is always much easier to live with and, in this particular case, the external objects of resentment were not difficult to identify. At the same time, the ailing Richard Weaver presented an ideal figure to draw both the emotions and the ideology away from the underlying fear. But, for Richard himself, it must have been a bittersweet arrangement.

Actually, Ben and Jock had argued that, given a spirit of open enquiry within the broader framework of humanistic thinking, Cold Mountain should encourage philosophical diversity. Ben's frequently cited statement "I would need a lot of information *not* to believe something" was reflected in the manner in which they set up their version of the Resident Fellow Program. They encouraged debate and engaged enthusiastically with those who came along with different ideas. But many others did not agree with disagreement, perceiving it to be treacherous to the most essential values of the community. So, however much the new Directors wanted to support the section leaders, the divisions and resentments continued to simmer beneath the surface. There was no doubt that the presence of Wong and McKeen was transforming Richard Weaver's Cold Mountain.

On the surface, the new Resident Fellow Program maintained its essential integrity under the new management. Once the plans had been finalised with the various group leaders, the direct participation of Ben and Jock was limited to sessions each Sunday and their own five day Self-Awareness workshop. Beyond these activities, however, the new Program Directors were able to exercise a profound influence on the tone of the proceedings through their daily meeting with the 'interns'—five leaders-in-training who ran the smaller evening group sessions monitored the personal experience of each participant and generally kept the two Directors in touch with what was taking place within the group.

So, while the format of the program retained its familiar narrative, a new and distinctive style was established at the very first intern's meeting. "People are in charge of their own process," Ben told them. They were seven in all, including the two leaders, pulled tightly around a rickety green-felt games table in the otherwise deserted lodge. "We are not here to force, confront, liberate or change them in some way. Our task is to use whatever skills and resources we have to create and support a climate in which they can do their own work in their own way."

"So what is that work?" The question was innocent enough, though the intonation had a precise and seductive quality, like that of a hungry lawyer ready to trap and devour an evasive witness. It came from a dark-faced young man who had introduced himself to the group as a "student of Zen."

Jock, who had already decided to keep watch on this particular intern, took the question as a challenge. "Put simply," he began, "we are concerned with the harmonic flow of energy that activates mind and body within a unified, self-contained whole. In the work, we invite people to experience and examine the ingrained patterns that serve to interrupt or block that flow." He paused for a moment and looked around the table. His face became noticeably softer. "It's sort of like clearing a log jam," he said, as an aside. When they nodded, he brought the edge back into his voice, re-set himself on his target and went on with his lecture. "Ben is asking you to remember that the people in the program are the ones doing the work. Deep down, they are the ones with the resources and the wisdom to know what needs to be done. Our job is to be there with them, inviting them to tap those resources and trust that inner wisdom." He paused, this time to take a breath.

Realizing that he had lost some ground, the questioner threw himself back into the fray with renewed determination, his eyes scanning the others as if in search of support. "So we don't intervene at all. You mean *we* just watch while *they* do whatever *they* want to do?"

Jock's response was immediate. "In the large group sessions, we expect you to be fully present and aware of all that's going on around you. Ben and I will be leading the work and we will call on you as we need your assistance." He was ready to 'process' the issue with the recalcitrant Buddhist right there and then. The man's feelings were right on the surface and it was the leader's task to bring feelings forward. But Jock also had some feelings and, as he prepared himself to take the risk, Ben stepped in.

"We want you to do more than just watch," he said quietly. At that point he had no interest in seeing the matter between Jock and the opposing intern become an exercise in experiential learning. "We want you to look beyond words and gestures, to acknowledge and suspend your own judgments or theories and to try to understand what each person is telling us about their inner experience. We want you to look at their world as if you were seeing it through their eyes. And we want you to do this with curiosity and humility, always respecting the innate integrity of that person's process."

With the exception of the young man who appeared to be at odds with Jock, the interns gladly turned away from the tension and began to consider Ben's more gently articulated, though no less demanding, instructions. "Oh yes," said a girl perched at the corner of the table. Throughout the confrontation between Jock and his adversary, she had looked on with an expression of confusion and distress. The others turned and waited for her to speak. "Well," she said nervously, "we try to be understanding listeners."

Jock transferred his stare to the girl in the corner. She had trivialized Ben's words. She had taken his simple gift, something she could have learned from, and transformed it into a crude cliché.

"It's more than that," he said sharply. "That kind of simplistic reductionism just leaves me cold. Listening is the art of really hearing the other person, respecting what they have to say. We tell you to stay in touch with your own experience because your own stuff is always there. You should know it as your own and not impose it on the other person's life. It takes all the qualities Ben mentioned to know where you end and the other person begins. If you don't work to acquire these qualities, then you will end up violating people with your own ignorance. As leaders it's our job to exemplify the principles of awareness, honesty and self-responsibility. At its essence the stance is simple but it isn't easy . . . and it isn't simplistic." He took a breath, vaguely aware that his own stuff had tumbled out over the naiveté of the smiling woman. "Dumb bird," he thought.

"Will you and Jock be teaching us how to do this?" asked another intern.

"No" replied Ben, "but we will be trying to create conditions in which you will learn."

"So, what tools do we need?" asked another.

"Your ears, your eyes, your hearts and the full depth of your experience in each moment," said Ben.

"How can we learn how to use these tools effectively?"

Jock, having finally out-stared the young Buddhist, jumped back in. "Through curiosity, honesty and respect. Remember what Ben told you."

"And what do we learn in this process?"

"Everything," said Ben, glancing sideways at his co-leader. "Everything you ever wanted to know."

Later, as they walked back along the path to Weaver's house, Jock silently reviewed his performance. He had been hard on them but it had to be said. They had to know that they weren't there to fix or enlighten others. Their challenge was to *be there*, in the moment, in the Tao. They wanted to be seen for their intentions and recognised by the leaders as the chosen ones, but they assumed their freedom rested on the permission of others. "To be free is nothing," said Fiscte, "to become free is heavenly." Ben had gently invited them to stay inside and respond to their own experience but they didn't seem to get it. They were looking for simple answers and trite prescriptions. They had to be told.

As they made their way down the drift-wood steps and onto the deck surrounding the house, Jock stopped suddenly. "Oh shit," he said, "that was all my stuff coming out in there. While I was preaching one thing, I was doing the exact opposite?"

Ben opened the front door, reached inside and switched on the porch light. "Well that seems possible," he replied, before stepping inside.

Jock turned and looked back at the roughly hewn steps rising up between clumps of gorse and juniper to the brink of the shallow cliff. Perhaps if he walked up backwards, along the path and back to the Lodge, the flow of events would also switch into reverse. He could try it again, without having to face his own recriminations.

There was no doubt that his work with Ben flowed easier now, but complementarity was one thing, equivalency was another. As he stood on Weaver's deck with the notes of Chopin's "Mazurka in D Major" drifting out through the open doorway, the images of his clumsy pretensions continued to plague him and desecrate the music. He remembered his first 'Gestalt.'

Christina had seemed like a prime candidate for the 'procedure.' A large neurotic woman in her mid-forties, she had spilled over into the group with a series of brassy, almost hysterical, outbursts. Her contact with the world around appeared equally fragmented. When she volunteered to do some work around her fears of being rejected by those she cared most about, Jock was ready for the challenge. Ben, who had sensed his enthusiasm, nodded for him to proceed.

Jock had studied Gestalt theory carefully and, on more than one occasion, actually had watched Fritz Perls, the father of the Gestalt method, in action. The technique most commonly associated with this brand of therapy was known simply as the "empty chair." In this procedure, the individual created a dialogue with split-off aspects of the self by externalizing one fragment, such as the abandonment by a parent, and talking to it 'as if' it really was a separate entity. Through this process, the person began to examine and, eventually, reclaim the detached element.

Now, as the memories of his work with Christina began to take shape, the past poured into the present.

Jock moves with Christina to the centre of the group where they sit, cross legged on the floor, face to face. He invites her to talk about relationships and her feelings of rejection, all the time searching for the content that might breathe life into the technique. He wants to make a connection with her but, above all, he wants to create a shining example of the Gestalt method. She jumps from experience to experience and topic to topic. He is tight in his stomach, fighting to maintain his own sense of integration. He begins to corral Christina's chaos into some order that will allow him to set up the 'empty chair' arrangement.

Finally, he manages to extricate Father from the jumble and places a cushion at her side to accommodate the absent parent. He invites her to tell her father about the pain and the anger, but her words are flat. For some reason the ebullient Christina has become disengaged from the whole process. Like a person watching a third rate movie, she refuses to suspend her disbelief. He invites her to take Father's place on the cushion and relate from this perspective but she becomes giddy and irrelevant, playing to entertain a disinterested group. So he closes down, with as much intensity as he can muster, and the two figures sink back into the group. Ben leans over as he resumes his place. "How does it feel to be a failure at twenty-eight?" he whispers to Jock's ear only.

Following that session Jock wrapped himself in resentment over Ben's rhetorical question. In the subsequent analysis, however, it became painfully clear that, in his desire to demonstrate his techniques and make something happen, he had created a neurosis all of his own. In attempting to 'watch his own creation,' he had managed to split himself off from the world he sought to impress and control. And somewhere among the pieces, Christina had continued to play her game undisturbed. Actually, it was *his* neurosis that had taken centre stage in the drama. It was *his* fragmentation that had kept them apart.

But, step by step, he was learning what he needed to know.

Now, standing on Weaver's deck, he wanted to assure himself of his progress. He settled into an old wicker chair, closed his eyes, and urged himself to retrieve the images of a subsequent session, one in which he could feel a sense of accomplishment. It didn't take long.

His place in the circle is safely assured by the presence of Ben sitting cross-legged on the cushion next to him. Today the group seems quiet, almost pensive. The round cedar session room flutters with the hushed murmurs of the assembly; twenty-seven of them sitting on a circle of cushions carefully laid out by the interns before breakfast. Above, streaks of early sunlight shines through a conical sky-light at the centre of a domed roof. Jock can actually feel Bennet Wong sitting on the cushion next to him, as if they were in some way attached. He imagines that he could reach out and join with the others also but, for the moment, he chooses to watch them from a distance; the usual odd collection of figures, some upright, others lying across their cushions. Some sit closely together, even touching or holding hands, others draw into their own space. The preferred dress is simple; cut off jeans with strands dangling, brightly coloured shorts, roughly fashioned skirts, loose tops and T-shirts, beads and bandannas. Most are bare-footed. And, as always, there are those who feel more comfortable in neatly creased dress pants and printed slacks sticking out over finely stretched socks or stockings, crisp-ironed blouses and carefully laundered shirts, even one with gold cuff-links. These are the ones whose presence most upsets the purists. But all bask in the same glow, all have brought their stories to this place and, over the next few days, each will share part of that mystery with the others. Now they look toward the leaders, waiting for whatever is about to happen among them.

As at the start of any group, Jock feels uneasy with the uncertainty of what is about to unfold. What will be his contribution and how will he been seen and judged? But Ben is the master of the unknown, it will unfold as it should.

They begin with 'group temperature-taking.' Thoughts and feelings of the moment tumble out into the centre. Some revelations startle, freezing breath and belly. Others touch common chords, bringing laughter, tears and murmurs of recognition. Attention shifts from one group member to the next as they talk about their excitement, their hopes and their fears. Many times they pause and look toward the leaders for reassurance. Jock is open and hovers on the borders of his own self-indulgence. He wants to touch their innocence with his tears and clasp the outstretched hands of their courage. But he is a leader. He is there to draw out and guide the process and he remains contained. He wonders how all of this is happening. What order begins to emerge through the trembling uncertainty of human vulnerability? What transformation is taking place through the spontaneity and revelations among this group of strangers? What is being revealed and what is being created? Who, or what, moves these people? He thinks back to the 'warm-up' last evening, the exercises that had invited them to throw aside the usual social rituals. Now, after the preliminary overtures, many are already doing what they have come to do.

Carol is speaking. She talks about her new baby and her fears of motherhood. Across the circle, Laura's body tightens and her face contorts. Jock notices.

"What's happening, Laura?" he asks.

"It's just . . . it's just what Carol said. I know about that." She draws her lips inside her mouth and bites down. The others watch and wait. "I just don't want to be a mother any more." She pauses and swallows. "I just can't do it. I don't even want to get up in the morning, its too much." Her face crinkles up again. "I can't even be a good wife. John's going to leave me, I know he is . . . then they'll take my daughter away and I'll have nothing . . . I'll be nothing . . . but I can't give any more, there's nothing left . . . I've got nothing left . . .Oh God, here I go." She pulls back her breath, her words caught in her throat. The man beside her places an arm around her shoulder.

"Laura, would you like to do some work around this?" Ben asks.

"I'm scared . . . I'm really scared. I thought I had it more together."

"It's okay to be scared here."

"What will I have to do?"

"Only what you want to do."

"Yes. I want to talk about it."

Ben picks up his cushion and invites her to join him in the centre. They sit cross-legged, facing each other, Ben leaning slightly forward, his elbows resting on his knees, she straight-backed and tense, her eyes darting anxiously around the group. They begin to talk softly, almost inaudibly, while the others strain to hear, exchanging anticipatory glances. Last night they learned how to move energy with their breath. Some of them remember. Others hold on. Ben talks to Laura about her fear.

"How are you right now Laura?" he asks.

"Scared."

"Tell me about the fear."

"I'm scared of what people will think if I really tell the truth."

"Are you worried about what we will think of you?"

"Yes."

She pulls herself in another notch but the words squeeze out anyway. "I hit my daughter with a kitchen chair. That's pretty shocking isn't it? John had to take her to the hospital. She's only four. They thought it was John but it was me. It seems so stupid. I told her she couldn't go next door so she went and got John's permission and did it anyway."

191

"And that really upset you."

"Yes, but it was the way she did it."

"And how was that?"

"By playing coy . . . little Miss Innocence. She can twist John around her little finger any time she wants . . . and she knows it. But that's no excuse for me hitting her like that. John says I'm making it up but I know exactly what she's doing and he can't see it. Maybe it was him I wanted to hit. I can feel the anger now and I don't know what to do with it."

"Where do you feel that anger now Laura?"

"Right in here." She presses the palm of her hand against her chest.

"You seem to know that place well."

"Yes I do, it was there a lot when I was kid."

"A kid like your daughter?"

"No. I didn't play innocent because I wasn't innocent . . ." She drops her head.

Ben watches the movement of her body. "What's happening now Laura?"

"I don't know. I don't know anything."

She is rigid, her face set firm. Her eyes shift from Ben to the floor, then she freezes.

Ben leans a little closer. "Would it be okay if Jock comes to join us?" he asks.

Her eyes circle the group until she finds the face of the other leader. Jock waits. He wants to be there beside Ben. She reminds him of Ann who died without him. Through her hesitation he struggles with an ego fearing rejection, a heart yearning to open and something, even deeper, searching to be recognised. He knows that the decision must come from her. Finally, she nods toward him. He reaches for his pouch of needles and moves his cushion out to join them.

Jock briefly explains acupuncture and Laura gives him permission to proceed. He checks the twelve pulses of the wrists, his fingers moving almost imperceptibly. "Metal high, wood low, water low, fire low, earth low," he mumbles. Ben nods. "Needle in the hand Laura, take a breath." Her eyes are closed, her legs crossed and her hands, palms upward, rest lightly on her knees. The two leaders sit side by side, their bodies now in contact.

A tremor moves through the group as Laura's body begins to move. Her head jerks to one side and her shoulders twitch alternatively as if engaged in some obscure form of somatic dialogue. Jock takes over. "Keep breathing Laura. Let the energy come. That's good . . . that's good." Sobs, heavy wrenching sobs, pump out the tears. "What's the feeling Laura? Talk about the feeling."

"I feel sad . . . I just feel really sad."

"What's the sadness about Laura. Let the sadness come."

She begins to shake, gulping to contain the spasms. Her body seems to pull back against the release and the paralysis returns. The group stiffens in response. Some force a breath. Laura stares back helplessly at the two leaders.

"We're ready to keep working if you are Laura." Ben's voice is soft and assuring. His eyes scan her rigid body. Jock nods in the direction of two interns and they leave the circle, returning moments later carrying a plastic covered mattress between them. They lay it down beside the three figures and drift back into the circle. Following a hushed discussion, Laura loosens the tartan shirt from around her waist and rolls her slacks up above her knees. Standing at one end of the mattress, her shirt hanging out and her pant legs crumpled around her thighs, she looks frail and exposed. At Jock's request, she lays down on the mattress, her knees up and feet apart. Ben sits cross-legged at her head as Jock and a young female intern take up positions on either side.

"I want you to take some deep breaths," Jock tells her. "Open your chest and take the breath all the way down into your belly. That's it. Keep a steady rhythm, just like waves moving in and out on the shore." He demonstrates with his own breath, his dark eyes watching the uneasy undulations of her upper body. Her legs begin to shake. Jock and the intern sweep their hands above her body. The strange ritual of energy work is underway.

Jock leans over, placing his thumb and forefinger at points high on her chest. Her body moves out to meet the pressure and she winces in pain. "Breathe into the chest, Laura. Breathe through the pain." Jock is now fully engaged, his body poised and his jaw set. She cries out and her throat opens. And again, this time piercing up from the groin and reverberating around the walls. The pulse of the group is broken. Some look away or reach to another for comfort. Others stare fixedly toward the middle of the circle. The 'old hands' breathe into their own pain. Jock has removed his fingers but she continues to fight against the pressure that is now hers alone.

As the crisis subsides, the belly that shrieked its fury at the world moves in spasmodic union with the sobbing contractions of her throat. Jock's posture has softened, his eyes wide and compassionate. She coughs, first in response to the stricture of the throat and then from the abating tempest of her chest. Ben, sitting behind the top of her head, reaches out and takes a Kleenex from the box at his side. Gently turning her head to one side, he wipes her mouth with the delicacy of a skilled and devoted parent. Jock watches him. Somehow Ben can bring symmetry and dignity to even the most basic human acts.

Her immediate discomfort eases, and she allows her head to fall back into the cradle of Ben's hands. He lowers his face until their cheeks are almost touching. "Keep the breathing going Laura, right down into the belly," he whispers. "That's good. Yes, just let the shaking go. That's all you Laura, it's your life." His thumbs move along the line of her jaw, meeting under her chin. He presses into the joint below the ears and she screams again, this time from the head. "Yes, let it go Laura," he says. "Ah yes, hmmm yes." Her face twists in rebellion. "Breathe through it Laura, just let it go."

"Oh Jesus, Jesus it hurts." She arches her back off the mattress, kicking out each leg in succession. Jock and the intern place her feet back on the surface.

"*You* hurt," Ben whispers.

"I hurt . . . yes I hurt . . . Oh Jesus I hurt."

Ben releases the pressure and cradles her head again. Coughing and sobbing intertwine as Ben reaches for another Kleenex, then another. Her breathing subsides into gentle modulation. Her belly, chest and head rise and fall in connected sequence as the energy flows through her. Her face seems softer. Ben, his mouth beside her ear, whispers a gentle assurance.

Jock and the intern take up positions on either side of her legs. Placing an elbow above each knee, they begin their work on her inner thighs, pushing their elbows in unison toward her knees. Her torso freezes again, straining up from the mattress in a desperate attempt to hold back the pain. Her mouth is wide open, lips stretched tightly across the teeth but there is no sound. "Let it go Laura, let it go," Jock says. Ben's thumbs press back into the hinges of the jaw. This time the eruption seems to come from a place deep inside and her body convulses.

"Words, Laura, what are the words?" Ben's inverted face is beside hers, their cheeks touching now.

"You bastard," she shrieks.

"Who is it Laura?"

"For Christ's sake get off me, leave me alone. I can't take this . . . get off me . . . get off me." She smashes her hands and forearms down on the mattress, the rest of her body writhing and buffeting. Jock leans forward. "Who's hurting you Laura? Who is it?"

"It's you . . . it's you. You have no right . . . you have no right. I'm your kid for God's sake . . . I'm your goddamned daughter, your DAUGHTER." She rolls over on her side, drawing up her legs and lowering her head into the foetal position. Now another voice, a young girl's voice, takes over. "I'm going to tell Mommy . . . I don't care what you say . . . I'm going to tell Mommy." She buries her face in her hands. "Mommy, Mommy, Mommy . . . " She rocks herself to the rhythm.

Jock stands up and hovers over her. "You won't tell Mommy anything," he says coldly.

"Yes I will, yes I will." The voice of the young child whispers out from between the fingers.

"You know what will happen if you do."

The fetal bundle tightens and moans.

"It's our secret Laura," Jock says.

Without warning her body uncoils in an explosion of fury; eyes staring, fists clenched, shoulders arched and jaw thrust forward, she hisses like a wildcat. Jock springs back lightly. The group watches in horror at the transformation. Ben gestures toward an intern who leaves the circle and returns with a large over-stuffed cushion. Another brings a baseball bat and hands it to Jock.

Laura is sitting cross-legged on the edge of the mattress, her breath ferocious. She is rigid and unyielding, staring out into space. Chin, breasts and pelvis are pushed forward. She seems far removed from the world occupied by the others, a demonic transfiguration of the timorous young woman who stepped into the centre less than an hour ago.

The blue cushion is placed in front of her by the two interns and they tighten their grip on the handles stitched into either side of the mattress. Jock, no longer at the centre of her rage, places the bat in her hand. "You have every right to your anger Laura. As you feel it deep inside, try to let it come out through your body and through your arms. When you feel it building up, take the bat up over your head and bring in down on the mat as hard as you like. Really let it go. Think about what he did to you. Think about the times you wanted to strike back and were afraid of what might happen. He had no right to do that Laura."

"You had no right to do that." The words are cold and deliberate, the expression on her face fixed and uncompromising. Her grip on the bat tightens but it hangs limply between her thighs and the cushion.

Jock moves in again. "Then tell him how you *really* feel Laura. Now, after all these years, you can finally let him know. He had no right to do that. Let him know Laura."

Slowly she raises the bat above her head and pauses at the top.

"Tell him Laura . . . now you can really let him know." Jock moves to her side.

Then, in a shattering instant, the demon returns and the bat cracks down on the mat with a force that causes the two interns to pull back reflexively, their arms straining to hold onto the handles. Then again, and again, the bat comes down as the group recoils.

"The words Laura . . . say the words . . . tell him how you feel." Jock is moving around her, his voice demanding as he calls upon her rage.

"Enough, you bastard," she shrieks. "No more . . . no more." The bat crashes down in a frenzied and unrelenting assault.

"It's our secret Laura," Jock says.

The bat smashes down again. "Never. You get the fuck out of my life . . . d'ya hear me? Get the fuck out. . . ."

"It's our secret Laura. It's our secret," Jock whispers.

"It's no fucking secret . . . I'll tell everybody . . . I'll tell the whole fucking world. He did it . . . he did it to me . . . his own daughter." She is screaming out at the group, unable to see the faces that stare back in horror. "And I loved you, goddammit . . . I loved you." Tears are breaking from her eyes and flooding her face. "I wanted you to look after me . . . I wanted you to love me . . . Oh God, I wanted you to love me."

Her body is losing its fury. She struggles to lift the bat above her head and it falls to the cushion. Her head drops and her chest heaves in sobbing convulsions. She curls over, grasping her knees in her hands.

Ben, Jock and the interns sit back in silence. They motion for the circle to move in closer. Jock allows himself to cry. The storm is over and he sits back on his haunches. Ben nods. They have worked well together.

Slowly Laura uncurls and looks up into the receptive eyes of Jock McKeen. She reaches out to him with both hands and, kneeling upright, he wraps his arms around her. In the silent sadness that connects them all, Laura's pain has affirmed the simple dignity of each life.

"Would you like to be rocked?" he whispers. She nods.

Sitting on the mattress, with Laura on his knees and an intern supporting his back, Jock begins to rock back and forth. Ben has left the group to add the final piece. Music begins to drift from the speakers mounted high on the session room wall. His selection blends perfectly into the mood, offering another medium through which feelings can be acknowledged and expressed. The group sways to a gentle tempo as a mellow female voice urges them to seek the love that lies behind the pain.

As the music comes to an end, Jock looks over the shoulder of his surrogate child and reconnects with the group. He unravels his arms and motions for them to come closer. "Laura, I want you to look into the faces of the people here. What do you see?"

Slowly she lifts her head from his chest and looks around, searching each face.

"I see people out there who understand," she says and nestles back into the body of her protector.

"Who would like to share some feelings with Laura?" Jock asks.

"Laura, I want to thank you," says Marilyn, an overweight young woman who has maintained an aloof distance from the group up to this point. Now, her tears draw them toward her. "I had a stepfather who molested me for years while my mother turned away," she says.

"I feel angry and ashamed," Jason says. "I don't want to be judged by the actions of other men but I feel in some way responsible for what we do."

One by one they share their thoughts and feeling around Laura's work. She is sitting up, allowing their experience to mingle with her own. Her face is soft and her eyes make contact with those who speak. Jock carefully extricates himself as the others move in to put their arms around her. Ben has moved back to the stereo and the music begins again. No words this time, only a gentle strain, the melody of being alive.

Jock joins Ben on the periphery and, with their arms around each other, they watch the group in silence. One person remains on the outside, bent over and motionless, where the others once formed their circle. They have noticed the isolated figure of David Mortimer but, for the moment, they allow the process to take its course. Gradually, the circle starts to re-form and the figure of the balding middle-aged man in the blue sweater blends back into the crowd, lost for the moment, but not forgotten.

"Some of you may have seen body-work before," Ben says when the circle is complete and settled. "I want to say a few words about this before we move on. We believe that the body and the mind are one entity. So, our experience of ourselves and the world are stored as much in our bodies as in our mind. We are connected through a single flow of energy. Physical and mental health are possible as long as this energy stream remains open to our experiences, past and present. Problems arise as we clamp down on experience by blocking this energy flow. In this way, we set up defences and create our own protective patterns for dealing with life. In the mind, these recurring patterns can be released through awareness or insight. In the body, they may be released through breathing and body-work. But we are always dealing with the same energy. So, in Laura's case, her early experience and her fears about the judgments of others created blocks held in place by fears of disclosure. Here we find the rage and the sadness that she has locked away. As we work to remove these blocks, the feelings are released and, in that moment, the energy is allowed to flow."

Jock takes over. "The energy begins to move with the simple act of taking a full breath," he explains. "The method we use is called Reichian breathing since Wilhelm Reich did much of the early work in this area. He referred to this energy of life as 'Orgone' energy and we'll be talking more about some of his ideas later in the program. When I used acupuncture needles at the beginning, I was using specific points along energy channels, or what the Chinese refer to as 'meridians.' This also helps to dissolve blocks in the same energy—the Chinese refer to this as 'Chi.'"

"The whole thing looks so painful. Does it really hurt that much?" asks Marilyn.

"Well, the person on the mat is always in control. Whatever pain is experienced comes from the resistance and not from the pressure. Even so, we will always stop if the person asks," Jock replies.

"How do you know what part of the body to work on?" asks another voice from the circle.

"From our perspective, our personal stories are written into our bodies as much as they are written into our minds," says Ben. "The key is in being able to read what the body has to say, as you might read a book, or a piece of music. It comes with practice. It's all there in the posture, the breathing and in the way the person moves in the world."

"Laura looks so different, so full of life. Does this mean that she is now free from the blockages?"

Ben responds again. "As I said before, the way we generate and deal with experience in our lives becomes patterned and, to some extent, predictable. This is what gives us our individuality, our own unique way of being in the world. While some of these patterns might be self-defeating, we still hang on to them even though we might know that there's a better way. In body-work, we may be able to release an energy block in the moment but this is only the first step. The tendency will be for Laura to go back to her old patterns. But now she has experienced an alternative. Over time, through awareness, she may shift her way of dealing with her experience and transform these habits. The energy shift you saw today is a step in that direction."

"So people don't change very easily."

"Well," says Jock, "at a deep level, we don't believe that people change at all. Ben used the word 'transformation' and that's what we believe can take place. But while we might change our ways of moving in the world, the essence of who we are remains basically unchanged."

There's confusion written into some of the faces, but nobody leaps in to seek clarification. There will be many opportunities for clarification through the course of the program. "So we'll talk some more about the work as we move along. We wanted

you to have some understanding of body-work at this stage."
He turns to Jock who has been carefully eyeing the group. Their
eyes meet. Ben has known no better time.

"So, how are you?" Jock asks the assembly. A flicker of energy travels the circle but nobody responds directly. Jock's eyes
search out David Mortimer; others follow. A balding man with
wire-framed glasses and pale blue sweater, his place in the group
has gone largely unnoticed. But now, as a focal point of attention, he looks oddly out of place.

"What's happening David?" All eyes are upon him now. He
looks back at Jock directly. He clenches his teeth and pulls at the
knees of his black trousers, raising the cuffs well above the top
of his socks.

"I'm one of those people," he says. "I did it with my daughter."

"Do you want to talk some more about it?" Jock asks.

Nestled in Weavers old chair, Jock continued to ponder on his
life and his future. The meeting with the interns had not gone
well but there were times, as in the session with Laura, when he
seemed to be finding his own place in the partnership. But they
were never planned or predictable. Now, as a cool evening breeze
off the ocean whipped up small eddies of sand and sent them
whirling across the porch, he wondered if his life would ever
settle there. Ben's music called him to the living room but, closing the door quietly behind him, he headed down the stairs to
the basement in search of his flute.

He continued to look for forms that might focus and contain
his learning within tolerable parameters. To this end, the
"Chicken Coop Rule" served him well. It was simple enough in
its formulation. Whatever feedback Ben might have for him after each group session was to be communicated before they
reached the Chicken Coop on the way from the session room to
the Lodge. In this way, he could be assured that the pain of criticism would be predictable, immediate and, hopefully, bearable.
The analysis could come later.

"I won't diminish you with contrived praise or condescending platitudes of encouragement," Ben told him one evening. "Rather, I'll recognize and respect you with the honesty of my experience. But I'll only do this if you'll take responsibility for yours." It was all perfectly reasonable and understandable at the time, but that was in the days when theories could be embraced without having to be lived.

"When I think you're really pissed off, my gut suddenly empties and my head rushes around trying to plug the hole," Jock said, placing his cup precariously on the arm of his chair. They had left the supper table to watch the sunset from the chairs on the porch. "I try to stay open and vulnerable but this automatic response kicks in every time."

Ben leaned over and delicately moved the cup toward the middle of the arm. "The strange thing is that I rarely feel that pissed off with you. But, short of unqualified praise, you seem to take all observations about you as criticism. You used to come back with justifications or apologies but now you just seem to shrink away. Like today, when we came down for supper and I was talking about your work with Barbara. You asked for my opinion and then, without really hearing what I had to say, you seemed to detach yourself from me and drift off into that sulky defensive place of yours. Where were you?"

"On my own, defending myself and feeling guilty," Jock admitted. "I'm even feeling that way right now because you just moved my cup. I'm holding you responsible for my feelings."

"Would you feel better if the cup had fallen?"

"No, I'd probably feel even more stupid, more judged. But, come on, fess up, you weren't pleased with the work with Barbara and I was the one who was leading the way. You were angry and I was the object of your anger. Isn't that the way it was?"

Ben wrapped his hands around his own coffee mug and thought for a moment. "If we're in this thing together, then I want to be able to talk about our work, about ourselves and about each other. What I offered was my response to that particular piece of work, because that's what you'd asked for. There was no anger involved."

"Okay, okay, but there have been times, many of them, when you *have* been pissed off," Jock insisted, not wanting his cause to be lost on the weakness of a single example. "That's what the bloody chicken coop rule is all about, isn't it?"

"So you want me to stop sharing my anger, is that it?"

Jock lifted an empty cup to his lips and took a long ponderous drink. It sounded like a trap, a reason to tread carefully, to choose words that would take him deftly around the hazards and back into the open. He took three gulps of decaffeinated air before presenting his considered response. "No," he said limply.

Ben knew that his anger could be intimidating and, on occasion, he was not above using it for effect. Never contrived, always contained and aware of the possible impact, such eruptions generally left the unfortunate recipient in little doubt about the nature of the alleged transgression. Many who had sought to be close to him recalled these full-bodied expressions of contempt as pivotal, if not transformational, experiences along the way. This was an integral part of Bennet Wong and he wanted Jock to know him well.

Ben moved his chair a little closer. "Of course there are times when I'm angry, even furious, but I'm always the subject of my own anger. It belongs to me as much as my joy and my sadness. But you don't seem to get too upset when I share these things with you, even if you do happen to be the object. Whatever we share honestly, openly and non-strategically is of equal value to me. So, when you try to capture my anger to feed your own guilt or self-hate, that value is lost to both of us. And, if you do happen to be the object of my anger, then it's because I care enough about you to make you a part of my personal experience. This doesn't mean that you're responsible for my feelings, and it certainly doesn't mean that you're supposed to do something about them. My intention is to include you, not to hurt you or to get you to do things differently. I'm quite capable of asking directly for anything I might want from you. But, if you start to defend yourself, then I can only assume that you consider yourself to be under attack, with me as your assailant. And if you start trying to make things better for me, then you must be arrogant enough to believe that you can fix me up in some way."

There he was again, the dunce in his own classroom. He knew the material, even the words. He could have delivered the same speech without thinking but, once again, something was blocked and it had to come from Ben. There was so much information in his head that seemed to run into the corners whenever he needed it the most. The nature of the material wasn't the issue since he had contributed many of the ideas. The problem was definitely in the application, the relentless scurrying backwards and forwards between his brain and his belly. Whatever the hang-up, it was strangling his options and turning him into a fool. Maybe it was some obscure form of learning disability that needed to be diagnosed and treated. To hell with the Chicken Coop Rule, he had to know for sure. It was time to move on, to put himself at the centre of his knowledge and demonstrate his willingness to withstand the fall-out.

"Curiosity," he said, "that's what I lose when I get into my defensive stuff, curiosity. I want to stay curious about your experience and my response, even when you are pissed off. Perhaps if I knew more about your anger, maybe that would help." He raised his eyebrows to transform the statement into a question.

"You really want to know about my anger, even around you?" Ben asked.

"Yes."

"Well, if we're still talking about our work, I get angry whenever, in my judgment, you act in ways that are disrespectful or thoughtless of people in the group, particularly when you are insensitive to their boundaries."

"So, what's behind the anger?" Jock asked, momentarily enjoying the illusionary freedom of the interrogator.

"Sadness," Ben said, his face suddenly heavy. "It's like slamming a door in someone's face. Whenever you throw away the possibility of making contact with others I lose my connection with you. I'm sad in my aloneness."

Jock's mind moved swiftly to avoid temptation. He could have lost himself in a thousand sins, but this was the test and his challenge was to break the habit. If only his belly had responded to the same logic, he might have been a free man.

"Tell me more," he said, "be more specific."

Ben hesitated. "Are you still interested in my anger, or are you trying to figure out how to deal with it?" Ben asked.

Jock smiled. "I'm not sure. How about both?"

"How about if I continue to stay with your original question while you try to stay with yourself and your curiosity about me?"

"Well, okay." The smile went the way of the imaginary coffee. Through some strange twist of mind he found himself standing alone. Something had severed his connection. Ben was still there, but oddly remote and lifeless. There was nothing in the space between them and there was nothing on the inside capable of reaching across. Whatever had created the vacuum, Ben would have to make the next move. But the wait seemed endless.

Ben tossed out a life-line. "You're still somewhere else aren't you? You can't be with me without being with yourself at the same time. If you cut out one, you'll cut out the other."

Of course. He was both the butcher and the surgeon of his own life. There was nothing for him to do but to be there and listen.

Ben began softly. "To me, our work is spiritual. What we do takes us to the most precious and vulnerable place in the human experience. When I was a kid, I would stand for hours in a church and speak to God out loud. But the voice that came back was only an echo, often with the words of others who had stood in that same place and asked those same questions. There were no answers, nothing of substance for a little kid who wanted to know everything. Finally I gave up, but I had this idea that what

I was looking for was hidden somewhere in the questions. And if it was there in my life, then it must be there in every other life. I couldn't live my life without, in some way, living their lives also. If I could only talk to those lives, directly, without having to follow the rules or the scriptures, then God would be there, speaking through all of us.

"That's why I chose Psychiatry . . . to learn the language of other lives. But as I listened to my teachers and later watched my colleagues, I saw how they had just created another language, as remote and detached as the language of the clergy. I saw how their beliefs and their rituals had been built into a religion, with themselves as the priests and the prophets. I saw hubris and self-righteousness in the place of humanness and humility; status and power in the place of curiosity and compassion. I would never accept this, not just because I found it personally offensive, but because it was all so diametrically opposed to everything the kid in the church was looking for."

He paused and looked out over the bay, as though he were looking for something that might be found somewhere in the mingling of sky and ocean. Then he turned back to look into the face of the man who was now daring to ask the same questions. Neither would ever find the answers, uncover the truth, for there was no truth to be had. But together they could explore the possibilities.

"You are so much a part of my life these days Jock," he said. "Yet, in our work together, the lives of the people we work with are no more and no less important than you, me, or our relationship. How can we respect ourselves and each other if we don't have the same respect for other lives? How can we talk about honesty and integrity if we change our colours from one moment to the next? As Jock McKeen, you are free to lead your life in any way you choose. But, as my partner, I will always let you know if, in my judgment, you have shown disrespect or insensitivity for another human life. I just won't have it any other way."

Once again Jock's mind ran over its litany of sins, but, this time, he was more interested in knowing the details of the case than in preparing his own defence.

"You know, I really did see Stewart trying to say something at the end of the session this afternoon. But I knew that we were running out of time and I wanted to finish the Lawrence quote. You knew that, didn't you?"

"Yes."

"And you were angry, weren't you?"

"Yes. In my judgment, you were trapped in your own head. You'd found some words to make your own dramatic impact and chose to abandon Stewart, and the rest of us, in order to make it happen."

Jock flinched. "Okay, so here I go. I'm feeling criticized and defensive . . . now what?" He sat for a moment, preparing an answer to his own question.

"You might begin by asking yourself what needs to be protected," Ben suggested.

Jock squeezed and let go, the release filling his eyes. Still, the thoughts made no sense and the feelings had no name. Anxious to let Ben in, he began to talk, hoping that the words might take over. "I'm defending myself . . . I think . . . but I'm not sure what about me needs to be so protected. I think I've always believed that I should be a certain way without really knowing what that way looks like. It keeps changing, depending upon where I am and who I'm with . . . or who I think I'm with."

"So you want to protect yourself from someone, or something." It was an answer in search of a question.

"Yes. The someone is you and the something is your evaluation of me." It wasn't very profound or revealing but, at least, it was clear.

"So, if you judge my evaluations to be positive, do you defend yourself against them as well? That would make sense to me."

This tossed another stone into the already troubled waters. "Probably, but not in the same way, perhaps, not to the same degree . . . maybe."

"Then whose evaluations are we really dealing with?"

Enough. The questions had become circular and the answers tautological. His unknown, waiting-to-be-discovered self simply couldn't converse in a way that made any sense to his postured, wanting-to-be-defended, self. They spoke a different language. Meanwhile, a foreign tongue at the centre begged for someone to listen, for somebody to translate.

Ben turned back to look at the ocean. Today it was playful and seductive, lightly running across the sand and around the rocks. Tomorrow it would be different, "high winds and swollen seas" they predicted, though nobody could ever be sure. Whatever the expectations and the reactions, the ocean would respond to changing conditions according to its own essence, as would Jock McKeen some day. Meanwhile, Ben marvelled at his friend's tenacity.

"You know I spend a lot of time trying to look at myself through your eyes," Jock said on his return to the moment.

"Yes, sort of like a blind man with borrowed glasses," Ben said, drawing himself away from his preoccupation with the ocean. "But the real challenge is to look at yourself through your own eyes, taking my perspective as a light that may shine on nothing."

Jock remained stoically analytic. "Ah yes," he conceded, "but to do this I have to know myself as separate from you and then open up to whatever you, or your experience, has to offer. This is impossible if I hold you responsible for me; if I spend my time trying to control you as a way of protecting me." It made sense, though he had to pause for a moment to think about it.

"And I need to know that you accept my experience as being about me and not about you," said Ben, turning the light up a little higher. "Only then can I feel free to share my experience with you openly in the spirit of being *seen* by you, rather than the fear of being *used* by you."

Jock took another incremental step into the light. "So let me use your anger one more time to see if I've got it. You were upset about the way I encouraged Sharon to do her work yesterday. Take me through this again and I'll try to stay with *your* experience." It was a sincere proposition, surrounded by apprehension.

Ben cleared his throat and began. "Well, without going over all the details again, I considered your cajoling of Sharon to be insensitive to her personal boundaries. Two or three times she tried to hold you back but you kept on coming forward. I assumed you were aware of the pressure from the group and this made your actions all the more offensive to me. And I was angry because, in my opinion, you were insensitive to whatever was happening for her."

Jock kept his apprehension firmly in storage and pushed on. "So, beyond my own defensiveness, I can accept that this was your experience, that it had nothing directly to do with me. So, now I can ask my next question about you which is . . . What does Ben's anger tell me about Ben?" The final step was to turn the question outwards. "So, here we go. What lies behind *your* anger? I'd really like to know." The question was terse, if not presumptuous but, having paved the way, he was determined to pull his projected shadow, this outlaw, this saboteur, from the corners and slay it there and then with the sword of reason. All Ben had to do now was to take back his anger and place it fairly and squarely in his own separate life. He denied himself breath and waited.

When finally it came, the answer was alarmingly brief. "When, in my judgment, you are disrespectful to people in the group, you are also disrespectful toward me. As you are with them, so you are with me. As they hurt, so I hurt."

On the strength of his long-awaited breath, Jock wanted only to scream. Another 'no man is an island' exhortation. After all the work, all the soul-searching, he was still stuck to Ben's anger like a fly on fly-paper. Why had the man refused to locate his anger somewhere in the story of his own childhood, freeing others of the burden? The lesson was supposed to be about not being responsible for the experience of others and here was his teacher reversing the entire thesis just as the bell sounded. He considered blurting out his protest but contained himself, fearing that his understanding might be revealed as inadequate. Clearly, something was missing and he searched in vain for the insight that had somehow escaped. For the moment, he settled for the glaringly superficial explanation that, since he and Ben were partners, the actions of one would in some way reflect upon the other. Yet, at the same time, a deeper, though stubbornly inarticulate, thought cautioned that he may have missed the point completely.

Clearly there was still work he needed to do. "What do you need from me?" he once asked Ben. "Nothing," was the reply, "I don't need anything from you." He felt dismissed, derogated and insignificant. Despite the illusions of partnership, it was always clear that Ben had the power. And, despite his protestations to the contrary, he was a very powerful man, unquestionably the most powerful that Jock had ever met. Whether he actively sought or even consciously used such power for his own ends remained a question. It certainly seemed that way whenever the punishing onslaught of criticism punctuated their journey down to the Chicken Coop. Preoccupied with the matter of his own potency, it was some time before Jock was ready to consider that he had actually created the Chicken Coop Rule as a poorly disguised attempt to wrestle power from his best friend.

While Jock was in no doubt about his student status, he dangled his co-leader shingle before the outside world. Not that representatives of that world were necessarily fooled. Most of the participants in the Resident Fellow Program regarded Ben as the primary leader. Those in closer proximity, like Jerry Glock, who had come to Cortes to be an intern in the program, considered themselves to be participating in a seminar led by Bennet Wong, *assisted* by Jock McKeen. With an attitude never far from resentment, Jerry watched the student's struggle for equivalency with the teacher.

"I don't see myself as your teacher," Ben told Jock. They were sitting in Weaver's garden, filled with the glow from the afternoon session and lulled by the distant sounds of their participants singing and dancing on the lawn by the Lodge. Beneath them, others lounged or strolled along the log-strewn beach, looking at themselves, each other and the world, as if the face of their new God was to be found hidden somewhere in every thought, behind every feeling and under every rock. Here at Cold Mountain, the innocent enchantment of the Sixties was more than a fun-filled romance, it was a dedicated and disciplined commitment.

The two leaders looked forward to these early evening talks. For Jock, they were times when he had Ben to himself. "Teacher or not, I certainly learn from you," he said.

"That's fine. There are things that you can learn from me," Ben acknowledged.

"Then you become my teacher," Jock insisted.

"No, because you have to ask first. Then I respond to your curiosity."

"And, in responding, you become my teacher."

"I become the vehicle for your curiosity. I can only offer you my personal responses. What happens then is up to you."

"Ah, but, however much you might understand my intentions, you're the one who decides what information will be offered," Jock said.

"Whatever I say, please take it for what it is . . . an expression of my ideas, my beliefs and my experience. It's you who must decide what fits and what doesn't. I don't have the slightest interest in convincing you of anything.

"Well, if you have no investment in me, then what's in it for you?" Jock asked, still hoping to salvage something from his position.

"When I know that you'll take full responsibility for your own intentions and interpretations, then I'll feel free to reveal mine. I just don't want to get lost in your expectations or projections. What's in this for me is the chance to be seen. I'm talking about letting the knowledge reside with the knower."

The distinction wasn't new. In fact, he had used it himself on several occasions. This was not the issue here, however, and he disliked being taught what he already knew. "Oh come off it," he protested. "I learn many things from your knowledge and your experience. It happens every bloody day, for God's sake."

"Then you have made me your teacher, for your own purposes," Ben replied. "But, come to think of it, I *did* teach you how to hook up the stereo yesterday," he added with a smile.

"The hell you did. Your method was just different from what I had in mind."

"Precisely."

For Ben, such exchanges were interesting enough but they were not at the heart of the matter. Of all the things that Ben had come to appreciate about his friend, this willingness to remain at the focal point of investigation impressed him beyond words. Jock's attempts to capture him were not a problem. On the contrary, this was an essential part of the process; a game of power in which Bennet Wong had nothing to offer and nothing to lose. But, in the revelation of such intentions, Jock became freer, Ben became wiser and they both became closer.

But, whatever moves they made toward intimacy, the matter of sexuality was never far away. Well before their commitment to the Resident Fellow Program, their collaboration with Margaret Woods and Lynne Vogel in leading the "Sex and Identity" workshop had paved the way along one particular avenue of investigation.

Margaret, a straight-to-the-point, fun-loving woman, had gained Ben's respect for her understanding of sexual issues and for her rigorous work in examining and stylizing the sexual forms of our culture. An avid student of Sigmund Freud, she rarely hesitated in casting discretion aside in her pursuit of sexual 'truth.' One evening, she suggested that 'the boys' should become more serious in exploring the sexuality hidden within their relationship. She had made no secret of her own curiosity in this matter and persistently asked them questions about their fantasies and physical contact. She jumped into the role of counsellor and made frequent suggestions as to how they might break through their inhibitions. "Well, did anything come up last night?" she would ask as they made their way down to the Lodge for breakfast. Then they would all laugh, though each for a different reason.

"Why don't you try kissing while I watch and we'll go from there?" she suggested as the three of them sat together in Weaver's living room that evening. "I'll be the safe therapist. You'll probably need to work on this stuff." From her sprawled out position on the floor, she waited for the two men on the sofa to respond.

Caught between his fears and the expectation that enquiry into the human experience should be unbridled, Jock turned to look at Ben for a response. He was impassive, clearly unwilling to take the initiative, setting out the conditions for yet another challenge. "Okay," Jock said, sliding toward Ben with the self-abandonment of a first-time skydiver. "What are we supposed to do?"

Margaret smiled, shuffled herself into a seated position and assumed the role of instructor. "Begin by kissing lightly on the lips . . . yes, that's good. Now, gradually increase the pressure and put your arms around each other's shoulders. Oh, that's great . . . open your mouths a little . . . ah yes. Now, whatever the urge dictates . . . Oh my God, I'm getting excited, what's happening for you?"

The two 'lovers' disentangled themselves and looked at each other in silence. Each secret called for the revelation of the other first. Finally Ben turned to face their instructor. "Nothing," he said, "at least nothing that feels remotely sexual." Jock was quick, perhaps too quick, to confirm the reciprocity of the experience. "Well, it felt okay to me, but nothing stirred twixt navel and knee-cap." Another ordeal over, another release.

Margaret was clearly disappointed. "Well, something happened for me," she proclaimed. "I still think you guys are hiding something from yourselves or each other. Maybe you're just hiding it from me?" She rose from the floor and left the room.

The following evening the three met again in the living room for their customary post-workshop analysis. When the babble of the inevitable 'high' had settled into a soft and satisfied silence, Margaret said, "I thought we might do some work from the manual."

Her beloved manual was a picture book of sexual forms that she had compiled to illustrate the commonly recurring themes and patterns of sexual arousal in Western culture. It was also an elegant example of unabashed erotica, a highly ingenious piece of work, used by its creator in sexuality workshops as well as in her own private practice. "There you go," she said, pulling it from a heavily embroidered bag beside her chair and handing it over to Jock. "If you can identify the particular sexual form that fits for your relationship, then maybe we can get somewhere."

Again, in the all-encompassing spirit of enquiry, the two men sat down at Richard Weaver's old writing table and began to thumb their way through a procession of illustrations depicting various motifs of sexual excitement and gratification. They talked in hushed and reverent tones.

"Don't just sit there nattering about the pictures like a pair of schoolboys," Margaret scolded. "Just stop when you find the one that best fits for both of you. You don't have to talk about it. You'll know when you come to it. Just let it happen."

Suitably chastised, the two voyeurs continued their erotic quest in silence, waiting for the truth to leap out from the pages and plunge them into irrepressible carnality. Time passed.

"Oh here, let me help you," Margaret said testily as she watched them return to the opening pages for the third time. She stood behind them, leaned over Ben's shoulder and proceeded to flick through the pages for them. "How about this one? I call it the 'Principal and the Schoolgirl.'" They glanced at each other and shook their heads. Margaret humphed and flicked on. "Then it has to be this one, 'The German Officer and Jewish Maiden?'" Again a quick glance, but this time a moment of hesitation passed between them. "That's the sign," she announced. "That's what we've been waiting for. It's a fascinating motif of power, seduction, surrender or submission. Oh it's so right for you guys. Now, just sit for a moment, breathe and let the imagery sink in . . . slowly now. As the scene builds up in your mind, just let your body respond in whatever way it wants. Now, I'm going to leave you to act it out in a way that fits for you. Don't think too much about it, just let it happen." She placed her arms around their shoulders and beamed down on them benevolently while they continued to stare blankly at the pages of the open book. Then, with a sigh of satisfaction, she floated out into the kitchen and closed the door.

Ben took one final look at the picture, rose from the table and sat in an old afghan-covered chair by the door. He carried the whole picture in his mind but, uncommitted to either of the roles, he could feel nothing that might propel him into some form of action.

Jock continued to stare at the picture. He tried to place himself in the body of the young woman but quickly wriggled free. He stood between them, thinking for a moment that he might stay in the middle, a champion defending the ground between innocence and infamy. But the woman was smiling, not around the mouth but around the eyes; not at him, at the damned Nazi. Yes, he could take the goon's place, with or without the uniform. He could stand like that, stare like that, sneer like that, if that's what was wanted. But Ben as the Jewish Maiden? The image brought a split response, first amusement, then panic. With almost any other person, male or female, he would be the one with the power, but not with Bennet Wong. It was interesting stuff, but none of this was making him feel horny, not even a jingle.

Meanwhile, Ben kept looking at the picture in his mind, becoming increasingly convinced that there would be no resolution until the action commenced. It would have been easier if Margaret had assigned the roles . . more fun that way. Perhaps she took it for granted that they already knew who was supposed to be who.

Still hunched over the desk, Jock considered the prospect of submission as mind and body recoiled in disgust. Someone once told him, a school counsellor he thought, that he was 'officer material.' Nobody ever told him that he was Jewish Maiden material. Perhaps it would take a battle for him to find out, hero or heroine. If only Margaret had given more specific instructions.

They were facing each other squarely; Ben poised on the edge of the afghan chair, Jock perched side-saddle on his seat at the writing desk. Ben was ready for action, any kind of action. Jock wanted to remove the ambiguity of no-man's land. Ben was curious to see what position Jock had chosen. Jock wondered if he would be giving up power should he allow Ben to make the decision. It could be a watershed moment in their relationship.

Ben placed his hands firmly on the arms of his chair and slowly rose to his feet. It was then that Jock realized that the roles would be determined through combat, rather than assigned through negotiation. In making the first move, Ben had taken the advantage, reaching for the gun belt rather than the garter belt. Only swift and decisive action would save the day. Jock sprang from his seat, flashed across the room and threw his arms around Ben's shoulders, not as a gesture of affection but as an undisguised method of restraint. Sensing the hostility, Ben pulled his own arms free and tried to push his assailant away from the inside. Flailing and hanging on to each other like a pair of drunks, they fell helplessly back into the afghan chair with such momentum that it toppled over, sending both of them to the ground in a tangle. Ben let out a scream, stifled by a shoulder jammed firmly in his mouth. Jock reciprocated with his own piercing howl, torn out of him by an arm twisted against the joint and pinned between the floor and the back of the upturned chair.

Out in the kitchen, Margaret Woods listened to the muffled mayhem coming from the next room. She could only guess at the particular form that might be emerging from the chaos, but smiled. It was almost time to take a peek.

Realizing that pain now stood between them and any hope of resolution, pleasure or enlightenment, the combatants struggled to extricate themselves from their entanglement. Once separated, they made their way over to the sofa that had miraculously escaped the blitz. Sitting down carefully, so as not to aggravate any injury, they muttered to themselves and commiserated with each other amid the devastation.

"My God, take a look at this." Jock had pulled his shirt up above his pants and was carefully examining a ferocious welt, low down on his belly. Reluctantly, Ben turned his attention away from his own wounds and leaned over to inspect the damage. Jock pulled down his zipper while the attendant physician peered closely into the abdominal area. "Looks like a carpet burn to me," Ben whispered and touched it with his finger. The patient threw his head back and grimaced, only to catch sight of an ecstatic Margaret Woods quietly closing the kitchen door. He looked down at the top of Ben's head hovering above his open fly. "Oh my God," he said. "Oh my God."

The following day, at breakfast, Jock tried his utmost to convince Margaret that what-she-might-have-seen-might-not-have-fit-with-what-she-might-have-interpreted. She laughed. "I know a blow job when I see one," she said. Jock was horrified and looked over for Ben to intervene. He didn't. He laughed too. "Oh what the hell," Jock said as they made their way toward the session room. "If that's what people are going to think I may as well move into your room if the offer still stands. At least I'll have a decent bed to sleep in." That evening he moved his stuff upstairs.

"As you are in sexuality, so you are in life." It was a simple proposition that had arisen from their more esoteric discussions, but over the course of the Resident Fellow Program it began to acquire increasing intuitive and empirical validity. Everything that Jock was beginning to see in himself he could also see reflected in his sexual adventures. It wasn't just the obvious power-related issue of dominance and submission, winning and losing, tension and release; nor was it simply the game of baiting and capturing the prize. Many times he had lost himself in the sheer physicality of his contact with a woman. He had felt a warmth and tenderness that stretched far beyond the watery-eyed sentimentalism of possessor and possessed but, for some reason, these feelings had seldom been recognized, nurtured or even expressed. In his relationships with men, he had never made any distinction between the sensuous and the sensual, always keeping his body at a carefully prescribed distance. Though memories of Uncle Murray could evoke an odd stirring of the senses, they were quickly turned into images and words that steered them away from any communion with the flesh.

In relationships generally, he had created a perfect prescription for a predictable, and short, journey. Even in the momentary delights of sexuality, he was more concerned with what could be taken out of the union than what could be retained, savoured and nurtured on the inside. With Ben, he had discovered the simple pleasure in touching in a way that was both receptive and expressive. Whenever he allowed his mind to step back from censoring his feelings, he realized that, from the soft massage around the shoulders to the tingling of another skin against his, and the reassuring warmth of a full-bodied embrace, Ben's touch was no different from that of a woman in the gentle moments of a sexual encounter; sexuality and sensuality became one and the same.

"In a way, I become the object through which your sensuality can be expressed," Ben said on one of their regular strolls down the road toward Manson's Landing.

"How do you figure that?" Jock asked, remembering to breathe.

"Well, through me you can reflect upon your sexuality and integrate it into your sense of who you are. In this way, I'm useful to you. And, the closer we are, the more useful I become."

A few weeks earlier it would have sounded either obscure or preposterous. Now it seemed like a perfectly reasonable proposition. Three weeks into the Resident Fellow Program and Jock was beginning to ease himself into the physicality of their relationship. The small and innocent things, like having Ben's arm around his shoulder as they sat listening to music, a light kiss before leaving the house for the morning session, a hug when they returned in the late afternoon, and now, holding hands along the road to Manson's. Their beds were closer now and they could lie together and talk, sometimes in each other's arms, sometimes not.

"I'm really hung-up on the Fag business," he said, as they walked along the road. "In spite of all you've said, and all we've experienced together, I still get spooked about your intentions. I've got to keep telling myself that you're not waiting for an opportunity to get into my pants."

Ben laughed. "Well I'm not. As I've told you before, I'm not that interested in developing a relationship around sexuality. Your own exploits should be enough to illustrate the shortcomings of that approach. As for homosexual relationships, the same dynamics seem to be at work—transient encounters trading power for immediate gratification. Whatever the content, the form seems to remain pretty much the same and, in my judgment, it usually turns out to be the opposite of what we've defined as intimacy."

"So tell me about your experience of sexuality," Jock asked. "Don't you have the same urges and preferences as the rest of us?"

"Well, there have been times when I've thought I might be gay. On the whole, I've found more sensuality in my relationships with men than in my relationships with women. But, now I think about it, this probably has more to do with opportunity than preference."

"But your sexual experience . . . I mean the physical, penetrating stuff . . . has been with women hasn't it?" Jock asked.

"Yes, but my relationships with women have been moulded so much by expectation and prescription that the kind of relationship I want has simply not been available. When it came down to it, none of them seemed particularly interested in the kind of sensuality I enjoy and I've come to the conclusion that the sexual dance makes intimacy virtually impossible. When it comes to the basic act of sexual intercourse, it really wouldn't bother me if I never did it again."

Jock breathed a little easier. "Well it *would* bother me," he said. "I've been celibate for a long time, but that's just experimental, it's my way of taking a look, but I agree with you about all the objectification and power stuff. I just think that sex can be more than that."

"Ah, yes," Ben agreed. "I think it's possible for sex to be a highly sensual experience. I also believe that intimacy can come from a sharing of sensuality. This just hasn't been my experience and I certainly haven't found any evidence of it in your ribald adventures."

They both laughed.

"Yea, I wonder why not?"

"Maybe it's because you spend half the time conjuring up tension with some form of power trip and forcing a release through your genitals. This isn't even orgasmic, at least not in the Reichian sense. It sounds more like self-denial than ecstasy."

For Jock, there was more to it than that. "Well, something must be lost in the telling," he said. "Hey, maybe you should be there instead of relying on my scanty descriptions. Maybe you could help uncover the lost sensuality . . . for both of us." Jock was serious.

"Well, it could be interesting for both of us." Ben was also serious but, since celibacy was the rule of the day, the topic did not warrant further investigation.

"What are you thinking about," Jock asked after they had walked in silence for a minute or so.

"I was thinking about your fears around homosexuality and whether you'd be interested in looking more closely at that."

Jock's breath caught somewhere in his throat. Their conversation was bringing in new light but it was no more than a flicker in a mine shaft. He knew that he would go no further without yet another leap of faith into the darkness. "Well, okay," he said, "we have a commitment to explore our issues. What do you suggest?"

Ben stopped, turned, wrapped his arms around him and kissed him firmly on the mouth. Backing off no more than an inch from his face he whispered, "Why don't you examine how it is for you right now?"

Jock's tormented mind finally decided that breathing, any form of breathing, would only intensify the agony of his final moments. Jock held his breath and he glanced from side to side. "Jesus," he gasped, "what the hell are you trying to prove?"

Ben kept the contact close, his arms still tightly clasped around Jock's middle. "What's the matter? What are you scared of?" he asked, his voice still a whisper.

Jock's lips were stretched so tightly across his teeth that his jaw could barely move. "Come on," he managed, "what if there are people watching us? We're in the middle of the goddamned road."

"So what? So why would you be worried about what other people think?" Finally, Ben released his grip.

"There you go . . . you're doing it again," said Jock stepping to one side and working through his case of lockjaw. "Like what other people think is no big deal because that's all their stuff. Well it all sounds very nice but that's not the way it is for most of us mortals. Our public face is attached to our skulls for God's sake!"

"You mean you have to keep up appearances," Ben said, turning and continuing to walk down the road.

Jock hesitated for a moment and moved to catch up. "Well, okay, if you want to put it that way, sure."

"And it's all based on how you wield your cock in the world?"

"Sure," Jock confessed. "Well, sort of," he added.

"Sort of what?"

"Sort of I'm your typical North American male. Why should I be any different from the rest? You're the deviant, not me."

"Yes, but staying with *you* for the moment, who handed you this program? And who decided that you should accept it?"

When Ben suggested they might borrow George's gay movie and watch it together, Jock accepted the idea as the next step in the investigative process. Still, the prospect of sitting down with Ben and watching a porno flick, with the same dedication they had given to "Citizen Kane" the week before, felt strange. To make matters worse, he knew that, whatever his experience was to be, Ben would want to know about it.

The Institute's movie projector was in good shape and the images of George's movie were sharp and graphic. Jock went in and out, taking in bits and then running back to the safety of his own objectivity. Generally he was very adept in this, but this lubricious visual parade challenged his skill to the limits. From the gentle caresses to the close-ups of anal penetration, he urged himself to stay present, splitting off only when the violence became intolerable. After a brief intermission during which Ben wondered what would happen if he imagined one of the participants to be a woman, his level of toleration increased significantly.

By the mid point of the Resident Fellow Program, the presence of Wong and McKeen had changed forever the rugged ecology of the Cold Mountain community. An ailing Richard Weaver had moved to Vancouver for treatment and there was a growing sense of anomie among the followers he left behind. In this uncertain climate, the two doctors with mainstream legitimacy and thirty-three participants, primarily drawn from the offices, apartment blocks and suburban dwelling of conventional society, were creating their own style of leadership.

The workshop leaders, who had trained and worked with Weaver, continued to come in and make their three or four day contributions to the Program, but they were not at all happy with the new Directors, or with the group that had been set up to respect personal boundaries and resist the intrusive confrontations of Encounter. Some of the old guard could smell the irony that these people, whose money was needed to save Cold Mountain, were not only destroying the heart of the organism but the heart of Richard Weaver also. To make matters worse, Jean Weaver was set upon implementing her policy of holding workshop leaders responsible for attracting their own participants, and paying them on a per capita basis. The fact that some of the leaders who resisted this idea could continue to benefit from the popularity of Wong and McKeen added another degree of irony to the discontent.

Even Jerry Glock was caught up in the stew. Having chosen to be an intern in the program, he found himself accounting to Co-Director Jock McKeen. And this was no benign formality. If Drs. Wong and McKeen had imported anything from the traditional medical model into this new form of institutional practice, it was the demands they made on those working somewhere between them and their 'patients.'

At the daily meeting of interns, each person was expected to report on what was happening with the participants specifically assigned to them. In addition, each was asked to disclose whatever was taking place for them personally. Every week, a full day was set aside for the interns to meet, as a group, with the two Program Directors. Here, the leaders guided and facilitated a group process dealing with matters of personal and professional development. It was a clear expectation that interns would be involved in their own personal work as a condition of their participation in the three month program.

So, with all of this, Jerry Glock would sit in the circle while Jock McKeen was elevated and dignified by the man who had once regarded them as equals. Screw the M.D. and the unfettered ambition, Jerry saw himself as being more experienced in the personal growth business, more knowledgeable about the mission of Cold Mountain, and certainly more committed to the cause of authenticity than his ex-roommate. So why was he now playing second fiddle to Jock? Perhaps because he had challenged Ben to make a choice between them; to insist upon some rank order within their relationships. Perhaps, at some level, he understood that Ben would never have defined things in such terms had the issue not been brought to him for resolution. Much as he continued to hold Ben beyond reproach, he was also convinced that fate, destiny and Jock McKeen had conspired against him.

From this deflated position, it was difficult for him not to side with those of his peers in the Cold Mountain community who challenged the authenticity of the Wong-McKeen partnership. With Ben seeming to accommodate his sidekick's prancing ego, there was an element of performance about their leadership that mocked the spontaneous purity of the good old days.

For Jerry, however, the problem was not with their obvious departure from the mind and methods of Richard Weaver, but with the barrier that was being created between himself and his mentor. Deep down, he despised Jock for his power games and resented Ben for playing along. In one vicious stroke of fate, father had abandoned him all over again and his partner had run off with his best friend. But, unlike many who were to follow in laying their stuff on the doorstep of Wong and McKeen, Jerry continued to chip away at his illusions, using whatever personal resources he could find within himself.

Meanwhile, the personal resources of Wong and McKeen were fully committed to their work and, of course, their relationship. Among other things, there was romance in the air and it had to be examined. They would walk, hand in hand, along the beach, pausing to enjoy a moment of dreamy sentimentality, before moving on again. They realized the absurdity of it all, but the fantasy still had a life that drew their curiosity and demanded investigation. "All such romance is a form of psychosis," Ben concluded, while allowing himself the indulgence. "It's using sentimentality to create an illusion, a refusal to come to terms with what's really there. Like Oscar Wilde said, 'sentimentalism is having the luxury of an emotion without having to pay for it.'" So Jock's wooing of Ben and Ben's fascination with Jock were held up before the ruthless and prosaic mirror of self-scrutiny and mutual revelation. Candy-coated projections from childhood and delusions of adulthood, all devious distortions of subject and object, were taken apart and examined with a candour that could, at times, be excruciating.

"Many people thought of them as ambassadors of the 'Love Generation' but, from where I stood, they always seemed to be fighting," said psychologist Lee Pulos after staying with them at Weaver's house during his contribution to the Resident Fellow Program. A long-time friend, whose practice had been associated with Ben's in Vancouver, Dr. Pulos was, himself, a noted contributor to the humanistic movement. He was intrigued by the Wong-McKeen experiment, though he could never quite come to terms with either the design or the methodology. "All the time I was there, they would stop in the middle of the most routine tasks and start to process their experience with each other. Sometimes voices would be raised and Jock would storm off for a minute or so. Then he'd come back and the cycle would start up again. For the most part, I just stayed right out of the way."

What impressed Lee Pulos, and other observers, was their clear commitment to the process. "During my visits with them, I came to realize that the fighting was an agreed upon process of sharing what was happening between them. The raised voices reflected the feeling content. Now I recognize that these guys were processing all the time I was there. At that time, I had no idea what they were about."

Sharing a bedroom was proving to be a workable arrangement, though it generated more stuff to be looked at. One morning, as he lay in bed listening to the clinks and clatters of breakfast being prepared Jock cursed his friend's lack of consideration. Then, when the stereo was turned on, he became convinced that Ben was implementing a strategy of guilt induction. He wrapped his pillow about his head and repeated his favourite mantra. When the music was turned up, he pulled up his knees, tucked the sheets tightly around him and screamed his hostility into the blankets. Later that day, he decided to bring the matter up. They were washing dishes at the time.

"Do you want me to get up with you in the mornings?" he asked, in a manner casual enough to allay any suspicion of a challenge.

"No, but I'd be pleased if you did decide to do that. It would seem more like a partnership." Ben handed over a plate to be dried.

"Then do you deliberately make a noise?" He wanted to guide his arrow to the target, not listen to yet another lecture on togetherness.

"No, but sometimes I play the stereo in case you're wondering if the world is worth waking up to." Ben handed over a soup bowl.

Jock pounced ahead of his own words. "Ah!...so...well... I think that's slimy and manipulative." He paused. "That's dishonest ... in my judgment, of course."

"Oh?"

"That's right," he continued, with growing confidence and satisfaction. "I'm only applying one of your own principles. If you want me to do something, then the honest way would be to come right out and ask directly. Is that not the case?"

Ben drained the sink and carefully folded the dishcloth across the faucet. "But I don't want you to do anything," he answered. "I would be delighted if you got up with me but I can live with it either way. My preferences are simply my preferences. Would you like a hand with the drying?"

"No," Jock snapped. It was slipping away from him again. "So why the stuff with the music?" He could have done better if he'd really thought about it but he sensed the inevitable turning of the tide.

Ben was looking at him with that 'surely-you-understand-such-a-simple-statement' expression on his face. "I just want to listen to the music," he said, "and it's also an invitation for you to join me."

"But I don't like it, damn it!" Jock threw the towel down on the counter. "In fact, I find it *very* disturbing."

"So you want me to not turn on the stereo in the morning when you're still in bed."

"Yes." It had all come down to this.

"Then why don't you ask me not to turn on the stereo? Now *that* would be honest."

Following the predictable outburst and retreat, Jock sat on the bare mattress of his old bed in the basement and fingered the keys of his flute, lying idly across his knees. But there was no music in his soul. It had all seemed so simple and self-evident once. Now, like Satan, this man Wong was inverting everything and making the perversions seductively plausible. Yet maybe it really was an invitation, a gentle request for him to share his world with another. Certainly he had been free to make his own decision, and this had always been Ben's way. Perhaps if he were looking for his freedom, he would find it buried somewhere beneath his own spluttering commitment. He returned his flute to its cushion without sharing a single breath and trundled back upstairs. Whether Ben had been right or wrong, artless or manipulative, was not the issue. Again he had looked at his own part and now it was time to take another look . . . together.

Without doubt, their belief in their relationship as a working laboratory was more than just a romantic notion. The 'Morning Music' incident, for example, was subsequently assigned to a broader category of similar events with the generic label of 'entitlement.' Also filed under this heading was Jock's reluctantly abandoned habit of flopping down in a chair after the day's work while Ben saw to the drapes, turned up the heat, and generally made sure that the house was ready for the evening. Jock was willing to do the 'manly' things, like chopping wood or fixing a door hinge, while never stopping for a moment to wonder how the sheets got washed or the toilets cleaned. In fact, whenever such oversights were pointed out, he was stunned and ashamed.

"Poor Jock," Ben said one evening as he watched his friend ease his aching body into the corner of Weaver's sofa after a long group session and a particularly fierce Chicken Coop exchange. "I've found my way into every corner of your life, and I'm loving every minute of it. So when I see you preoccupied and self-involved like this I just want to keep going, but I'll leave you alone, or just be here with you if you wish."

"No, I want you to know what's up." Jock straightened himself up and puffed up the cushion next to him. "I feel like shit— raw guts, light head, all that kind of stuff. If you really want to join me, we can ride this one together." He patted the cushion again.

Ben sat down beside him. "You talk, I'll listen," he said.

Jock talked for almost an hour. He talked about his 'field dependency'—a term they used to describe the tendency of people to respond to the demands and expectations of others, rather than their own inner cues. He described how, even in his rebellion, he had always waited for the world to tell him what to do and had looked back to that same world for its evaluation. Though the unveiling brought bursts of emotion to the surface that, at times, choked his words, he spoke with clarity. When immersed in the cause of science, Jock was a dedicated scientist. Shuffling between shame and guilt he said, "You know I'm a habitual liar. Not always consciously but, at some level, I'm lying most of the time. Sometimes I'm withholding information I know is pertinent. Sometimes I'm just being strategic and filtering information toward some particular end. And, Jesus, I still take bloody candies when you're not looking."

Through it all, Ben listened. Then he spoke. "It's not about truth Jock, I don't even know what that word means. But, when I see you, as I do now, my heart opens. I don't want to capture *your* pain, or assuage it with my words. I only want to understand that you hurt, as I hurt. When you lose yourself in your obsessions and I show you my anger, it's because I've lost you too and I want you to know how I feel about that. Nothing is lost or taken away in the showing. If I hold you in my arms, it's because I recognize you in your pain, or in your joy, or in your love, and because I feel close to you. But yes, none of this is possible if you cheat yourself with lies and deceptions. With these things you keep us forever apart." Ben's pain was right there, in his face and in his tears.

Jock saw, and his sadness deepened. He understood, despite the urge to take Ben's tears as his own. "I know," he said, taking Ben's hand and holding on gently. "When I get into this stuff I'm running from my own fear. On the surface it's my fear of you or, at least, your criticism of me. But it's me despising myself. It's not you I'm afraid of, it's me. It's me I'm deceiving, not you." He paused as if the words had suddenly taken hold of his senses. "I'm afraid of myself," he said. "That's why I'm afraid to look. And I'm afraid of what might happen to us if I did look and you saw what I saw. That's why I've screwed up so many relationships, even though I didn't think I wanted to."

There was a time, not too long before, when Jock would have balked at the idea of assuming responsibility for his unconsciously driven actions. He had always equated responsibility with blame, even though they had long since written the word 'response-ability' into their ever-expanding glossary of terms. Now it made perfect sense. "I chose to tuck it away in there and it's my choice to dig it out again," he told himself. To believe otherwise would be to split himself down the middle and make each side a victim of the other. "What kind of freedom is that?"

Many of his deceptions were not born in the unconscious, however. They were deliberate attempts to protect himself. By conventional standards, they were small and insignificant moments of slippage, completely understandable and readily forgiven. Yet each transgression threw a pellet of poison into the well. It seemed almost inevitable that Ben would discover the deception and withdraw. Invariably, Jock would escape into guilt and attempt to atone for his misdemeanours. But forgiveness was a lost cause. Eventually, Ben would come back but it was never quite the same; it was as if some part of the relationship died with each offence. Jock knew that his addiction to deception needed treatment, however painful the withdrawal, and to this he dedicated himself.

Sometime later, when the young pansies fluttered and bobbed their mottled heads around the vegetable gardens of Cold Mountain, they walked together along the gravel pathway and devised a more fitting analogy. A single pansy may be trampled and, even though the garden may appear to flourish, the life of that single pansy is lost for ever. At that moment, Jock made up his mind to become a very careful and protective gardener.

As the hour of disclosure drew to a close, Jock sank back into the sofa and breathed easily into the silence. Ben watched and waited, his own feelings running softly now. They were alone on their islands. He loved this bright young buccaneer who had clambered over the sea-swept rocks to shake his hand. Now, on the journey inland they could sit together in silence, gazing out at the mountains beyond. For Jock, the words of his valedictory address drifted back to define the moment: ". . . hills peep over hills, and this summit which looked so large and imposing from below, now appears only as a stepping stone—a little rise from which we see more and greater ascents."

Ben shifted closer and waited until their eyes found a soft meeting place. Then he spoke, very quietly, as a person might speak to a creature suddenly encountered on a walk in the forest. "You know, all my life I've wanted to be with someone who was willing to let me see them as they really are. Before you came along I met a lot of people who seemed to do this quite easily, but there was little risk involved, nothing was really on the line—like the possibility of a relationship with me. And then, when all was revealed, it seemed to me that there wasn't very much there, no real substance, nothing that hadn't been revealed many times before. But you, Jock, have so much to lose . . . you take great risks. In your relationship with me, you've already given up more than most people acquire in a lifetime, many things I once wanted for myself. And you go on taking risks, making sacrifices.

"Those who stand back and judge you from their place of safety will never see what I've seen. Their judgments are about them, not about you. I'm so full of respect for your courage as you push open the doors and stand in awe of what I see behind. Sometimes it's so hard for me to believe that you have chosen to do this with me . . . I . . ."

Jock recognized the familiar tremor in the voice as Ben's words disappeared into his feelings. Their hands reached out, touched, and took hold.

On reflection, Jock described his life during this period as "a hideous nightmare punctuated by periods of grace." With a ferocious determination to conquer whatever mountains appeared on the horizon, however, he thrived on the challenge, if not the pain. Ben, on the other hand, found himself "swimming in what I had always wanted." Well aware of the concerns being expressed about their style of leadership in the program, he assumed that, in time, the Cold Mountain community would come to tolerate and respect the differences.

CHAPTER SIX

As the three month Resident Fellow program drew to a close, they decided to give up their practices in Vancouver and continue their work together among the cedars of Cortes Island. Ben was making a choice to do exactly what he wanted. Jock looked at the world he was slowly coming to reject and based his decision on what he didn't want. They had only a week before the next program was due to begin.

Corinne had little to say about the matter. It had been clear for a long time that her hopes for the family were not going to be realised, and the departure of her husband to some unknown island merely confirmed all that had already come to pass. Behind the unflinching composure of this beautiful and stoic woman, however, an undisclosed being cried out against a world that had broken so many promises.

Kevin Wong, aged twelve, stood ready to challenge his father's decision. In the week between the two programs, Ben flew to Winnipeg for a meeting of the Moffat board, taking both boys with him in order to discuss his decision and the circumstances. Good boys as they were, they listened quietly and attentively to their father. On their return, the family spent their last two days together at the house in West Vancouver. After supper on the second day, Kevin came into the living room where mother and father sat discussing the practical details of their separation and stood respectfully before them. Already a serious and purposeful young man, his face was particularly solemn and his stance resolute. "I want to have a meeting with you and Mom," he said, eyeing Ben grimly. "There are things that need to be talked about." They agreed to meet in fifteen minutes.

True to his nature, Kevin returned at precisely the appointed time, with brother Randy following closely behind. He sat on a high-backed dining room chair, assumed a posture of dignity and resolve, and gestured for Randy to sit on the chair beside him. Making sure of his parents' undivided attention, Kevin then issued his challenge.

"When you got married and had us kids, didn't you feel you had a responsibility to us as well as to yourselves?"

"Yes, of course we did," Corinne answered truthfully.

"Well, when you made that decision, you built a roof for us to grow up under. Now you believe you can take that roof away."

Corinne waited for Ben to respond. "Well, things have changed Kevin. There's nothing holding the roof together any more. There's no love between your Mom and I to keep it in place."

Kevin stared back at his parents, first at one, then the other. "That sounds fine for you," he said, "but what about us?"

Ben looked at his two sons, the sadness swelling in his chest, but at this stage in the process, the release of such emotion would only paralyse Corinne, strip Kevin of his authority and create incalculable confusion in the mind of young Randy. So the man who had intimidated so many in his quest for openness and revelation, drew himself in, and stepped back from a family struggling with uncertainty. He knew that Corinne would be a competent and dedicated mother. His place as a father would have to be defined as events unfolded and there were many decisions yet to be made.

On the other side of town, Jock was making his own preparations. He sold his once beloved MGB without a trace of regret and, with the money, purchased a red and white half-ton truck to facilitate, and symbolize, his new life-style. Having loaded it up with personal possessions from his Vancouver house, he drove over to the Wong residence to pick up his partner and friend. On the surface it all seemed so pragmatic. Jerry Glock would be there to help load the truck, along with David Aitken, another young architect searching for meaning beyond a life of 'doing.' On the one hand, they would collaborate in this most common-place of tasks, on the other, they were like conspirators, collud-ing to dismantle a family, the most revered institution within a society from which they were setting themselves apart.

The Wongs were an established family and, for Jock, Ben's separation from Corrine and the boys seemed far more drastic than his own separation from Cathy and Justin. Whatever his ambitions, there was something about the sanctity of families that gave him a sense of security, an assurance about how things were and should be. Just as his own family in Ontario had been the solid context that affirmed his role, framed his adventures and contained his rebellions, so the Wongs, with their everyday values and routines, had brought a sense of familiarity and pre-dictability into his relationship with Ben. Whenever he found himself floundering in ambiguity, he could always slot Ben back into the roles of husband or father and return to solid ground. Now there would be no such anchor points, nothing to hold things together. And what about Corrine and the boys? How would they manage to reconstruct their lives with Ben no longer at the centre? As the magnitude of Ben's decision began to sink in, Jock worried for them all and, in particular, he worried about his own part in the proceedings.

Jock felt strangely disconnected; a sense of floating above and beyond the familiar terrain of life. Sitting in the cab of the un-familiar truck and driving through the congested Denman Street traffic he felt chilled and alone, like a small boy suddenly separated from his mother. Perhaps it would all be just a passing phase, another experiment that, once conducted, would find its place in the realm of normality. On the other hand, they may have been dangerously close to the point of no return. The familiar blend of excitement and fear ran through him as the red and white truck crossed Lion's Gate Bridge and drove to West Vancouver.

Jim Sellner was another good-looking, power-seeking young man who found his way to Bennet Wong's door. A City Planner by profession, Jim had become part of the group that sprang up around Ben's practice in Vancouver. Like many of the others, his life on the surface had seemed full and successful while his inner world remained empty and bleak. By 1974, his marriage to Judy was in trouble and, even in his faculty position at the University of British Columbia, he could find little meaning in his day to day encounters.

At his first Wong and McKeen workshop, he had watched in amazement as people volunteered to lie on a mat before a circle of onlookers and subject themselves to the probing thumbs and fingers of the two leaders. He had attended one workshop led by Richard Weaver some months before but this experience was different. Like most people who witness deep structure body-work for the first time, he was stunned by the ferocious blend of apparent pain and catharsis. "People just screamed out their shit to the world," he told a friend some days later. But Jim Sellner was not about to recoil from the challenge. Lying on the mat and looking up into the faces of Wong and McKeen, he wondered what sediment might be piled up behind the sluice-gates in his own belly.

Jim laughed. At first the giggles of a ticklish school-girl, followed by the snickers of a smutty adolescent. Then, as sinew pressed against bone in his chest, the comedy of his life ran before him in crazy images, and laughter brought tears to his eyes. Much as his body resisted the pressure, the energy convulsed its way past his kicking legs, banging torso and flailing arms. Around him, the twenty-two people who had borne witness to incest, parental abandonment and ritual abuse issues that morning now held on to each other and shook with uncontrollable laughter. Ben and Jock sat back on their haunches and laughed with the rest.

Meeting over coffee after the workshop, Jim Sellner wondered how the world would judge him and what might have been lost in the hilarity of the body-work. Perhaps he was so shallow and lacking in substance that his performance was no more than a joke. "Those who work at the centre work not only for themselves, but for all of us," Ben told him. "Through your humour, we were able to find our own." Rather than dismiss his contribution, Ben went on to suggest that Jim might give consideration to working with people. So, at their invitation, Jim began attending the evening men's groups and, on Wednesdays, he would see Jock at his office in the mornings and Ben in the afternoons. Again, there was no particular plan, other than to enjoy the communion, support and encouragement of like-minded people.

In the Fall of 1974, Ben suggested that Jim might want to enrol in the Master's Degree program offered by Cold Mountain, under the auspices of Antioch University. As part of this training, Ben also invited him to work as an intern in one of his own Cortes programs. Jim knew little about the degree program and was tired of the academic shuffle, but the prospect of being around Bennet Wong had great appeal. "Ben was my male mother," he said, some years later. "He accepted me for who I was; he confronted me about my undeveloped self; and, in his presence, I felt both comfortable and fearful."

At that point, Jim and Judy lived separate lives under the same roof, while sharing the parenting of their young daughter. When he discussed the Antioch idea with Judy she was fascinated. A school teacher with a degree in psychology and a marriage going nowhere, she was also taking stock of her life. With a speedy decision that was to change both of their lives, the Sellners sold their house in Vancouver and, with the proceeds, prepared themselves for graduate school. They went their separate ways in the summer of 1975, Judy to continue her graduate studies, Jim to be an intern in the second Resident Fellow Program to be co-directed by Drs. Wong and McKeen.

Richard Weaver remembered Jim Sellner as a participant in one of his own workshops. When he learned of Ben's interest in this young man, Weaver responded in much the same way as he had around Ben's association with Jock. He saw the same dangerous mixture of power and narcissism lurking in them both and, having declared, "There's no place for the narcissistic personality at Cold Mountain," he went on to suggest that Ben was "crazy" for encouraging such people. Now "such people" were taking leadership roles within his beloved Cold Mountain community and this, combined with the different style of participants and methodologies, was pushing that community to the limits of its tolerance.

To the uninitiated, it might have appeared that the factions simmering beneath the surface could be characterized more by their similarities than by their differences. Collectively they were all part of the West Coast humanistic movement that stretched from southern California to Cortes. Allegedly, their concern was with the ability of human beings to reach their full potential through awareness, authenticity and personal autonomy. They talked of "love" as a force binding Self to Other, and challenged the social order to respect, if not embrace, the simple state of being human. But, behind the appearance of synonymy, the differences of philosophy and practice ran deep. It was also becoming increasingly apparent that these differences were being clustered around the leadership of Richard Weaver, on the one hand, and Wong and McKeen on the other.

Unlike Richard Weaver, Bennet Wong had no carefully articulated philosophy. He reflected an approach to life that was open to whatever each moment and each experience had to offer. He was interested in the ideas of Eastern thought, and his stance was undoubtedly Zen-like, but he would never buy into Weaver's notion that "the world is a lost cause that must be transcended." On the contrary, he spoke of celebrating each moment and found great joy in whatever transformations were taking place in people's lives. Still harbouring the romanticism and chivalry of the Arthurian Legends, Bennet Wong rejected Weaver's cynicism, along with his curative prescriptions for change. When he and Jock talked of "love" it had little to do with the hippie state of benign benevolence to all. "Love is a verb," they insisted. "It isn't a commodity to be traded but a process to be experienced through responsibility and intimacy."

While they incorporated many diverse ideas and approaches within their own practices, they firmly rejected any model of a human potential movement created and maintained by the experts, whether they be Richard Weaver or Fritz Perls. Their stance was that each person was responsible for finding her or his own answers and that there really were no experts in the tricky business of doing life. By the same token, they maintained that in any humanistic practice there could be no clean division between the professional and the personal. Had it not been for their indisputable formal qualifications, they most certainly would have been accused of being unprofessional by those who were in the habit of wrapping the shroud of Zen around their own assumptions of professionalism. "You will never experience intimacy or love until you abandon your need for security," said Bennet Wong to those who cared to listen.

For Jim Sellner, the young intern with no formal qualifications in the business, and very little experience, security needs dissolved into undiluted panic. "What am I supposed to do?" he asked the leaders on the night before the program was due to begin. "Do whatever you're going to do," he was told, "but let's talk about what's happening for you." The fear did not diminish with self-analysis. His only consolation was that with no theoretical models or prescriptions in his head, he carried no professional baggage into the arena.

Yet, he really *didn't* know what to do. He knew from his own experience that when people begin to learn from the inside out, they become involved in a personal process that is essentially autonomous and self-directed. This was reassuring, but he also knew that this process brought forward aspects of the self that appeared as alien to the learner as they were to the observer. Confused, and often fearful, the neophytes looked to the leaders for security and the leader who looked back with equal confusion might well become an enemy of the people.

"Stay with it and breathe," was the thing to say. He had heard it so many times and, as long is it came with authority, it had always worked for him. Ben had once explained that when people are stuck in any body-mind issue breathing will generally move them through, just as rocking a car back and forth will free it from a bed of mud.

So, over the first few days of the program, he said it many times, sounding more authoritative with each successive utterance. What most participants saw was a brash young intern who seemed to have a close association with the two leaders. What most failed to see was the uncertainty in the eyes and the fear in the body. "If that smart-ass tells me to 'stay with it and breathe' once more, I'll make sure he never breathes again," someone said. "Perhaps he doesn't know what else to say," suggested another . . . and she was right.

Ben and Jock understood the fear and, since they knew it as nothing less than the exhilarating fear of life itself, they worked toward keeping it alive and well during their daily meeting of interns. They had another full group of thirty-five people and each, at some point, would discover the longings of the undisclosed self. Those who had the courage to face the unknown and move beyond would create their own form of transformation. For some there would be monumental insights, highs and lows experienced and expressed. For others, the process would be slow and incremental, shuffling and stumbling forward towards a new sense of integrity. And, along with the rest, Jim Sellner urged himself to "stay with it and breathe."

Meanwhile, the two leaders were following their own particular destiny. Their work on Cortes Island was no longer a brief respite from their practices in Vancouver and the inevitable blend of excitement and anxiety was woven into the emergence of a new phase. Preparing for the return of the Weavers, they purchased an old house on twenty four acres of land on the rim of Cortes Bay. With the prospect of turning this neglected wooden structure into a home for themselves, their quest to discover the messages within the mundane would be given full licence. Anticipating the energy that would serve their cause, they named the property "Ch'i." As they made their final trip with their belongings from the Weaver residence, Jock brought the truck to a halt at the splintered relic of their new gate. "Let's put a sign on it," he suggested. "A Wong and McKeen sign would look pretty good right there . . . once we fix the damned gate, of course."

"Leave the sign to me," Ben said, as they trundled down the rutted grass driveway.

Two days later, a bold "McKeen & Wong" sign was mounted on the freshly painted and proudly perpendicular gate post. Jock was outwardly embarrassed, and inwardly delighted at Ben's gracious gesture.

Gates, fences, kitchen cabinets, electrical wiring, plumbing, cedar siding, septic fields and vegetable gardens; thankfully, the format of the Resident Fellow Program was generous in allowing them the time to play with their new property. And with it came a new sense of contentment, a profound belief in their being together, and an awareness that they were sharing their lives with all that surrounded them. Though many of the tasks were foreign and they lacked the knowledge and skills they needed, they approached each project thoughtfully and executed it meticulously. It was their way of translating their principles and beliefs into the doings of life, from the most rudimentary to the most expansive. Each task performed contributed in some valuable way to the whole. All resources were respected for their place in the scheme of things. Each moment of work required a careful and parsimonious blending of these resources around the investment of the self. Each obstacle encountered was the voice of the physical world inviting them back into harmony. As in all of life, it was a 'process' in which 'outcomes' were little more than arbitrary rest-stops along the way. Their property was not something that simply demanded their attention, it was something that invited their intimate involvement.

And, throughout it all, they continued to prod and probe each other, drawing their inner creation out into the world they were creating on the outside. Jock continued to clamber on the roof and bring in the firewood while avoiding laundering sheets and cleaning toilets. Ben listened to his friend rummaging around in the workshop and wondered why he was alone. Washing the dishes together brought them into a regular union of purpose. Every interruption in the flow was something to be acknowledged and examined: a break in the natural harmony; a moment of non-presence; a hidden expectation; an undisclosed thought; an errant value. But, in this traditionally mundane ritual, they also discovered the joy of moving lightly together in the effortless communion they called "grace."

In growing their own food, they thrust themselves into exploring the nature of their union with the earth. As in most sought-after relationships, there was an anticipatory romance that veiled their early encounters, a mindful separation of subject from object. But their own style of investigation and expression involved an uncompromising commitment to direct experience. In their vegetable garden they nursed the tender plants and, with their hands in the soil, sought their connection with nature's most basic designs. From this place, there would be no taking or sacrificing of life. The fresh green shoots that responded to their care, eventually would serve to nourish that same life within themselves, not as substances to be greedily consumed by senseless bodies, but as willing participants in the partnership of all things, moving with a single purpose. What they were discovering within themselves, they rediscovered in this silent little garden.

In preparing their own food, they became conscious stewards of wondrous transformations, deliberating over each procedure taking place between the soil and the cooking pot. The life that converged in their kitchen could, through its delicate textures, exquisite shapes and colours, subtle sounds and rich aromas, draw them into an order that their senses recognized as ecstasy. For their part, all they had to do was be there, fully involved with themselves, with each other, and with the pulse of the life that surrounded them. But it was their being together that seemed to open the channels, a sort of primal sharing that induced the unspoken world to become known.

Then came the meal itself—a sensuous indulgence of the palate that transformed the dulled demands of the stomach into an adventure, the sheer joy and contentment of something created in harmony and shared through direct encounter. No farmers, grocers, cooks or waiters had to be called upon to mediate any part of the experience. It was their creation, whole and complete, a far cry from the sanitized eating places of restless Vancouver. As the evening candle burned low and flickered its light across their faces, there were no mumbled words of gratitude to some remote and unseen provider. The Grace that blessed their table was a simple appreciation for the life they were coming to know.

Meanwhile, their minds would vacillate between reflection and dialogue, using the raw data of their senses to speculate about the universal order. And beyond the infinite realities created by the uncertainty and confusion of the psyche, they saw patterns . . . the same curious configurations of experience and events occurring and reoccurring whether they looked inward or outward. At first glance, each pattern seemed to have its own independent existence but, once examined and placed alongside others in their expanding atlas of observations, the images became blurred at the edges, each part seeming to dissolve into the whole. Then, when the part was isolated and re-examined, it bore the unmistakable characteristics of the whole, irrevocably transformed in a fleeting moment of association. Something much larger seemed to be peeking through; something that could assume a myriad of different forms and expressions.

Once their minds had grasped the implications of what they saw, it didn't seem to matter where they looked. Whether looking back into their histories, washing dishes, leading a group, or staring up into the night sky, the same whispers of a hidden order seemed to spring from what they had once assumed to be random. But, if all that occurred in the universe was in some way already sketched out, what then was the nature of their freedom? And what of their cherished attachment to the principle of response-ability?

As scientists, they could shape their explanations within the framework of the emerging 'new physics.' As philosophers, they could invoke the principles of 'structuralism' to communicate their emerging beliefs. And, as musicians, they could access metaphors that would keep them firmly in the realm of the senses. In this, the order might be represented as a basic harmonic around which many melodies could be created and woven back into the universal theme. The nature of any blended harmony would reflect the familiarity of the players with their own essence, their sensitivity to their place in the orchestra and their willingness and ability to improvise. So the most primitive elements could be bound to the original score while the more complex, the more creative, might sing and dance with varying degrees of 'freedom.' But always, their nature and their relatedness could only be revealed in relation to the central theme—the music of the spheres.

From the most mundane event to the most sublime adventure, this framework seemed capable of containing the stuff of their experience. Making the bed together was a simple procedure that held an infinite variety of possibilities and potentials. And to this performance, each player brought his own distinct patterns, developed over so many years, in so many ways and at so many levels that the possible permutations were incalculable and, essentially, unpredictable. Only by seeing these patterns, through revelation, would their bed-making be understood. Only through their conscious commitment could such understanding be used to create the foundations of a new melody. And only through their sensitivity to the basic universal theme, could their creations strike a chord that would affirm the existence of their duet within the symphony.

Despite the complexity of the enterprise, the data they used were stunningly simple and readily apparent. The dropping of a pillow case, the tangling of a sheet, an interruption in the flow of a blanket passed from hand to hand in a moment of non-presence, revealed an order disrupted. Each incident was worthy of examination, not from a judgmental or moralistic stance, but as empirical evidence of the implicit order. In fact, many things that initially appeared as discordant interruptions in the flow turned out to be quite the opposite when their essence was revealed and their place in the broader realm seen and understood. Some years later they wrote:

"As proposed by the philosophy of structuralism, each person is already whole, although the wholeness is usually being expressed in a lower state of resolution. There is nothing to be rid of, added to, or punished for; there is only more Self-awareness and Self-responsibility to be experienced. The Self is not striving toward perfection; it is already whole. We are attempting both to know and accept ourselves more, in order to better reveal to ourselves and to others what already exists within. Ours is a process of revelation and unfolding wholeness, rather than a striving toward perfection set before us by authorities greater than ourselves. We are forever in a process of creating the expression of ourselves rather than attempting what others want us to be."

Between their work on the property and their directorship of the Resident Fellow Program, they maintained a varied schedule of daily activities, often extending until late into the long summer evenings. Then, one evening after supper, the telephone rang. Richard Weaver was dead. The man who had personified the other side of the uneasy balance at Cold Mountain had died of heart failure in Vancouver while sitting in a chair borrowed from Jock McKeen. Two days later, his body was cremated and the ashes brought out to the Cortes property.

During the week following the internment ceremony, Ben was disturbed in his sleep at two a.m. Jock too was startled into consciousness by the stirring of his friend in the next bed, and by the sudden chill that seemed to hang in the bedroom. "Who are you talking to?" he asked.

Ben was sitting up in bed, seemingly transfixed. "It's Richard," he said.

"What does he want?" Jock's voice was barely a whisper.

"He wants me to make sure the educational program continues."

"Oh Jesus, tell him to go away." Jock stared out wildly into the darkness.

"You tell him." Ben's voice was a frozen monotone.

Jock's eyes darted about madly, trying to find a focal point for the communication. He drew a breath and prayed that it would carry the words. "Go away Richard," he said. "You never came to visit us in life, why do it in death? If you want to talk, come back in the daytime." It didn't seem to make much sense but it was worth a try.

Later that morning, as they went about their bathroom routines, the telephone rang again. Jock picked it up with some trepidation. It was Clem, the island mystic and spiritualist. Banned from the Cold Mountain property by Richard Weaver many months before, this strange reclusive woman had continued to maintain a sporadic and unusual friendship with Ben and Jock. "Richard Weaver came to my house last night," she said, as if he had dropped in casually on his way home from work. "He was trying to get in touch with Ben.

"He came here too," Jock answered, trembling at his own words. "What did he have to say?"

"He had a message for Ben. Something about looking after the university program . . . or something like that."

Jock was horrified by this kind of stuff. Even Ben had proclaimed how his own childhood fear of ghosts could still be invoked under the right conditions. "We'd better invite Clem over to deal with this," he told a shaken Jock McKeen, who was pacing the living room floor after putting down the phone.

"I just don't want to get back into this business," Jock said, pausing in the hope of securing immediate agreement. "I'm scared, for God's sake. Our times with David Young and Clem were enough for me. I'm still struggling to stay present in this reality." He swept his arm in a wide arc, intending to symbolically consecrate the living room, their property and, hopefully, the whole of Cortes Island.

He was referring back to a time in 1973 when, with one tentative foot in the reality of human relations, he had been blissfully, and blindly, confident enough to step out with the other to explore the 'other' reality. In the open spirit of enquiry, they had participated in a five-night workshop entitled "Listen to the Spirits," led by David Young, the well-known British spiritualist. The sessions were held on the Cold Mountain property and, with Richard and Jean away in California, Ben and Jock had been press-ganged into staying at the Weaver residence to play hosts to the workshop leader.

At the first session, David Young explained to the group that each of them had a "Spirit Guide" and that, in the dim light of the room, he could often see these protectors hovering around the group. Ben's guide was, apparently, particularly prominent. He was a massive black man named "Towahaya." When Jock asked for the name of his guide, David, for reasons that were never disclosed, instructed him to leave the room He then told the others. It was two years later when Ben finally told him that the name of his guide was "Hassim."

At the mid-point of the workshop, Ben was called away to attend to a very sick father in Vancouver and Jock was left alone in their bedroom . . . all alone. With the session ending at 2.30 a.m., three hours of darkness had still to be confronted. That night, David had been teaching participants how to open up and call upon the spirits. Jock was fascinated and, at the same time, scared out of his wits. Playing his own version of 'chicken,' he inwardly rehearsed some of the procedures before pulling the bedcovers over his head and calling upon the sleepfairy to take him quickly. But, as he flashed back into consciousness, she was there in the room with him . . . Marilyn Davis from Oakridge High. She'd died of cancer many years earlier.

"What are you doing here?" he asked, before any rational thought had entered his head.

"I'm here because you asked," she replied.

"Well I want you to go away now . . . I'm scared," he said, remembering David's assurance that spirits generally do as they're told.

She left.

In a sequence that seemed to lose the order of time and logic, he threw back the covers, climbed out of bed, crossed the room, switched on the light, left the room, went back in, left again and entered David Young's room. "David, are you awake? There's a spirit in my room," he whispered.

David slipped out of his own sleep to behold the trembling figure of Jock McKeen standing by his bed. "Yes, I know," David said quietly, "they're all over the place." And with that assurance, he went back to sleep.

Approximately one year after the David Young workshop, Jock agreed to participate in a séance. They had been working on Cortes with a young man from Nelson, B.C. who, by all psychiatric diagnostic criteria, was schizophrenic. With a symptomology that would have later been classified as "Multiple Personality Disorder," Ben had the notion that they might be dealing with a case of "possession." At that time he knew of Clem only by reputation but called her in for an opinion. It was Clem's belief that the man was being "occupied" by a brother who had recently committed suicide. She suggested that they needed to do some "rescue work."

When it became clear that this man knew nothing of his brother's death, Ben agreed to the proposed "rescue work" and a circle of eighteen people was quickly brought together on the Cold Mountain property. Prior to the session, Clem had determined that Ben was a "passive medium." This, she explained, is someone whose light shines on the other side and spirits may follow that light into the earthly realm. She also told him that he was protected by a large black man named "Towahaya."

*

The group assembles and forms the ritualistic circle, sitting cross-legged around the perimeter of the room. At Clem's behest, Ben and Jock move to sit on opposite sides. "Their relationship could unbalance the circle," she tells the others. Lights are dimmed and a nervous silence saturates the room. They look at each other; a strange mixture of island oddities and mainland seekers, waiting anxiously to confront the unknown together.

The session begins with Clem conducting herself as the central medium. She calls upon all spirits present to hear her words. Her calm voice informs the brother that he has died; that he must now leave his sibling alone and move through to the other side. All eyes are on the shadowy form of the young man sitting motionless between Clem and Ben. The young man's head is lowered, almost to the level of his knees. He begins to speak but the words are indistinct, barely audible, tumbling out in a stream punctuated only by the quivering uncertainty of his breath. The words evaporate into silence. His breathing, heavy at first, now seems to come from his belly and the rhythm becomes gentle and regular. As his head rises and his body begins to unfurl, a new ripple of light dances lightly around the circle. There is a sense that, whatever has happened, is now complete.

From Jock's perspective it is a remarkably undramatic piece of work, and he is thankful. He sends out a smile of relief toward Ben on the other side. Suddenly, this gentle encounter with the spirit world takes a turn that is unexpected and disquieting. While the others have stepped back, Clem has remained ominously engaged.

The group sits in silence, waiting for Clem to make some sign that might release them from their clandestine mission of mercy. She is swaying gently from side to side, seemingly oblivious to their hopes and expectations. "Why am I swaying?" she asks. Her eyes are closed, her expression quizzical. "Because I've been hung, and I'm still hanging here," comes the reply.

The words are from Clem's mouth but the voice is deep, coarse and tormented, totally incongruous with the blank expression of her face and the easy attitude of her body.

The group is frozen now. Breath is held in and released sparingly. Something is happening around her but nothing is clear. Suddenly, Ben feels that he is somehow being drained from his own body. It's as if his inner self is being liquefied and evacuated from an aperture somewhere deep within the centre of his belly. Now, percolating up into the vacuum is an overwhelming sensation of agony. It fills his inside, pushing up relentlessly until his lungs can no longer withstand the pressure. As blackness engulfs him, a scream that seems to come from the bowels of the earth sears through his body and fills his lungs to the point of bursting. In a violent convulsion, his mouth is torn open and a scream of insufferable torment rips through his throat and out into the world.

The others watch in horror. They see the involuntary contortions of Ben's body and can only imagine what might be taking place on the inside. They watch as his lungs struggle to release the pressure, his eyes bulge out and his mouth breaks open, as if he were about to vomit. But what they hear is only the sound of choking, followed by a stifled gasp. Now his face remains fixed, his mouth still open, his eyes straining and staring ahead.

Jock is terrified. There is absolutely no doubt in his mind that Ben has gone. The man he has come to love is no longer there, no longer with him.

With little thought for the forces that might tear him apart, he scrambles over and, taking both of Ben's hands in his own, drops to his knees. He searches the eyes in wild desperation but can find no trace of the being who had moved so gracefully to the centre of his life. He begins to shout, demanding Ben's immediate return. He releases the hands and, taking hold of the shoulders, begins to shake them vigorously, repeating his frenzied demands.

Ben hears the shouting, but the frantic voice is distant, disconnected. He has a sense of being shaken. Finally, he finds himself looking into the familiar and desperate eyes of the man who was ready to walk into the shadows to find him.

The next day Ben continued to look pale, as the colour of life literally had been drained from his body. Jock was protective, in a loving way, drawing some obscure satisfaction from being the strong one for a time.

In the days that followed, Ben experienced episodes in which he felt himself slipping back into the void and a pervasive fear would swell within him. Two or three times he had to hang on to Jock in order to support himself through waves of nauseous disorientation. It was then that Jock decided that they should restrict their exploratory activities to 'this side' of reality. They had no reason to doubt Clem's explanation that Ben had been "used" by a robber, hanged during the latter part of the nineteenth century, but this was filed away as interesting information to be left in the file marked "spiritism."

So, when the late Richard Weaver crossed over to express his posthumous wishes, Jock was understandably dismayed at the prospect of another excursion into the realm of the spirits. He was comforted, however, by Ben's assurance that they would resist any further dialogue with the deceased. Instead, they agreed to be firm in telling Richard to abandon his earthly ambitions and follow the pathway before him.

Then, they unwittingly tossed another ingredient into the stew pot by telling participants in the Resident Fellow Program about Richard's visit and message. Their simple intention was to tell a story and to push the exploration of personal experience toward yet another frontier. In the unfolding of the larger picture, however, it is impossible to predict how any single event will find its place within the whole.

With the death of Richard Weaver, the divergent interests within the Cold Mountain rose quickly to the surface. Some members of the old guard openly suggested that Bennet Wong had dreamed up the story of Richard's visitation as a ploy to take over Cold Mountain in a way that even Weaver's most devoted followers would be compelled to accept. Ironically Richard Weaver, a purposeful person throughout his life, had, through this one simple request, created the final wave of resistance to his deepest wish. Such was the legacy.

"They shit on me at every opportunity," said Jim Sellner, reflecting upon his experience as an intern in that particular Resident Fellow Program. He was not referring to the participants but to the regular leaders and residents of the community. "They had the idea that I was close to Ben and Jock and that was enough to prove my complicity. I can see how I contributed to their fears though. Hell, Ben was the most important person in my life at that point and I was a devoted student of their way of working. I made no excuses for this. After the first month I got sick of living in fear all the time and decided to let people know what I really thought. As an intern, I challenged the beliefs and methods of the other leaders and obviously they were pissed off. Ben backed me in all of this and I'm pretty sure the others knew that. Still, they were *my* questions and it was *my* attitude they were really dealing with."

The tide had turned, however. A few months after the conclusion of this Resident Fellow Program, Jean Weaver met Jim at a party in Vancouver and invited him to become the site manager of the Cortes operation. At that time, the pragmatic Mrs. Weaver was the sole owner and executive officer of the Cold Mountain Institute. From the time of its creation she had been the organizational mind behind the dream of her late husband but, alone now, she was beginning to spin her own dreams. Much as she wanted the work of Cold Mountain to continue, she knew that it would require a new leadership and she was well aware of what Ben and Jock could offer.

Like Jim Sellner, David Aitken also exemplified and personified this energy. Another young man in his early thirties, he had risen quickly to stardom as an architect in Manitoba and capped his short and illustrious career by creating his own highly successful corporation. So, at the age of thirty-one, having created considerable wealth, and being involved in an increasingly fragile marriage and a future that seemed to have little substance, he headed out to Vancouver where he was drawn into a workshop entitled "The Failure of Success." The leader was Richard Weaver. A few weeks later, having decided that the real David Aitken could be found somewhere in the glittering debris of his own achievements, he reconnected with his old university associate Jerry Glock and learned of the work of Wong and McKeen.

Walking confidently down the receiving line at an elegant affair hosted by the upper echelon of Vancouver society, he stretched out his hand to be greeted by an oriental psychiatrist with silver shoulder-length hair and an ethereal young man with eyes that drew him in and held him for intense scrutiny. He disengaged with the sense that he had met them both at precisely the same time, within the embrace of a single gesture. During the course of the evening he caught himself watching them from the safety of trivial conversations and felt strangely envious of his friend Jerry who seemed to know them so well. He watched them leave before the party had moved into its second hour and decided that he would follow them . . . in his own way and in his own time, of course.

The time seemed to be right when his wife Mary, after eleven years of marriage, requested an amicable separation in which she would assume custody of their two young daughters. Suddenly, without the roles of husband and father, the associated role of 'provider' seemed redundant. In an emotional state of confusion, he abandoned his professional activities and, from his accumulated earnings, made arrangements to pay himself a modest monthly allowance.

Stripped of the doings that had made up his life, he exchanged his sports coupe for a motor cycle and set out to reclaim whatever had been lost on the inside. At first, he played on the edge, attending the odd session led by Wong and McKeen in Vancouver and dashing down to Mexico "for all the wrong reasons." His estranged wife Mary had completed the Resident Fellow

Program and she encouraged him to 'take the plunge' also, but he was afraid.

When Wong and McKeen announced their intention to take up residence around the Cold Mountain Institute, David was there to assist with the preparations. As he watched the old red and white truck leave the driveway of the Wong residence in West Vancouver it seemed that, once again, the 'boys' were leaving the party early. But this time he decided not to be left behind. Calling once more upon the freedom of his spirit, he turned his motor cycle in the direction of Cortes Island and went off to sign up for the Resident Fellow Program.

"Just stay with it and breathe" Jim Sellner told him, but the words made no sense. For five days he sought invisibility in the circle of thirty-two fellow travellers, wondering what grand design had brought him to this place. There were women, some of them fragile, recoiling from the harshness of the words and rawness of the issues; others pushed themselves forward, demanding to be heard in a world that had negotiated their silence. There were men, soft spoken and conciliatory, questioning their right to step boldly through the pain. And there were other men, some of them criminals, with angry eyes and hostile words, always poised to desecrate the sensitivity of any moment. These were the ones he feared the most.

At the end of the first week, the carrier bags on his motorcycle were still packed and he took comfort in a daily ritual of warming up the engine and checking the machine over meticulously for faults that might restrict his mobility. On the Saturday, Ben and Jock suggested that some of the men might want to form an extra curricular group for body-work. They told David that he should participate. Sessions would be held in the Chicken Coop after supper.

The first session was held on "blind day." This was a standard workshop practice in which participants wore blindfolds in order to bring forward the other faculties of sensory awareness. With this one anomaly, the program proceeded as usual.

*

David has been 'blind' for almost seventeen hours. Holding onto the arm of a young female kitchen worker, he makes his way from the Lodge to the Chicken Coop. She eases him gently through the door and, with a reassuring touch on his shoulder, detaches herself and retraces her steps alone. He gropes his way around the inside perimeter of the building and, sensing the presence of others, sinks cross-legged to the floor. There's the image of a circle in his mind. Ben and Jock are close by. He hears their voices but their words are lost among the muffled sounds of other bodies shuffling around to find a place in the blackness. He strokes the moisture from the palms of his hands and listens to the pounding of his own heart. He is terrified.

He listens while Ben explains the body-work procedures. There's nothing new here. He's been on the mat before but, with all the visual cues removed, he feels lost and powerless. Finally Ben asks for a volunteer to do the first piece of work. David raises his hand and imagines that the others have done likewise. The hand on his arm and the familiar sound of Jock's voice in his ear tells him that he is the chosen one.

David Aitken, architect, provider, manager and warrior, has squeezed out every drop of his courage to get to this place. Now he must find a way to step back into immunity or surrender to whatever might lie beyond. Removing his clothing and lying down on the mat, he understands that, in some unfamiliar way, he has made his decision.

"David, it's Ben." The voice is warm, offering a gentle haven in the emptiness.

"David, it's Jock. Bring your knees up and start the breathing from your belly."

The instruction offers more assurance that the void can be confronted and traversed. In a moment of sudden clarity, he understands that, while he must travel alone, he can never be lost or disconnected from this strange collection of men gathered together in the place they call the "Chicken Coop."

For over an hour David challenges the spectre of his own shadow, sometimes in the pain of acceptance, sometimes in the anger of confrontation, and sometimes in the ecstasy of walking through the soothing mists and gentle rain of his Soul. It is a journey that he alone can undertake, understand and appreciate while those who witness blindly from the outside follow with their own experience. And through it all, the ubiquitous presence of Wong and McKeen moves around the nakedness of their friend, their distant voices reaching down into the abyss with words to ease him along the way. Fingers in the chest, thumbs in the thighs and the occasional needle in the hands and feet, they deftly go about their work monitoring the life force in its struggle to connect the body with the images of the mind. Matching David's absence with their own profound level of presence they maintain the connective balance among them, even at the innermost reaches of his being.

In returning from the darkness, David learns that the experience of light has little do with the optical system of the body. As he rises from the mat and the arms of Ben and Jock embrace him he can 'see' that they are themselves embraced by a shimmering light that radiates out to invite the others to come forward. And come forward they do, moving in concert toward the centre of the room like a single organism contracting in the simple pulsation of life. Yet not a blindfold has been removed . . . not even his own.

There is music beyond the ears. The simple blending of melody and lyrics reaching out from the speakers at the back of the room to fill and connect the senses of men. "I made it through the rain"; the words lilt and etch themselves into hearts hardened against a world of unrelenting expectations. In the moment, he understands fully why he has followed these unusual men to this strange and wonderful place. He has glimpsed the paradox of connections created from stark aloneness and wonders where his relationship with Wong and McKeen will go from here.

Arm in arm, the shuffling brigade leaves the Chicken Coop.

David Aitken nestles himself among them and happily relinquishes his life as a warrior. Now, as a blind man, he can see far beyond the dreamless Presbyterian eyes of his father. He wants to touch and know that which he had always driven himself to conquer and possess. Outside . . . or is it inside? something is gently urging them toward the unseen light of the Lodge. He is moving with the river, willingly, knowingly and contentedly.

For the remainder of the program he dedicated himself to the cause of self-awareness. But this time, the experience was richer and deeper than anything that had gone before. Going inside to examine the texture of thoughts and feelings still carried its legacy of fear, but now it was mingled with excitement . . . the potential for discovery. And, more than ever, he brought himself forward without the crippling concerns for the expectations and judgments of others. He wept without shame or embarrassment and laughed from his belly without inhibition. He sang, played his guitar and entertained with a level of spontaneity and quality of performance that amazed him and delighted the many who stopped to listen.

But, in the greatest revelation of all, he discovered that this was no simple adventure into unabashed narcissism or self-indulgence. From this deeper place he could be more honest, available and present with others. In the sessions he reached out as others did their work, giving them ownership of their lives without hooking them to the judgments of his own issues. And, in the process of making such distinctions, he was beginning to appreciate the logic of what had always seemed like a contradiction—a true awareness of others can only be created from an emerging awareness of self.

There was no doubt in his mind that some bond existed between himself and Ben and Jock. He had been around long enough to understand the processes of objectification and transference that inevitably weave their way into psychotherapeutic relationships, but these notions seemed trivial and unsatisfying. Of course Ben was a wonderfully wise, accepting and challenging father figure and Jock was everything he could hope for in a brother, but such superficial ideas could shed little light on the connection he had felt from his place in the darkness. Certainly he had been alone and afraid, but he was not a child looking to them for survival in a hostile world. However inhospitable it seemed to be, it was *his* world and *he* alone could be at home there.

In his life as an architect and entrepreneur there had been times when he had revelled in his own ability to step forward, make his own decisions and take full responsibility for the consequences. This was freedom. In his life as a husband and father, however, there were times when he seemed to be flying blind, mindlessly repeating old patterns and dancing to the tune of unconsciously held archaic messages and other people's expectations. Consequences, like the break up of his marriage, often appeared as the unjust designs of an unpredictable world. This was imprisonment.

Lying on the grass plateau beside the beach, with the warm afternoon sun warming his body, he stared into the eternity of the blindfold and decided that he was ready to examine his own experience, embracing and taking responsibility for whatever he found there. Only then could he guarantee himself the freedom of his own decisions and actions . . . his own will. For the remainder of the program, and probably beyond, Ben and Jock would be there to support, mirror and encourage the process. His challenge would be to keep them close without falling into the trap of making them responsible—a challenge that many others failed to confront.

For their part, Ben and Jock challenged, and were challenged by, the expanding presence of David Aitken. His energy generated a focal point in each group and brought a vibrancy to the program as a whole. They grew to like him and trust him. More particularly, he exemplified and personified what their work was all about. As they had looked beyond the prescriptions and illusions of their own lives, so he was calling upon his own courage to follow the candle of his curiosity. As they worked together to dismantle the armour protecting them from each other, so he was moving to expose his own vulnerability to the world. As they uncovered and revealed that which lay at the core of self, so he was bringing himself forward to test the waters. In the terminology of the times he was a man 'in process,' and this was the essential dynamic of the laboratory that Wong and McKeen had created.

There were other creative souls at work. In an ingenious workshop designed and led by Lilly Jaffe, participants were invited to create living masks upon their own faces, using theatrical make-up and grease paint. The meaning of each mask, as a projection of the wearer, was then explored in the context of the group; yet another opportunity for revelation within the mosaic of the Resident Fellow Program. David Aitken, no longer blindfolded, took up the challenge.

He saw the fear in the painted face that stared back from the mirror. It was blue, dark blue, with a white band stretching across, separating the top of the cheek bones from the brow of the forehead. Suspended in the void, two disembodied eyes stared out in wild desperation. In the cobalt hollow beneath the nose, tight-lined lips were stretched and frozen across tomb-stoned teeth.

He was not inclined to run from the fear. Nor was he taken by the antics of those who chose to turn the exercise into a charade. Deep within the staring eyes, a kaleidoscope of reflections drew him through the fear, beyond the postures of manhood and the desperate struggles to become the wishes of his parents, pulling him inward to the place where it all began . . . the essence of David Aitken. More than anything in the world, he wanted to know that place again, to cast off the rusted armour of the years and allow the fearful eyes to re-open in the wide-eyed wonder of his infancy, ready to comprehend a world that would accept him joyfully and unconditionally.

The workshop leaders came and went, John Enright, Gregory Bateson, Will Schutz, each offering David a different context, a new perspective for experience and reflection. Ben and Jock moved in and out, like master weavers, gently urging him to draw together the fragmented elements of his life. They held up a mirror, inviting him to examine his own truth. This was not the agenda-laden feedback to which he had always felt compelled to respond and comply, but the simple sharing of other selves stimulating him to seek only that which he knew to be true. The patterns were becoming clearer, richer and more intricate, as he saw himself being drawn out across a stretcher of time. And he grew ever more fascinated.

The motorcycle, its carrier bags now refilled, stood ready to take him back to life on the Lower Mainland. It would be the same life. He was still David Aitken, architect, father and achiever, but the mission had changed and the experience would be profoundly different. From now on, it would be David Aitken in action and not some idealised, and despised, facsimile chasing the external symbols of success. Having discovered a self that needed no external validation, he was determined that his external persona would work in the service of his inner truth. Any other way would be a lie, an act of self-deception that could only re-create fragmentation and self-hate.

As he checked over the machine that had once been his vehicle of escape, he was amused by the thought that it had actually brought him to a place of unrelenting reality. Now he wondered how he would manage to transport this reality beyond the of Cortes Island. Ben and Jock had invited him to return, to work with them as an assistant in their programs but, after serious consideration, he decided that his challenge was in returning to the world of lost meaning. In a strange and ironic twist of perception, it occurred to him that Cold Mountain now offered him the greater potential for escape. At the deeper level of truth, however, he knew that his need for escape had little to do with the external context.

As always the motorcycle supported his decision, immediately responding to the thrust of his foot on the kick start. Then, without turning to consider the past or reaching ahead beyond the rutted tracks, David Aitken left Cortes Island, taking his context with him to create another family, a highly successful business and a long-term relationship with Drs. Bennet Wong and Jock McKeen.

"The Courage to Be is the ethical act in which man affirms his own being in spite of those elements of his existence which conflict with his essential self-affirmation." At first blush, the words of Paul Tillich may seem prescriptive, but the sentiment stands as a simple proposition.

When Ben first read Tillich's book *The Courage to Be*, he did not stop to ponder what the author might have meant by such words. The meaning was already there, forged from the stuff of his own life and flowing from the lives of those who had allowed him to see them. Laura, David, Jim, Jerry, had all said the same thing, not through the intellect of carefully considered words, but through the unexpurgated openness of their hearts. They, more than Tillich, had touched the chord. Their voices rang out across the waters and echoed through the valleys of his island. Their stories mingled with his own, and their courage reached out to him through the blackness of the night. Many times he had been alone and afraid, cut off from his lifeline to God. He had imagined himself as a single link in a fragile chain stretching out to some unseen meeting place beyond the horizon. Now the horizon was no further than his own boundaries and the meeting place was a myriad of reflections, in which each life held a mirror for every other life. To hide would be an act of self-deception; not to look would be to choose blindness. Whatever Tillich had meant by his words, it was in this place, and with these people, that the self would surely find the "courage to be."

In his own struggle to "be," Jock continued to draw upon the same inner resources that had served him so well in his pursuit of recognition and power. In his determination to lay aside such ambitions, his commitment to revelation became even more intense. He was a zealot for precision and clarity, imposing fastidious expectations and unforgiving judgments upon himself.

He strained to pry open the doors of enquiry, even if the immediate pain caused him to draw away for momentary respite.

"What do you feel?" Ben would ask.

"Nothing," he would reply in response to the numbness. Then, since the numbness might be a lie, a convenient form of self-deceit, scrambling the senses to ward off the fear, he would delve into the unknown.

"You've gone distant," Ben would say.

"Yea, I wonder what that's about," he would reply.

It was all part of being at one with the self, with Ben and, finally, with the world in general. He struggled to be precise in his use of language, clear in the formulation of his ideas and, above all, deferential to the man he continued to regard as his teacher. The style was known and well-practised but now he was determined to work from the inner subject, transforming success into mastery and power into strength, looking to his teacher for guidance and to himself for integrity. By any standards, it was a remarkable and monumental project. For Jock McKeen, it was his way of choosing life.

Following their second Resident Fellow Program they introduced a five day variation on Ben's original Self-Awareness seminar. Giving their new creation the laconic title of "Come Alive," the format was simple and effective. Participants met as a large group every morning and afternoon, dividing into smaller groups for the evening sessions. Ben and Jock led the large group sessions while their assistants, or interns, were in charge of the evening meetings. With over twenty participants, there was little opportunity to use group process, in the traditional psychotherapeutic sense, but this was never meant to be part of the design anyway.

The program commenced with warm-up exercises common to most forms of group encounter. In this particular case, they were used to break through the usual impersonal rituals of social interaction, establish the place of the leaders and help create a personal environment in which participants could experience a sense of safety and support. The principles of being present, respectful and responsible were introduced and exemplified through this process. Then it was down to the basic structure that was to become the hallmark of all Wong and McKeen workshops—individual work within the context of a group.

By this time in their career, they were fascinated by the process through which groups establish their own unique 'personality' and the first session provided them with an opportunity to assess, and influence, the blending of the individual parts into the emerging whole. The task of bringing out the characteristics of the group, while attending to what was happening for each group member, called for considerable awareness, sensitivity and skill from the leaders; and this was something that Bennet Wong did very well. To the casual observer, his presence might have seemed unobtrusive but his attention to each person's experience was readily sensed by those who participated. His ability to gather and analyse vast amounts of information enabled him to move straight to the heart of the matter, leaving many wondering how their complex and covert lives had suddenly become so simple and apparent. Some were convinced that Ben had pushed aside their mask of survival and stared unflinchingly into their soul. Others regarded it as some form of magic and stood back in awe. What these participants really experienced was their own ability to discover themselves through the presence of others, but such insight often takes time and commitment to unfold. In the meantime, the wisdom remained grounded on the outside and the magic attributed to the magician.

Unlike individual psychotherapy, the nature of their work made it impossible to move through the personal projections of each participant. More importantly, they were engaged in short-term intensive group work in which moments of insight or awareness, along with somatic energy shifts, offered only brief glimpses of each person's particular patterns. These were the building blocks of a learning process that needed to be seen, owned, and taken back into the melange of everyday life. It was never intended to be a controlled therapeutic process contracted between therapist and patient. Above all, their work was founded upon a model of personal responsibility leading to personal growth, rather than one of diminished personal responsibility requiring 'treatment.' And, for this, there were some risks that had to be taken.

Ben continued to be surprised by the frequency and intensity of other people's projections toward him. "I just can't be *that* important," he said. Working with Jock, he was less likely to be the sole and central transference object, but this also brought a new element into the arena—the partnership itself. In this, people saw the same kind of magic and the kind of relationship they had always wanted. Some even revealed their fantasies about being in an intimate union with one or both partners. While Ben and Jock were prepared to use their own experience in their teaching, they were not about to lay their relationship wide open for public scrutiny; so others simply filled in the missing pieces from their own lives. Even when the two leaders talked about their own relational struggles, the revelations were often seen as evidence of openness or vulnerability, and the idealisations continued. There was no way to predict when such positive attributions would turn negative, but, as Ben and Jock knew full well, it was bound to happen.

As it was, the "Come Alive" program provided the ideal context in which the professional partnership of Wong and McKeen could flourish. Working from whatever their participants brought forward, the form was necessarily spontaneous and creative. Their most basic contribution to this creative process was in forging the most optimal conditions in which each person would have the opportunity to be seen and heard.

From this perspective, each piece of work was unique. Over the five day period, however, it would become apparent to most participants that, beneath the surface, the same issues would present themselves with amazing regularity: anger toward parents; guilt around undisclosed feelings or actions from the past; unreflected grief for someone or something lost; dissatisfaction with a primary relationship. Looking still further beyond the personal contexts and the particular expressions, the more discerning observers would be drawn to the conclusion that even these matters were manifestations of a much smaller number of issues, so deep, yet so universal that they could only belong somewhere at the heart of the human condition.

In the matter of universality, Ben had come to believe that the central concern was the struggle of each self to find full expression and resonance in the world. This grew from his deep respect for authentic expression in all its forms. But, unlike many who sought or claimed enlightenment, he placed no relative value on any given person or expression. Whatever attributions others might have made toward him, his own concern was not in the acquisition of wisdom, awareness or proficiency, but in each moment of discovery and revelation. He could love the bristling ego of young John Creston who paraded himself through a "Come Alive," but when the same lost soul stood nervously before the entire gathering to sing on the final evening, it was the tentative unpostured tremors of the voice that brought tears to his eyes. When that voice swelled up and took the young man's heart out into the world, he was overwhelmed. It was as wonderful and profound as any Caruso aria. "When you sing," he told John later, "you carry the voice of God." That Ben's own tentative warblings were less than melodic or inspired was irrelevant to his appreciation. He had his own talents, and singing wasn't one of them.

"Watching Ben and Jock from my hiding place in the circle, I was overwhelmed by the caring, commitment and sheer artistry of these two men," said botanist Russel Milner, commenting upon his first 'Come Alive' experience. "My own fears began to disappear on the second day and I found myself wanting to rush out into the middle and say 'Here I am, do you care about me too?' When Jock played the part of this young woman's father . . . I've forgotten her name now . . . he came out with all the stuff my own Dad put out to me. I got so pissed off, I wanted to scream. I was screaming inside anyway. When she finished her work and they asked us to gather round her and give feedback I tried to speak. I opened my mouth to say something but this lump came up from my belly and I just sat there with my mouth open and the tears streaming down my face. At the time I thought I was crying for her but, Jesus, it just hit me that I was crying for myself. Then Jock, who'd been holding her in his arms, looked up and said, 'Russ knows something about this.' Then I was in the middle of the circle. Ben, Jock and the rest were all there for *me*. I remember thinking, 'Christ, I wish Margaret (his wife) was here.'"

One of the many reasons why the 'Come Alive' survived to become a cornerstone for their practice was its infinite portability. A short term program, accommodating a manageable number of people at an affordable, though profitable, cost could be taken anywhere, particularly to people who had neither the time nor the money to travel to Cortes Island. So, as Cold Mountain began to crumble, the work of Wong and McKeen became increasingly self-contained and they took to making more and more decisions on their own behalf.

Taking their programs on the road was a decision that fit for them, although it provided yet more ammunition for their resident critics. By this time, however, the situation clearly was irredeemable. Any indication that they might wish to preserve the legacy of Richard Weaver was taken as confirmation of their covert take-over aspirations. On the other hand, any move to promote their own particular brand of work was judged to be an act of abandonment, committed in the service of crude opportunism. As it was, they continued to step carefully through the potential hazards, offering their support for the others while protecting the integrity of their own work. In fact, through their workshops across Canada and in the United States, they continued to work as ambassadors for all Cortes programs, with little or no acknowledgement for their efforts.

In the Spring of 1976, they experimented with another variation on the portability theme by taking a group of adventurers to do a 'Come Alive' at a health spa in Rio Caliente, Mexico. Lilly Jaffe had recommended the facility to them and, at seven dollars per day per person, their shared pleasure in parsimony triumphed over Ben's graphically expressed misgivings about intestinal discomforts and unfamiliar washrooms.

With professionally appropriate glances of indifference, the staff watched them arrive, two unknown Canadian doctors standing together in the lobby surrounded by a motley collection of twenty or so fellow travellers still sorting out suitcases, tote bags and backpacks. Nobody at the spa seemed sure about why they had come or what they were about to do now they had arrived. From her place in the shadows of the kitchen doorway Anna Maria watched with particular interest. She was a dreamy, soft-skinned Mexican girl who had worked at the spa for almost a year. Her dark eyes locked onto the figure of an oblivious Jock McKeen.

"Oooo! Who's dat man at de desk . . . de one in de red shirt and tight black pants?" she whispered as Peggie Merlin, the Spa Director, emerged from the dining room. "Hmmmm! I'm not sure, but I know what you mean." The two women exchanged brief smiles of shared appreciation and parted to attend to their respective duties.

Peggie Merlin had assumed the responsibilities of Spa Director some months before when the owners, a husband and wife partnership from Los Angeles, had returned to the United States to seek legal advice on the Mexican Government's challenge to their ownership of the property. A spirited, bright and articulate woman in her early thirties Peggie originally had taken up residence as a yoga instructor, escaping from a broken marriage and changing the course of a career that included being the first female producer with the Merv Griffin Show, in New York City. When her friends asked her to oversee the operation, she had taken it as an opportunity to push her talents in yet another direction. A former graduate student of anthropologist Margaret Mead, Peggie was fluent in Spanish and, having been involved in setting up the National Anthropological Museum in Mexico City, she was no stranger to the culture. Hence, she was admirably qualified for the role and she carried it off with great skill.

She was curious about the group from Canada but, unlike

Anna Maria, she was too preoccupied with her own projects to give them her full attention. She was surprised when, after dinner on the day of their arrival, they went straight to whatever business had brought them there, closing themselves off in the large gymnasium that had been set aside for their use. The following morning she joined with the rest of the staff in speculating about the strange noises that emanated from behind the hand-carved double doors.

"What do they do in there?" Anna Maria asked, distancing herself from the door in response to Peggie's unexpected arrival in the hallway.

"Just a group of tourists doing whatever tourists do. Are you still gasping after the young doctor in the black pants?"

"Oh yes. Did you see him in those shorts this morning?" She placed her hand over her heart and blew a kiss toward the doorway.

From lunch time until the middle of the afternoon, the Canadians roamed around the property, some in small groups, some in pairs and some in solitary contemplation. At every opportunity, Anna Maria glided and giggled her way to Jock's side and he seemed to delight in her presence, melting into whispered episodes of romantic Spanish and gyrating around her with the flowing intentionality of a flamenco dancer. As the workshop participants indulged in their inevitable speculation about the relationship between their two leaders, the staff of the establishment began to speculate about the prospects for their amorous colleague and the man who stirred her passions.

Late in the evening of the day following the workshop she sat in Peggie Merlin's office, venting her anger through blazing eyes and torrential words. "That other man," she spat, "he wouldn't let him come to my room, even though he really wanted to. Why would he do that and why would Jocky listen to him?"

"I'm not really sure," answered Peggie. "How did he explain it to you?"

"First he said he would need his partner's permission and I asked no questions. Then he came back to my room to tell me he'd be sleeping in his own room and in his own bed. Who are these man, and who the Hell does he think he is?"

"I'm not really sure," Peggie repeated calmly.

"They gotta be faggots. Why else would he do this thing? Please tell me why."

Peggie nudged herself to come up with a new line. "Perhaps they have some kind of arrangement," she suggested.

"What kind of arrangement?" Anna Maria demanded. "One that hurts people? They're supposed to be doctors, helping people not hurting people." The anger dissolved into tears only to rise up again. "Perhaps he's not a man at all," she screamed. "Perhaps he just fakes it. No real man behaves like this. He's a weirdo, a zombie. That Chinese guy, I bet he's some kind of Voodoo person."

After breakfast the following morning, Peggie watched Jock as he made his way out of the dining room and across the foyer. "Hmmm," she thought, "I can certainly understand what she was so upset about."

CHAPTER SEVEN

Working under the auspices of Cold Mountain, their combined monthly income was a far cry from the lucrative returns of their practices in Vancouver. In deference to the fiscal integrity of the Institute, however, they decided to draw only one leader's fee, while proposing and practising a 'minimalistic' attitude to the consumption of all resources. Philosophically this blended well with the Zen-like traditions of Cold Mountain and the new property managers, Jim and Judy Sellner, together again, took up this cause with the same enthusiasm they used in bringing 'personal process' into their staff meetings.

Uncluttered by many of the standard features and fixtures of the world, the rough-cut reality of "Chi" was becoming an ideal setting for their own personal work. Sorting through the minutiae of their daily lives, they found themselves in places where even the most fleeting thought or whispered word would be a contamination. Unlike many of their Cold Mountain colleagues, their sense of relation with the eternal was not sought through transcendental rituals. On the contrary, it lived within them, rising out of the mundane to be grasped and released in the blinking of the mind's eye.

Having peered beneath the leaves to find themselves staring

back from the fleshy fibres, they assumed a profound respect for even the most primitive resources of the planet. They talked about 'walking lightly on the earth.' Money, they reasoned, has no inherent value. It serves as a vehicle between self and the world, benignly available to express any state of being. Insatiable demands for power give rise to heavy-footed and wasteful practices, disrupting the pre-existing harmony. Alternatively, a self moving toward its place in the relational order may use money in resounding the harmonic chord.

Prior to the development of these ideas, money had played a relatively pragmatic role in their lives. Beyond the necessities of daily living, Jock would spend money as a form of cautious and systematic self-indulgence. Ben, on the other hand, had gone along with the social prescription of doing what seemed right for a successful psychiatrist with a young family but, beyond this, money had little intrinsic value or relevance. As practising physicians, they both had managed to accumulate a significant excess of income over expenditure but were equally unsure about how these surpluses should be handled.

So, when Mike O'Kane arrived on the scene, his timing was brilliant. Jock was beginning to question many of his old indulgences and Ben, who had more material possessions than he had ever really wanted, was quite ready to hand over financial management to anyone who was trustworthy and seemed to have workable ideas. Mike was qualified on both counts. A vibrant and eloquent man in his mid-thirties, possessing a fortuitous blend of Irish charm and American determination, he seemed to glow whenever he talked about money.

He had made his first appearance at their Vancouver offices in the Fall of 1974, presenting himself to their receptionist as an Insurance Advisor. Over coffee, he convinced them that their life insurance policies has been designed almost exclusively for the benefit of the insurance company and recommended that they convert immediately to term insurance at considerably reduced premiums. The savings, he told them, should then be invested in mutual funds. Almost without question, they agreed with his analysis and gave him full authority to handle the transactions. The benefits were obvious and immediate and they were delighted that this neglected aspect of their lives could be handled with such expertise and enthusiasm.

In the months that followed, their investments flourished and they became increasingly fascinated by Mike's thesis that money could be applied to almost any conceivable purpose. Riding in the back of his white limousine, with Mozart and brushed leather caressing their senses, they listened while their driver explained how idle or misdirected finances where symptomatic of societal waste and personal irresponsibility. He took them to a place where they could look down on the city of Vancouver. "Look how nature has blessed this town," he said, sweeping his arm to cover the entire territory from Mount Seymour to the U.B.C. peninsula. "But you can see, hear, even smell, the alienation of Man from Paradise, and it's all been done with money. Now, if we wanted to, we could use that same money to challenge this entire city to participate in a completely different form of urban life . . . one that embraces, rather than opposes the nature of things. Of course it's just a dream but . . . what a dream."

Such words and thoughts flowed easily from him and he checked his audience through the driving mirror to make sure that he had their undivided attention. An astute businessman, Mike knew how to match his presentations to the carefully researched backgrounds of his clients. With Drs. Wong and McKeen, he had been particularly tenacious, constantly questioning them about their ideas and reading up on matters of humanistic psychology, eastern philosophy and contemporary ecology He spent hours playing chess with Jock on the beach while seeking Ben's opinions on almost everything over coffee or lunch. Yet, in all of their dealings with Mike, it seemed that his curiosity was more than that of a financial opportunist nurturing a potentially lucrative proposition. He was readily available with his feelings. He shared his own story in a way that could hardly have been designed to promote client confidence, like the details of a recent financial disaster for which he was held entirely responsible. They liked Mike, they trusted him and, as they grew more excited about his ideas on fiscal creativity, they gave him increased licence over the management of their own financial affairs. So, as they drove across the Second Narrows Bridge and headed back toward the down-town core, the two would-be investors began to consider how money might be incorporated into the equation of their partnership.

While Ben was not particularly interested in transforming the city of Vancouver, he did have some thoughts about how people might live together more responsibly and harmoniously. In a casual conversation with one of David Aitken's partners, Ben had challenged the popular contemporary concept of 'open communities,' suggesting that people need privacy along with options to participate in community life in their own way. He proposed an architectural design for 'vertical strata' titled apartments built side-by-side around a common courtyard, providing opportunities for personal autonomy, relationships and shared responsibility. In this way, he argued, architecture could be blended with humanistic thinking to support a particular way of life.

The idea sparked considerable excitement within the Aitken organization and a collaborative deal was established, with Wong and McKeen as the principal investors. They brought Mike in on the arrangement and, within a week or so, they were the co-owners of a sizable lot at the corner of Willow and 7th, close to downtown Vancouver. The investment was an immediate success and, on Mike's advice, they decided to re-sell this property for a profit before any building actually took place. Some months later, an apartment complex was constructed, incorporating Ben's ideas. Mike, an enthusiastic supporter of the concept, moved into one of the units.

When they made the move to Cortes Island, they were far from wealthy but, with Mike's help, they were able to close down their practices, cover the costs of their on-going domestic responsibilities and still retain some of their investment potential. In purchasing their island property, he showed them how to use their Retirement Savings Plans to raise the necessary capital and actually handled the entire transaction on their behalf. Then, with their remaining investment funds, they agreed to become part of a major project to establish a horse ranch and riding arena in Langley on the lower mainland.

For Michael O'Kane, an avid horse lover, this scheme was an affair of the heart and he went after the necessary capital with exceptional tenacity. In the process, he gathered together a consortium of physicians from among his clientele and, by having them all countersign for each other in the acquisition of bank loans, he created a substantial investors club. In pursuit of his dream, he would fly up to Cortes in his newly acquired airplane to discuss developments with his "favorite clients" and have the necessary papers signed.

In the final consummation of the deal, he flew Ben and Jock back to Vancouver to meet with the overseeing bank manager and to participate in the ritual of signing the final documents. There was a spirit of adventure about the whole affair. The two renegade doctors, giddy from their trip and bowled over by the sudden and unexpected appearance of department stores and theatres in their lives, purchased large Stetson hats and cavorted about the city streets like ebullient teenagers on an annual school outing. When they finally arrived at the bank, they presented a memorable sight.

Though Mike O'Kane made many trips to Cortes, he never showed the slightest interest in the affairs of Cold Mountain, financial or otherwise. By 1978, even Jean Weaver's interest was waning but, as the sole owner of the Cortes property and, with a lingering loyalty to the wishes of her late husband, she remained stoically at the helm. This was sufficient for those who continued to cling on to a family that no longer seemed to care about them. As Jim Pryor observed, "The patriarch is dead, mother doesn't want to keep the nest and the kids have become proprietary about who they are and what they do."

Jean Weaver tried to keep the pieces together, bringing the business talents of David Aitken and Jim Pryor onto the Board to blend with the therapeutic skills of Margaret Woods and Lee Pulos. Then, in a move that left little doubt about her own inclinations, she appointed Ben to serve as Board Chairman. In hiring Jim and Judy Sellner to manage the property, she assured everybody that the Wong and McKeen influence was there to stay and announced that her own attention would be dedicated to the programs operating from the Barge in Vancouver harbour. For the most part, the Board of Directors upheld Jean's position that workshop leaders should be responsible for promoting their own work and creating their own markets. While this issue continued to be a focal point of the power struggle, and the vehicle for a wide range of discontents, it was also a matter of basic survival.

Again, Jim Pryor said it well. "Most of these people (the workshop leaders) were eking out a marginal living. They had shifted their lives out of the standard mould and were clinging on to the idea that they were practitioners in their own right . . . and in the Weaver days, they were. But things were changing, not only at Cold Mountain but in the big world beyond. Ben and Jock, particularly Ben, could make it anywhere they chose. They didn't need a place where they could become the experts, they already had that. And Ben offered what people seemed to want . . . softness and grace, rather than harshness and confrontation."

There was no doubt in anybody's mind that the form and flavour of their work was markedly different from anything that Cold Mountain had seen before. While their version of the Resident Fellow Program continued to incorporate the workshops of the other leaders, their own influence was becoming increasingly central to the experience. They attracted groups of over forty participants and six interns, filling the session room and generating a new energy, along with much needed funds, for the struggling organization. At the same time, the kitchen, cleaning, gardening and maintenance crews were becoming well-versed in the Wong and McKeen style through the regular 'process' sessions conducted by their supervisors, Jim and Judy Sellner.

None of this served to soothe the discontent. On the contrary, the relative success of their programs provided the discontented with unequivocal support for the 'take-over' hypothesis, while the new brand of participants fuelled the conviction that the very heart of Cold Mountain was being torn apart. "These people belong on the Barge in Vancouver," observed one of the perennial program leaders to his group of eight as they sat huddled together on the lawn watching the interlopers file out of the session building. "This place used to be a very special place for very special people. Now we seem to be in the business of titillating the masses." They shook their heads and stared in silence.

In spite of the valiant efforts of the Sellners, many members of the resident staff were vocal contributors to the disharmony. While they shared a common respect for the work of Wong and McKeen, they were dismayed at what was happening to their beloved community and the blame had to reside somewhere. Ben became an instant target for their malcontent whenever he articulated his view of how staff should relate to the program participants. "When there are programs taking place on this property," he said at one general staff meeting, "this place operates for the benefit of those who have paid to do their work here. And *you* are paid to support that work in any way you can."

Characteristically, he had chosen words that tore straight to the belly of the matter and they sat in stunned silence. Many, like Xanon Jensen, had come to Cold Mountain in search of some personal dream of 'community.' "For the first time in my life I felt like I belonged somewhere," he said, some years later. "Finally, I'd found a place for myself where I was somebody, doing something useful, and people cared . . . shit, they cared a lot." Prior to leaving Vancouver, he had watched in horror as his girl friend was stabbed to death by another friend; an episode in an acid trip that would last a lifetime. When he signed on as a maintenance man at 'the Mountain,' it was to reconnect with a life that seemed to be slipping away.

"I didn't really understand what Ben was saying at that time.

I just remember feeling cold and empty again, like someone was taking something from my insides. Hell, we were a community no matter what this guy had to say. When people came out to do programs, they came to *our* world and we had something to offer them . . . something different . . . something real. We were important, man. We believed in ourselves and each other. And here this guy was telling us that our lives just weren't that important . . . that we were there to serve the visitors. We began to understand why some of the leaders were so pissed off. If I'd really understood all this at the time, I would've split then and there."

Whether or not Xanon and the others understood or appreciated the principle, the implications of Ben's position were becoming increasingly clear. Myra Brundle, a young kitchen worker, became a reluctant and resentful student of this new philosophy one morning when she forgot to blow the traditional carved horn to summon the residents to breakfast. At eight-thirty, a furious Bennet Wong and a stern-faced Jock McKeen appeared at the kitchen door. Three women looked up from their duties at the work table. "Whose job was it to blow the horn?" he demanded, freezing their chatter in mid-stream. Myra glanced quickly at the others and held up her hand. Ben turned on her without hesitation. "Your lack of consideration and respect for people in the program here will not be tolerated," he barked. "People who come here are in a totally unfamiliar world. Many of them are at a critical point in their lives, feeling scared and vulnerable. It's our job to offer a responsive and caring environment. I'm absolutely horrified by your thoughtlessness."

She stared back in fearful disbelief. "I just forgot," she said nervously. "It was a mistake . . . . Anyone can make a mistake. I didn't mean to. . . ."

"We're not talking about mistakes," Ben snapped. "We're talking about negligence. We're talking about disrespect. We're talking about thoughtlessness."

"Jesus, such a small thing. I don't understand what all the fuss is about," said one of the other women.

Ben turned toward her. "If you don't understand what the fuss is about, then you shouldn't be working here. It's as simple as that."

In the silence that followed, he glared at each of them in turn but the challenge was over. He left, with Jock closely behind.

With Myra sobbing, the others moved to her side and wrapped their arms around her. "So there goes Dr. Sensitivity and the Black Disciple," said the one who had remained silent in the exchange.

"He's got no right to pull that kinda stuff around here. He's no better than anyone else," said the other.

"I just made a mistake . . . I forgot . . . it could happen to anyone," sobbed Myra from her protective cocoon of arms and bodies.

But, for Bennet Wong, there were no 'its' to 'happen.' There were only people making personal choices, taking personal actions and accepting personal responsibility.

With Jean Weaver's move to Vancouver, the Barge at False Creek became the centre of Cold Mountain operations. Over the years, this large floating structure in the heart of the city had undergone many modest transformations to accommodate the changing needs of the Institute. Now its task was to provide an urban sanctuary for the ailing spirit of the island community. As the base for the Antioch University programs, it had an established raison-d'être and, with registrations for the M.A. degree on the increase, it was by far the best bet for carrying Richard's educational ambitions into the 1980's. Reflecting its centrality within the enterprise, the Barge was also the venue for monthly meetings of the teaching faculty and the Board of Directors.

As the new Chairman of the Board, and the target for much of the insecurity and resentment, Ben was acutely conscious of the organization's state of fragmentation and instability. But he was no zealous corporate chief, ready to tackle the collective malaise with carefully articulated goals and cool, efficient strategies. Beyond the primary objective of creating a context in which participants and practitioners could come together to do their work, in their own way, he offered no sense of 'mission' for the others to cling on to. There was no defined Wong and McKeen method to be followed. "It should be possible for people with different philosophies and ideas to work side-by-side in a climate of mutual respect," he said, oblivious to the fact that such a stance flew in the face of contemporary organizational theory, and in spite of the prevailing attitudes within Cold Mountain itself. "Personally, I just want a place where Jock and I can do our own work together. It's that simple," he told them.

For most of the players, however, it was not that simple. At the Board level, there was a growing belief that Cold Mountain should re-group under the umbrella of a shared 'mission statement' that transcended individual hopes and aspirations. Ironically, the business minds of Jim Pryor, David Aitken and Lee Pulos were more inclined to accept Ben's definition of how things might be. Yet they sincerely believed that the work of Wong and McKeen should provide the basis for a new era of development and were frustrated by Ben's refusal to articulate the terms. They considered his position to be overly accommodating, democratic and laissez-faire.

On the other side were those who were convinced that Wong and McKeen were actually using cleverly disguised strategies to take over all of the programs and impose their own brand of practice, including the selling of personal growth 'packages' for personal profit. In this confusing and paradoxical organizational milieu, the Board's decision to hire an Executive Director seemed rational and timely.

Anticipating that there would be more political tongue-wagging generated by this issue, Ben excluded himself from the search and selection procedures. The shortlist was drawn up by Jean Weaver and she, along with other Board members, interviewed the final candidates. Their unanimous decision was bestowed upon a bright young American woman whose recent professional experience included operating a spa at Rio Caliente in Mexico.

Peggie Merlin had never heard of the Cold Mountain Institute prior to the telephone call from Jean Weaver inviting her to an interview. Lilly Jaffe, who had used the spa for a number of her own workshops, had tossed Peggie's name into the hat shortly after the Board announced its intention to find a full-time administrator. By that time she was living in Minnesota, having long since returned the responsibilities of running the spa back to the original owners. In the process of working through a period of personal chaos, her therapist had suggested that she might consider counselling psychology as a profession and she had responded by enrolling in a Ph.D. program. Challenged by her own confrontations with her sense of self, she had become fascinated with the "untapped energy and resources of the human spirit," but the academic menu was failing to tempt the palate or satisfy the appetite. The opportunity to direct a personal growth institute came as an unexpected delight.

When the offer was made, she accepted the position without hesitation and, in response to the Board's urgent request for immediate action, she presented herself at the Barge three weeks later.

From the comments of those who had interviewed her, she understood that the organization had struggled with its own sense of identity and purpose since the death of its founder and that there were some concerns about the financial aspects of the operations. But, with an eye for an opportunity, a heart for a challenge and a mind to "do something different," Peggie relished the prospect of directing the resources of such a noble and mysterious enterprise. "I was very excited," she recalled, "but my excitement was tinged with a certain awe about working with a group of highly evolved people who I expected to be elegant communicators."

She sat in Jean Weaver's office conducting her first cursory review of the financial statements. With many workshops leaving deficits, and many expenditures out of control, it was clear that the internal systems and states were totally incapable of carrying this organization toward its humane and noble objectives.

"I need the full picture," she said to the photograph of Richard Weaver planted beside the "in" tray. "I've got to find my way to the heart of this thing."

She stood up, peered over the dust laden window ledge and out toward the congestion of False Creek and Granville Island. Propelled by the new wealth of the early 1970's, and fashioned by the tastes of a new generation of spenders, the old industrial areas were being destroyed to make way for open markets, theatres, restaurants, marinas and trendy condominiums. Skeletal cranes hovered over dilapidated warehouses; mud-caked backhoes and dump trucks waited idly among the debris of buildings, and old tugs and fishing boats bobbled beside brightly painted vessels. Wherever she looked, she saw a world in transition.

Then, as she considered how such a future might look for the Cold Mountain Institute, a mast freed itself from the entanglement. Borne upon the shadow of a sleek black hull, it slipped out into the middle of the channel. Three figures moved lightly around the decks. As the vessel slid silently beyond the barnacled wharfs of Granville Island, she pried open the window, sat down at her land-locked table and welcomed whatever destiny had to offer.

With the arrival of Peggie Merlin, Jean Weaver sought her own respite from the burden of carrying Richard's dream. She commenced graduate studies in Business Administration and was already withdrawing from the day-to-day operations of Cold Mountain. Her presence at the helm had been essential to maintain the truce. With her departure, some new order would need to either break through the surface or be imposed from above.

News of Peggie Merlin's arrival and the further separation of the matriarch sent another shudder through the Cortes community. When the new Director's questions centred around matters of financial viability, rumours began to spread. This American woman, with her head in the accounts, was obviously hell bent on peddling personal growth products to the mindless masses of the middle class in pursuit of ever-increasing profit margins. "The McDonald's of Human Development," somebody said, and the term stuck.

Peggie Merlin was given no forewarning of this dissatisfaction. In the early days, her secretary responded to certain topics with downcast eyes, the program co-ordinator went about her tasks with well-practised diplomacy, and the motley crew of characters—faculty and students—came and went. But there was no sign of the elegant communication, no sense of the noble mission and no evidence of the evolved human interaction she had expected. Rancour began to ooze from the timbers of the old Barge.

Still, she remained convinced that the larger picture would contain the aspirations and dedication that she so desperately wanted to embrace. "I'm really not sure what people are doing or where Cold Mountain is heading," she admitted to her Board Chairman as they sat sipping coffee in her office after a meeting. "I'd like to come out to the island and experience the programs first hand. What do you think?"

"Well, I can't tell you where Cold Mountain is heading," Ben admitted, "I can't even say for sure where Jock and I are heading, but we do know what we're doing at this point."

"I see you guys have a 'Come Alive' starting next Friday evening. Can I come up and participate?"

"Of course, we'd love to have you."

She *was* there, she *did* participate and, like most of the others, she found herself tumbling through the uncompromising mill of personal process. "Ben and Jock offered a gentle invitation and I just accepted," she recalled. "I didn't know what to expect. I'd heard stories about Encounter groups and I was ready for whatever happened. But it was all so delicate and respectful. People felt safe from the very beginning and there was a magical quality about how each piece of individual work blended into the experience of the whole. It was quite different from anything I'd experienced before, or even read about in my studies. I was so happy and thrilled to be part of an organization that offered such rich opportunities."

Also, like most of the others, she was intrigued by Ben and Jock and curious about the nature of their relationship. She noticed how, as leaders, they responded in concert to the unpredictability of motion and emotion within the group, while maintaining their individual integrity in their personal contacts with the others. They made no secret of their caring for each other and, on a number of occasions, she found herself "delighted and touched" by gestures of affection that passed between them. After the brief musical interlude and celebration following each piece of work, they would move together and talk, sometimes holding hands, sometimes in a loose embrace. She wondered what they were saying.

"During the first two days I commented upon how wise Ben was and how gorgeous Jock was," she said some years later. "Then, as the program drew to a close, I began to see how wise Jock was and how gorgeous Ben was. Most of the others could see the beauty of Bennet, yet nobody seemed to appreciate the wisdom of Jock. But I was struck with the sensitivity with which he saw what was there to be seen in the revelations of the others and by the finesse of his movements around them. His brightness was clear to everybody, but I also saw his pain. It was like a dark red mask that filled up behind his eyes whenever he hurt. To me he was much more readable than Ben and I couldn't understand why some of the others were so scared of him. Some of them seemed to feel gypped if Jock led their work rather than Ben, as if they had to settle for second best. I couldn't understand that either."

So, Executive Director Peggie Merlin returned to the Barge in False Creek, happily reassured that, in spite of its troubles, Cold Mountain was worthy of her dedicated attention. At her next meeting with Jean Weaver she asked, "Are they gay?"

"No, not exactly," replied Mrs. Weaver.

"What the hell does that mean?" she asked abruptly.

"Well, it's difficult to fit their relationship into any category,"

Jean answered. "They're really important to each other and they certainly know each other very well."

"Well it's true that they live together and share the same bedroom isn't it?" Peggie continued, with obvious frustration.

"Yes that's right."

"And do they sleep together?"

"No, I don't think they sleep together. If they did, they probably wouldn't make any secret about it. I don't think that's what their relationship is about. My God, look at the time . . . I've got to be at the university by three-thirty."

Peggie's curiosity about the sexual activities of the two workshop leaders was neither idle nor moralistic. She was attracted to Jock and, had it not been for professional protocols, she might have followed the charge. More significantly, however, her sketchy picture of their relationship was challenging some of her most fundamental perspectives on the world and she was searching for information that might tie everything back together again.

There was something alarming about the sight of two men openly acknowledging and displaying a committed and loving relationship, without an equally open declaration of homosexuality. There was something disturbing about their commitment to total self-revelation when Ann Landers had told the world that, for relationships to survive, some things are best left unsaid. And there was something strangely incongruous about a highly respected psychiatrist and a brilliant young physician choosing to closet themselves away on a remote island in order to practice their version of intimacy while conducting programs that seemed to mock the traditions of their respective disciplines. But Peggie Merlin had other things to think about and the Cold Mountain Institute was screaming for her undivided attention.

Jean Weaver was right, they didn't sleep together . . . well, not exactly. Though Jock had long since abandoned his insistence upon separate rooms, their beds remained adamantly apart . . . well, almost adamantly. Jim Sellner, who occasionally took time from his managerial responsibilities to visit their house and snoop around, claimed that he could always take the temperature of their relationship by measuring the 'degrees of separation' between the beds. Then there was their habit of 'visiting' one another before going to sleep at night and upon waking up in the morning. Sometimes they would lie next to each other, reflecting again on the events of the day, or anticipating the day ahead and, sometimes, they would simply hold each other.

For Ben it was a time of peaceful union, while Jock was learning to relax into sharing a simple pleasure with a best friend who was not afraid to make contact at any level. To touch physically and be touched was an intimate and caring experience. To sustain 'soft eye' contact in the passing of a single moment could stir the deepest emotions. To allow his body its full and shameless expression in the presence of another could free him from his web of words.

Though Jock maintained his rule of celibacy, sexuality continued to contaminate the purity of his senses. This disturbing reality rose to meet him whenever he fought to draw his eyes away from the women who drifted along the pathways of Cold Mountain, and whenever he withdrew from the untimely protrusions of Ben's pelvis. With women, he could always draw back, invoking the rules of professional conduct. With Ben, he could close his senses down by casting the demons onto his friend's intentions. But these rationalizations only served to offend the self and stifle their relationship. In matters of his own sexuality, he still listened to the voice of a morality that strangled him.

It spoke through his behavior. There was a time when he had pushed himself to be open with Ben about his sexual exploits, painfully grinding out the details of his lust. Now he sought to avoid the issue, denying whatever feelings and fantasies he did have and bringing yet another undisclosed strategy into their dialogue. Standing naked in the bathroom one morning, he became conscious of his half-erect penis and acutely aware of Ben shaving at the adjacent sink. Rather than suffer through another ambiguous silence, he drew Ben's attention to the matter with a less than elegant "Hey, look at this" invitation. Consciously, it was little more than a flippant gesture, though his belly told a different story. When Ben responded with a brief sideways glance through the steam-fogged mirror, followed by a perfunctory grunt of acknowledgement, he was left with the unmistakable symptoms of shame.

Sharing the same bedroom and holding hands between the beds became a pleasurable ritual. Spending time together in the same bed was simply a practical arrangement. Then, when they pushed their beds together, this too was more in the spirit of convenience than experimentation. Before sleep, Jock would slide over and enjoy the innocent closeness of friends on a long-awaited camping trip. But when he awoke one morning to find himself in Ben's arms, he felt invaded and resentful. He said nothing. When it happened a second time, he could see the trap but could see no way of escaping it without creating a new distance between them. On the third occasion, he lay stiffly in Ben's embrace and considered his options. In the course of his deliberations, he unearthed a shattering insight . . . he was lying on *Ben's* side of the bed.

The implications did not dawn on him immediately. Eventually, however, he had no option but to confront the obvious; it was *he* who had made the nocturnal advances; it was *he* who was seeking closeness; it was *he* who wanted to be touched. The stark realization that he had been blaming Ben for his own unacknowledged desires filtered through slowly and painfully. Then, he was ready to tell all.

"My fear of being dominated by you reflects my own craving to surrender," he said. "My celibacy isn't really a spiritual quest, it comes from my fear. It's a moralistic statement, for God's sake. The more immediate issue is that, between us, I don't seem to know where closeness ends and sexuality begins . . . or vice-versa."

"If you're talking about feeling sexual, I don't think there's any clear division at all," Ben said. "If you're talking about fucking someone, about penetration, then I believe you're talking about a particular form, a particular expression. Intimacy is about revelation, not about sex as such. Fucking isn't the physical expression of closeness. In fact, as you know from your own experience, it can be the very opposite."

Jock did know. Yet there was nothing he could do to anaesthetise his compulsion to manoeuvre women into surrender. On the other hand, there was now evidence to suggest that, at some level, he was also seeking to reverse the equation. Interestingly, the few months of analysis over his sexuality had been punctuated by approaches from three men—a program participant, an astrologer and his flute teacher. It was as if they sensed the questions that haunted him since, up to this point, there had been no time in his life when other men had shown any such interest.

Ben cut into his speculations. "Perhaps you should think about finding a woman to have sex with," he suggested. At the time, they were working to replace some of the rotting timbers in their old barn.

"Where did that suddenly come from?" Jock asked.

"Well you've been so preoccupied, like a man grieving. I just thought you might be looking for something that I can't offer." There was that unmistakable trace of sadness in Ben's voice.

Jock paused for a moment and watched him carefully gathering up the old nails for re-use. He didn't want more from Ben. How could any human being offer more? Whatever he had ever wanted was there in abundance. All he had to do was ask. Even in the days when he was searching for Ben's secrets, the only barrier was created by his own duplicity and his inability to formulate the questions. Ben understood his need to have sex with a woman and Jock was closing him out through his preoccupation. The rebirth of his sexuality was something that he could bring back to the pulse of their relationship. He didn't have to take anything away. "Would you be jealous if I did?" he asked.

Ben straightened a nail with a pair of pliers and dropped it into a leather pouch hanging from his belt. "Yes, but not because of the sex," he said, bending down to pick up another.

"What then?"

"Because of the remote possibility of intimacy . . . the thought that you might share something with her and not with me," Ben explained, continuing his search among the debris. "As things stand, it's your obsession that gets in the way of our relationship rather than your sexuality."

"Ha! So you think that sex and intimacy could come together then?"

Ben turned and looked at him for the first time in the discussion. "I think it's possible, but it would have to involve full disclosure. Then it would be interesting."

Jock laughed. "Not much to worry about in my case then,"

"Not really. What do you call it? . . .Foreplay and fulfilment?"

"Guile and deception, followed by abandonment and guilt, actually."

"I know, but who ever said that jealousy is rational?"

Over dinner Jock began to pick away at his poorly concealed frustrations. Later, as they washed the dishes, he tried to reclaim some of the sexual issues that he had conveniently dropped on Ben's doorstep, beginning with his judgments about his own sexual conduct before delving into his homophobia. "Why in Hell's name do I make you the agent of my own disowned morality?" he asked rhetorically. "In spite of all I now know, and all that you have come to mean to me, I still turn you into an object for my own protection."

Ben sighed. While there was nothing new in Jock's latest bout of self-recrimination, the issue of being objectified, of not being seen by his best friend, cut deep into his own fears. In this, he was no different from the women Jock was about to fuck. Laying side-by-side on Ben's bed, the remnants of an unusually quiet and gloomy evening leading them into sleep, Jock spoke again of his perplexity. "I sense your hurt," he whispered, "and I'm struggling not to take on the responsibility. You know, sometimes I feel so ashamed of how I draw you into my deceptions that I don't know who I'm crying for."

Ben's voice came back softly from the darkness. "I'm always

open to you," he said. "Your thing with women is an invitation for me to look at my jealousy, my possessiveness . . . my abandonment. If you continue to stay open with me, then I'll continue to feel blessed."

That night, they held each other for a long time. The following evening, a pensive Jock McKeen stood alone on the ferry to Quadra and watched the familiar outline of Cortes Island melt and finally disappear into the melancholy mists of Autumn. Another piece of the puzzle had found its way back into the mosaic of his consciousness . . . a known piece, but irrevocably transformed on the journey. He had acted swiftly. A brief telephone call, a hastily renewed acquaintance, and a frankly worded proposition were all it had taken. Throughout the day, his anticipation had been strange and confusing but, whatever else was happening, his commitment to celibacy was about to be rescinded.

He eased his way back into the practice, euphemistically referred to as 'dating.' with a modus operandi that he would once have considered unthinkable. In the first place, he was scrupulously clear in explaining his single minded purpose—sex. Secondly, he dedicated himself to accepting and respecting the woman's decision on the matter before throwing himself into the provocative pleasures of seduction. For the most part, the chosen ones claimed to understand, and accepted the terms of the arrangement with few questions. There was nothing forbidden or clandestine about the engagements and Jock rarely hesitated to bring his date back home to 'meet the family.' Usually, there was a genuine overlay of friendship involved and, in some cases, Ben was considered to be included, though never in a sexual sense.

In this way, Jock was able to reclaim his discarded sexuality and bring this detached aspect of himself back into his primary relationship. In fact, the addition of a third person served to add more interesting variables to their experimental design. His diligent attention to clarity and his understanding of personal boundaries made it possible for him to create and maintain this unusual relational configuration in a manner that would have been impossible a year or so earlier.

But there were times when the 'third person factor' began to raise more issues than they had bargained for. While the common dating paraphernalia of false promises and romantic illusions were surgically removed at the outset, the generalized symptoms of the disease usually began to manifest themselves after the third or fourth visit with the good doctor.

"You have no commitment to me," she said tearfully.

"You are my only sexual partner. That was the commitment," he reminded her. "I tell nobody other than Ben about our time together. That was also the commitment. And I will never try to persuade you to act against your own wishes—that too was the commitment."

"Don't you feel anything happening between us?" she asked.

"Yes, and it's wonderful."

"Well it's not enough, not for me anyway."

"Then we'd better stop seeing each other."

"Oh sure. So I end up being used." She pulled away.

"I don't think so." He lay on the bed staring up at the ceiling.

"You can't spend the rest of your life with *him* you know," she said from the silence.

"Right now that seems very possible to me."

"So you're AC-DC, right?"

"No."

"Then how is he holding on to you?"

"He isn't."

"He's some kind of weird father figure then."

"Oh sure . . . sometimes." He was bored, waiting for it to end.

"Then someday you'll grow up and get over it."

"I hope so . . . then we'll be even closer."

"You guys are sick." It was an acceptable Parthian shot.

Then there were times when a confused and despairing date would turn to Ben for comfort. In spite of the loose threads of jealousy that occasionally trailed across his mind, he was always gracious and available. On more than one occasion he shared her pain, holding the forlorn lover in his arms with the tears of his own abandonment in his eyes. But, in the aftermath, a curious and often painful inversion seemed to take place.

"Ben doesn't like me at all. I think he resents my being around," she complained.

"How can you say that after the time he spent with you last week," Jock protested.

"Well that was just my crying," she moaned. "Most of the time he's really distant."

"I don't think so. He's probably closer to you than I am."

"Are you kidding? What about last night? Now *that* was close."

"Well our genitals were close."

"So! Now you're trying to say that he cares more about me than you do. Is that it?"

"I think his heart is open where mine is all wrapped up in our sex."

"That's not the way it is. Why are you protecting him?"

"Why would I want to protect Ben for God's sake?"

"Because deep down he doesn't like women . . . and you know it."

"Not so. He cares as deeply about women as he does about men."

"Well, being with him isn't like being with a *man* at all."

"That's because he doesn't play the sex game."

"He doesn't go in for sex, is that what you're telling me?"

"I'm telling you he doesn't play the game, that's all."

She seemed lost. "Sometimes I don't know where you're coming from," she muttered. "You make things so complicated."

"You and I make things complicated," Jock corrected. "Ben's position is ridiculously simple."

"Well I, for one, don't understand it. I think it's perverted."

In spite of the confusion, Jock conducted many of his liaisons in an amicable, lustful and, at times, tender manner. Terminations were mutually agreed upon and separations were generally friendly, adorned with well-wishes for the future. There was one glaring exception however and, as so often is the case, the exception came back to swallow the norm.

There was nothing exceptional in either the flavour of the union or the circumstances of the departure. She was introduced to Jock by her brother. She initiated a series of visits during which they explored each other sexually. At an early point in that journey she made it known that, some thirteen years earlier, during a particularly stressful period in her life, she had seen Ben as a patient. Of course, Ben remembered. Since that time she had been married, given birth to two children and separated from her husband through mutual agreement. The frequency and duration of her trips to Cortes were limited by the demands of her children as well as her full-time job in Vancouver.

Known and befriended by many within the community, she was intrigued by the work of Cold Mountain. Jock was particularly delighted that she was willing to examine the ideas of humanistic psychology within her own life, without choosing to become involved as a participant in any of the programs. While he was quite prepared for her to make this decision, he also knew that their sexual union could never have been maintained, or even consummated, under such circumstances. It was a cardinal rule of their leadership.

He liked her and relished her visits in a way that extended far beyond the repetitive rituals of sexual gratification. Unlike most of the others, she was prepared to take a close look at her own sexuality, sharing their common interest in self-discovery and revelation, even in the presence of Ben. In this, she proved to be remarkably open and analytical. To this extent, she carved out a place for herself as another scientist-participant in their study of relationships.

For Jock, she offered a fortuitous and timely opportunity through which he could explore his sexual fears and fantasies. But this was no detached 'Masters and Johnson' analysis of sexual behavior. As always, the learning was drawn from the pleasures and pains of direct experience but, as always, the process had to reflect the integrity of the self and the autonomy of the other. In this spirit, they made a decision that seemed perfectly appropriate at that time and in that context. The decision was made following their review of a sexually explicit movie . . . one that had received considerable acclaim from the most sophisticated critics of erotica. As an adjunct to exploring the specific themes portrayed, they set up a video camera and, casting themselves in the roles of the performers, they filmed sequences of their own sexual encounter. Once this project was completed, the tape was carefully stored away in Ben and Jock's bedroom closet, on the strict understanding that it would never be made available for outside viewing and that it would be destroyed at the request of either party. It quickly became a relic in the archives of their sexual experimentation.

Early in 1982, she telephoned Jock to say that she wanted to break off the relationship. She had met another man and, given Jock's obvious unavailability, she had decided to opt for a more complete and full-time arrangement. With mutual expressions of sadness and appreciation, they agreed to terminate their activities. In wishing each other well, neither gave a moment's thought to the time bomb innocently tucked away in the bedroom closet.

At that time, Bennet Wong and Jock McKeen had more pressing matters occupying their thoughts.

CHAPTER EIGHT

Early in 1978 there were rumblings among the investors that the project initiated, designed and administered by Mike O'Kane was in some kind of trouble. In the months that followed, a series of strange legal documents arrived at the McKeen-Wong residence seeming to confirm the suspicions, and the telephone calls from the other physicians grew increasingly bitter and blaming. There was a growing consensus that Mike had mismanaged the whole affair and that their funds were in jeopardy.

In his brief and infrequent dealings with Ben and Jock, Mike failed to confirm or deny such speculations. Following a few weeks of silence, a telephone call from the bank manager in Vancouver resolved all ambiguity. He told them that the bank was calling in the loans and that they would be well advised to come over and discuss the situation at their "earliest convenience."

It wasn't until the bank manager had completed his summary of the case that the severity of their circumstances hit home. The project itself had collapsed and their own investment lost forever. On top of this, there were outstanding loans taken out by the consortium in the amount of three hundred and fifty thousand dollars.

"So, what's our share of the outstanding debt?" Jock asked nervously.

"All of it," he replied with the cold stare that distinguishes bankers from social workers.

In the wake of their stunned silence, he went on to explain how the others had all systematically absolved themselves of the obligation through declarations of bankruptcy. Since they had all co-signed for one another, the responsibility now rested with the only remaining solvent partners to the agreement, Messrs. Wong and McKeen.

"What just happened here?" Jock asked, as they shared an appropriately inexpensive lunch in Chinatown's most unassuming restaurant. "Yesterday we were rich and today we're in debt for this unimaginable sum of money. Like, what the Hell do we do now?" He hovered somewhere between denial and grief.

Ben reached over to ladle another helping of soup into his bowl. "Well, nothing has changed really," he said calmly. "We're still here together. Our work is still the same and nothing is standing in the way of what we want to do. We just carry on as we always have. Nothing changes . . . nothing to be done." He slurped his soup and smiled.

"Well I'm pissed off," Jock spluttered through a mouthful of heavily seasoned noodles. "Those other guys should carry their share of this." He swallowed hard and pointed a chopstick in Ben's direction. "They bloody well know that all the contractors and trades people who worked on that fucking horse ranch won't get paid if we all throw in the towel. Surely they thought about that before they went on their bankruptcy trip." He was prepared to live by his own principles, whatever the cost, but now they would be paying off the debts of those who lived by a different code. Behind the resentment, there was a delicate dilemma waiting to be addressed, but this was not the time.

"I don't know," Ben said thoughtfully. "You know a lot of other people have lost their investments too . . . I mean the ones who weren't even involved in the co-signing arrangement."

"Including Corrinne," added Jock, without pausing to recognise that the dilemma had just been addressed.

"Yes, I'm not happy about that," Ben continued. "A lot of the money she received in our divorce settlement went into this project. I had no idea Mike was going to call on her. I wish he hadn't done that."

"Well Mike's enthusiasm was pretty damned contagious," Jock recalled.

"Yes it was his big dream wasn't it? Whatever he did, or didn't do, it was his idea and his commitment, but we all wanted a piece of it. I don't think the others really understand that. When things were going well he was their hero, now they're ready to kill him."

Jock's thoughts followed. "And Mike's been in this position before. He must be feeling devastated by all of this. Should we give him a call?"

They ordered coffee and went over to the public telephone in the restaurant foyer.

"How are you?" Ben asked.

Mike burst into tears. "Only you and one other person have even bothered to ask," he sobbed.

"We all took this risk together," Ben told him. "It's not a question of finding someone to blame, we're all responsible. Jock and I believe that you acted with integrity. Just know that you're welcome to come and be with us anytime." Mike seemed genuinely touched, but he never took them up on their offer.

There was never any doubt that they would assume responsibility for the outstanding loans. Despite Jock's lingering grief around the financial losses and his resentment around the actions of the other investors, it was a decision that generated very little discussion. Before leaving Vancouver, they made arrangements with the bank manager to make monthly payments, based upon a significant percentage of their projected income. It would take them years. It was of little concern to them that their bankrupt partners would replace their lost sail boats and Mercedes within a matter of months.

Decisions around the future of the Cold Mountain Institute remained confused and chaotic, however. Still reeling from the bitterness of the internal conflicts, Peggie Merlin organized three meetings of the professional staff in the hope of achieving clarification, if not resolution. "Those gatherings were so rough and vituperative," she recalled. "A number of the staff were into heavy-duty macho encounter and I could hardly believe how such venom could be unleashed in the name of authenticity. It took me a year of reflection to really understand the dynamics of what was going on . . . a full-scale personal and professional power struggle dripping with jealousy and resentment."

After only six weeks, she presented a written report to the Board. Ben, as Board Chairman, complimented her on her efforts, saying that it was the most comprehensive analysis of the operation ever conducted. In general, however, the report was seen by many to reflect the already tarnished reputation of its author. Her participation in the 'Come Alive' served to confirm existing suspicions about her allegiances and her glowing reports of the experience left little doubt about her visions for the future of the organization.

"I was seen as some monster from the corporate world," she said. "I was dismissed as being slick, not ecologically correct, not philosophically correct, not spiritually correct and not personally correct. They were convinced that I was about to open the 'MacDonald's' of the human potential movement in the most crass way. It really was some kind of fantasy . . . a bizarre projection . . . because I would have loved to have been more effective. Within myself I felt so unsure. I was longing for us to create a collective vision to secure our future."

In an attempt to carve out such a vision, she challenged all staff to respond to their circumstances with submissions to the question, "Who are we and where are we going?" But those who chose to respond took it as another self-serving opportunity to reaffirm their own positions and solidify the existing climate. By this time, Peggie was battling her own personal and professional crisis.

Striving to move beyond the inertia of helplessness, she took a week out from her responsibilities to attend a self-development program offered by Context Training Inc. In a program aptly named "The Wall," she was encouraged to confront the question of her own self-efficacy and concluded that, in the service of her sanity, it was time for her to act on her own behalf.

On her return to the Barge, she made calls to Board members David Aitken, Jim Pryor and Lee Pulos before asking Ben to call an extraordinary meeting of all Directors. At that gathering, a motion was passed dissolving the Cold Mountain Institute and dividing its financial assets, approximately sixty thousand dollars in total, between the Weaver Institute in Vancouver and the Cortes Centre for Human Development. While the former was to continue operations from Jim Pryor's Barge, Ben and Jock's programs would be folded into a new operation, governed by its own independent Board and renting the old Cold Mountain property from its owner, Jean Weaver. As its final executive function, the battle-weary Board of Cold Mountain considered, and accepted, the resignation of its Executive Director, Peggie Merlin.

Whatever else was created through the demise and dissolution of Richard Weaver's experiment, Wong and McKeen were left with a place in which to continue their own work. While many symptoms of the disease found their way into both segments of the divided organism, people now had choices, and few hesitated in making their decisions. Jim Pryor and Lee Pulos, along with Don Mainwaring, Harriet Denison and Shelagh Baillie, formed the Board of the new Cortes Centre, while perennial supporters like David Aitken and Jim and Judy Sellner, who were now living in Vancouver, readily reaffirmed their commitments to the work of Wong and McKeen.

They were joined on the island by a small number of staff regulars who were prepared to do whatever was necessary to provide physical labour and administrative support for whatever the new Centre was going to be. Jane Sternberg, who had taken over from the Sellners, remained in the role of Property

Manager. With roots reaching back into the idealism of the sixties, their primary mission was to create and sustain a simple interpersonal community, away from the rampant materialism of the dominant culture. For them, personal growth programs provided an ideal philosophical and economic vehicle for their community aspirations, but their general belief that the former should serve the latter was not always shared by the breadwinners . . . the program leaders. This latent tension, common to most residential human development facilities, certainly contributed to the crumbling of the old Cold Mountain. Among the group that chose to create community around the work of Wong and McKeen were Jim Kearney, Dianne Anderson and Xanon Jensen.

Ben and Jock continued to make their relationship the focal point of their activities and their rambling acreage on Cortes Bay provided the primary context for this work. The new Cortes Centre for Human Development was a convenient and, hopefully, more stable place in which to practice their chosen profession. As the world shifted about them, unpredictably and beyond their control, they began to appreciate their shared ability to become the authors of their own lives amid the chaos of hidden designs and confused meanings. Their quest for intimacy was clearly focused and carefully contained. On the one hand, they were committed to participating in whatever was happening around them; to do otherwise would be to detach themselves from the energy of life. On the other hand, they knew better than to throw themselves into the fray and blindly follow the endless scrambling of other lives.

Even Jock could be momentarily surprised by the strength of his commitment to their relationship. Seduced by a special three year subscription offer from *Time* magazine, he had filled out the application form with unquestioning enthusiasm. Only when he casually tossed the return envelope into the outgoing mail tray at the Lodge did the significance of a three year contract hit home. "My God!" he said to Ben, as they went in for breakfast, "I thought I was just making a commitment to *Time*." Ben grinned and wrapped his arm around Jock's waist. "Perhaps you should consider making the same commitment to *Life*," he suggested. "Oh, I don't think that's published any more," Jock replied in all innocence.

From the outside, the unity of their friendship was receiving constant recognition and the actions of one were rarely mentioned without reference to the other. The staff on Cortes, as well as the program participants, simply assumed that, in talking to one, they were in some way communicating with the other. Casting them as a single entity within a single thought— "Ben and Jock believe that . . . According to B and J . . . 'The Boys' are going to . . ."—became part of the taken-for-granted reality that was the Cortes Centre. It was also the hallmark of a reputation that now stretched far beyond the shores of Cortes Island.

With the constraints of Cold Mountain tucked away into the archives, they were more prepared to work on their own behalf, accepting invitations to give talks and conduct workshops across the continent. Since they did little to market themselves directly, usually such invitations were initiated by people who had participated in their workshops.

After a rather formal presentation at York University, they found themselves in an unusually hectic rush to catch their flight from Toronto to Vancouver. As they gasped through the door of the plane, a wide-eyed female flight attendant welcomed them on board and closed the hatch behind them. Given their disposition to always fly at the cheapest rate, they made their way to their seats at the rear of aircraft and, once settled, became aware that the young woman was still staring at them. By this time, the aircraft was pulling away from the terminal and she had taken her seat at the front, facing the first-class passengers but leaning to one side in order to maintain her view of the two men at the back of the economy section. Then, with the pre-takeoff instructions in full swing, she rose from her seat and walked down the aisle toward them. As she drew alongside, she paused and smiled before easing herself into the folding seat on the rear bulkhead. When they were off the ground and the engines had been cut back, making conversation possible, she leaned forward and spoke.

"I've been watching you two since you came aboard," she whispered.

Jock leaned back in his seat and turned until their eyes met. "Yes, we noticed," he said.

"You guys didn't walk down this aisle, you glided," she said, her deep blue pupils dilating with the intensity of the stare. "It was like your feet were off the floor and you were floating through the air. It sounds weird, but I don't know how else to describe it."

"So you came all this way to check out the carpet?" asked Ben, who had been listening from the centre seat.

She giggled nervously. "No I came to check *you* out," she answered. "It just occurred to me that you guys know something that I should know. Now that's really weird isn't it?"

Between her responsibilities for the other passengers, she visited them frequently during the course of the flight, gathering information about their work and committing herself to taking programs at the Cortes Centre. She never did.

Had they concocted any transcendental illusions following their encounter with the starry-eyed flight attendant, such indulgences would have been shattered a week or so later during their presentation to a large community gathering in Halifax, Nova Scotia. Whenever they addressed such audiences, Jock's aspirations for equivalency were savagely assaulted whenever it came time for the customary question period. No matter who happened to have captured the balance of air time during the performance, invariably it was Ben who drew most of the questions and, thereby, the recognition. The pattern was so entrenched that Jock had taken to keeping score for his own perverse amusement.

On this particular occasion the score was a devastating twelve to zero before a faceless voice rose limply from the ranks with an irrelevant, if not inane, question about 'fatigue' for Dr.

McKeen's brief consideration. But the wills and wishes of others matter not to a man who truly believes that his time has come and, swooping out from the shadows of his own inconsequence, Jock filled the room with his indomitable presence. Whatever the questioner *thought* she wanted, the question was really about energy, the universal substance of life, the Tao, the wind upon the water, the permissive yet restraining arm of God that granted freedom with one stroke, and swept it away with the next.

Six and a half minutes later, his arm struck the water jug perched on the lectern and sent it flying across the stage. Had it not been for the unfortunate position of Ben, the force and trajectory would have taken it well into the audience. As it was, Jock could only stare in horror at the sight of his partner, with head bowed, watching the water drip from his black leather vest and collect in a pool around his feet.

"Well, you all saw what happened," he began, taking one more glance at his dripping partner. "Now I want you to know what was taking place behind the obvious. I was peeved by the fact that Ben was getting all the questions. It's not unusual for Ben to get most of the questions, and it's certainly not unusual for me to be peeved about it. But tonight I really had to wait for my turn and, when it came, I decided to make the most of it. I completely lost the question, I lost you, the audience, and I lost Ben standing here on the stage. I was so wrapped up in myself until finally I lost my own sense of presence. I want you all to know this, and I also want you to know that I feel ashamed." The audience applauded.

At this point, Ben moved to his side and, together, they discussed the importance of 'presence' in the context of relationships. Then, when they called again for questions, the first enquiry was addressed to Ben. They all laughed. "You didn't seem particularly upset by getting drenched. Were you angry on the inside?"

"No," Ben answered. "We were swimming in the pool this afternoon and I was wet all over. I have no reason to be upset about being a little wet this evening." They laughed again.

"But this was with your clothes on," the questioner persisted.

Ben patted his vest. "My clothes are dry already, there's nothing left to be angry about. I did think about being mad for a moment but I couldn't find any hurt looking for a cause. As I was telling you earlier, Jock and I discuss our hurts and resentments with each other all the time. We just don't allow them to fester, waiting to flood out on unrelated issues. The secret is in acknowledging the hurt as soon as possible, focusing upon the actual issue and not holding the other person responsible. When we express and own our own hurt in this way, we can stay current with our partners, sharing our feelings in a self-responsible way."

Then, as they were about to launch into their closing ritual of poetry and music, a man in the second row rose to his feet. "Since you've been talking about the importance of honesty, will you tell us honestly whether you staged the water-spilling trick as a way of bringing your points to life?"

"Are you kidding?" Jock replied in amazement.

By the mid 1970's, humanistic psychology, and its various forms of expression within the human potential movement, had grown to challenge the neo-Freudian psychoanalytic schools on the one side and the popular cause of empirical behaviorism, brilliantly explicated by B.F. Skinner, on the other. The adventurous, though at times bizarre, experimentations of the National Training School in New York, the Esalen Institute in California, Quaesitor in London, Findhorn in Scotland and Cold Mountain in Canada, were being transformed into legitimized concepts and practices in the fields of Psychiatry, Clinical Psychology and Social Work.

Beyond this, some of the prominent early pioneers were promoting these approaches in many locations across North America. Will Schutz, the self-styled radical of the encounter movement, had turned his attention to the workplace while Theory Y and Organizational Development (OD) were gaining ground on the more traditional authoritarian practices of industry. In education, A. S. Neil in England and George Leonard and William Glasser in the United States were some of the powerful voices that sought to place the subjective experience of the student at the heart of the learning process. Virginia Satir was leading the way in promoting a humanistic orientation toward the most sacrosanct of all institutions, the family. From her 'systems' perspective, the traditional idealistic and moralistic models were being dismantled and replaced by therapeutic practices that viewed each family as a unique creation of interacting selves. Some chose to take their examination of human potential directly into the spiritual domain, turning away from the dogma of western religions to seek enlightenment through the transcendental methods of eastern mysticism. British humanist Paul Lowe and American psychiatrist Len Zunin, for example, cast aside their personal and professional attachments to join forces with Rajneesh, first in India and later at his controversial community in Oregon. Meanwhile, the growing popularity of philosophers like Christmas Humphries and Allan Watts was introducing a whole new generation of scholars and seekers to Zen Buddhism.

Given the decidedly non-spiritual nature of western society, it was predictable that the quest for enlightenment would continue to be dismissed by many observers as a ridiculous, if not dangerous, fringe activity. The more secular aspects of the humanistic movement could not be that readily dismissed, however, and even those who continued to express disdain for the 'flaky,' 'touchy-feely' manifestations of 'California Dreaming' served to legitimize and strengthen the challenge with their persistent hostility. Clearly, Abraham Maslow, Harry Stack-Sullivan, Carl Rogers and Bruno Bettleheim had become legitimate contributors to be reckoned with.

In moving out into the world, Wong and McKeen were quickly and conveniently tagged as proponents of the 'new psychology.' Many disciples, drawn to their particular brand of humanism, set out to delineate their style, to set it apart from the rest. Some even attempted to replicate their version in their own practices.

While Jock was ready to wear the badge of affiliation and had some interest in a 'Wong and McKeen Model,' Ben viewed such classifications as arbitrary and restrictive.

He shared this concern with their friend Virginia Satir, as the three of them sipped coffee at the Lodge. "I see the danger in the fact that you communicate in a form that I would see as the 'Satir' form. Once I can say there's a 'Satir' form, and I see your forms as being very creative, very dramatic and very impactful, then it seems to me that people lose sight of the essence of you. They become hooked to the form. *You* have the essence but, in order to communicate it, you had to develop the form, the words, the language and the concepts. Then you deliver it in an understandable way to the majority of people. In the process, however, the forms are ascribed with importance by so many people. You become famous because your forms are so well received and understood and, more important, they work. But how many people get to know Virginia personally, get to know that beneath all that form, there is a person, Virginia, who is very human?"

In listening to Ben, Jock took yet another look at his own ambitions and offered a thoughtful response. "You know Plato and Socrates wrestled with that. I guess my cynicism or my bleakness comes out here. It seems that some people have some kind of spark, or some kind of enthusiasm that is native to them and are stimulated to say, 'Oh yes, that's Virginia's form and I can't take her form, I have to get mine.' Yet so many people don't have the self-motivating spark. They take the form and then don't make the next necessary step."

"Even though I don't know of anything that can change that whole process," said Ben, "I feel compelled to do what I can. What I respect about you, Virginia, is that I believe I see the same kind of attitude in you. Whether or not we are all going to blow up, you still continue doing what you do. I think that out of that is born courage."

"That's right, that's right," she replied. "But if I did not believe that human beings have a wise part in themselves and a connection with the universe, I'd give up what I'm doing."

Virginia Satir finally gave up with her death in 1989. For many of her closest associates, she will always be remembered as a remarkably courageous, creative, insightful and charismatic woman who, from her own place of loneliness, inspired thousands of people to look beyond.

Through his own deliberations, Jock gradually abandoned his notion of being involved in any particular 'cause' or 'movement,' although Ben and he both recognized that they were not alone in emphasizing the hidden potentials of the self. Having generated a belief that causes are the politically motivated contaminations of original thought, they wanted no part in the collective ideology. Even their tenuous affiliations with the associations of humanistic and transpersonal psychology were uneasy arrangements with little commitment on either side. Nevertheless, they were unceremoniously tagged with the popular labels and those who came to see the show were not always impressed.

At a large gathering, sponsored by the University of Calgary, they blended their didactic presentation on 'Relationships' with the live music of a singer-guitarist and offered brief experiential exercises for those who wished to participate. Following this event they received a letter from the academic sponsors questioning the propriety of their behavior. It was alleged that 'many in the audience' were displeased with the 'theatrical' titillation of emotions, shocked by the unexpected deviations from the lecture format and horrified by the flagrant flaunting of their homosexuality.

Deeply concerned by this reaction, they managed to obtain a copy of the evaluations submitted by this reportedly hostile group and found no supportive evidence for the allegations. The thirtieth evaluation, referring to them as "two very powerful people," was the only hint of ambiguity in a highly enthusiastic collection of appraisals.

Virginia Satir, an ex-school principal herself, observed that school teachers, individually and collectively, present the greatest challenge to anyone who chooses to advocate for a more personal approach to human relationships. Addressing over two thousand educators at a major conference in Alberta, Wong and McKeen stunned an already uptight audience by inviting them to tweak each others noses as a non-traditional way of making contact. Three hundred delegates walked out.

On the other side of the equation, their work on Cortes, along with their many workshop, conference and television appearances across Canada and the United States, had given birth to a growing network of followers. Within this circle, one of the most committed and zealous promoters of their work was Carol Stewart, a young woman from Ottawa who, along with her husband, Steve, had relished their participation in the Cortes programs. Her unconditional enthusiasm captured the curiosity of friends and, directly or indirectly, led to a number of Wong and McKeen speaking and workshop engagements in various locations. At their home in the Gatineau Hills, Carol and Steve attempted to incorporate the principles of intimacy into their relationship, while inviting their friends to examine the notions of revelation, vulnerability and self-responsibility within their own lives.

"Carol was so totally taken with what Ben and Jock had to say," recalled Mark Fraser, a young disenchanted social worker from Ontario. "It was virtually impossible to be around her and Steve and not be drawn into their enthusiasm. We were all curious about these guys Wong and McKeen. So, when she organized for them to come to Ottawa for a presentation, followed by a one day workshop, we all showed up to take a look for ourselves. And, really, I've no words to express what I experienced. From my inertia in social work, I suddenly saw life in two professionals who were prepared to open themselves up. I couldn't believe or understand it but, whatever it was, I knew there was something very important here for me."

Coincidentally, the evening presentation was Mark's first date with Louise Belisle, another social worker who had come to question the nature and efficacy of the helping professions. She had been working in a large general hospital where a small group of psychiatrists led the way in prescribing textbook cures for diagnostically-packaged patients. "The shrinks themselves were so closed down," she observed. "None of them showed any sign of personal development. Instead they just showed their arrogance. When Ben and Jock talked about their work, so many of the missing pieces seemed to fall into place. I attended their workshop the following day and watched them work together. I'll never forget that experience. They worked with two nuns, bringing them face to face in the most sensitive and elegant piece of work I'd ever seen. It was all so open, yet so human and respectful."

Soon after this brief encounter with the two west coast 'therapists,' Mark gave up the practice of social work in order to work on the Stewart's property and participate in the new way of being. In this context his involvement with Louise broadened and deepened and their relationship became infused with many of the ideas expressed and exemplified by Wong and McKeen. Though their new mentors would have been appalled at the idea, Mark made no bones about the fact that he was a "follower."

On the other side of the continent another human service practitioner was laying her own foundations for a long term association with Ben and Jock. Joann Peterson was the Director of Children's Services at the Mental Health Clinic in Bellingham, Washington, when she first heard of the Cortes Centre for Human Development. A colleague of hers returned from the three month Resident Fellow Program and, in relating the experience, touched a timely chord in the cacophony of Mrs. Peterson's life. At that point Joann's marriage was in the process of falling apart and she was wondering how she had managed to lock herself into the roles of wife, mother and professional without ever understanding the glue that was supposed to hold them all together. Unlike Mark and Louise, she was quite satisfied with the modes and morals of professional practice. In fact, she considered herself to be a firm adherent to the schooled traditions of her trade and was meticulous in their application. At a personal level, however, she felt "empty," "lonely" and "lost." She understood from her mysteriously re-energized colleague that something called body-work would help her to get into her feelings and draw some meaning from her generalised sense of despair. She registered for a 'Come Alive' program that was scheduled to take place on a barge in Vancouver harbour.

"I felt like a moral, tight and square woman landing in the middle of hippiedom," she said of her first exposure to the waiting group, "but I struggled to keep an open mind. Then, when the two guys walked in, there was an immediate sense of purpose about the whole event. I'd never seen anyone take charge of a group like that without saying anything; it was like some instant transformation had taken place. It was as if they moved together with one energy that brought us all to the edge. I was in awe and desperately scared. I noticed the bounce in their step, as if they were skipping on water. As they sat down in the circle, my fear began to channel into a sense of excitement.

"During the early part of the workshop I was drawn particularly to Jock. It sounds funny now but I found myself watching his hands. They seemed to move with such compassion and skilful directedness. I just loved his energy. As the workshop went on I found myself more and more in awe of Bennet. He kept coming up with these truly profound observations and I couldn't figure out where they were coming from. There were times when he would laugh and giggle and I saw the possibility of making contact. I puzzled a great deal about him. Where Jock's own personal struggle was quite clear and available, Ben just seemed to address himself to each moment. It was years later that I came to the conclusion that Ben *is* process."

Joann noticed, as had many others, that Ben frequently made reference to Jock in his examples. Given Ben's liberal use of humour, it was a given that many of these references to his friend generated laughter. Like many others she "felt" for Jock and wondered about Ben's motives in "using" him in this way. Joann had to come a long way to see how, in a relationship where each person expresses the whole, there is no "use" of the other.

Joann found that she could not continue her journey of self-discovery while maintaining a distance between her professional and personal experiences. Very early in the process, she realized that the elusive glue of her existence was nothing less than her unreflected self and that her confusion was its struggle to participate in all aspects of her life. It was a simple matter of integrity. "My entire belief system was up for grabs in those days," she recalled.

She remained in relationship with her husband Pete and, though they moved with their two young children to San Diego, she continued to strengthen her association with Wong and McKeen, flying in for three consecutive 'Come Alive's' on Cortes and maintaining a regular correspondence with Ben on issues relating to her work with the victims of physical and sexual abuse. "At the personal level I think it was the first time I really felt that I mattered to someone beyond the roles I'd created for myself," she said of her relationship with Ben and Jock. "I have a great nose for 'B.S.' and I knew from the beginning that what they offered was real. I had never met people, particularly professionals in our field, who were so honest. I was absolutely amazed at the way they were able to match their expressions of honesty with what was going on in the other person. It was uncompromising, yet totally sensitive to the other person, without being tentative or patronizing. As a professional, I wondered how they did this."

Professionally Joann found herself in a situation in which her stifled sense of self was challenged to the core. "I had trapped myself into being a judgmental bitch, working with male perpetrators and deifying the victims. I was losing my own sexuality in the process. I wondered how I could see people and live myself in this environment without going down the tubes with my own belief system. I knew I had to find something beyond victimization but needed help to get through the blocks. Ben and Jock were the only people I knew and respected at this level who were not invested in attributing blame and politicising issues. Ben helped me to see the person beyond the act, without taking away from the principle of personal responsibility. Through his letters I began to make my own distinctions between anger and violation, to learn how to understand and respect personal boundaries and how to support victims without feeding into their victimhood. In one sense it was all about my clients, in another, it was all about me."

Like many who find their way into the helping professions, Joann had a compelling need to make things right for others, and the price she was paying for this impossible quest was the loss of her self. The closer she looked, the more she could see the source of her self-abandonment. There, in the mirror that Bennet Wong held up, she saw the stuff that, for years, she had been seeing in the troubled lives of her clients. Much as she was committed to the responsibilities of her work and her family, she knew that neither would be served unless she was equally committed to her own self-liberation.

Her attachment to Bennet Wong went straight to the heart of the matter. "Ben was a mentor at a very critical period in my life," she observed. "I'd like to say that I saw him as a friend but that would be bullshit. I saw him as the wisest man I'd ever known; a very caring and compassionate man who seemed to understand me at the deepest level. I really wanted to make him a father figure but never quite got there. In this half-baked fantasy, I imagined myself related to Jock as a very special kind of brother. Sometimes, when I was struggling at the very bottom in San Diego, I'd close my eyes and dialogue with them; not really in Guru form, but as a way of bringing my most personal feelings into the world. Still, I couldn't be with them and be fully who I was. My lifelong fears of abandonment and rejection constantly rose to the surface in one form or another and I continued to protect myself with roles. They were the mentors and I was the inadequate student, always worrying that I hadn't quite got it. I know that much of it was transference but it was more *personal* than anything I'd known before."

There was nothing unusual about Joann's *use* of Ben as the idealized parent. From a psychoanalytic perspective the re-creation of parent figures through such 'transference projections' is considered to be a universal phenomenon. What is unusual is that, by striving to remain open to what was happening on the inside, she was able to see her own part in the process. "I knew that I was using them for my own purposes but I went along with it anyway. As it turned out, I was able to take so much of what I was learning back into my own professional work. I was learning to simply be with people while they cried, and even died. It began to dawn on me that I no longer had to be the person to make everything right, or even play the role of neutral template for their pain. I could be myself . . . and I was learning to be personal."

Joann's insights into her own 'process' made it possible for her to create a relationship with Ben and Jock that few others had managed to achieve. Had she continued to fill them with her missing parts, they would have remained as distant idols. But, as every competent therapist knows, sooner or later such idealizations begin to tarnish, leaving the 'patient' feeling let down, resentful, angry and vindictive. In psychotherapy, this shift from 'positive' to 'negative' transference is part of the process through which the 'patient' eventually comes to take ownership of his or her projections. In less monitored and controlled relationships, however, this reversal can be diabolical. Fortunately, Joann Peterson had the insight to understand what was going on and the courage to do something about it.

As professionals, Ben and Jock understood the dynamics of this convoluted process. On a personal level, however, it wasn't that simple. If anybody knew what it was like to become a father figure for the unresolved childhood issues of others, it was Bennet Wong. Yet, time and time again, he ended up feeling hurt and asking himself why. Sometimes, in facing a venomous stream of anger and accusations, he would feel helpless. In his own way, Jock also knew the experience of being objectified for his charisma, his medical expertise, his intelligence, his good looks and his sexuality. But, step by step, he was learning how to become the master of his own inclinations and willing to turn away from the seductive prospects of using this power as an elixir to fix others. Through this work, he was creating his own way of protecting himself from the projections of others, both positive and negative and, with the noblest of intentions, was coming to the conclusion that it was his responsibility to protect Ben also.

But, in the middle of it all, a new twist in the transference game was slowly coming to light, one that was not so well documented in the psychoanalytic literature. Thanks to the openness of people like Joann Peterson, Ben and Jock began to see how a new object was being cobbled together in the minds of their 'audience.' Rather than force some differentiation between their leaders, workshop participants simply created a third object, one that could accommodate the very deepest issues and the widest possible range of projections—the *relationship* between Bennet Wong and Jock McKeen.

With the dissolution of the Cold Mountain Institute and the creation of the Cortes Centre for Human Development, the late Richard Weaver released his tenuous hold on the destiny of the small island community. With a thirty-thousand dollar capital base derived from the division of the Cold Mountain assets, the new Board rented the Cortes facility from its owner Jean Weaver. There were no leaders, as such, although it was commonly understood that the work of Wong and McKeen would provide the cash flow for the new venture. Meanwhile, the new Weaver Institute operated from the Barge in Vancouver and, as a totally separate entity, assumed complete responsibility for the university programs.

Many of those who left Cortes were in no doubt about who was responsible for the pain they carried with them. Some would never forget. Meanwhile, Jim and Judy Sellner, Carol Stewart, Xanon Jensen, Jim Kearney, Dianne Anderson and a handful of established residents settled in to create the new Cortes Centre while Lilly Jaffe and Lee Pulos, along with some of the other leaders, committed themselves to offering segments of the new program.

"Ben and Jock had by far the greatest involvement," noted Peggie Merlin who, at the time of her resignation, had declared herself to be a 'friend' of the Cortes Centre and was now investing much of her own time around the property. "Lee was preoccupied with the 'Spaghetti Factory' (his highly successful restaurant business) and Lilly had her own practice in Vancouver, so 'the boys' became leaders by default. It was obvious that they weren't that interested in the business and organizational stuff. Management didn't seem to be their thing. They just wanted to get on with their own work. They had an established clientele and were committed to making sure that the people who came out for the programs were well looked after. They broke the programs down from three month chunks to one month chunks, calling them 'Phases One and Two' and created a more theoretical course they called 'New Horizons.' And of course, they continued with the five-day 'Come Alive's' both on and off the island. Since most of the people who came to their programs had their own living and working commitments in places like Vancouver and Seattle, this was simply a sensible marketing decision."

In the company of the new settlers, Peggie discovered that she wasn't the only person curious about the nature of the relationship between the two men. In fact, the issue of 'relationship' was a central theme in the daily life of the community and the word 'intimacy' was as ubiquitous as the word 'peace' at a love-in. "I just didn't get it," Peggie recalled. "I believed it was important for people in a close relationship to understand one another but seeing a relationship as a 'laboratory' seemed distinctly strange. I'd always believed there were things better left unsaid if you want a relationship to work. I thought it was quite bizarre, although there was a tinge of excitement about it."

To her amazement people were not just talking about intimacy but actually trying to do it. "It looked as if they were all trying to copy Ben and Jock. They were all involved in the programs and it was obviously the thing to do."

When Ben and Jock suggested that she might work on such a relationship with Jane Sternberg, Peggie actually took the first step. Jane, one of the property managers, had been developing such a relationship with Carol Stewart but, with Carol moving off the island, the project was left in midstream. When Peggie broached the subject, Jane sprang at the opportunity to continue the quest but, staring into the prospect of uncensored intimacy, the cautious Ms. Merlin backed off. "I couldn't see the value of having such a relationship with someone I didn't want to sleep with," she said later. "For some reason, it just didn't cut it for me in those days . . . so I turned her down."

Whatever the others were doing, the two program leaders continued to pursue their mission of intimacy. Each morning before breakfast, during the three hour lunch break and again in the evenings, they 'processed' the stuff of their lives. By this time they had resolved not to bring their own issues into the workshop sessions; a decision that was made after Jock had declared some feelings of 'shame' during the course of a workshop. He had lusted after one of the women in the program and, in his obsession, had separated himself from Ben. He acknowledged this distance, along with the assurance that he wanted to be close and would be. His intention had been to offer a simple declaration that would allow him to move through his self-preoccupation and be present for the session, but his unnecessarily long explanation scattered irrelevant seeds upon the fertile minds of his audience. To his dismay, and despite his protestations, members of the group became involved in the insidious task of therapizing him . . . telling him what a 'good' person he was and generally trying to make him feel better. Some idealized him by saying how 'great' it was for a group leader to be that 'open,' actually practicing what they preached. Shame faded into repulsion as he struggled to make amends for his self-indulgence with a stilted lecture on self-responsibility.

In the final analysis, it was an event that helped them to clarify what the role of a group leader should, and should not, be. "We're here for those who come to our programs," Ben said, "our own state of disarray usually isn't helpful to the group." And Jock agreed. All he really had to do was reveal his own lack of presence; the details were irrelevant. In this, and in many other ways, they were issuing their own challenge to the "let it all hang out" ideals of humanistic liberalism, but rather than joining the reactionary backlash of the 1970's and 80's they preferred to develop a new framework in which the core values could be preserved. Their own alternative to the 'New Morality' was being constructed around the pillars of personal boundaries, inter-personal respect, and self-responsibility. These things, they believed, would offer the widest range of choices for people living in harmony.

So those who remained fascinated by what was going on between the two leaders, continued to watch and fill in the gaps with their own speculations. Most residents and participants wanted to know more but were afraid to ask. Some did take the risk and were given direct and truthful answers, small delicacies to be taken back into the dreams, fantasies and theories of coffee breaks, beach gatherings, bedtime chats and leisurely strolls along woodland trails.

Within the informal hierarchy, those who were judged to be closest to 'the boys' were offered, and usually accepted, a special status and a share of the mystery. Collectively they represented an impenetrable barrier but, individually, they could be drawn into sharing time and words with outsiders. For most casual workshop visitors, all of the resident staff were insiders and even the most recently hired and lowly serfs were offered respect and, in some cases, power by wanderers seeking to replace their group leaders between sessions. An outsider who spent considerable time in such company could then be granted a third-level status by carrying the shared secrets back to the waiting ears of the uninitiated. Workshop participants who had become 'regulars,' enjoyed the tacit privileges of affiliation with the community in accordance with their assumed significance to Ben and Jock. Then there were the stars, old friends and workshop leaders from the outside world, who remained in their company and even slept over at the house down the bay. Who knew what secrets they carried? Who would dare to ask?

To most of the observers it seemed clear that Ben was leading the way and, to many, it seemed that whatever his long term ambitions Jock was under the control of his mentor. So they identified with Jock and stood back in awe from the man who might lead them also. Some were even jealous of the guitar-strumming, flute-tooting hippie doctor and would fantasize about taking his place, and his privileges.

But the most dedicated Ben watcher of them all was beginning to get the picture. The illusion of Ben leading was being created by Jock's own dedication to following; Ben himself had absolutely no interest in leading anybody anywhere. What others saw as control was based upon the manner in which they distributed power in their own minds, and they gave it to Ben. But Jock was finally becoming convinced that Ben really didn't want it, so whose illusions of power were being addressed? Such insights were changing his views on the dynamics of power . . . leaders and followers, tyrants and oppressed, diseases and patients . . . who is really in charge? . . . and of what? From such questions, came more questions and more ideas.

In a vague and abstract way, Ben and Jock saw themselves as participants in the human potential movement, but their experientially based ideas frequently found them in direct conflict with other notable contributors. When most of the heavy voices were proclaiming that their followers could become anything they wanted, simply by putting their minds to it, Wong and McKeen proclaimed that, in their opinion, "change is not possible." From their own experience, they had come to conclusion that trying to change the self, at the deepest level, was a cop-out, a way of anaesthetising the anxiety of non-being. When Martha Crampton, the mother of psychosynthesis, announced at a symposium in Washington, "You're not your body and you're not your mind," they stood up from the third row and chorused "yes we are." And, when popular humanist Ken Keyes told a large gathering in Oregon, "Your behavior is not you," Ben immediately stood up and said, "Well, if my behavior isn't me, then I don't know who it belongs to." On this occasion, Keyes responded to the challenge. "When you have evolved to my level of consciousness, you'll understand my point," he replied. Jock fumed. Ben walked out. Jock followed. Meetings with Ida Rolf, Fritz Perls and Jean Huston ended in a similar way. "If they're not going to engage with us personally, we may just as well read their books," Ben concluded. Jock, who was painstakingly dismantling his deified image of 'the teacher,' agreed. "What really pisses me off is their arrogance, their belief that they have the 'truth,'" he complained. "Jesus, not one of them has presented any evidence for their claims."

As Jock struggled to relinquish his hold on Ben as his teacher, he could certainly appreciate why the spectators of the Cortes Centre for Human Development would see Ben as the leader. By this time Jock's quest for professional equivalency had become a sincere search for the potentials of his own contribution, though he continued to make comparisons. "Ben does things so elegantly," he pondered, "how can I be seen in his positive light without being over-shadowed?" But such questions did not detract from his appreciation of the aesthetics of Ben's work. There were many times when Ben seemed to be moving so completely with the unfolding revelations of a person, that it became one flowing process.

"How the Hell did you do that?" Jock asked during a mid-session coffee break. As usual they were the first to arrive at the Lodge, had drawn mugs of freshly brewed coffee from the old urn on the foyer table, and had gone to the small meeting room, before the others began to arrive. This ritual, replacing the old Chicken Coop Rule, was designed for them to 'check-in' with each other, clear any matters that might linger between them and discuss whatever plans they might have for the rest of the session.

"You want to know why Norman finally chose to talk about his father in my work with him this morning!"

"Yea . . . and while you're at it, how the Hell did you know what my question was about?"

"Because I know you well enough to understand the function of your question."

"Function?"

"Yes, function. Remember the carport affair? Let's talk more after supper. Right now, I'm off to the bathroom." He left Jock searching for the point. Surely he wasn't going to be subjected to another bout of senseless ridicule over the damned carport. He had already paid the price on that one. He had designed the simple structure, to blend with the rustic architecture of the house, using materials that were already available on the property. He had selected the tools they would need and calculated the approximate time it would take them to complete the project. He had set the time of construction according to their schedule and arranged for the additional lumber to be delivered the day before. Only then, with the new timbers stacked neatly alongside the driveway, did Ben point out that, with that design, in that location, no car could ever be driven in or out. "Okay, then I'll do another design and we'll build the fucking thing somewhere else," he had said.

"Oh no, let's build it your way and not drive the car into it," said Ben.

"Very funny."

"No really," Ben had persisted, "let's turn it into a storage room, or a solarium, or a . . . "

"Oh, go to Hell!"

Now it was all going to be dragged up again for Ben's amusement. Ben returned from the bathroom with the unmistakable anticipation of pleasure on his face.

By the time they had finished supper that evening, Jock had rekindled his curiosity about Ben's intuition. Dabbing the last remnants of chocolate mousse from his mouth, he decided it was worth one more try. "I want to go back to the question I asked this afternoon," he began. "It wasn't just about the work with Norman. It's something that often happens between us, but it becomes even more obvious when I stand back and watch you work with someone else. You begin with a question and the other person completes it, as though they know already what it's about. You make an observation to someone else's question and the door suddenly opens. Somehow, you're able to see exactly what the other person is after, even when they're not sure themselves. I've been trying to figure out what you mean by the word 'function.' My guess is that you ask yourself, 'what does this question, or this gesture, mean in the life of this person, right now. What's its function?' Where I would treat the words or behavior as abstractions, requiring some response from me, you keep the person as your focus and they make the connections. So, where I find myself dealing cerebrally with one abstraction after another, you're working with the structure as a whole. I end up looking detached and obtuse, while you remain personal and insightful." He slapped the palm of his hand against his forehead. "There I go. You see? I just did exactly what I'm theorizing about. I took you out of the picture, went off into my head and left you sitting there. Hell, instead of coming to know you better, I actually abandoned you."

Ben thought for a moment. "Yes," he said finally, "I think the question becomes a theoretical issue for you and you respond like a scientist. You may finish up with the right answer, but it may have nothing to do with the question. When we work on projects around the property, you seem to need a fully fleshed out, nicely sequenced, design before you can take the first step, whereas I sense what the task calls for and move straight to the action. But then, when you do get the plan, you work with such beauty and precision. What really interests me is that you're quite different when you write poetry. Here you seem to begin with an inner knowing . . . an immediate sense of the whole, and you just express it. It's the same with your music. Where I need the order of notes and the sheet music, you just play. And when you're fully invested, the sounds are just beautiful, like your poetry I think you're probably this way in your sexuality though, in this area, I'm still trying to figure out how you got there."

"It's something to do with creativity isn't it?" asked Jock. "Your work with people and my poetry and music are creative acts. They come from a different place. It's hard to describe or account for them and yet they're just there, in form and function." He paused to let the thoughts seek their own destination. It didn't take long. "Ah, so now going back to my question at coffee break today, I *know* how you do it, but I don't *understand* how you do it."

"Okay, so that deals with Norman this morning," Ben said. "Let's talk about the carport affair. It's a great example."

"No, forget the bloody carport. I'm now trying to figure out how you move so easily to the whole picture and I get caught struggling with the pieces."

"Well if you drop a stone in a pond, you get carried away with watching the ripples, where I'll watch the stone sink to the bottom."

"Ah, so you ignore the ripples."

"No, of course not. I'm well aware of the ripples."

"So how do you attend to both?"

"Go and dig out your old carport plans and we'll talk about it."

"No."

"Okay" Ben said, rising from his chair. "Let's have another coffee."

Over coffee the carport incident was buried again under a series of light-hearted exchanges. Then, sitting by the fire, Jock started the wheels turning again. "It always seems to me that I'm following your lead, whether we're sitting here at home or working together in the session room. I'd like to feel that our contributions are more equal. It must be so obvious to everybody else that I'm not where you're at and I'm scrambling to get there."

"Yes, " Ben said. "I think you want to be on my island but you never really arrive because you're so preoccupied with trying to find and interpret the charts. My island becomes the objective and I become the elusive object. It's as if you were trying to capture me and take over the island, even though you know that's impossible. You can only find me by exploring your own island."

"I know that too," said Jock. "But being in relationship with you is such a relentless process of self-scrutiny. You set such standards, have so many expectations."

Ben tried again with a familiar refrain. "I have my own standards and expectations, but, by letting you know about them, I don't *set* them. You make me into an examiner and I've no interest in that. By doing this you make me the reason for your self-scrutiny and I become the externalized object of your own morality. I don't want that either."

"Yes I do," Jock agreed, "but so many people seem to do that dance around you. Do you remember Margaret Wood's comments about you carrying morality and me carrying excitement?"

"Yes, and I agree with that. Because of who we are, we attract particular people and particular issues. It's all part of the fascination," Ben said, his body moving gently with the music in the background.

"So you don't blame me when I use you in this way?"

"No. Sometimes I feel sad about not being seen for who I am, but if you keep the issue open and on the table, I know we'll find our way back into harmony. That's what this thing is all about. It's not about being right or perfect, we are both right and perfect to begin with . . . just like Chopin. What we hear is all Chopin, and when we allow ourselves to move with his music, we live in accord and the experience is beautiful. Just as what we have is beautiful."

"It doesn't seem very beautiful when you get pissed off."

"When I really hurt is when you give up on what we have. When you leave me, I assume that you don't attach any importance to the moment, so you kill it. That moment, and that opportunity, can never be re-captured because it was never allowed to be. All you can do is begin again." He got up from his chair, took the old iron poker from the hearth and gave the fire a perfunctory prod. "Any relationship can only take so much before it dies or, even worse, becomes embalmed in senseless repetition." He propped the poker against the cobbled mantle and sat down again. "I see so many people who have embalmed their relationships. The relationship has died but they embalm the body and, for some reason, keep the other around. I won't live that way. I would kill my own life energy if I did."

"Well you don't do that, so I must be to blame for each death along the way," Jock said with more than a hint of self-derogation.

"No I don't do that, but I don't blame you for the killing either. Your choice is simply your choice. I just hurt for each moment killed and I withdraw. It's like a mourning for something beautiful that was never allowed to live. This, I think, is where the issue of control comes in. When I do this, you sense that something's wrong and you want to correct it, but that can't be done, no matter how much effort you put into it. The more you dance, the more you create an energy that people interpret as me controlling you, but that's not the issue. You used to get upset because I refused to accept apologies, but what's the point of an apology? There's nothing to forgive. Again it may look from the outside like I'm controlling or manipulating you. But I want a certain kind of experience of being with people. If it's not your choice to do this I don't blame you, but I will find someone else. And that may sound like 'either love me or else' but in my heart it's just a fact of life."

"But you do get into punishment and revenge, we both know that."

"Oh, I'm perfectly capable of punishing to assuage my own hurt," Ben acknowledged. "And I'm sure there's an element of revenge in there somewhere. It's like wanting you to feel a little of how I feel. Sometimes when you storm off and come slinking back I'm inclined to stay with my contempt, just to keep the pot boiling."

Jock knew the scene well. So many times he had wanted to throw off his feelings of inadequacy and escalate the fight with his own weapons of abandonment. He could go anytime, anywhere, to Hawaii maybe, and leave this arrogant despot to live alone on his own bedrock of contempt. What a lesson that would be!

"I hate your contempt," Jock continued, "particularly the sarcasm, but I never experience it as revenge. You always seem to keep it contained and on topic. God knows, if you really wanted to unleash your wrath, if you really wanted me to hurt, you'd have more ammunition than I would want to deal with."

"Yes, I do play with revenge," Ben admitted, "but I never really live it."

"God, you're so diligent in your stance that people must make their own choices and you have so much love for the world, but your contempt has to live in there somewhere,"

Ben rose again and placed another log on the fire. "Well I see so many people making their own choices and I rejoice in that. But then," he added with a laugh, "I seem to have contempt for so many of the choices they make. It's like they're totally invested in creating their own unhappiness. And I think, 'If only they would see things the way I see them, then they'd be happy.'" He sank back into his chair and they laughed together.

Jock watched the bright new flames burst and curl up around the blackened log. Were they really new, or simply the rejuvenated spirits of those that had gone before? What did it mean to declare a fire dead anyway? "Yea, I see the same stuff," he said, "but I become invested in what they *should* do and end up falling flat on my face." They laughed again. "So many of the choices I make around you and around our relationship must be painful for you, even though I might learn to take no direct responsibility for your pain. I'm glad you hang in with me, even though I continue to fret about my contribution."

"That's *my* pleasure Jock. I try to understand how difficult it must be for you to stay in relationship with me. You know, nobody has stayed with me the way you do. Working with you is an exciting and aesthetic experience for me. What you experience as playing second fiddle is you learning to play your own instrument, in your own unique and creative way. The more you do this, the more our music becomes syncopated. Right now I think you're searching for the perfect score, just like you looked for the perfect carport design, but when you allow the poet and the musician to come forward, our felt experience becomes harmonic. When you bring all of this into our life and our work together, then we create together. I've experienced this in some of our work in the sessions and, when that happens, all of the hurt and all of the pain just becomes life along the way."

"But why does it always seem so painful and harsh?" Jock asked, trying to make it not sound like a complaint.

"It's not harsh," said Ben, "it's really quite beautiful. You know Chopin's music has been playing even when we haven't bothered to listen."

In the summer of 1982, Jock received a telephone call from his ex-girl friend, the one who had left him to work on an alternative relationship in Vancouver. She was obviously distressed. Her new boy friend was beating her up, breaking into her house and issuing threats against her and her children. She wanted know what she should do. Jock was troubled and empathic to the young woman's plight. On the other hand, he realised that he was in no position to intervene or give advice. "I'm not your therapist," he told her, "but, as your friend, I think you should get some professional help." He gave her the names of Judy Sellner and Joann Peterson and suggested she get together with one of them. Immediately after the call, he spoke to Joann about the situation and they waited for the contact. None was made.

Some weeks later, when Ben and Jock were leading a five-day 'Come Alive' in Edmonton, Alberta, a friend who had been looking after their property on Cortes telephoned to say that the house had been broken into. The break-in occurred while the friend had stayed overnight in Campbell River to take an evening course. "The house is a bit of a mess inside, but I don't know if anything's missing," he said. "Well, you'd better call the police and we'll be right back," they told him.

Going through the house with an R.C.M.P. officer, they looked helplessly at the disarray of their personal space and were overwhelmed with a sense of violation. The police officer was puzzled. There were no signs of forced entry and he concluded that the intruder had used a key. From that point, the intruder had been quite systematic; telephone and computer modem lines had been cut; office drawers had been rifled and left open; and, in the bedroom, the closet had been broken into and video tapes had been taken.

In the week following the incident, there was much speculation among the staff of the Cortes Centre. The most commonly held belief was that the boyfriend of Jock's ex-lover was responsible. One staff member, who knew the young woman well, claimed to have conclusive evidence to this effect.

This hypothesis became an unequivocal reality a few days later when the boyfriend telephoned to confirm that he had the 'explicit' video of Jock and the woman. Giving no details as to how he acquired this tape, he told Jock that he wanted to erase and return it to them. In consultation with the police, it was decided that they would not press charges if the tape was returned as promised. Three days later the blank tape arrived in the mail. For a time the tape, along with the spectre of its missing contents, was returned to the darkness of the bedroom closet. Still shaken, they returned to their business.

It was Peggie Merlin's suggestion that they should consider the national television talk shows as a legitimate outlet for their educational aspirations. Ben was not overly enthusiastic about the idea but the prospect struck a chord with Jock. A week or so later they received an invitation to appear on the syndicated "Alan Thicke Show" taped in Vancouver. Jock telephoned immediately and accepted.

"Alan Thicke and I were in pre-med together at Western," he said with the telephone still in his hands.

"Oh really," said Ben with apparent indifference as he continued to sort through the shelves of his record library. "How come he made it and you didn't?"

Jock ignored the remark. "As a matter of fact," he said, "I gave Alan his first real break in show biz."

Ben had the next line. "No kidding," he said scrutinizing the jacket of a rediscovered LP. "What did you do, lend him your lecture notes?"

"No, that would have meant instant stardom. All I did was let him take my place in introducing Simon and Garfunkel at a

University concert. It didn't seem like a big deal at the time. I doubt he'll even remember."

"Perhaps you should remind him," Ben said, returning the record to its place among the rest.

During their first on-air appearance, Jock did remind him and Alan Thicke did remember.

The Denman Hotel in Vancouver provided flowers, fruit and champagne, courtesy of an attentive hotel manager. A chauffeur-driven limousine, surrounded by a group of giddy young girls seeking autographs, waited to take them to the studio. They scrawled their names with appropriate humility, slid into the back seat and giggled. When they arrived at the studio, they were met by a studio host who showed them to their dressing room. On the door was a star-spangled sign with their names embossed in gold. Fighting back the urge to clown around, they went in, closed the door and stared at themselves in the mirror. "Do we look like stars?" Ben asked.

After visiting the make-up artist, they were ushered into the greenroom to await their call to the studio set. "You're Wilt Chamberlain," said Jock, looking skyward and holding out his hand. "Yea, how'ya doin?" came the voice from on high. "Fine, how are *you* doin?" Jock asked with the deepest voice he could muster.

It was the first of many experiences in the greenroom. "Hi, I'm Michael J. Fox."

"Hi, I'm Bennet Wong. What do you do?"

"Oh, I'm an actor."

"Hello, my name's Jock McKeen, what do you do?"

"Well right now I'm doing a show called 'Mission Impossible.'"

For Jock, it was all captivating and dream-like and they would chuckle and snigger together in their dressing room about their own illusions of playing among the stars. But over the space of three or four shows they began to recognise how lonely many of the famous guests seemed to be. Some would come down to their dressing room for brief chats or an opportunity to experience acupuncture. The illusion was beginning to fade.

Then, in one fleeting episode, Jock stepped in and out of his Hollywood romance. It was late at night when the elevator doors opened and a group of guests from the show were standing together in a state of obvious inebriation. With rolling eyes and slurs of acknowledgement, they greeted him as one of their own. One of them, a young blonde actress whom Jock had coveted many times from his seat in the movie theatre, was in particularly bad shape. In an effort to extricate herself from the elevator, she stumbled and fell at his feet. He helped her up and then escorted three of the revellers back to their rooms and quietly closed the door behind him. "I was just horrified at the dehumanization and indignity of it all," he told Ben later. "It wasn't a moralistic stance on my part, only doing what I thought should be done. Whatever fantasies I might have had just turned to nausea. I was actually stunned by it all."

Jock continued to foster relationships with the television in-crowd and they maintained a sporadic schedule of appearances on other talk shows. At the same time, requests for them to give presentations to various groups and at conferences across Canada and the United States reflected a growing interest in their work and their ideas. Those who attended their itinerant workshops or made the journey to take the programs on Cortes island were also drawn in to the charisma of the men themselves and many, of course, were fascinated with the nature of their relationship.

The financial viability of the Cortes Centre for Human Development continued to be based upon the success of the Wong and McKeen programs. The initial thirty-thousand dollar carry-over from Cold Mountain swelled to a capital reserve of seventy-thousand dollars but, increasingly, the new revenues were being derived from a single source. "It was their earnings that kept the place afloat," observed Board member Jim Pryor. "Many of us on the Board were convinced that they should move out on their own but they seemed committed to the joint-enterprise. As it happened the costs of maintaining the Cortes facility were very high and, when Jean Weaver announced that she wanted to sell the place, there seemed no point in keeping the thing going. As a fiscally responsible Board, we were concerned about the amount of rent being paid out each month. Eventually, three of us decided to resign from the Board to underscore our belief that Wong and McKeen should establish their own base of operations."

Jock took the first step by acquiring a 'do-it-yourself' business incorporation kit and filing an application with the Province of British Columbia. To assure themselves of a place to work, at considerably less cost, they rented the April Point Lodge on Quadra Island in the off-season for particular programs. Here the newly incorporated company of 'PD (personal and professional) Seminars Ltd.' began to establish its own foundation. Unencumbered by the trials and tribulations of other agenda, April Point was a place where they could focus exclusively on their work, and they loved it. Dianne Anderson joined them to provide kitchen and registration services and Jim Kearney came along as Site Manager.

Through their work at April Point, they began to realise that planning and operating programs could incorporate the same aesthetic principles and qualities that had become so important to them in other aspects of their lives. Here again the thoughtful blending of resources and the efficient flow of energy could generate pleasure and satisfaction. For them, this was not the driven business ethic of cutting costs, increasing production, achieving targets and maximizing profit margins. Working without waste, operating to the extent of their potential, making their work as widely available as possible and providing a secure foundation for the continuation of their ambitions were matters to be appreciated and enjoyed for their own sake. Money, as a resource, was to be carefully blended into the whole. The whole operation was designed and monitored in an office that once served as a carport on the "Ch'i" property.

The early success of PD Seminars was applauded by many at the Cortes Centre. When that property was put up for sale early in 1982, some members of the existing community tried to raise the necessary capital but the price was simply beyond their reach;

it was also beyond the reach of Wong and McKeen who were still paying off the final dregs of the debt incurred through their association with Mike O'Kane.

On the other hand, April Point could offer only limited accommodation for the programs of PD Seminars. A highly popular fishing lodge, its availability for other purposes was restricted to particular times of the year. In addition, it's physical characteristics were far from ideal for personal growth purposes. They considered using "Ch'i" as the centre of operations but, again, the restrictions of the existing physical facility appeared monumental. Another location and another facility had to be found.

Though still personally in debt, PD Seminars had risen rapidly to fiscal viability. In addition, the sale of "Ch'i" would raise enough capital for a healthy down payment. It sold quickly. With the money in their pockets and a sense of urgency in their hearts, they boldly went off to knock on doors and present offers, regardless of 'listings' or For Sale signs.

They began their search on Quadra but could find nothing to suit their purposes. Moving over to Vancouver Island, they explored the possibility of purchasing the Silver Springs Motel, a six unit complex on a half acre of land in the middle of suburbia. Then, while applying for a loan at the bank, the manager told them of a resort on the east coast of Quadra Island that had been taken into receivership. It was far more extensive than anything they had imagined; five acres with a hotel, a dock, a marina and a restaurant. But the bank was anxious to sell, although, for whatever reason, the manager refused any loan and referred them to the manager of another bank in Campbell River. Their application was successful and within a matter of weeks they would be the legal owners of Taku Lodge.

But there had been conspiracy and deception in the deal. On taking possession they discovered that the facility had no foreshore rights and that, without such access, the business prospects for the resort were dismal. Through questioning local government officials they discovered that these rights, acquired through a simple application and the payment of a fifty-dollar fee, had been retained by the bank. Returning to the realtor who had sold them the property, they were told that the bank would be prepared to relinquish the rights to them for fifty-thousand dollars. At that point, there was nothing the bank manager could say or do to preserve the sale. Immediately, they took the matter to court, the judge found in their favour, and they resumed their search.

By this time, the excitement was being overlaid with a growing desperation. It was June and registrations for their Fall programs, to commence on September 15th, were substantial. Their brochure had contained the ambiguous invitation to "come to a Seaside Resort on the sunny west coast," but would-be participants had every right to know where to find this place. Dianne Anderson, now the Registrar for 'PD Seminars Ltd.,' was perturbed. Running a gift shop on Quadra, that also served as a clandestine Registrars' Office, she waited anxiously for something that would replace her beloved community on Cortes.

Without appointments, they dropped in on any hotel, motel or resort that looked remotely suitable for their purposes. Many were experiencing hard times but none of the startled proprietors were ready to hand over their businesses to the two strange men on the doorstep. Sipping coffee at 'Schooner Cove,' a multi-million dollar four-star hotel and marina complex near Nanoose, they found that the owners of that establishment were prepared to make a deal. With a substantial bank loan levered from the success of PD Seminars Ltd., together with the money from the sale of "Ch'i" they could have bought an equal partnership in which they would have been responsible for the total operation of the facility. Under any other circumstances it would have been a wild proposition, but time was running out. They negotiated to keep the offer open; "As the last resort," said Ben (pun intended) and resumed their quest.

On the way to a meeting of the Humanistic Psychology Association in Toronto, they glanced through the newspapers at Vancouver Airport and came across an advertisement that promised to solve their problem. "Looking for a Hotel or Resort?"

it read. "I won't stop until I find exactly what you're looking for. Please call Laurie Pochinko." So they did call, and he did promise.

A week later they began another tour of Vancouver Island, this time in the company of Mr. Pochinko. Old beer parlours, broken down motels, renovated pig farms, dilapidated hostelries and a variety of unclassifiable establishments were paraded before them, but now at the end of July, none could have been converted in time for the September programs. Despondently they began to consider portable trailers, and even tents, as a makeshift way of keeping PD Seminars in business.

At first glance, Taylor Bay Lodge on Gabriola Island was not promising. The Lodge itself was little more than a broken down shack with a dingy restaurant, seedy bar and dubious sleeping accommodation for thirteen. An adjacent wooden structure with an outside bathhouse and two small cottage-type buildings made up the rest of this dejected settlement on the rocky shores of Taylor Bay. Whether from inspiration or fatigue, they both agreed that the place "felt good." So, they bought it.

They took possession on August 1st, 1983. Immediately they invited Jim Kearney, who had been acting as the manager of PD Seminars, to join them as property manager for the new resort. It was clear from the outset that this facility would be legally and fiscally separate from their Seminar business. Although much of the revenue for the former would be provided through a contract with the latter, they were determined to ensure that both enterprises would be financially viable and self-sufficient.

With the demise of Cold Mountain and the Cortes Centre, Jim Kearney was looking for a new place in a world that, for the most part, he rejected. He had found his niche as a participant in the 'tell it as it is' community. This was his mark of recognition in the only world that made any sense to him. Here he could be openly judgmental, confrontational and stubbornly committed to his ideals. In this place he was fully engaged and, with his many practical skills, had proven himself to be an excellent contributor to the collective spirit of both Cold Mountain and the

Cortes Centre. He was also an unabashed admirer of Dr. Bennet Wong, and the prospect of creating a new community on Gabriola, along with the opportunity of continuing his association with 'the boys,' was a lifeline. So, when they invited him to become a partner in the new business he was constrained only by his own lack of money. A loan from Ben and Jock, and another from a relative, enabled him to buy a ten percent interest in the future of the Resort business and, with his property manager's salary assured, Jim found himself investing in a different kind of world, and a different kind of future.

Initially the challenge was pragmatic. Taking over the existing operation of Taylor Bay Lodge, Jim cooked for the restaurant, Dianne Anderson worked as general helper and barmaid, while Ben and Jock served tables. At the same time, they all knew that, without extensive modification, the facilities could never be stretched to accommodate the programs due to commence in six weeks. Trailers and tents seemed to be the only solution.

On a whim, Ben and Jock dropped in at the Lyndal Cedar Home Sales Centre in Nanaimo, a short ferry ride from Gabriola. These pre-designed and pre-cut packaged buildings would have blended well on the property but the salespeople were adamant that a construction time of six weeks was impossible. By chance, a representative of the Vancouver branch became involved in the discussions and he introduced the idea of bringing in a ready-made building by barge from the Lower Mainland. Having examined the specifications, they concluded that one of these buildings would be large enough to provide them with adequate space for a session room. They drew up site plans, obtained the transit permits to haul the building through the streets of Vancouver, and made arrangements to float the building across to Gabriola Island. Then, as the final preparations were being made, their calculations revealed that, even with the most ingenious procedures, the anticipated high tide would be a foot too low to ensure a successful landing. The only other alternative was to bring the building ashore at a cove around the corner but, since they balked at the prospect of cutting a sixty foot swath through the forest, the project was abandoned.

Finally, the developer hired to locate and finish the structure said, "Oh Hell. Let's just build the bloody thing from scratch." And they did. Working miracles, he obtained all of the necessary approvals, transported all of the necessary materials and, on September 15th, an almost completed building stood ready to welcome workshop participants and other visitors to "Haven-by-the-Sea."

CHAPTER NINE

Father Jack Sproule quickly caught the gossip around the happenings at Taylor Bay Lodge. As priest of the Nanaimo Parish of St. Peters, Gabriola Island was part of his territory and it was his business to know of such things. The news that Bennet Wong and Jock McKeen were setting up shop at the ailing resort stirred an old excitement.

A year or so earlier, he had been discussing the life of Christ with Sister Marie M. when the good Sister had told him how two men had offered her glimpses of what Christ might have been like; one was the philanthropist John Vanier, the other a psychiatrist named Bennet Wong. Fascinated and horrified by the comparisons, he had decided to investigate. He had heard that Bennet Wong and Jock McKeen worked in partnership at a place they called the Cold Mountain. Allegedly their story was one of relationship, something he had longed for as a boy and had sought, to no avail, through the Church. So he had gone to Cortes to find out for himself. Rather than meet with the two men, however, he had been handed a pamphlet through the door of the lodge without greeting or invitation. Then he had left.

Now Bennet Wong and Jock McKeen had come to him and he was ready to try again. "I enjoyed a total responsibility for the spiritual well being of the people of St. Peter's," he recalled. "I wanted to be prepared for any questions regarding the Centre. I puffed up my sanctimonious self and went to Haven to inspect, or according to my religious language, I went on a 'visitation.' Over the years I have often been struck by the prevalence of coincidence in my life. I take this to be a confirmation of my belief that all things are trying to be one. In spite of this fact I never imagined what was in store for me."

Immediately in store was the delightful experience of Ben and Jock suspending their manual labours to welcome him. Open to his enquiries, they matched his curiosity with their own questions and observations about the Church, the priesthood and, most specifically, about Jack Sproule. It was an easy encounter and words and laughter flowed into the sunset of late afternoon.

He accepted their invitation to stay for supper. "That evening we talked about the Church, spiritual growth, presence and relationship. To my astonishment their activity is a fundamentally priestly activity. I was entering into what was foreign to me, as I discovered them recapturing the original priestly task of 'calling people forth.' In this they were keepers of a most original and universal faith. We laughed about my watchdog intent in coming over to Gabriola. They seemed to pull their weight with God and their spiritual stance and posture challenged me as a priest. I sensed they were not primarily about religion, although they valued the best in religion. I quickly realized they were about life—followers of life! The world for them was open. In the seminary, I grew up in a fix, my soul muscle-bound."

Sitting in the modest dining room of the old lodge he found himself moving comfortably beyond the demands of his calling. "I soon realized they were able to see the integrity of differences and had no need to identify themselves as Christians or members of any religious tradition. They were open to my own and familiar with the best within it. In our conversations, I discovered my narrowness; that I worshipped the sky but stayed indoors. Eventually they challenged me to reclaim elements of my own tradition that I never fully appreciated. In fact I had disowned some of it, claiming a different birthplace . . . I wasn't always a Roman Catholic. I returned to Nanaimo, tuned up but had no place to go."

What Father Jack took with him was a sense of communion. Nothing had to be created, it was already there with two pairs of hands outstretched, inviting him to participate. "Time was away and somewhere else," he mused. "Three people, with one pulse, talking deeply. Wearing my halo cocked, I decided 'They are of the Kingdom.'" It was a romance he had once wrapped around the Church.

Ben and Jock enjoyed their meeting with the parish priest. Both had experienced long associations with the influences of the established church and were deeply involved in the matter of their own spirituality. For Ben, the encounter rekindled his childhood fascination with religion, although he had long since abandoned his belief that God might speak to him directly through the gospels and sermons of other men's words. But he remained curious about the Church as another institution that assumed its authority through the illusion of protecting uncertain life from certain death. Though he continued to value the Church's reverence of the spiritual, he had no personal need for such an institution. He had come to believe that all life is revealed through its full expression and its continuity affirmed in its relatedness to all other life.

Jock, who had come to regard the established Church as the distant watchdog of a questionable morality, was intrigued by their encounter with Jack Sproule. Through his spontaneous and personal revelations, the priest had presented his religion as a fallible and distinctly human enterprise. He talked about the Church in a manner that seemed almost heretical, and his theology appeared to be more embedded in his own experience than in the exhorations of the Gospels. Having considered Gnosticism and Buddhism as possible resting places for his own elusive spirit, Jock was taken with the idea that Christianity might not be as alien to his soul as he had come to believe. On the one hand, his interest was abstract and academic, on the other it was personal and profound. But, when Jack Sproule said, "You and Ben are doing God's work here," Jock detached himself from the Sacred. The idea that they were the missionaries of some undisclosed authority made no sense to him. For Jock, their work was simply their work and, if there was any grand design behind it all, it could only be revealed in the doing. There was no goal to be attained and no manual to be followed.

For his part, Father Jack was convinced that, in Bennet Wong and Jock McKeen, he had found the combination of innocence and courage that he had once hoped to find in the Church and, ultimately, in himself. "Their version of intimacy, the unmediated revelation of one self to another, must surely breathe life into the sinner," he told himself. It was an exciting prospect that filled him with fear. From the safety of his priesthood, he chose to hand the project over to them, to stand in awe of their relationship, to wonder at their innocence and fear for their lives.

Caught up in his fascination, Jack Sproule became a frequent visitor to the Haven property, sometimes appearing unannounced, sometimes to keep appointments. When Ben and Jock invited him to sit in on a body-work session he held his breath and accepted.

Unsure about the legitimacy of his place in the group, he watched the strange ritual unfold. It was gentle at first, like soft music calling the congregation into communion. He noticed how the two doctors spoke in whispers as they went about their business and the voice of his fear became silent. When the young man lying at the centre began to tremble, the priest was ready to reach for his robes and declare his place as a healer. But, as the groans turned to screams and the man's fists hammered down on the mat, the healer recoiled. "Where is your ministry now, priest?" he asked himself. "Can you fix this man's agony with your words and your prayers? You're not needed here. Why don't you run away like you always do?" But, without his priestly vestments, there was no place for him to go. So he sat, with his own fear, his own loneliness, his own pain and waited for the young man on the mat to pull him through. Only in the final minutes, when the music played and the three figures wrapped their arms around each other, did Jack find his way back into the sanctity of his calling.

"Maybe body-work is about real presence, about pain and rebirth, about communion," he suggested, as Jock walked him to his car. "Sure," Jock answered, "I can live with that." They embraced and parted.

As the ferry pulled away from the Gabriola pier, Father Jack sat in his car and savoured his acceptance at Haven-by-the-Sea. Ben and Jock, were able to laugh at his snobbery, inviting him to take the courage to look inside. He had been seen and accepted in this arrogance, pulled out of his pain of loneliness. He giggled to himself about the presumptuous and arrogant shadow that once had seemed so burdensome and intolerable. He glanced at himself in the rearview mirror and laughed out loud.

"Haven" rested gently in nature's hands, waiting for whatever designs its new inhabitants might have in mind. Jim Kearney was there, content in the legitimacy of his new association with his old mentors. Dianne Anderson was there, ready to replace the lost community of Cold Mountain. Carol Stewart was there, bringing her Tarot Reading gifts to the new programs. And others followed.

Xanon Jensen came. After completing his term as maintenance undertaker for the corpse of Cold Mountain, he spent a few months teaching English in Japan, but returned ready to resume his quest for "family." Mark Fraser and Louise Belisle came. This was their chance to break free from the chains of tradition and learn a new way. Joann Peterson came, committing herself to longer periods of time away from her family and professional responsibilities in Washington. They were joined by a number of Cold Mountain refugees who transferred their homes, and their allegiances, to do whatever was needed in seed-ing, nurturing and, hopefully, harvesting the produce of the new enterprise.

Others committed themselves to various program contributions. Jerry Glock, having established a counselling practice in Vancouver, brought his partner Shirley Ronner to intern workshops and lead groups together. Peggie Merlin, now a leader with the Context Training Organization and a close friend of Jerry and Shirley, threw her impressive teaching and administrative skills into the collective effort. Trish Grainge, a professional actress, and her partner, lawyer/writer Leslie Pinder, came to weave their own dramatic style of enlightenment into the Phase One Program, along with Lily Jaffe and her masks of the unconscious. Physician Peter Nunn and his wife Heather came up from their 'Pain and Stress Centre' in Victoria to show Phase One participants how the New Medicine was bringing the patient back into the healing.

And behind it all, Ben and Jock involved themselves in every aspect of the project while planning and overseeing operations. Beyond their work with the programs, they occupied themselves with the pressing issues and problems of establishing life in a tired out facility that seemed determined to resist their occupancy. Countless holes in the lodge roof played hide-and-seek with strategically placed buckets until, finally, the basement flooded and the heating system failed. Plumbing and electrical systems were in dire need of repair; doors and windows were rotting; and the grounds bore the unmistakable signs of years of neglect. Only the new session building stood strong and proud, though starkly naked and incomplete. For Jim Kearney and his staff of trouble-shooters, these were merely the fascinating overtures of things to come.

Ben and Jock were happy. Finally they had a place of their own where they could live and work without the constant accommodations to competing agenda. They had no business plan in the traditional sense, but they had learned much from their experiences at Cold Mountain and were determined that the new organisation would serve to express their own principles and beliefs. To this end, the notion of 'responsible responsiveness' was central to the scheme. Rather than set targets for rate of growth and margin of profit, this principle guided them toward creating an environment in which they could respond personally to those who spent time on the property. To draw in more people than they could reasonably relate to would result in a shift from a climate of personal contact to one of anonymity. They had no interest in offering an impersonal service designed to accommodate the demands of its 'clients.' "We're a pair of skunk cabbages," Ben said. "If people want to come and spend time with us skunk cabbages, we'll make them welcome, provide a comfortable environment, offer them our programs, respect their privacy and expect them to be responsible for their behavior. If people don't come, then we'll know that skunk cabbages are out of favour and we'll do something else." The Sheratons and Club Meds had nothing to fear from such competition.

But people did come. In fact, they came in numbers that stretched the human and physical resources to the limit. On one occasion, Xanon found himself kicked out of his humble room in the Lodge in order to make way for a visiting program participant. "This really pisses me off," he told a sympathetic ear. "I feel like a dispensable commodity around here. I hear them talking about personal respect and personal responsibility, well I'm a person too. It's not like we're all here for the fucking money." But, saying nothing to 'the boys' about his discontent, he quickly settled into his new accommodation in a dilapidated outbuilding and resumed his commitment to building the ark. "It was a long time before their philosophy finally hit home," he said many years later.

In fact, Xanon had briefly stirred up a matter that dated back to the days at Cold Mountain. The issue was the distinction between 'responsiveness' and outright expediency in dealing with the changing client demands and market conditions. Since Ben and Jock did adjust some of their methods in line with changing social values, and since they continued to attract increasing numbers of mainstream participants, there remained a covert suspicion that some intrinsic value was being sold over the counter. "Sure times have changed," Jock said at one staff meeting. "What we did in the sixties and seventies no longer fits for people but that's no sacrifice on our part. Our principles don't necessitate three month programs or semiclad encounter groups, these are only forms, infinitely varied and infinitely changeable. That's not what our work is about. Responsiveness is about understanding where the other person is at; making it clear where you're at in ways that they can hear, and moving from there. This is quite different from selling what you think other people want."

It was a difficult distinction for people to grasp, particularly in the light of Ben and Jock's constant assertion that both PD Seminars and Haven-by-the-Sea were businesses committed to achieving independent and sustainable levels of economic well-being. Many assumed that this made money the central value and, since this was offensive to those who believed that they had already purged the materialistic bile from their souls, the message was resisted or distorted. What they failed to understand was that the central value was not about money at all—it was about aesthetics. At its core, it addressed the simple pleasure of creating forms that could stand alone, without losing their relatedness to other forms. As with an individual life, so with a painting, a symphony, a building, or a business enterprise. In this sense, the two revisionists stood accused of abandoning principles that were never theirs in the first place.

At its very essence, Haven was intended to be a place of work. Again, those who had rejected the traditional idea of work as a means of earning money to support their non-work pleasures struggled to find an alternative. "We were expected to go way beyond the call of duty," Xanon recalled. "We were supposed to love the place, doing whatever was needed to be done. We were given shit for not picking up cigarette butts or ignoring a visitor to the property. Yet the wages were minimum and, as far as Ben and Jock were concerned, it wasn't our show. It was easy to feel exploited at times. But we were all committed to them and, somehow, we managed to create our own reasons for sticking around." But those who used loyalty as their reason, were given little in return for such devotion. "Loyalty, like morality," they were told, "is a commitment to some external frame of reference. The idea usually involves some form of self-sacrifice and we want no part in this."

The idea that work on the Haven property should have its own intrinsic worth was part of a value that made perfect sense to Ben and Jock. Whatever the popular theories of management were proposing, they did not see it as their task to motivate people through external rewards, group generated commitments, or threats of deprivation. The staff were there by *choice* and for them to care and be responsible was a commitment to the self more than to the organization. This, after all, had been at the heart of their teaching from the outset. Contrary to some speculations, this expectation was not driven by financial considerations, although efficiency of effort and the parsimonious use of resources were passionately advocated. Paradoxical as it appeared to those who wanted to work *for* someone or something, this type of diligence was the only way to fully experience the aesthetic value of work for its own sake.

"You just dropped three nails," Jock said to a young contractor who was working on the roof of the Lodge. "Do you know where they fell?"

"Probably not," came the reply, "but it would take me ten minutes to come down and find them. That would be a waste of my time and your money."

"You can protect that time and money by being more careful. Meanwhile, those nails will be lost for ever. I'd like you to come down and find them."

"This doesn't make any sense," he muttered on his way down the ladder.

"It makes all the sense in the world to me," Jock said.

At that time, business management across North America was picking the bones of the humanistic movement in psychology, creating Theory Y and methods of Organizational Development (OD) designed to revolutionise management practices. Many advocates found support for these trends by examining the success of Japanese industry with little concern for, or understanding of, the cultural context. At the heart of these ideas was the belief that organizations could replicate a family mentality and that productivity would increase the more the workers had a sense of involvement in the overall operation of the organization. It would have been so simple for Wong and McKeen to jump on this popular bandwagon and appeal to democratic family values but, typically, their own style of humanism brought a distinctively different set of values into the equation. "I've never seen a democratic family," Ben said. "I have no idea what it might look like."

Dianne Anderson remembered the death of democracy well. Ben had decided that it would be a good idea to have peacocks on the property but left the decision to a vote among the first group of pioneers. This was not untypical of Ben. He had tried to create consensus throughout his chairmanship of the Cold Mountain Board and he had been sincere in his desire to ensure that all points of interest be considered in any decision. When the peacock vote was registered as a resounding "No" he left the room saying, "Well, I'll live with that one decision, but from now on there'll be no voting around here." It was abundantly clear that the ethic of majority rule would not operate at PD Seminars and Haven-by-the-Sea any more than it operated within the programs.

Occasionally they would use the terms "family" and "community" to describe the ethos of the enterprise but, here again, their definitions were quite different from the interpretations made by many staff members. Time and again they insisted that this was not the surrogate family that Xanon had been searching for, nor was it the intentional community that would replace Dianne's loss of her Cold Mountain support group. But people held onto their dreams and struggled to create their own versions of Utopia. Beyond these illusions, nobody really disputed Ben and Jock's influence or their leadership and in this lurked the most dangerous illusionary monster of them all. They were natural leaders; highly charismatic, brilliant in their work, graceful in their ways, caring in their relationships and powerful in their presence. Together they became the internal voice for those who felt unsure; the secure footing for those who felt unsafe; the validation for those who felt unworthy; the mirror for those who felt unseen; the alternative for those who had dropped out with nowhere to go. Tempted by power they could have pronounced themselves gurus and created a closed cult community. But such a prospect was the antithesis of their ambitions.

"It took me years to begin to understand what they were really about," Xanon acknowledged in his reflections on the old days. "I used to think they were cold and calculating when they told people to get on with their own lives. I wondered how they could be so close at one time and then so distant, like nothing had happened between us. I loved them, man, and they seemed to love me but then they'd disappear. Sometimes, when I thought I needed them the most, they'd just walk away and get on with their own lives. Sometimes, when I felt really fragile, they'd come down on me like a ton of bricks. I'm still trying to figure out some of this stuff, but Jeez, like I'm still learning man. What I do know is that if they'd done what we wanted and allowed themselves to be all the things we wanted them to be the whole thing would have turned sick."

Had they not been so contained within their relationship, the demands for Ben to become the universal father would have flooded in from all directions. On the other side, the temptations for Jock to be drawn back into the seductive opportunities for power and influence were there in abundance. Without each other, both were destined to be alone, though each in different ways and for very different reasons. As it was, Ben had the relationship he wanted, Jock had the mirror to keep himself clearly in view and, together, they worked to establish and maintain a carefully delineated contact boundary with the rest of the world.

Both were aware of the potential dangers, but where Ben felt no need to take evasive action, Jock found himself becoming increasingly vigilant and protective. From the garrison of their relationship, he assigned himself the task of 'Master of the Gate' and, somewhere within this self-designed job description, he had incorporated a mandate to protect Ben. In this role he could be arrogant, dismissive and abrasive, calling on the rich resources of his contempt to keep intruders at bay. "Can I have a minute with you guys?" asked one presumptuous intern. "Yes, and this is it," Jock replied. While the intentions might have changed, it was the same outward presentation of self that had turned so many people away during the early days at Cold Mountain.

However the official position was interpreted, those who lived and worked at Haven-by-the-Sea did experience a growing sense of community. True to the nature of social life, status hierarchies, sub-group affiliations, in-groups and out-groups, personal personae and individual roles began to shape the patterns of everyday interaction. And, however close or distant 'the boys' seemed to be, they always were securely placed on the central pinnacle . . . the ultimate point of reference for individual and collective realities.

Some, like Mark Fraser, were delighted to be there and relished each new opportunity to learn. Along with Louise, he participated in the programs, interned whenever possible, and paid for the privileges by working around the property. "It was a great deal for us," he said. "Where else could we have learned so much with such honesty and generosity? We were not part of the 1960's Cold Mountain romance and we were in our own relationship. Our vision was to create for ourselves rather than just be with Ben and Jock. We saw how others were building their whole lives around them and those of us who understood the transference stuff, like Jerry and Shirley, Joann and Peggie, Trish and Leslie, could see what was happening. Not that there's anything inherently wrong with transference. Hell, I'm just a little duckling waiting to transfer myself, but I know I don't have to sign up for life. It's the awareness and the commitment to individuation that makes the difference."

345

Louise understood. She had been with Rajneesh in India, and lived in an ashram in the Kooteneys of British Columbia prior to meeting Mark. She too was searching for her own vision of community but discovered the trap in the illusion. "I found that I had to hate the Swami before I could bring myself to break away from the ashram," she recalled. "I could have stayed and worked it out, but I don't think you can work out all the transference with the transference object. It's great to have other relationships and other realities to do this. Ben and Jock seem to understand this; they have their lives and we have ours."

Having completed their commitment to the first nine months of training, Mark and Louise spent a considerable amount of time in Vancouver, forming close and lasting relationships with Jerry Glock, Shirley Ronner, Peggie Merlin, Trish Grainge and Leslie Pinder. Together they shared the stuff of their own personal work and practised their versions of honesty, vulnerability and intimacy. With lives and relationships beyond the shores of Gabriola Island, they enjoyed the very best of what Haven had to offer.

There is no doubt that Mark and Louise understood the phenomenon of transference far beyond the understanding of most psychologists and psychotherapists. Acknowledging their own susceptibility, they made a conscious and dedicated commitment to exploring its place within their own personal and professional lives, while searching for ways to reclaim themselves from its seductive clutches. Yet, some years later, they detached themselves from Wong and McKeen in order to follow Paul Lowe, a renegade disciple of Rajneesh, who appeared at Haven-by-the-Sea in 1994. Jerry Glock and Shirley Ronner joined the parade. As one long-serving member of the Haven community remarked, "If Mark, Louise, Jerry and Shirley are still looking for gurus, what chance is there for the rest of us?"

Back in 1984, the resident 'community' continued to welcome guests, register participants, make beds, clean rooms, cook meals, serve tables, repair buildings, plant gardens and take the programs that urged them to bring together the joy and pain of their lives in an integrated and responsible way. Most were fully dedicated to the task and, together, they found themselves creating a world in which vulnerability, honesty, responsibility and caring replaced the more conventional norms of defensiveness, strategic deceit, selective blaming and conditional affection.

Delving into the substance of their lives, most of the residents looked to Ben and Jock for support and guidance. But the co-directors were not that interested in becoming involved in the affairs of their employees and found themselves cast as distant role models, to be observed and emulated. While their apparent detachment stirred up some resentment, most staff members knew that by changing their status to that of 'program participant' they could be assured of Ben and Jock's undivided attention. So, like everybody else, they saved up their money and paid their fees—it was all part of their commitment to their own growth. Many went on to become interns, contributing to the Haven programs and taking their newly acquired knowledge and skills out into the 'real' world.

Business boomed. Registrations for the one month Phase One Self-Awareness program necessitated a waiting list, even though the number of participants was increased from the mid-twenties to the mid-thirties. Many of these people stayed over for Phase Two, a program of the same duration made up of a series of shorter workshops designed to explore the self in relationship with others. Again, the registrations for the whole program, and for each component, began to surpass the number of available places. The other four week residential program, "New Horizons," picked up many people who had completed both Phases and were ready to look at the more theoretical and philosophical aspects of the work. This was particularly popular with physicians and other health professionals interested in holistic practices, Chinese medicine and, particularly, the theory and practice of acupuncture. Many practising therapists came to learn the Wong and McKeen styles of Gestalt Therapy, Psychodrama and, of course, body-work.

The flagship of the fleet continued to be the five-day "Come

Alive" program and, though they experimented with larger and larger groups, the waiting lists continued to grow. In responding to such interest, they continued their practice of taking this program on the road as their calendar permitted. In diverse places and venues across Canada and the United States, groups of people explored themselves and each other and many of these people wanted more. Invitations to speak and give media interviews came in a steady stream and, where possible, they continued to respond. And, of course, all of this translated into more registrations for the programs at Haven-by-the-Sea.

By the Spring of their first year, every program was stretching the physical resources of Haven to the brink of discomfort. Finally, they managed to pay off the debts of the Mike O'Kane fiasco and were ready to invest in the development of their own project. They took a small business loan through a Government sponsored program but the banks refused to provide additional loans for further property development. "If you were a trucking company we'd have no problem in advancing you money," they were told. "But, even though your business is booming, we know nothing about what you guys do and we can't take the risk." Jock, particularly, was distressed and offended by such ignorance. "To Hell with them," he said, "let's do this thing on cash flow and projections." So they did.

Conscious of Jim Kearney's ten percent partnership in the property, they invited him to maintain his proportion of the ownership. Jim had no savings of his own and was not inclined to incur more personal debts so, with the construction of another large building, his actual stake in the business of Haven slipped from ten to three per cent. "Let's call it five per cent anyway," they suggested and Jim agreed.

The new building, christened "Kingfisher," provided them with another large session room as well as many more double rooms for program participants. This made it possible for Ben and Jock to move out of their rental accommodation down the road and create a modest on-site apartment for themselves. It was the start of a building and property development that subsequently created new residential buildings, session rooms, hot tubs, swimming pools and a theatre.

Some of those who had participated in the programs and who went on to 'intern' with Ben and Jock became involved in a formalised program of training leading to the "PD Diploma in Counselling (Dip.C.)." Of these, Joann Peterson, Mark Fraser, Jerry Glock, Shirley Ronner and Peggie Merlin in particular, emerged as leaders in their own right and their involvement in workshops and training became integral to the work of PD Seminars. Lilly Jaffe, Carol Stewart and Trish Grainge continued to develop their own personal growth seminars to complement the work of Ben and Jock within Phase Programs. Receiving professional fees for their contributions this group established what was to become known as the "Core Faculty."

In addition, Ben and Jock looked around for notable leaders in the humanistic movement who might draw their own followers to Haven-by-the-Sea. Jim and Judy Sellner, now well established specialists in couples work; Lee Pulos, widely recognised for his work in the field of human consciousness, and Paul Reps, the Zen Master who often appeared from nowhere, could all attract enough people to their own workshops. Virginia Satir, disenchanted by recent developments at Esalen and discouraged by her followers in affiliating with any other 'growth centre,' chose to grace the Haven property with her substantial presence in a number of scheduled workshops. "This is where I feel truly cared about," she said and even contemplated purchasing a house adjacent to the property. As a gesture of their own regard, Ben and Jock renovated the lounge in the old Lodge and, in a touching ceremony, proclaimed it to be "The Satir Room."

Jim Kearney worked hard. Each day he and his maintenance crew added to their list of required repairs, replacements and renovations. With the face and function of the property changing by the week, each new development brought another set of challenges. Jim worked with the kitchen and cleaning staff, played host to emotionally charged groups that descended and departed en masse, and catered to those who had chosen Haven as a place to relax or recuperate.

Then there were the expectations of his senior partners, rigorous Zen-like standards drawn from their own work and translated into prescriptions for life around the property. But Jim had dedicated himself to 'the boys' and committed himself to living the philosophy to the full. He interned programs to keep himself sharp and rarely hesitated to show his disdain for any staff member or program participant who failed to respect the principles. For him it was a very serious business. "Jimmy was my intern in Phase One," recalled Mark Fraser. "He could be a self-righteous son-of-a-bitch at times, particularly around the issue of self-responsibility. He would jump on people; it didn't matter who they were."

Jim's grim determination to make the philosophy live at Haven was not matched by a similar level of commitment to the overall organizational design, however. To operate as an independent business, Haven-by-the-Sea would need to draw revenue from sources other than PD Seminars, but Jim always seemed less than enthusiastic about the prospect of non-program people hanging about the property. Even ideas like "Agatha Christie; Find the Murderer" weekends were met with an indifference that, left unchecked, would have closed the bar, cancelled the Saturday night dances and encouraged the public to stay away. In Jim's world, there was no place for frivolous escapes from the work to be done. Ironically, this was a commitment to Ben and Jock as much as to himself.

For many people, Haven was indeed a serious place to be. Some who came to the programs talked of being afraid as they entered through the gates of the property. And while Jock or Ben might ask innocently, "What are you afraid of?" they rarely heard the only answer that made sense: "I'm afraid to die." People came to face the pain of issues long denied and pushed themselves to higher levels of personal awareness and responsibility. Some found themselves groping helplessly in the existential blackness, while others tentatively picked away at the layers of deceit, even allowing others to see what was behind. But in every pain there is a gift, in every fear lies a freedom and behind every closure is a gate waiting to be opened.

When darkness turns to light and the complex gives way to the simple, the human spirit soars. And so it was at Haven-by-the-Sea. Through the work of PD Seminars, participants who entered the mythical 'abyss' generally found their own way through and came out smiling. Some giggled, others roared with laughter. And, together, they celebrated; not so much the celebration of something achieved as the unrestrained acknowledgement of simply being alive. In her own celebration, participant Judy Burrows wrote:

And there it was, the laughter,
bubbling up from the pit of my stomach,
beneath the sadness, under the fear.
I am alive, I know life.
No need for harps or angels,
no saints needed here,
no day of judgement . . .
only lights, only colour, only now,
stretching forward, past forever.

And, as always, Ben and Jock, along with the others, were there, supporting the travellers, witnessing their anguish, rejoicing in their ecstasy and applauding their courage. This was the work they loved and the place they always wanted.

But they also had to deal with the dark side. In October, 1983, the matter of the video tape stolen from their Cortes property came back into circulation. The husband of the woman on camera called Jock to say that a copy of the original tape had been sent to him, along with a threat that other copies would be distributed unless money was paid to the ex-boyfriend. Having reestablished his relationship with his wife, the husband was appropriately outraged and suggested that he and Jock should 'get' the blackmailer. Wondering if the issue would ever be laid to rest, Jock let the caller know that he had no interest in getting anybody. He explained that, technically speaking, there had been no theft since the original tape had been returned. He suggested that the husband may wish to call the police and make a complaint of blackmail. Taking this as a refusal to co-operate, the voice on the line became resentful and the man hung up.

But the caller did follow Jock's advice and, in lodging his complaint, handed the tape over to the police. Unaware of the implications of this seemingly rational decision, Ben and Jock went back to their work.

By this time, there was a definitive tone and structure in all of their workshops that could be, and frequently was, replicated by other leaders, both within and beyond PD Seminars. What could never be replicated, however, were the contributions made by each man through the spontaneous and creative properties of their partnership. And it was their ability to bring these resources into the moment, and respond to whatever was taking place that gave their work its unmistakable trademark. Drawing from the wealth of their own experience, they incorporated many of the standard tools of their trade—techniques established in the fields of bioenergetics, Chinese medicine, encounter group training and psychotherapy—and added many of their own creation. But these were only the vehicles; what really mattered was the direct experience of one self in relationship with other selves. This is what the sessions at Haven-by-the-Sea were all about.

Nobody has bothered to turn on the session room lights. Nature has set a mellow tone for the morning and her melting mood draws the gathering into a hushed communion. Outside, dark saturated clouds drift over a heavy ocean and shred themselves among the spiky firs and cedars of Taylor Bay. Alone, or huddled together in twos and threes, the final stragglers pull themselves away from the warmth of the Lodge with its glowing log fire, french toast, granola, coffee and herbal teas, and slide through the drizzle to participate in this, the first full-day session of another residential program. Hanging their damp outerwear on rough wooden pegs in the lobby, they place their shoes side by side along the walls and pass quietly into the darkened session room to find a place for themselves within the waiting circle of bodies and cushions.

Last night they broke the ice with warm-up exercises, defying convention through strange personal exchanges, looking shakily into each others eyes, tweaking noses and giggling with embarrassment. They were urged to 'breathe,' to take in the fullness of the moment, to feel the energy shifting through varying degrees of 'presence.' They took risks, feeling the first rushes and blushes of life beyond the defences. Then, before retiring to their shared accommodations, they clustered back in the Lodge, lingering in the glow of their nervous self-revelations and assuring themselves and each other that, whatever might lie ahead, Ben and Jock would be there to guide them.

But today another reality has set in and the mist of this January morning wraps itself around the hopes and fears that the night protected. Only a week ago it was Christmas.

Jack Sproule is here. Now confident in his relationship with the leaders, he has taken a cushion adjacent to the four interns and close to the spaces respectfully reserved for Ben, Jock and the supervising intern, Joann Peterson. Bev Brown, a parishioner who had taken it upon herself to look after the parish priest, had given him the registration fee as a Christmas present. "It's like open heart surgery without an anaesthetic," she had told him. But the cautious Father still used his special status with the Haven authorities to find out if any of his parishioners had registered before making up his mind to take the plunge. Even with their amused assurances, he spent much of last night scanning faces, listening carefully to each personal introduction and concocting the parish emergency that might call him back to Nanaimo should his priestly persona be in need of protection. This morning he is more at ease.

Allison, Bob and Madelaine, the other three interns, stare out into the circle. The group is still raw, its embryonic personality waiting to be fleshed out and moulded with the stuff of individual lives. Talk is still shallow and tentative but, to the sensitive eye, much is already being revealed. Joann has asked the interns to look beyond the shrouded faces and scattered patterns; to speculate about the underlife, while acknowledging their own expectations and fears. It's a formidable challenge.

Allison, twenty three years old and nervously playing on the edge of her first internship, finds herself avoiding the assignment. Perhaps they will see her watching them and wonder what she's up to. Judy Burrows is too preoccupied to notice the intern's hesitant gaze, however. The doctors say Judy has Multiple Sclerosis, an elusive and incurable disease. Ben and Jock have talked about this being something to do with the ingrained patterns of her life and Allison believes them. But it's easy to believe such things when your own life isn't on the line . . . at least not in the same urgent way.

So what convinced Judy, at the age of fifty, to select Haven as her primary treatment option? Was it desperation, or courage? Listening attentively to the man sitting by her side, only the strain in her face and the weariness in her eyes bear testimony to her story. For years she watched her father's growing desperation as his body closed down on life, first on the outside, then creeping slowly up from the core. In the final moments she had looked into his eyes and seen the terror. Then, some years later, the haziness in her own eyes and the tingling numbness in her arms and legs seemed to herald the same journey into helplessness. This she fears more than death itself. Already she has made arrangements with a physician friend to administer medication that will put an end to her impotence should the final trail become inevitable.

A psychologist by profession, Judy has tried to make things right for others since the day her father walked out of the door and commanded that she, a lonely six-year-old, take care of her mother. Four years ago she saw Ben and Jock work with a small group of people in her home town and had made up her mind that, should any of her own family require the resources to confront serious illness, she would find a way of getting them out to Haven-by-the-Sea. Now she is here in the service of her own frozen spirit. In her mind, the genetic explanations and prognosis sympathetically put forward by the hospital neurologist compete with a growing belief that, in spite of the medical evidence, her diagnosed condition has something to do with *her* at some profoundly personal level. She has heard Ben and Jock talk about physical disease as a 'process' involving body, mind and spirit and, typically, she wants to examine whatever options may be open to her. This particular course puts the controls back into her own hands. Perhaps her battle to control life can somehow be transformed, setting her own life free. "Life is not your enemy," Ben told her. "Maybe it's time for you to stop fighting and learn to surrender." At dinner last night, she heard of another woman with the same diagnosis who had managed to bring the life back into the stuttering circuits of her nervous system. Her name, she was told, was Peggie Merlin.

Bob, a dedicated therapist and seasoned intern, easily sniffs out the dis-ease lurking inside Chris Channing's meditative posture. Sitting erect with eyes closed, legs crossed, hands on knees, palms upward, Chris's body is tightly held as his unquiet mind tugs down on the corners of his mouth. He breathes from the chest. There's an energy around him that holds others at a distance. A twenty-seven year old computer technician, he let some of his troubles be known in a carefully worded letter in which he described himself as a "loner," an "introvert" and "emotionally labile" . . . a term picked up from a therapeutic consultation. Earlier this morning, the interns were told how he had become chronically depressed when his marriage fell apart after only three months; a recent evaluation raised questions about his competence at work; and, somewhere in all of this, was a suspicion that the police were interested in his week-end activities. Bob has decided to take a particular interest in the life of Mr. Channing.

Madelaine, a practising physician from Eugene, Oregon, is

attending her fourth program as an intern. Struggling to contain some of her own personal demons, she scans the group and urges herself to become present for the work of the morning. Last evening she was drawn to Frances, a young social worker, and Brian, another physician in general practice, but both are lost in the fog of her preoccupation. In fact, Frances is sitting only two cushions away, her body angled forward, her eyes alert and her mouth set in a fixed, ambiguous smile. She seems to sense when others are looking at her, responding with an almost imperceptible nod of the head, a raising of her black eyebrows and another painful push on the smile. Frances has trouble relating to men and has heard that Ben and Jock are specialists in the art of relationships. She also suffers from a crippling array of allergies, but that's not why she's here.

Jock switches on the lights as he, Ben and Joann enter the room and take their prescribed places. The session begins.

Joyce, a resident of Gabriola and frequent visitor to Haven-by-the-Sea, is the first to work in the centre. In a delightfully flowing and at times humorous gestalt, she turns Bob into her brother and, under the direction of Jock, plays out an archaic pattern of sibling rivalry that has found its way into her marriage. Her laughter, shy and tentative at first, then bold and extravagant, ignites the comedy of other unfinished childhoods and the others laugh with her.

But Frances can only nod and smile. While the group gathers around Joyce, Frances remains on the outside. The music ends and the others move back to their cushions. Frances remains motionless, peering around the circle like an unwanted child at a birthday party. Finally, her sadness finds its own reflection in the waiting eyes of Jock McKeen and the energy in the room becomes hushed and centred.

Frances is afraid of men. She's afraid of Jock, though she has now moved willingly to be with him at the centre. She finds him strange and exciting. She thinks he must be gay and feels safer. Her smile returns but his sadness stares back at her. Men . . . she wants to talk about men. She talks, but the words skirt

356

the issues. Acupuncture, yes, she'll try that. He's a doctor. Needles and more words, but this time with tears. She is shaking. They're saying things she doesn't understand. More words, the sense doesn't matter any more, only the fear must be contained. They are all around her now, closing in like a net around a captured salmon. Where's Daddy now? Only the doctor can save her. She reaches out and the net dissolves into an endless ocean.

Jock, on his knees, his arms around her, rocks gently backward and forward. There's music from somewhere. She wants to curl up until every shade of feeling has been drained away. On his lap now, her face buried in the softness between his chest and shoulder. "I feel very close to you right now," he whispers. She looks up and weeps for his tears. "I want you to look at the people Frances," he says, but the idea repels her and she burrows in deeper. "Look at their faces Frances, what do you see?" She wants to be left alone, to disappear down the slipway again, never see their faces, never see another face, but she knows he will leave her, they always have. She raises her head above his shoulders and her eyes turn inward. There's nothing to see and nobody but Jock to see her. She is trembling again. The music is louder but nobody moves in. The doctor has saved her.

"We believe that each person is born with an essential self," Ben explains. "In order for this self to express its unique characteristics it works to create a boundary within which it can grow and develop through experience. The skin is one boundary, but the self stretches outward into the world and back inside the skin according to the particular state of exploration. This self boundary is in constant motion, like the pseudopods of an amoeba, reaching out into the environment and then withdrawing back into the core. Its surface can be imagined as a semipermeable membrane that reaches out to make tentative contacts with the world. In relationships, it touches other boundaries, returning each contact to the experience of the central core. What happens at this contact boundary is taken into the self experience and, when the self is allowed to speak, it will instruct the boundary to respond in a particular way. If the self is silent and unknown, the boundary cannot respond, it can only react, sensitised to the outside world but oblivious of the inner core. At the most elementary level you can probably understand how unpleasant contacts will create a tendency for a child to withdraw and pleasing contacts will stimulate the child to move out. As we move through our experience of life, the process becomes more complex, though the basic patterns may remain fixed."

Jock takes over. "Many of the problems we see in our work with people are actually boundary issues," he says. "People who give themselves away by not saying their real 'yes's' and real 'no's,' for example, have poorly established boundaries. Some people will distance themselves from the world with extensive boundaries, while others will not insist on their boundaries being respected, ignoring the fragile centre of life on the inside. There are people who create inflexible walls rather than sensitive and malleable boundaries in order to protect themselves. For them, the world is a potentially hostile place and, in fear, they literally wall themselves up. From this perspective, then, Frances's work was very much about boundaries or, in her case, the lack of them."

She nods in agreement.

"But she seems so alive and engaged in the world," says Joyce.

"I judge this to be more vigilance and fear of the world," Jock says.

Frances nods again but has nothing more to say, nothing more to give, not even her smile. The others nod back. She has taken her first step.

The mid-morning break is over and the group settles. Outside, shafts of sunlight break through. In the session room someone has slipped a soft rock tape into the stereo and the steady rhythm moves the bodies of the early arrivers, some of them dancing in self-engrossed gyrations at the centre; others flop casually around the disordered circle of cushions, rapt in conversation or alone with their thoughts. Again, Chris Channing sits behind his mask of meditation but this time he is less concerned with the immediacy of his surroundings. In a brief exchange with Bob over lunch, Chris let it be known that he is ready for some individual work and this information now rests in the hands of Ben and Jock.

The leaders arrive and the group settles into the customary process of 'clearing' (issues and experiences carried over from the morning brought back into the collective pulse of the group) and 'temperature taking' (an opportunity for people to become present by reporting their inner experience at that precise moment). By now they already understand that thoughts and feelings held back may become as flotsam and jetsam jamming the flow of energy.

It's Jock who conducts this procedure and it's Jock who finally looks over toward Chris. "Bob tells us you want to do some work this afternoon, Chris." Jock is very much the initiator and choreographer these days. Not too long ago it was Ben who generally took the lead and many felt short-changed if their work was delegated to the assistant. Now Jock's confident presence draws the eyes and the energy into the centre. And behind him Ben presides, always watching, always visible, always there, providing the frame for the delicate tapestry of their work.

Chris lays lightly on the mattress—the uneasy lightness that comes from a body-felt terror of touching down. Jock, on his knees at one side, and Joann, sitting on a cushion at the other, urge him to 'breathe.' He looks up at them through pale hollow eyes, his mouth turns down in an expression of disgust. He forces breath through his lips. More instruction, more resistance. Jock moves closer, whispers softly and reaches for the box of needles at his side. Joann continues her gentle encouragement. His belly contorts in a burst of energy and he slams his legs down on the mattress, stemming the flow at the groin. They pull back.

"I can't do it," he gasps.

"You want us to stop what we're doing," suggests Jock.

"I want . . . I want to let go but I can't."

"Why don't you just breathe and let it come in your own way Chris? Joann and I will stay here at your side," Jock says.

They watch his body soften as the breath in his chest begins to thaw and melt into the tight drum of his gut. "That's good Chris, just let it go," Joann says, checking Jock with her eyes. They take his wrist pulses, Chinese style and, with permission, Jock delicately slips a needle beside each knee. There will be no more body-work. There's a flow now but they let him move to his own rhythm, rolling gently from side to side. Jock stays with him, rocking backwards and forwards as if pulled by the same invisible chord. "So you can do it Chris," he says. "It seems hard for you to know that." Chris looks up at Jock.

With Joann slipping discreetly back into the circle, the two men begin to talk together, Jock crossed-legged on the vacated cushion and Chris perched on the edge of the mattress. With his body breathing easily now, the story continues, Jock gently nudging the action along as a master actor might massage meaning from the lines of a lifeless script. Whenever he pulls his energy back, however, the words trail off into silence. Carefully, Jock extracts and repeats three lines from the heart of the story and invites Chris to repeat them, filling them with whatever feelings might be found in the expression.

"I'm nobody's servant." Mother's shadow at his bedroom door and images of a childhood traded in for fleeting illusions of love.

"I hate the word 'girlie.'" The torturous journeys home past sneering bullies and tittering tarts hanging around the school yard.

"I'm a dreamer, not a loser." The faces that turned away from the student who never quite made the grades for law school.

His head down and face hidden, he plays with the lines, slowly and tentatively at first. But Jock urges him on, "Tell *them* Chris," he says. "Tell them all, look at them, they're all listening now. Look at them." Chris raises his eyes to the group but the energy runs out. "Let them know, Chris," Jock continues. "Now it's your chance to speak. Let them know how it is for *you*." Chris's eyes turn crazy as the fear pushes through. His lips curl back from his teeth and they wait for the sound to come.

"I'm nobody's servant . . . I'm nobody's fucking servant," he screams.

Jock looks across at Bob and gestures with his hands. A baseball bat is efficiently and unobtrusively delivered. Chris needs little tutelage or encouragement. Once in his hands the bat cracks down onto the mattress, the words ripping into the silence. Then again, and again, wave after wave pounding against the walls of judgment with each swing of the club. "I HATE the word 'girlie.' I'm a dreamer not a godammed loser. I'm nobody's. . . ."

Finally it breaks, the bat falls to the mat. Chris unlocks a hand from his knee and reaches out. Jock takes the hand into his own. "It's good to be with you here," he says quietly.

Chris comes back through his tears. "Would you say the words again?" Jock asks. Chris meets him with his eyes. "I'm nobody's servant. I hate the word 'girlie.' I'm a dreamer not a loser." The words are clear now, the voice full. The faint glimmer of a smile plays in the young man's cheeks and Jock joins him with an unrestrained grin of his own. "Play it again Sam," he says and the laughter breaks between them. "I'm nobody's servant. I hate the word 'girlie.' I'm a dreamer, Oh God am I ever a dreamer. . . . " The scene has shifted into the absurd.

"ALRIGHT!" screams somebody from the edge. "BRAVO!" cries another and, on that cue, twenty-five fellow losers cut loose with laughter and applause.

Chris beams back at them as Jock helps him to his feet. Music, bright carnival music, courtesy of Ben, springs from the speakers. Still hand in hand, they stand before their delighted audience, swaying together like figure skaters after a gruelling routine. Jock moves easily to the cadence, his hips nudging his partner into a reciprocal motion. Clapping hands, banging feet and screaming encouragement, the circle drives the tempo along. "Okay, let's do it one more time Chris . . . I'm nobody's servant."

"And I hate the word 'girlie,'" Chris sings, breaking from Jock and wafting his arms in the air. The audience screams its approval and Jock slips quietly into the wings. "I'm a dreamer not a loser." Chris's voice warbles with the music and he punches out the words to the rhythm, rolling his head from side to side while shifting his pelvis to the off-beat. It's his audience now and he's playing them like a trouper. Conjured up from the prop cupboard by one of the interns and passed through the choreographer, Jock McKeen, a straw boater and silver-tipped cane are slipped into the hands of the performer. Tossing his head back and dropping his jaw in a gesture of comic surprise, he dons the hat with a jaunty tap, thrusts the stick beneath his arm and proceeds to cavort around the circle. "I'm a dreamer, I'm a dreamer," he sings. "You're a dreamer, you're a dreamer," they tell him in spontaneous unison as the music moves to its final crescendo.

Suddenly its over. He stands in front of the mattress, makes a sweeping bow, boater in hand, and then, in a dramatic expression of exhaustion and finality, he throws his arms and legs out to the side and collapses backwards onto the mattress.

In a single motion they rise to their feet, some with hands raised above their heads, others whooping deliriously. Peeking out from behind his imaginary curtain, Chris sees Jock smiling in his direction and amid the surrounding din, the partnership is reawakened. Rising from the mattress for the last time, he goes over to acknowledge the bond. The two men embrace. The music strikes up once more, the circle breaks, and the dancing begins.

At the final session of any Wong and McKeen program, many emotions are stirred. For some, the anticipation of returning to the familiar evokes an excitement of new potentials. For others, the prospects are laced with apprehension, even fear.

This time, the leaders have invited the participants to devise their own parting ritual. Jock has agreed to be Master of Ceremonies. A makeshift stage has been set up at one end of the session room. Stage left, Jock McKeen watches the audience settle onto their seats. Stage right, Judy Burrows is preparing to make her entrance. Jock moves to centre stage and faces the audience.

"If you look at life from a structuralist perspective, seeing all things in their state of relatedness, then saying 'good-bye' becomes really important in the continuity of our experience of self and other. Many of us don't like saying 'good-bye' so we avoid or deny the experience. You have chosen not to do that today. Rather, in your ceremony, you have chosen to investigate the experience. . . ."

Choosing to investigate. That's what these last few weeks have been about for Judy. Weary from a lifelong struggle of trying to make things right for others and facing the diagnosis used to account for the death of her father, she came here looking for options. She had hoped that Drs. Wong and McKeen might have some answers. Now she knows that her disease comes from the inside, that she is at the centre. She is no longer a helpless victim of nature's designs. And it all happened here, in this room, with these people.

Jock leaves the stage, Judy moves to centre. According to the script, she is to say nothing—just stand there and take in the experience. She scans the audience until her eyes meet those of Jan, her roommate. Judy has never had a woman friend before, at least not one who was prepared to delve beyond the illusions and into long-forsaken wisdom. With this woman, Judy has found the strength she was seeking.

A few seats away sits Jack Sproule. Three weeks ago, Judy asked him to participate in her healing ceremony. She wanted him there as a priest and he wore his vestments for the occasion. But, rather than call upon God to intervene, Father Jack waited patiently for the spirit of Judy Burrows to lead the way. And it did, through the sensuality of her body and the opening of her heart.

Behind and to the right, she picks out the face of John Taylor. A humble and self-effacing man in some respects, he can also be arrogant, bombastic and crude when the mood takes him. But, around her, he has been gentle and caring, curious about her experience and adamant in his belief that she is not bound to follow in her father's footsteps. They are unlikely friends, their worlds and beliefs running far apart, but Haven is a strange and unexpected meeting place.

She looks for Ben. He is standing at the back but without the familiar figure of Jock at his side. There's a warmth in her stomach but her head is empty. She takes a breath and a strange sadness dampens the glow. So many times he has been there to fill the empty places but now, when she seeks only to acknowledge his presence, her mind is blank. How can she detach herself from something still unknown, yet to be discovered? Perhaps she's not yet ready to say 'good-bye' to Bennet Wong. The idea intrigues her.

She turns to face Jock, still standing in the wings. She recalls a time when, emerging from a piece of body-work, she found herself staring into the face of this man who, in most circumstances, would have sent her scuttling behind her well-manicured defences. Yet, seen through the openness of her own heart, his eyes were alive with the love and compassion that, she decided later, must have sprung from some universal source. Perhaps his poetry and his child-like love for Ben were drawn through the same channel. Perhaps Ben walked with him in the place where she spent that brief moment in time.

Judy Burrows crosses her hands over her heart, smiles gently through her tears and leaves the stage. Phase Two awaits.

CHAPTER TEN

The two-man police station on Gabriola Island was, by law-en-forcement standards, a relatively benign and friendly place. On the walls, posters of local regulations mingled with notices of upcoming community events and letters from classes of local school children thanking their 'friends' for showing them around and telling them about "poleese work." Sitting at his desk, be-hind the counter that separated the simplicity of the law from the chaos of the world, the lone officer sighed and scribbled into his book of 'facts," muttering each word to himself before com-mitting it to posterity. The door opened and closed but his dedi-cation to duty kept him engaged to the completion of the sen-tence. Then he looked up. Behind the counter, two figures pa-tiently waited.

"Well if it isn't the good doctors from Heaven," said the Ser-geant, drumming his fingers on the desk to the tempo of his own good humour. "So what brings you here? Last time was when you and your cronies were up here singing carols at the door . . . must 'ave been Christmas." He laughed. But this was no festive occasion and the two visitors were obviously anxious to push the conversation into their current business. Becoming suddenly official, the Sergeant closed his notebook, picked up another from the shelf behind and walked over to the counter. "So what can I do for you gents?" he asked.

Jock spoke. They had received a telephone call from a friend whose daughter had once dated an R.C.M.P. officer. Some months after the dissolution of this relationship they had met again by chance at a bar in Vancouver. Over a perfunctory drink, the off-duty officer had interrogated her about the "goings on" at Cold Mountain and about these guys Wong and McKeen who were now "peddling the same stuff" at this place called "Haven" on Gabriola Island. He said something about a porno tape handed over to the police by the outraged husband of the woman who "co-starred" with Jock McKeen. An ex-boyfriend of the woman had obtained a copy of the tape and was threatening to show it publicly unless the husband agreed to pay a considerable sum of money. Adding insult to injury, McKeen had refused to assist in bringing the blackmailer to justice. It seemed that the police officer was more concerned with the "touchy-feely degenerates who brainwash people into immoral and unnatural sexual practices" than with any allegations of blackmail or extortion. His questions and comments seemed to imply that the R.C.M.P. was involved in some official investigation and that Haven-by-the-Sea was now at the centre of their enquiries.

For almost an hour they poured out the story of making the video tape, the break-in on Cortes, the calls from the ex-girl-friend and the bitterness of the aggrieved husband. The Sergeant, now officially involved and appropriately detached, sat on his stool at the counter and scribbled his version of the tale into his notebook, pausing only to ponder the odd point or ask the occasional question.

"Well that's about it," Jock said, glancing at Ben for final veri-fication. "We want this thing out in the open. Feel free to ask us about anything that's not clear." It was clear. In fact, Jock had peeled off a factual chronology that could have been transferred directly into the official records; he was good at that sort of thing.

The Sergeant closed his notebook and looked back at the two men on the other side of the counter. "This is all news to me," he said, his eyes moving from one to the other. "If there is some kind of investigation underway, nobody's said anything to us. I'll make some enquiries." His manner was still amiable but they were carol singers no longer.

On the short drive home, Jock silently cursed the damned video tape that seemed to be sticking to his life . . . to both their lives. From the passenger seat, Ben watched the black asphalt of Taylor Bay Road rush by under the headlights. As the car passed through the property gates and made its way along the gravel driveway to their apartment, Jock wondered if anything had changed. Ben sank back into his seat and allowed the weariness to seep through him. He placed a hand lightly on Jock's knee. "It's good to be home," he said.

A few weeks later, the sanctity of that home was desecrated without warning. In the Lodge, Louise Belisle stopped her sweeping, put down her broom and stared at the sight of four staff members being corralled and hustled into the barroom area by three uniformed police officers. Inside the maintenance barn, three plain-clothed officers burst in on Mark Fraser and two other maintenance men ordering them to "come with us." A marked police cruiser blocked off the driveway at the gates and three of its occupants spilled out, disappearing into the bushes around the perimeter of the property. Inside the session room, participants nudged each other and pointed to the strange faces peering in through the windows.

At the centre of it all, Ben and Jock knelt over the prostrate form of Xanon Jensen. They were aware of the energy shifting uneasily around them but their task of remaining present, to welcome a vulnerable self back to the contact boundary, was a serious commitment. When the detectives walked in and took up positions along the wall, the leaders motioned for the group to move in a tighter circle around them. They conducted their business in whispers, inviting the others to be there for Xanon, to offer feedback and reaffirm the sanctity of life within the circle. When all had been said, Ben walked over to the stereo, selected the music and returned to the centre. Xanon sat up, looked around, stared at the darkened figures, wrapped his arms around Ben and Jock and wept. The intruders stood in silence.

In the Lodge, those rounded up by the police eyed their captors in disbelief, but no questions were asked and no explanations were offered. Footsteps crunching on the gravel pathway heralded the arrival of the program participants, the armed guards ushering them into the crowded foyer. At the rear, the officer in charge held the door open while Ben, Jock and a wide-eyed Xanon shuffled their way into the crowd.

"This is a raid," the cop announced, standing squarely in the doorway. "We have warrants to make a full search of the premises. You are not under arrest but we ask you to remain here to allow the officers to do their job. At this stage we will need only your names and addresses. Should we require more information from you, we will acquaint you with your legal rights. We will be asking some of you who work here to let us into the various areas."

"I didn't know what the Hell was going on," recalled Mark Fraser, "but for some reason I found myself staring at Ben. I couldn't believe what I saw in his face. It was as if all of the life had been drained away . . . like he wasn't there any more. I was just horrified. Jock was standing at his side like a bodyguard but he must have felt as helpless as the rest of us."

Louise was selected to help with the search. "This policeman came with me to my room. He lay on my bed and began searching through all my private possessions. Any item of a vaguely sexual nature he placed in a bag with some rude offhand comment. I was more scared than angry at the time. I remember wondering about what was going to happen to my professional career as a social worker."

While Louise faced the indignity of her own personal violations, Ben and Jock sat together on the sofa in their apartment and watched as two strange men in dark suits poked through every nook and cranny. "Look at these," said one holding up three copies of *Playboy* retrieved from Jock's bedside drawer. "Obviously they're a couple of fags," he said, opening up the centrefold picture and displaying it to his colleague. "Huh," belched the other as he filled his bag with the video tapes used in the "Sex and Identity" workshops, "I'll bet this filth gets 'em going around here."

On the other side of the property, more evidence was being gathered from the props room. Articles of women's clothing, wigs, a riding crop, leather pants, black boots and a Bishop's mitre were carefully tagged, listed and placed in large white laundry bags.

The raid went on until late into the evening. As darkness fell and the last squad car drove out through the gates, small groups of men and women gathered in the shadows or huddled together in dimly lit rooms and whispered their speculations and assurances into the night.

For two days following the raid, the people of Haven and PD Seminars followed the direction of their leaders in supporting the current workshop through to its conclusion. On the surface, the police action was categorised as a reflection of mainstream paranoia but, beneath the collective indignation, individual reactions were ambiguous. Angry voices announced that basic human rights—*their* rights—had been violated and loudly demanded their own versions of justice. Timid souls mouthed words of protest while anticipating the possible consequences of being 'known' to the police. Drawn faces bursting into tears of sadness and helplessness posed questions that would never be answered. Around the inner circle there were those who knew more—odd bits of tattle handed down from the days of Cold Mountain and pieced together in countless ways.

But, at the very core of this enterprise, a handful of people, known only to one another, wrestled with secrets they had hoped to contain. All had friends or relatives 'on the other side'—people who, for whatever reason, had chosen to disassociate themselves from Wong and McKeen. All had tried to wrestle with their judgments of stories about abandoned lovers and stolen video tapes, personal rejections and professional impropriety. They heard about meetings where grievances were sympathetically and supportively orchestrated into choruses of resentment. And they learned of interviews with the police following the handing over of the ubiquitous video tape. Choosing to retain their own affiliations with Haven-by-the-Sea they preserved a delicate state of open-mindedness with closed-minded strategies of delusion and denial. Now the police raid had dragged it all into the open and they were under pressure to make their own positions known.

Rationally speaking, their options were clear. On the one hand, they could choose to detach themselves from the accusers and uphold the integrity of the work at Haven. On the other, they could disown their affiliation with Wong and McKeen and leave. Less rationally, they could attempt to bring the two opposing forces together, either in their own minds, or through some attempt to facilitate a reconciliation. Their only other recourse would be to push the matter further out of awareness and hope that, in time, it might all go away.

When all the program participants had left, Ben and Jock called a staff meeting. Jock, his face tight and his body uncharacteristically rigid, punched out the storyline as it had been given to the Gabriola police sergeant a week or so ago. Then the interview in the apartment on the day of the raid; the dossier on Cold Mountain with its allegations and speculations of sexual experimentation; the questions directed at Ben about his training in clinical hypnosis and the lightly veiled suggestions of professional misconduct. Then came the matter of the video tape.

"Do you guys deny having sex with patients?" the cops had asked.

"Yes," they had answered.

"But there were all kinds of sexual orgies taking place on Cortes, we have the information right here. Are you trying to tell us that you weren't involved in that stuff?"

"Yes."

Immediately after the interview, Jock had called the head of the College of Physicians and Surgeons and informed him of the raid. Once again he repeated the details of the story along with the allegations. The man on the other end seemed neutral. Since the woman in the video tape had been a patient of Ben's many years previously and never a patient of Jock's, he was clear that there was no professional misconduct involved, at least as far as the College was concerned. "This is a police matter," he concluded. "The College would have no interest." But all who listened that day in the Lodge *were* interested.

Most of them listened very carefully. "Ben and Jock were on the line," Xanon Jensen said. "It was a tough time for all of us but, for them, it was everything. I didn't know what the truth was and at that time I didn't care. Hell, all kinds of things went on at Cold Mountain that never involved Ben and Jock. There were rumours all over the place. I just pushed the politics and moralistic stuff aside. They were my friends and I loved them. That's what it came down to. When you live on an iceberg you've gotta understand that all that stuff underneath keeps you upright and all that stuff around is what keeps you afloat."

Those who remained stuck on the ice listened with their ears and waited for the thaw to take them back to safety. "Many of us were trying to get our heads around something that just didn't make sense," Louise remembered. "There was something going on in the inner circle but, in those days, Mark and I were on the outside. We tried to understand but there were so many stories. It was very confusing. I couldn't believe how desperate Ben was. I couldn't even bring myself to look at him during the meeting." Voices on the one side cried out for the plight of a friend who had been abandoned by her husband, abused by a boyfriend and used by Jock McKeen. On the other side, the same 'facts' were being marshalled into a conviction that the same woman, in attempting to reconcile her relationship with her husband, and unable to wreak her scorn on a boyfriend who had left the country, turned her anger toward Jock in a classic manoeuvre of 'displacement.' For all of them, the compass needle trembled and pointed. Some responded fully to the moment and found a truth that reached far beyond the facts. Others turned frantically to the security of their time-tested beliefs.

And, for a few, the needle pointed toward the only truth that mattered . . . the truth of their own complicity.

Dianne Anderson was well aware of the turmoil among her friends, although her own commitments remained firm. "The raid stunned us all," she said, "but as time went on, it was the growing sense of betrayal that created the deepest wounds. Ben and Jock withdrew from us but I could see their pain. Jock seemed more judgmental and remote but I think Ben's heart was broken; I could hardly contain my own sadness around him."

In the weeks following the invasion, the ongoing routines and encounters at Haven contained an unfamiliar tension. Personal experiences of the raid were replaced by more speculation about the larger story and reflections on the broader issues. Nonresident members of the PD fraternity dropped by to check out the rumours and add their own conjectures and commitments to the proceedings. Peggie Merlin, Father Jack, Jerry Glock, Carol Stewart and many others came to participate in the reappraisal.

Joann Peterson found herself in the role of an informal counsellor to many of those seeking an understanding ear for their concerns. "Most people were willing to look beyond politics and morality and examine their own personal issues," she noted. In some ways, the crisis provided them with an opportunity to look at themselves, particularly in relation to Ben and Jock. We were all dealing with transference issues of one form or another. This is what connected us in the first place and there was a general understanding that working through our own parental stuff was very much a part of being at Haven."

But now a different version of Mommy and Daddy had been imposed from the outside and the 'children' had to find ways of assimilating the new information. Ironically, it was a perfect opportunity for them to see and acknowledge the humanness of their heroes, to relate to them as fellow beings, and to take one more step toward their own autonomy. And many, including Joann herself, took the risk to explore their archaic illusions of childhood. Among those who resisted such a challenge, however, were some of the most long standing followers and disciples of the Wong and McKeen way. Some had abandoned the way of Richard Weaver and Cold Mountain in favour of another ideal, but now their carefully preserved images of perfection were under attack. Denial and resentment were the reactions that could best protect them from the painful alternatives of personal introspection and responsibility.

Beyond her own turmoil, Joann Peterson was intrigued by the broader context. "Times were changing. Ben created enemies when he broke from the traditions of Cold Mountain. In the sixties, sexuality was something to be explored openly in the human potential movement but, somehow, the sexuality of Ben and Jock was locked out of people's minds as the new humanism began to emerge. Then the sexual forms of those times became the sounding ground for the trumpets of a new morality, particularly where women were concerned. In the early days of their so-called 'liberation' many women regarded themselves as victims of male dominance and some who came to Haven were clearly upset by Ben and Jock's position on choice and personal responsibility. Such women held onto a belief that, as women, they had no choice and that men were responsible for their distress. In this particular case, had the alleged 'victim' not been a woman and had Ben and Jock not been men, the whole scene probably would have been entirely different."

Soon after the raid, the scene became a tense juxtaposition of 'rightness' and 'wrongness' and the fallout began. Individually, those who were the most wronged left. Many of their Haven friends expressed empathy for their position and, while their departure seemed amicable, a number of observers noted that their behavior was similar to that of "kids who had found a reason to break away, even though the permission to leave home had been there all the time."

Joann continued to be troubled by what she saw. "I had the belief that there were forces outside of Haven that were out to destroy Ben and Jock. They weren't focused or organized but, given an appropriate cause and conducive circumstances, they could be mobilised. Many of these people considered themselves to be in close relationship with Ben and Jock but the heroes no longer lived up to their fantasies. In order to have their own differences, they had to make Ben and Jock wrong. When this stuff becomes collective and political it can be very dangerous." Joann's fears were not unfounded. When the police investigators expressed their conviction that Wong and McKeen had power over people and that Haven was a cult designed to serve the self-interests of the leaders, they held up a banner for anyone looking to do battle.

With friends in both camps, Carol Stewart tried desperately to hang onto both sides of the widening chasm. "Carol went through agony," Louise Belisle said. "She was convinced that the differences could be patched up if only the parties would get together and she tried desperately to find some grounds for a reconciliation. But Ben and Jock seemed to have retreated to their own place of survival and there was no middle ground."

Mark Fraser was also aware of Carol's struggle. "She had lost herself in Ben and Jock's ideas and thought she had learned so much from them but here they were, seemingly tarnished and somehow out of integrity. She was very idealistic about them but, if you're going to grow, you have to go into the transference and move through it in some creative way, or make a break. Perhaps this was the only way for Carol to get out."

"Carol had a need to make them wrong," Joann concluded after an all night clearing session. "They had let her down, but if they were ready to acknowledge their guilt, reveal their dark side, then it might have been possible for her to forgive them. Then, the karma would change. But they would only acknowledge their participation and this wasn't good enough. In her mind, Carol wanted them to be non-sexual beings and the illusion had been destroyed."

In many ways, Carol's struggle expressed the pain of a deeply divided community—a community founded upon the willingness of its members to reveal the nature of their experience. Diane Anderson summed it up eloquently. "At Haven, when things matter, they matter a lot. Here, everybody's process is shared in one way or another." While only Carol herself had access to the truth of her dilemma, the process of her extrication from Ben and Jock, and Haven-by-the-Sea, was there for all to see.

As events unfolded, Jim Kearney, his own dreams for a community revolving around Ben and Jock already ragged, empathized with the dissenters and absorbed his discontent into his role as manager. "Jim had become a wet blanket," explained Xanon. "What he wanted for Haven was very different from what the boys wanted. Ben confronted him once in public about something stupid, I think it was about keeping the salt shakers full, and Jim blew. He decided not to accept any more feedback from Ben. Kent, who worked in the kitchen, also blew up when Ben suggested we should open up a restaurant for the island. He called Ben all kinds of names and took off." Meanwhile Xanon tucked away his own fantasies and threw his abundant energy into property maintenance, attending programs and running Saturday night dances in the Lodge." Actually most of us created a cosy sense of togetherness, with us as the heroes and society as the villain. As far we were concerned, some disgruntled person had gone for revenge."

As the others struggled to find their place, the two men at the centre of the controversy chose to distance themselves from the proceedings. While Jock's alleged actions may have precipitated the crisis, most of the reactions eventually clustered around Ben. Jock was incensed by the injustice. As far as Jock was concerned, Ben had taken nothing for himself; his only felony had been that of taking a hearty interest in others, including those who now seemed ready to condemn him. In the uneasy silence that settled between and around them, Jock became painfully aware that Ben was considering taking his own life. On reflection he wrote:

Outrageous atrocity!
They are taking life
in their ignorance

No more! Don't commit such savagery!
This is arrogant taking of life
A needless shedding of blood.

I stand by
in outrage
and pain
and shame
for my own complicity
for I have done this too.

What Jock saw, as nobody had seen before, was that Bennet Wong was essentially defenceless. As a vulnerable human being, Ben knew that his place on the planet carried no assurances and he feared the forces that would render him helpless, that would strangle the flow of his life. "I've sat with many women who have been raped," he told Jock, after the police raid. "Now I think I know something of how they must have felt. I feel as though someone has entered me personally and trampled all over my soul. It's like I have no right to any life . . . nothing left to live for." Then, when the accusations seemed to be coming from all directions he asked, "Why do people choose to do these things and why are they so upset with me? What have I done to hurt them?" Behind the man of strength and substance, an innocent and curious child peered out on an alien world.

For Ben, it wasn't a question of defence, it was the matter of meaning. The possibilities of life and death implied options, decisions to be made, and suicide would be a simple confirmation of lifelessness. Alternatively, to channel the precious resources of his life into the service of its own protection would be to shackle his self and imprison his soul. To demand justice would be to collaborate with the forces of destruction, while a cry for help would merely acknowledge their power. Yet, behind the pain was his irrefutable faith that he would continue to be part of the whole, if not in his present form, then in some other. Within the universal realm, his place in the scheme of things was written by a hand that would not be pressed by fear or ignorance. While his mind pondered and his heart ached, Ben waited for his soul to speak.

Jock watched and waited also. In confronting his own helplessness, Jock had been trained to strike back, but as witness to his friend's despair, there was nowhere for him to go, nothing for him to do. There were moments when he could convert his anguish into anger and turn it upon the wrongdoers but he could do little to assuage his own impotence. There were times when he turned the anger inward, but this only took him further away from what now mattered the most—the urgent and profound desire to be with Ben, whatever the outcome.

Many times, Jock, like so many others, had distanced himself from Ben with the belief that he had to match him in some way, to know what Ben knew, to feel what Ben felt, to be what Ben was. Now it was time for him to let go and stand at his friend's side. But there was something else, something vague and voiceless, pushing up behind his desperation. The first glimmer of truth came without warning, a sudden calmness that passed quickly through his body while his head maintained its preoccupation with the enemy. Fight to survive or surrender to the unknown? He had fought his way to get here, now there was another option. He took a breath and allowed whatever was stirring on the inside to come to the surface and wash over him. His body trembled and his mind floated in a blissful union.

On the third day of his vigil, they sat side-by-side on the sofa. Jock, his head bowed, caressed Ben's hand.

Ben was silent. He heard the clock chime, felt the fingers stroking the back of his hand and let the warm sun from the window sink into his body. He was home.

"Jock," he whispered, "where are you now?"

"I'm here," Jock answered.

"No you're not." The voice was clear and emphatic.

"Well what's the point if you're not going to be here too?"

Ben grasped Jock's fingers. "But I *am* here with you," he said firmly, "and this is where I want to be."

377

No more words. Jock looked into the familiar face and saw all that he had been waiting and hoping for.

"I love you Ben."

"I know."

The police raid, though it sparked many personal reactions, created no fundamental transformations in the operations of either PD Seminars or Haven-by-the-Sea. If anything, it reinforced the leaders' commitments to their original designs. Both organizations would continue to operate as businesses, only now, any illusions of 'family' or 'intentional community' would be confronted from the outset. "If people don't want this, then they won't come," Ben said at a staff meeting, "so we'll move on and do something else."

But people did come, lining up for the five-day "Come Alives," swelling the four week Phase programs to unprecedented levels and stretching the leaders to the limits of their responsiveness. New programs offered under the leadership of Joann Peterson, Mark Fraser, Louise Belisle, Jerry Glock, Shirley Ronner, Peggie Merlin, Jim and Judy Sellner, Trish Grainge and other former students, added depth and variety to the menu, while visiting leaders in the humanistic movement, like Virginia Satir, Paul Reps, Bunny and Frederick Duhl, Lee Pulos, Carl Whitaker, Ervin and Miriam Polster, Morris Berman and Marjorie Rand contributed to Haven's growing reputation as an educational centre.

Meanwhile, many of those who worked on the Haven property continued to be enthusiastic participants and interns. Whatever their individual issues and mythologies, they shared a common commitment to take the principles of awareness, vulnerability, honesty and self-responsibility into the flow of everyday experience. And, despite the fragmentation of recent events, they continued to believe that Ben and Jock were the models to be watched and emulated . . . masters of this way of being.

Some months after the raid, Ben and Jock received a telephone call from the R.C.M.P. A congenial voice told them that after careful deliberation the Attorney General's Office had determined that there had been no legal wrongdoing at Haven-by-the-Sea and that no charges would be laid. He invited them to come over and pick up their confiscated belongings.

Entering the police station and walking over to the reception area, they found their way blocked by a young detective sergeant who ushered them into one of the interrogation rooms off the main foyer. Once inside, he slammed the door, sat in the only available chair and began reading a file. They stood before him like kids waiting for the principal's judgment. "Perhaps we should come back another day," Jock whispered.

"You wanna know what I think?" the young cop snarled, leaning back in his chair and clasping his hands behind his head. "I think you people are worse than murderers . . . that's what I think."

They stared back blankly. Calmly, Ben explained that they had come by invitation, that it was their understanding no charges were to be laid and that their property was to be returned. The cop swung himself forward so that the front legs of his chair cracked down on the linoleum floor "You must think you've got away with this," he said, slapping the palm of his hand on the open file, "but it's not going to be that easy, I've already seen to that."

"Oh?"

"Oh . . . yeah," he said, drawing in breath through his teeth and blowing it out through his nostrils. "I've already spoken with your friends at the doctor's college. They wanted a copy of the porno tape . . . you know, the one that got away . . . so, since our hands are tied, I'm letting them carry the ball, at least for the time being." He slapped the file one more time and stood up. "You can check the inventory and sign the release papers at the desk," he said.

As the echoes of personal and moral indignation swept through Haven-by-the-Sea, most of the inhabitants were far too preoccupied with their own internal disarray to notice yet another storm building along the horizon. Long before the story of the stolen video came to light, friends in the medical profession had been alerting Ben and Jock to the rumour that the College of Physicians and Surgeons was keeping an eye on the activities at PD Seminars. In spite of their apparent disregard for the traditions of their profession, however, the precise nature of their transgressions was always difficult to pin down. They were undoubtedly men of medicine and there could be no doubt about the legitimacy of their qualifications. But the radical nature of their work attracted an odd assortment of physicians who had come to question their own professional efficacy and whose personal lives were ill at ease behind the white coat and stethoscope. Many referred their unresponsive patients to the programs at Haven and came to extend their definition of psychosomatics when the symptoms of cancer, multiple sclerosis and allergic reactivity appeared to respond to a treatment generically referred to as 'personal work.' Some came to find out for themselves, taking programs like "New Horizons" to learn about the principles of traditional Chinese medicine while being introduced to the techniques of Reichian breathing, bodywork and acupuncture. Others came to immerse themselves in their own 'process.' Within the profession at large, Drs. Wong and McKeen were called upon to address medical conferences and even the College of Family Practitioners invited them to present their views on the philosophy of medicine. But, in general, the relationship between their work and the mainstream of their profession was tenuous and they were never surprised by stories that the College of Physicians and Surgeons regarded them with suspicion. Now, courtesy of a tenacious detective, the medical authorities had something to sink their teeth into.

The following week the two doctors received a letter from the College requesting their attendance at a tribunal to answer charges of 'gross misconduct' vis-à-vis their participation in the making of the video tape. Since the hearing was scheduled three days hence and, given that they had workshop commitments at that time, they decided to have their lawyer attend and seek a delay of proceedings. On his return, the lawyer offered his opinion that a 'guilty' verdict had already been reached. The five members of the panel had viewed the tape, reviewed the dossier containing the allegations, and already were offering their opinions. When the lawyer raised objections, it was made clear that the rules of 'due process' did not apply. Given that fact, he wondered how he could be of any help.

Ben and Jock wondered also. As far as they were concerned, they had been open with the police, the College had declared neutrality and, from their understanding of medical practices, no breach of conduct had taken place. "What are we actually being accused of?" Jock asked. The lawyer shook his head. According to his research, the medical establishment seemed to be conducting some kind of nation-wide purge but none of his colleagues could discover the reasons.

Jock called the Medical Protective Association and asked for their assistance. Once acquainted with the circumstances, they quickly concluded that, regardless of the allegations, the fifteen year time lapse between the woman's status as a 'patient' of Dr. Wong's and her subsequent involvement with Dr. McKeen would rule out a charge of 'misconduct' on medical grounds. For them, the issue was more personal than medical. A call to the British Columbia Medical Association was met with a similar response.

Meanwhile, the lawyer retained to represent the two physicians continued to pursue whatever avenues he could find. Having spoken with representatives of the Medical Association, he remained firmly of the opinion that a "Morals and Standards Committee," held in camera at the College, would pronounce the two practitioners guilty. He was willing to take the matter to court, submitting the paralegal procedures of the College to an open investigation. While he was convinced that Wong and McKeen would eventually win, he anticipated that the College would fight hard, that the time would be lengthy, the media coverage extensive and the costs monumental.

They considered this option very carefully. "I'm ready to go for justice," Jock said, "but they're my actions that have brought this thing down on us and it could get worse. If we start the ball rolling, the media will be onto it like a pack of wolves and God only knows what the consequences will be from all of that. It would cost us a bundle and could go on for years."

"And we could lose Haven," Ben said, "but for what? Absolutely nothing would be gained by us throwing away our work on some meaningless cause. I'm just not that interested in beating the College in some moralistic public debate."

The lawyer accepted their decision not to counter formally the allegations being levelled against them. But when the Vancouver press reported that the College of Physicians and Surgeons had been investigating the practices of two unnamed members, and threw a few morsels of tantalising information into the pot, he acted quickly. With the consent of his clients, he arranged an in camera courthouse hearing. Before the judge, he shared his concerns and argued that, since proper safeguards were not being employed, the court should ensure that the identities of his clients would not be made public. The judge agreed and ruled accordingly.

But now another institutional servant of the public interest had a stake in the action. Using the "Freedom of Information Act," a tenacious investigative reporter took his own cause into the courtroom and succeeded in having the 'gag order' lifted. Now the public's right to know, the media's right to publish, the College's right to govern and the accuser's right to speak called upon the rights of the accused to defend themselves against the torrent of allegations and innuendo.

They were chatting over breakfast in the Lodge with a handful of staff members when one of the kitchen workers brought the morning papers to their table. "It's quite a splash," she said, turning to hide her tears and then running back through the doorway. Jock read the article aloud, his voice clear and steady. Ben sat in silence, the others groaned, shook their heads and mumbled in the background. When it was all over 'the boys' rose from the table, took their dishes over to the washing-up tray and headed back to their apartment. From the Lodge, the others watched them make their way along the pathway. As they passed the gymnasium, Ben slipped his arm around Jock's shoulders and they disappeared from view.

That morning the wire services carried the story across the country. The telephone rang with constant invitations for the two doctors to make public rebuttals or declarations. But whatever they had to say was being said only to each other. Three days later, a local radio station broadcast the personal revelations of a man who claimed to have taken one of the Haven programs and to have been exposed to wild sexual displays, including public masturbation during the sessions. Somewhat desensitized to the kerfuffle by this time, Ben and Jock managed to draw some amusement from the fact that the only program taking place on the dates cited had been led by Virginia Satir. On her next visit they eagerly drew this matter to her attention. Virginia was not amused.

In the midst of all the publicity, the College summoned Wong and McKeen to a meeting—an 'arraignment' they called it. On the day before the event, however, they received a call from the lawyer representing the College. Reviewing their billing records, the College had discovered that Drs. Wong and McKeen had not used their licences to practice medicine for quite some time. If they would now accept the withdrawal of the licences and agree never to apply for reinstatement, then the College would drop all further action. They readily accepted the first condition but refused to agree to the second. On this basis, a deal was struck and the drawn out offensive came finally to an end.

Almost a year following the surrender of their licences, Ben and Jock were contacted by a representative of the national television program "The Fifth Estate." While she appreciated that their lawyer would advise them to say nothing, she wanted the two doctors to hear the story as their researchers had pieced it together. Over the telephone she proceeded to relate the circumstances and events as Ben and Jock had always understood them, citing evidence and details that took even them by surprise. Taking the position that the actions of the B.C. College were part of a broader purge undertaken by Colleges across the country, she asked them to consider participating in a program designed to investigate the reactionary forces of the medical establishment. They thanked her and declined the invitation.

Chapter Eleven

In February 1985 I joined twenty-seven others in a three week Phase One program at Haven-by-the-Sea. At that time, I had little interest in the story of Bennet Wong and Jock McKeen and no knowledge of the turmoil that had occurred only a few months earlier. In fact, I would probably have remained oblivious to the whole affair had the two leaders not taken the time to review briefly the episode with some of their workshop participants, me included. They were obviously still shaken by it all but I was impressed with the way they refused to present themselves as targets of malice or victims of circumstance, despite the friendly ears in the room. Having been involved in the human relations field for most of my life, it seemed obvious to me that it would be impossible for these two controversial figures to pursue their particular interests without creating serious kerfuffles along the way. Anyway, it all sounded much more interesting than the petty little intrigues and blowups that had punctuated my own career.

But I was not there to hear *their* story. I was there because my own story had become *nothing but* circumstance. I needed to find the author and hold him accountable for his neglect but, true to form, I continued to search in all the wrong places. In

Bennet Wong and Jock McKeen I found a pair of exquisite ghost writers who knew all about the life I wanted. Whether they liked it or not, they would lead the way and, after a few perfunctory gestures of rebellion, I would follow. I didn't have to go digging on the inside after all. I could find my authenticity in their words, my choices in their methods, my acceptability in their presence and my potential in their approval. Of course there would still be holes in my performance but, with a little creativity, I could take pieces from each and stuff them into all the right places. "A changed man since he went to Haven," they would say. Finally, I understood what my wife Judith was on about when she returned from Haven earlier that year demanding a 'relationship.' She wanted one just like Ben and Jock's and I would get it for her because I loved her, because she deserved it and, above all, because then she would never leave me. I had three weeks to put it all together.

Of course it was all nonsense, but I believed it because I wanted to believe it. I abandoned that part of my mind that was usually so adept at sniffing out my sporadic pretensions and God only knows what happened to all that academic and professional training on the subject of 'transference.' Once or twice my intellect did attempt to intervene but it was met with solid denials reinforced with quick shots of rebellion. Whatever they were doing I could replicate. I slid behind my Ph.D. and cocked a professional ear to those who turned Ben into the father they always wanted and Jock into their idealized brother, without ever stopping to consider that these needy souls might be further along the pathway to self-actualization than I was. For me, it was still a game. If I was ever going to move to the centre of my life, it was going to take longer than three weeks.

As I watched others moving forward to 'do their work,' I knew that my turn would come and I became locked in fear. It seemed that people had to come unglued for the stuff on the inside to flow out; the unknown into the known, the dark into the light. Then, after the pain and the release would come the transformation, the bright eyes, the clear voice, the sturdy presence and, finally, the tributes of the group. But what if there had been nothing on the inside, nothing to fill the gaping holes in the self's empty shell? Would transformation then turn to decomposition? Would reverence turn to pity? Why would I want to take such a risk? Better to wrap my hollowness in thoughts and words than disappear for ever into its murk.

But, the more I watched the others, the more my body seemed to detach from my mind's instructions. I laughed and cried along with them and my body trembled, though there was nothing to hold it all together. When their work was over and they returned to their place in the circle they would take their feelings with them and my body would have to relinquish the excitement it had stolen. Ben and Jock told us that we can do our own work by watching others do theirs, but they weren't talking about me. After each piece of work, when the observers were moved to share their feelings, I held back, always fearing that my treachery would be discovered. In the evenings I would pull myself together by drawing my roommate, a disenchanted physician, into a lengthy analysis of the day's proceedings. I particularly liked to talk about techniques.

The first time I stepped into the middle of the group was in response to Jock's invitation. We sat cross-legged facing each other and talked. It didn't matter what we talked about, I was simply going to go wherever he went. So long as I didn't take the lead, I would be safe. After a few minutes of chatter, Jock stopped the flow and looked at me. The man was staring straight into the hollow. I could feel his eyes searching for something that, I knew, wasn't there. Suddenly he seemed to give up and a tear ran down his cheek. So now *he* knew too. My belly convulsed but I held on. Ben joined us and gently reconnected me with my words. He wanted to know why they were so important and what they meant? So I told him. I told everybody and they listened respectfully.

When the time came for the others to offer their response to my performance, I was ready to sneak off again but felt obliged to return their respect by hanging in for the opening statements.

The first two or three were easily dismissed as common clichés. "I feel close to you," "I resonate with your sense of emptiness," "I found myself delving into my own sadness," went past my ears although, on reflection, they were probably honest. But, just as I was about to disappear, the man I most distrusted in the group began to speak. A perverse curiosity kept me hanging in. He was English with an accent that came straight out of the upper drawer and an aloofness I have always associated with the ruling class. He talked of his struggle to find a place for himself in the world through his achievements, about the judgments he still made of himself for not being good enough in a world of relentless expectations. He had rejected himself without ever knowing what he was rejecting. Though his emotions were contained and his words precise, everything he said seemed straight and uncensored. He talked far longer than anyone else and I began to resent him for saying so much about himself with no reference to me. Yet it was about me, it was *all* about me. This man, who I had tried so hard to distance myself from on the outside, understood so much about my life, or lack of it, on the inside. Could it be that my avoidance of him was just another way of avoiding myself? I had real feelings, but I held onto them for fear that, through their expression, I might lose him in some way. When he finished, I wanted to leave my place at the centre and wrap my arms around him. Instead, after the session, I went over and shook his hand.

As the program moved toward its close, my mind and body seemed more and more determined to tear each other apart. Bizarre dreams, bouts of despair, crazy thoughts and brief moments of elation were woven into what I imagined to be a form of transitory psychosis. I felt sick but in a way that demanded my full participation.

In the third week I volunteered to do some body-work. It was no act of courage, driven by curiosity or commitment to self. It wasn't even an attempt to surrender to the chaos on the inside. It was a cop-out, a form of self-abandonment that would get me through without having to take responsibility for the outcome . . . a strategy I had employed many times before. I have no idea what really took place as I lay on the floor stripped to the waist while people probed my body for the 'right points.' I just know that when I finally sat up to face the circle I felt as though my body was filled with something odd, yet indisputably mine. It tingled . . . no . . . I tingled. I ran my hands down and across my torso. I listened to what others had to say without expecting or wanting anything from them.

Within a matter of hours, the euphoria had subsided, though my mind remained hooked to the strange sensations that continued to flow through me. If, as the humanists say, body and mind are one, then perhaps I was taking the first tentative steps toward an existential reunion. I thought this might be what the initiated refer to as being 'in process.' Certainly, I was self-absorbed, with little concern for how I might be judged from the outside . . . and that I liked.

On the final day of the program, we organized an impromptu concert in the dining room, for ourselves and for anyone on the property who cared to show up. The room was packed and, for the most part, the 'entertainment' drew the audience into spontaneous participation. When I stood up to play my clarinet, however, there were only eyes surrounded by silence and I immediately regretted my decision. I struggled through the first few bars, my vibrato being little more than an amplification of my anxiety. As always, my mind cut into my performance, but this time its message was stunningly different. "This is for you, go back to the feeling, nothing to prove, just be with your music," then it was gone. I could feel the shift immediately. My breathing settled, the knot in my stomach dissolved and my heart took its place at my centre. It was the feeling I had as a youngster when I played in jazz bands, but then I had the music to turn me on and other players to draw me out. Now, after discarding the instrument for many years, alone and without accompaniment, I had only myself to draw from. I played a simple tune in a simple key, but the improvisations began to curl around the melody with little or no effort on my part. Whatever it sounded like from the outside, it was all me and I loved it. I loved it that there were others who were there to hear whatever was coming out. Then, when I felt myself filling the room, it suddenly occurred to me that I was overdoing it, imposing myself in some way, and I finished off with a prearranged flourish that I remembered from the old days. I was overwhelmed by the enthusiasm of the response and, with only the mildest protest, agreed to play some more. Ben asked for a jazz version of "A Closer Walk With Thee," so I played it. Someone else wanted "Petite Fleur," so I played that. Then came "Stranger on the Shore" and "Memories of You." Somehow I managed to play them all.

Later that evening I was invited over to Ben and Jock's apartment for a small private jam. Jock went off to get his flute while Ben dragged out some sheet music, sat down at the piano and started to tinkle his way through old favorites. I did my best to follow his lead, or at least transpose what he was playing into some kind of harmony, but it was useless. Whatever I had an hour ago drained out of me as I struggled to perform to some uncertain standard. He was gracious about it all but, somewhere inside, I believed that I had let him down, spoiled his fun, failed to meet his expectations. Jock never did get a chance to play his flute. As I made my way back to my room, I knew that I still had a long way to go. It was clear to me that the work to be done was *my* work but that, somehow, I would find ways to include Bennet Wong and Jock McKeen along the way.

In August, 1993, Judith and I accepted an invitation to Haven's tenth birthday celebrations. By the time we arrived, the place was jam-packed with people and we had to make several trips through the woods and around the residential buildings to find a parking spot. "Just look at this place," Judith said on the second go-around, "it's hard to believe that ten years ago there was only the old Lodge, one session room and some odd cabins scattered about. Now it's a sizzling resort with hot tubs, swimming pool, gymnasium, auditorium and enough accommodation for an army. You've got to hand it to the boys. They sure put their hearts into everything they do."

"Individualism in harmony," I said smugly, still searching for a place to park. "It's all tied together. Look how everything you see has its own unique character yet remains defined by the whole, and how easily the whole sits with nature."

I was about to launch off into my own version of *Feng Shui* when Judith tapped me on the shoulder and pointed to a perfect spot by the "Swallow Building." "That place over there was designed specifically for this car at this moment," she said with a grin. "It would be bad karma not to take it."

I ignored her. "The interesting thing is that there was never really any grand design, yet every time I come here, something new has been added. I know it's Ben and Jock who keep the pot boiling but it's more than that. Other lives are also reflected here."

"Yes I do know what you're getting at," she admitted. "Everything here is interactional in some way."

"Ah . . . yes," I said. "That's good, I like that."

Walking along the pathway from the woods, smiling at strangers, pausing to acknowledge familiar faces and embrace old friends, we made our way down to the Lodge. I was particularly struck by the number of Asian people, the distinctive lilt of their voices seeming to come from all directions.

"All these folks," I said, "where have they come from?"

"All from the same place," said Judith, "just like us." I had no idea what she meant but it sounded profound, so I nodded.

We squeezed past the crowd at the registration desk and headed for the lounge. While Judith immediately moved into conversation with three or four people (a social skill I have never managed to cultivate) I glanced hopefully toward the bar. I have always been ill at ease walking into large groups and find comfort in having a glass of something in my hand. Of course it's a way of avoiding contact and if the something happens to be alcoholic the quality of any connection diminishes with every swig. For this reason, the consumption of alcohol, like tobacco, has always been something of a fringe activity at Haven and, even to this day, the bar is little more than a token gesture, a few bottles languishing behind a counter with nobody showing much interest in actually peddling the stuff. Yet it remains a choice.

I managed to catch the eye of Trudy Hammond, one of the front-office staff, and conveyed my desires by raising an imaginary glass to my lips. She understood immediately and, taking a set of keys from her skirt pocket, went over to unlock the glass-fronted beer and wine cooler. She removed a bottle of local Chardonnay and placed it on the counter, drawing the attention of a number of others in the room. I considered reversing my decision but waited too long; the glass was already full. Realizing I was reacting to what others might think and that a sudden change of mind would only serve to complicate the matter further, I paid her and quietly slipped out of the scene. By the time I returned, glass in hand, Judith and her group were inventing their own history of PD Seminars and Haven-by-the-Sea. I listened to their creations with great curiosity. "How's the book coming?" someone ventured to ask during a rare lull in the proceedings. "These things take time," I replied, taking a drink long enough to arrest the flow of attention until it found some other location (a social skill I have tuned to perfection).

Having filled our plates from a buffet of fine delicacies, our group settled around a large table in one corner and continued to weave personal memories into yet another history. The dining room filled quickly, each table chattering to the rhythm of its own agenda. Before long, only the table by the door, the one reserved for Jock, Ben, their closest colleagues and guests, still had vacancies. For the two leaders, this was a very pragmatic arrangement, a way of ensuring that they could eat together, catch up on whatever was happening within their organization and invite whomever they wished to share a meal. Having been welcomed at this table on many occasions I had always enjoyed making connection with the leaders, sharing ideas, discussing the book, or simply joking around. It was a great table to eat at.

Linda Nicholls, then General Manager of PD Seminars and

Haven-by-the-Sea, and her boyfriend Bill Leuze, the property manager, were already seated at 'the table.' If I was looking for a Goddess for *my* mountain, I would enthrone Linda in a palace at the summit. Apart from her classical good looks, she has a sensuality that seems to draw wisdom from innocence and substance from vulnerability. It never came as a surprise to me whenever my informers, boldly or sheepishly, told me how they had 'fallen in love' with Linda at some point in their Haven experience. I particularly love her self-conscious giggle in the face of the unexpected. She is intelligent, astute, engaging, unpretentiously honest and comfortably at one with her own principles. Throughout my investigations, I never came across one person who spoke negatively about this woman or cast any slurs on her integrity—a remarkable phenomenon in this place of constant gossip and speculation.

As a senior executive with a multi-national technology corporation, Linda Nicholls first came to PD seminars in search of Linda Nicholls. Like corporate leaders David Aitken, Jim Pryor and Donald Mainwaring, she also came to see how the philosophy of Wong and McKeen was as applicable to organizational development as it was to personal and professional development. Taking over the reigns from the disenchanted Jim Kearney in 1988, she worked closely with her two mentors to mold the joint ventures of PD Seminars and Haven-by-the-Sea into an efficient and thriving business. But the talents and aspirations of Ms. Nicholls could not be contained within her managerial and supervisory responsibilities. Working alongside some of the best in the business, she had come to be a respected workshop leader in her own right.

I was now gawking at her from across the room and waiting for events to unfold when Joann Peterson slid into her seat by the wall. Now Director of Education, with her own apartment on the property, she had earned her place at 'the table.' Such was the quality of her work that she was able to fill workshops once offered exclusively by Wong and McKeen, a truly remarkable achievement. Ben and Jock were delighted. The 'personal growth' side of the business was flourishing and it was in their minds to create more opportunities for those who wanted professional training beyond the established Diploma in Counselling. Joann was equally adept in both areas and, like so many developments in this unusual enterprise, her role as Director of Education slipped quietly and easily into the organizational matrix.

No sooner had Joann sat down at 'the table' when 'the boys' floated in through the adjacent doorway. I have always been impressed by how quickly they move without ever seeming to hurry. As a program participant, I was curious about how they managed to get from the session room to the Lodge before anyone else and began to suspect that there were secret trails around the property that enabled them to disappear from one location and reappear somewhere else as if by magic. So I made a point of following them, only to discover that they move quickly. In fact, I found myself almost jogging to maintain my few feet of separation. They also move in unison. In the early days I often felt awkward around them, not in an awestruck way, but for fear that I might disrupt their delicate choreography. Their arrival completed the gathering around 'the table.'

I looked around the dining room. It was nothing like the Haven gatherings of old. Men dressed in tailored casuals and women in suits or summer dresses ate and chatted away with folks in jeans, Nike T-shirts and tattered shorts. There were children of all ages, some sitting sedately beside their parents, others zooming around the tables, pausing only to bask in the transitory attention of beaming adults. Trudy and two other members of staff drifted in and out, bringing wine and beer to those who chose to indulge.

It was a scene that could have been playing in any resort or conference centre almost anywhere in the world. On the surface, at least, there was nothing to suggest that this was, or ever had been, a place where people came to transform their lives. There were no groups silently holding hands, no tearful couples locked in soft eye contact, and no isolated souls enduring the private agony known as 'process.' I did notice a number of people who had 'been there' dotted about but they all seemed quite content to go with the silky flow. It was, after all, a celebration.

But, celebration or no celebration, there was no doubt that Haven had indeed changed since that time, ten years ago, when a small handful of Cold Mountaineers scrambled to put together the first session building in time for the first workshop. Yet times had also changed. By the nineteen-eighties, the concentrated energy of the 'human potential' movement was already diluted, its radical propositions and 'far out' experimentations dispersed into forms that could be incorporated into commercial enterprises, educational institutions, self-help formulas and almost every brand of counseling and psychotherapy on the market. In California, even the mighty Esalen Institute set about changing its image from a place where 'anything goes'(or went) to that of a responsible educational facility offering a wide range of learning options to an even wider range of learners. Sophisticated marketing strategies, including glossy brochures with pictures of star performers promising startling results and supported by testimonials from the rich and famous, became a sign of the times. Up on Cortes Island, the old Cold Mountain facility was doing pretty much the same thing in the guise of Hollyhock Farm. In the face of these changing conditions, many personal growth centres across North America and Europe closed their doors for ever, rather than compromise their humanistic ideals.

As I sat there picking at my roast turkey and eyeing the guests, it struck me that Haven had found its own way to move with the times, *without compromise*. If people were coming for different reasons, Ben and Jock were no less dedicated to their work; and the principles and beliefs that had guided them from the outset remained firmly at the centre of the enterprise. Certainly it was a business, but there was nothing in their world view that had ever mitigated against such entrepreneurial ambitions as generating revenues or expanding current operations. Rather than view money as a pollutant in the stream of consciousness, they saw it as a neutral resource that could be put to use in an infinite variety of ways. For them, the challenge had been to bring their notions of authenticity, awareness, self-expression, personal responsibility and interpersonal relatedness, along with their Zen-like dedication to 'walking lightly on the planet,' into their own way of doing business. And this they did with great finesse. I wondered what transformations might occur on this planet if such ideas and practices could be assimilated into the frenetic grab bag that we now refer to as the global economy? I realized, of course, that this could never take place unless we delve into our own personal resources and transform ourselves. But this, Wong and McKeen would argue, we could do at Haven-by-the-Sea.

Oddly enough, as these thoughts were going through my head, the talk at our table was drifting into a sentimental reverie about how things had changed since the 'old days.' Margie McKeacheran, a psychotherapist from Winnipeg told us that, in those days she learned far more at Haven than she had ever learned in graduate school. "We really delved into the phenomena of our selves," she said. "It was the deepest form of personal therapy and now it just isn't available, anywhere." Barry Redinski agreed, although he could understand why Ben and Jock would not want to "bring out the shadow" in people, given the sensitivities of the times. Jan Pottinger offered a third proposition. "I think it's simply a matter of economics," she said. "What sold then, doesn't sell now. I have no problem with that." She smiled and went back to eating her cream pie.

I really disliked this kind of old school elitism that showed up from time to time and I might well have confronted the issue had Judith not returned from her preoccupation with helping a stray toddler find his table of origin. "I'm not sure this place has changed as much as *we* have," she said quietly. "Haven has its own life. Sure Ben and Jock are at the centre but think of all the people who have opened up their lives here. I certainly don't come here to be serviced, God knows I can pay for that anywhere. I come here because, whether I'm in a program, or just hanging about, there's some kind of mutuality involved." She paused for a moment, "I think it's about respect. I've always felt that my life is respected here and I have a similar respect for the life of this place. Perhaps Haven is the way it is today because of all the people who continue to come here and if that doesn't always match my fantasy, well neither does Gerald. So what?"

With the possible exception of Jan, who continued to finish off her cream pie, everyone seemed in agreement.

Over at the next table, a familiar Asian face separated itself from the others and smiled in my direction. I raised my empty glass and smiled back. The owner of the first smile was Feng Zheng, known to all at Haven as "Sean" Feng. In a remarkable way, his very presence at this gathering exemplified the principle of responsivity. This story is embedded in a slice of Haven history that deserves to be told.

They first met Sean in the Spring of 1987 when Jock and Ben were asked to present a paper at the World Acupuncture Conference in Beijing. Given Jock's long-time fascination with eastern medicine, culture and philosophy, and Ben's Asian roots, they responded affirmatively and enthusiastically to the invitation. Linda Nicholls and Ben's son, Kevin, now Research Scientist at Cambridge, joined them on the trip. True to form, the expedition contained all of the ingredients of a full-scale Wong and McKeen investigation; Jock searching out the facts, Ben fleshing out the meanings, everybody contributing their personal experiences.

Feng Zheng was assigned to them as their guide in Xi'an, and Jock took copious notes on whatever this local expert had to say. One morning, when Jock was busily scribbling down information about the Dynasties, Linda leaned over to him and whispered, "Have you noticed he's also taking notes from you every time you make some reference to Taoism or Confucianism?" During the Cultural Revolution, when the Chinese authorities rewrote their nation's history, they determined that traditional philosophies, along with the ancient cultural traditions, were irrelevant, if not hazardous, to the development of the 'modern' China. So Jock, with his substantial knowledge of these things, found himself to be the unlikely guardian of China's philosophical and ideological past, and Feng Zheng was his equally unlikely student. It was an act of courage for him to own up to his curiosity. Given his position of trust with the authorities responsible for the eradication of pre-Maoist ideas, he placed himself in considerable jeopardy by asking questions about his own lost culture. But he was anxious to learn and obviously considered the risk worth taking.

On their return to Gabriola Island, they sent Feng Zheng a copy of the *Yi Jing* (*I Ching*) and a steady correspondence developed between them. Through this dialogue, they devised the idea of having him come to Haven as a student. It was an unprecedented notion that was bound to become stuck in the bureaucratic and diplomatic machinery in both Canada and China. Finally, after years of wrangling, filling in forms and exchanging documents, Feng Zheng arrived at Haven to begin his studies. In a microcosmic way another connection had been made in the fragmented sphere of the collective conscious. (Sean Feng went on to study at Malaspina University College in Nanaimo and Simon Fraser University in Vancouver. On his return to China in 1998 he was given a high ranking position at a Chinese college with responsibilities for promoting educational collaboration with the West. At the time of writing he was negotiating educational contracts with Malaspina University College and other post secondary institutions.)

As it turned out, Ben and Jock's presentation in Beijing opened a door that refused to close. Later that year, they were invited to Hong Kong to conduct a personal development workshop for forty Chinese participants, most of them drawn from the clergy and the helping professions. The sessions were held in a small nunnery. On the second day, members of the group brought spouses and other family members, doubling the size of the gathering. Once again, people were surprised and fascinated by Jock's knowledge of eastern philosophy and cultural traditions, stuff that their grandparents used to talk about, and they lined up to receive acupuncture from this strange western practitioner of the eastern arts. In their personal work, they were polite and reserved, carefully checking out the leaders before and after each encounter. Ben, with his Asian heritage and a presence that always seems to inspire confidence in anyone who seeks to reach beyond the familiar, had their trust from the outset. Between sessions, they sought him out for a shoulder massage and sank blissfully into the rare experience of physical contact with a stranger.

For me, the image of Bennet Wong sitting cross-legged in a Hong Kong nunnery while a group of locals stand in line, waiting patiently to be touched, is particularly poignant. For years I tried to understand this man by contextualizing him, constructing him from the arbitrary details of his life and arranging them around his childhood ambition to find a place for himself in the world. For much of that time, I was caught up in the notion that he had found that place in his relationship with Jock, but it gradually dawned on me that this was nothing more than a romance, imposed for the sake of a story line. There never was a place set out for Bennet Wong in this world, anymore than there was a place waiting to be inhabited by Jock McKeen. The self that seeks its own expression will persistently create and re-create its own place and I can't imagine why I assumed that this particular self would ever settle for some convenient niche in the scheme of things. As a distant observer, I came to the conclusion that Bennet Wong, like Rousseau's "marginal man," can never be defined or contained within any context, cultural, social or relational. Wherever he happens to be, he is constantly creating his own life in his own way. Jock came along as the covetous eye of the beholder, carefully studying the forms in the hope of emulating them. But, however strategically he tried to position himself, there was no place for him on the inside. Only through the arduous process of disentangling himself from his gallery of trophies could he begin to carve out the place that was his, and his alone. Then, and only then, could they bring their creations side-by-side, to establish the 'equivalency' that Jock had always longed for.

So there sat Bennet Wong, somewhere in Hong Kong, beckoning the next person in line to come forward and experience a gentle shoulder massage. And there, on the other side of the room, sat Jock McKeen meticulously needling one 'patient' after another. Two very different men, each fully engaged in the world, contained in their separateness, incorporated in their union and, together, creating yet another place to *be*.

The Hong Kong workshop was judged to be a great success by all who participated and, in response to many requests, they agreed to make it an annual event. On the second occasion, the gathering included Kris Huang and Sara Liuh, founders of the Shiu Li Liuh organization in Taipei, a group dedicated to promoting personal development opportunities for Chinese people. But their quest was not simply to import western ideas and methods. Chinese culture contains no equivalent to the revered notion of the 'self' found in European and North American traditions. In the Chinese language, the smallest unit is the family and the term 'self' is translated as 'deep nature,' which is shared by everyone. They had learned of the workshop through their association with Maria Gomori, a close friend of Ben and Jock who had been continuing the work of Virginia Satir by conducting seminars in Taipei. "You should check out these guys," she told them. The following year, the first Wong and McKeen workshop was held in Taipei and this, too, became an annual commitment.

Again, it was a matter of responsivity. They loved their work in the east and felt a deep affinity for the Chinese people. But those who came, nurses, nuns, priests, psychiatrists, social workers and business people, were hardly Cold Mountaineers ready to strip themselves of their defences and release the soul in cathartic communion. On the contrary, these were, for the most part, gentle and respectful people and the work needed to be equally gentle and respectful. This was particularly important to Ben who became profoundly upset by what he considered to be the influence of Caucasian arrogance and cultural insensitivity. Crossing Hong Kong harbour in a high-speed motor launch, he was outraged by the driver's lack of concern for those attempting to guide their more humble vessels through the crowded waters. Later, when other leaders from Haven went along to assist in the workshops, he would assail anyone whom he judged to be disrespectful of participants, and this included the common sin of not being 'present.' They were amazed, and mortified, by the sheer intensity of a confrontation that came all the way from Strasbourg, Saskatchewan.

Lunch was almost over. A steady stream of people paused at 'the table' on their way out and smiled or chatted with the occupants, some even leaned over and pecked the odd cheek. By the time our party was ready to suspend operations, the dining room was all but deserted. We drifted out in single file to deposit our plates in the appropriate receptacles and make our way to the Phoenix building where the celebrations were about to begin. On the way out of the Lodge, I noticed that the bar was well and truly closed, locked in fact.

The design of the Phoenix building is actually based upon the structures of the old session rooms at Cold Mountain but, for the dwindling few who still yearned for the good old days, this particular bird arose from the ashes as a mockery of its former self, another symbol of Haven's slide into the mire of mainstream illusions. But, to its designers, Wong and McKeen, Phoenix was not intended to be a symbol of the past but a creative and functional representation of the present. To all intents and purposes, it is a theatre, and a rather fine one at that. Massive wooden beams support its conical roof, offering an unrestricted open area capable of seating hundreds of spectators. The place is adorned with artifacts, paintings, sculptures, carvings and tapestries, collected by the co-directors or donated by those who came to appreciate them and their work. The stage area consists of a basic proscenium with extensions to create a multitude of presentational options. On the technical side, lighting, sound and special effects are controlled from a booth constructed along the left-hand wall. From the time when the first stereo system was installed in the Lodge to accommodate Saturday night dances, Ben always seemed to find reasons to be messing about with the equipment. Now there is this booth crammed with switches and levers. I don't recall ever attending a function in Phoenix, and I attended many, when he was not directing technical operations from the booth, peering through the windows that look out onto both the stage and the audience, or popping out to give yet another set of direction to whoever was operating the main floods from an elevated platform at the back. Jock, on the other hand, always seemed to gravitate toward the stage.

Like all of the developments at Haven-by-the-Sea, this remarkable facility is an expression of Wong and McKeen, their relationship and their work. In their seminars, they constantly encourage participants to bring the self forward and the public performance, whether spontaneous or rehearsed, can be an ideal vehicle for channeling expression and containing risk. A multitude of costumes and props are available for all who wish to tremble on the edge of their own creations. In the Phase Programs, and on special occasions like Christmas and New Year, these performances are incorporated into talent shows and improvised plays that attract appreciative and, at times boisterous, audiences drawn from the Haven community. In those days, many of these productions were directed by the legendary Trish Grainge, a multi-talented drama therapist and workshop leader from Vancouver. While the consummate performer and the polished performance are highly regarded, the neophyte who summons up the courage to walk into the spotlight to play a part, recite a poem, sing a song, play an instrument or dance to a well-worn recording, can always be assured of an equally enthusiastic response from all who are there to bear witness.

As we strolled past the Raven building and on toward Phoenix, my mind drifted back to a time in the Phase One program when my own thespian fantasies were front and centre. Struggling to find the essence of my missing self, I came to the conclusion that I was no more than an actor in my own life, a performer walking the boards of other people's expectations. I was determined to uncover the person behind the persona but no matter how many times I found myself groping around in the darkness, I could find no sign of my spirit. The energy that was my life became heavy and ponderous. At this point I dragged myself to a meeting with Ben and, with no concern for the words I was using, I told him of my crisis. He placed his hands on my cheeks and raised my head until our eyes met. "You might want to consider the possibility that the actor *is* you," he said. Such is the genius of Bennet Wong. The following day, I strutted around the Haven property dressed as a medieval troubadour, strumming on a three stringed lute and singing bawdy songs to anyone with a heart to listen. "Good to see you being yourself," said Ben as we passed each other in the woods. "Fuck you very much," I replied and continued along my circuitous pathway to authenticity.

As we filed into Phoenix and took our seats for the first round of birthday celebrations, I wondered how many others had similar stories to tell. I didn't realize that over the next two days I was actually going to hear many of them. Some were told on stage, brief anecdotes, poems, dances and musical compositions, all expressing some aspect of the performer's experience at Haven. Others were shared informally, around meal tables and at spontaneous gatherings that sprang up everywhere around the property. The scheduled entertainment was spectacular and heart warming. The people from Taiwan sang in their own language and performed traditional Chinese dances. Accomplished musicians like Tom Northcott, Morry Stearns and David Aitken sang songs for the occasion and Haven's favorite entertainer, the inimitable Peter Joyce, brought the house down with his deadpan humor.

Toward the end of the afternoon's proceedings a huge crate was carried into the building and onto the stage amidst a flurry of excitement. One of the four carriers breathlessly explained that, despite many obstacles along the way, they had finally managed to convince Canada Customs to release the package in time for the party. In an atmosphere of hushed anticipation, Ben and Jock slowly and meticulously removed the protective packing to reveal an exquisite oriental screen carved in oak and set with precious stones. It was a gift commissioned by the Shuih Li Liuh Foundation in Taiwan. When all the remnants of the crate had been removed, Ben and Jock stood on either side of the screen and beamed with delight. The audience oohed and aahed, finally breaking into spontaneous applause. Later that evening, with the screen proudly on display in the corner of the auditorium, the crowd danced to the music of a band led by drummer Justin McKeen, son of Jock.

The following morning people gathered in Phoenix. Ben and Jock talked about PD Seminars and their lives at Haven-by-the-Sea. Others rose to reflect upon their own experiences and offer birthday wishes in their own way. Jack Sproule contributed a moving blessing to the occasion and Xanon Jenson sang a hymn with the voice of an angel. But, for me, the most memorable moment came when a man from Taiwan rose to his feet. "I used to think of myself as Chinese," he said, "and later, when the world seemed like a much bigger place, I began to think of myself as a Buddhist. But now, as I sit here with all of you in this room I know that, above all, I am a human being. Thank you." Then, he sat down. I reached over, took Judith's hand, and cried. Suddenly, my reasons for writing this book had become clear.

During the years that brought the twentieth century to a close the programs of PD Seminars continued to expand in many diverse directions. Workshops for people interested in writing, dancing, music, psychotherapy, relationships and organizational development were added to the curriculum. Many program graduates became successful workshop leaders, some creating their own variation on the basic themes. Meanwhile, increasing numbers of people were coming to Haven to simply relax in this peaceful spot by the ocean, enjoy the fine food, swim in the pool, hike or cycle around the island and languish in the hot tubs. All received the same warm and respectful hospitality.

But the old timers began to sense that something was amiss. It seemed to them that the conjoined spirits of Ben and Jock no longer presided over the daily life at Haven-by-the Sea. More and more they saw them delegating the work to others while becoming preoccupied with their personal projects. They wrote books. First came *The Manual for Life*, a review of their philosophical and theoretical perspectives. This was followed by *The Relationship Garden*, a treatise on human relationships drawn from their own experience. Jock published a collection of his poems in *As it is in Heaven* and Ben's well-loved stories were brought together in a volume entitled *In and Out of Our Own Way*. They travelled. They went off to eastern Europe with Maria Gomori and made frequent trips to New York where they indulged in their love of the theatre. They continued to maintain their commitments in the Far East and took the time to visit other countries like Laos and Vietnam. They studied languages. Through the use of an interpreter, Marie Lam, their Eastern workshops were translated into Cantonese and Mandarin and, in typical fashion, Jock dedicated himself to serious study, attending classes in Chinese at Malaspina University-College. As always, he was an outstanding student. They danced. Under the direction of a professional instructor, classes in ballroom dancing were held each week in the Phoenix auditorium and they participated enthusiastically. Again this revived a passion in Jock. He found himself a teacher and, while Ben beamed with approval and admiration in the background, he committed body, mind and spirit to the art of modern dance. And, throughout it all, they continued to lead Phase programs and special interest workshops under the auspices of PD Seminars.

Meanwhile, their closest friends and associates knew that there was trouble brewing and they watched anxiously as the storm clouds gathered. Once again, events that took place twenty-five years earlier were centred around allegations of sexual impropriety with Jock as the alleged perpetrator and Ben as the alleged accomplice. While some of the supporting cast remained the same, the accusations, and the woman who made them, were completely separate from the video tape affair that brought the storm some years earlier.

On the advice of their lawyers, Jock and Ben kept the matter to themselves, offering only perfunctory responses to anyone bold enough to ask questions. People gossiped, as people do, but there was no public debate and people waited, friends and foes alike, knowing that this particular drama was going to be played out in public, to wit, the Supreme Court of British Columbia. Those closest to the accused knew that, despite appearances, the mingling of hurt and anxiety on the inside was intense. The energy between them and the rest of the world became uncharacteristically stifled as they prepared themselves, emotionally and pragmatically, for their ordeal. Their sense of being unjustly accused weighed heavily upon them. Some, who knew little or nothing of these circumstances, saw this as a sign of their dwindling passion for their work with PD Seminars.

The months leading up to the court hearing were filled with apprehension and, above all, caution. In consultation with Ben and Jock, I suspended my work on the book fearing that it might stir the pot even further. I resigned myself to the possibility that this work might never be finished, let alone published. There was nothing to do but wait.

When the Supreme Court ruled that Drs. Bennet Wong and Jock McKeen were acquitted on all charges I, like so many others, sighed with relief. But there was nothing to rejoice about in this grim affair where nobody won and everybody lost. Whenever the sword of justice is thrust into the tender flesh of human relationships, all parties are left carrying the scar. As Ben and Jock left the courtroom to be confronted by the anger of their accusers, it was clear that, in human terms, nothing had been resolved.

In October 1999, I had a call from Jock to say that Ben had

been hospitalized with a serious heart condition. This turn of events came as a shock to those who had come to regard him as the personification of health and well-being, a man through whom energy flows freely. I will let Ben tell his own story:

In October, 1999, in the middle of a 'Relationship' workshop that Jock and I were leading at Haven, during a very emotional interaction that was occurring, I suddenly felt a pressure in my chest, accompanied by profuse perspiration and a sense of weakness. Not wanting to interrupt what was happening, I quietly left to lie down on the floor in the adjacent room. In a few minutes, Jock and another physician group leader were by my side, diagnosing my symptoms as cardiac angina. Through a rapid series of events, I was rushed to Nanaimo and hospitalized for treatment of cardiac insufficiency. I failed my stress test on the treadmill, thus placing me on the waiting list for an angioplasty (wherein a long catheter is inserted in an artery in my wrist and directed to the coronary arteries where a balloon is inflated to ream out the vessel) which is performed in Victoria.

Ideally, I should have had this procedure done immediately. But as you are aware, this being British Columbia, I had to wait in the hospital for almost three weeks, moving from bed to bed as they would become available. Actually, although I continued to have some difficult symptoms of pain, I could have taken care of myself at home, with the help of nitroglycerine tablets. However, if I left the hospital, I would have lost my place in the queue of patients awaiting angioplasty. So I was subject to a sort of forced bed rest for three weeks.

In the hospital, part of my time was occupied with visits with Jock each evening, getting updated on the process of 'our' group that he was leading at Haven by himself. It was gratifying to learn that I was not an 'essential' part of our work together. However, I continued to interact with the participants through the messages sent back and forth through Jock— sort of group leading from a distance.

A 'crunchy' issue arose over a commitment we had to put on

a weekend workshop in Seattle. Unfortunately, the date coincided with the date of my angioplasty in Victoria. Jock and I had long talks about 'commitment' versus personal considerations, ultimately opting to fulfill our commitments. This meant that Jock would not be by my side during this mildly risky procedure; son Randy and Father Jack had sworn that they would be there, so Jock and I both agreed that he should proceed with the workshop in Seattle (which he did). This little episode precipitated fervent criticism from some close friends who were very concerned about me. They seemed to suggest that if Jock was not by my side when I needed him the most, it would indicate some deficit of loving. Strangely, to both of us, that Jock was prepared to fulfill our commitments by himself (and that I preferred that he do so) was an indication of the depth of our love! Few people seem to understand or appreciate this.

Most of my time in hospital was occupied with getting to know the ever changing population of patients. I often felt as though I was leading a group on the ward. It is evident to me that wherever I go, I bring my pattern of aiding people to communicate, wanting them not to feel isolated or frightened.

When I was quiet and alone, my thoughts centred around an attempt to 'understand' just why I (of all people) was not well. I started off by reasoning that the energy and message of the heart was related to caring, loving and joining. If this be so, I was firmly convinced that I had no 'blocks' in this area. I believe that I love easily and readily. My sense of compassion is and always has been strong. My heart symptoms made no sense. Then one day when Jock was visiting me, he made a move to help me with some little thing; I immediately took over and did it myself.

That reminds me of when I was being wheeled back into my recovery room after the angioplasty The nurse was questioning Randy and Jack at my bedside. She said, "Who will take responsibility for seeing about his recovery (medications etc.)?" Randy laughs as he remembers me rallying out of my post-procedure drugged state to rise up in bed to answer firmly "I will."

So these episodes gave me a strong clue into the genesis of my heart blockage. As I said, I think that I can love easily; but I don't easily receive love from others! The resonance (not the flow of energy) is incomplete. Hence the constriction— precipitated by the static situation of being unwilling to receive. It's not as though I have not known this; I just never had connected things in this way. Jock and I have been aware of this as a problem from the very beginning. I have even tried to practice fitting into his arms to be held, since I had so little experience of such as an infant and child. We just never took this to the somatic level of understanding.

The angioplasty (and stent) performed in November 1999 was a success. Over the three weeks of hospitalization (on a low fat diet), I lost close to twenty pounds of weight. Strangely enough, so did Jock! Now both of us continue with a low fat diet. And each day, we exercise on our treadmill and rowing machine. Furthermore, Jock has undertaken ballet lessons, and practices over an hour each day, above and beyond our hour each morning. We both feel great.

Given what the man himself has said, the question of whether being open to the love of others might have nurtured his spirit through times of rejection or hostility is redundant. For myself, I hope that this loving soul finds ways to receive and cherish the love that I believe surrounds him. Bennet Wong knows love from the inside out and there is little chance that he will ever be deceived or seduced by its self-seeking impostors. He will continue to be admired, worshipped and, in some cases deified, but these are crude objectifications with which he is very familiar, thanks in part to the revelations of Jock McKeen. But he has also known a quality of love from the outside that has no other agenda than its own expression, thanks largely to the loving soul of Jock McKeen.

(July, 2000) The last major event I attended at Haven prior to the completion of this book was the eightieth birthday celebration for their friend Maria Gomori. Once again the place was packed and the feeling within the Phoenix auditorium was much like the tenth birthday of Haven six years before. It was as if the spirit had returned. Ben and Jock dedicated themselves to the celebration of this remarkable woman's life, drawing out the history of her escape from persecution in Eastern Europe, her quest for knowledge and her personal and professional commitment to others.

In honor of this occasion, Jock performed a solo dance. It was a piece choreographed especially for him by his teacher and first performed publicly at the Exhibition of Modern Dance in Winnipeg in June 2000. At that performance nobody in the audience was aware that they were watching a fifty-three year old physician with relatively little formal training and absolutely no professional experience. It didn't matter; the crowd and the professionals standing in the wings applauded enthusiastically. Ben watched in admiration. Two months later Jock reprised the piece for a dance festival in Nanaimo and the response was the same.

I watched him glide across the floor, his face set, his eyes dark and intense, his body stretching and recoiling, drawing the music through him, transforming every nuance into motion, sometimes precise and tentative, sometimes bold and decisive. I had the strange sense that we were now seeing what Bennet Wong has always been willing and able to see. It wasn't that I suddenly grasped some new version of Jock McKeen out there. Even many of the movements were oddly familiar, the sweeping of the arms, the delicate turning of the wrists to reveal the open palms, the light prancing steps that would transport him easily from one place to another. These I recognized from countless seminars, workshops and stage presentations. The difference was in the intensity, the way in which he seemed to inhabit his own expression without ever pausing to step outside. I was spellbound. I had come to know Jock McKeen as a complex man of many talents and remarkable qualities but now I understood for the first time that, behind it all, Jock McKeen dances. When his performance ended and he turned to face his audience there was a brief silence. It was as if he, and we, needed a moment to shift from one reality to another. I saw what I judged to be the reflection of that transition in his face, from the stoic stare of the dancer to the shy smile of the schoolboy. When he bowed his head to acknowledge his audience the place erupted. Amid the pandemonium, I looked around in search of Ben and there he was, standing alone on the platform outside his beloved booth. The grin on his face told the story.

A large crowd has gathered around the freshly painted totem pole that stands on the lawn facing the western ocean. A steady stream of latecomers trickles down from the residences, circles the assembly and becomes absorbed into its ranks. Ben and Jock stand in a small space that has been delineated at the centre, talking with a large Maori women dressed in her magnificent traditional costume. Next to them, a young man carefully inspects the totem, occasionally moving his hands across its deeply carved surface and nodding his head as if to express some form of approval. He is Michael Runningwater, a First Nations man who came to Haven on a Vision Quest. He is the one who suggested that the totem pole needed attention and invited the participants of a New Horizons program to join him in a repainting ritual. And so it came to be.

People talk in hushed tones. Out on the horizon, the sun is beginning its final descent into the water, blending sky, mountains and ocean in a soft pink glow. The crowd becomes silent. From the Lodge the wail of the Highland Pipes breaks into the stillness. "Amazing Grace." This is the sunset ceremony that takes place at Haven every summer's evening. The pipes continue to play until the sun disappears. As the first cool breeze sweeps gently off the ocean, the crowd turns its attention back to the totem pole.

After a few brief words from Jock and Ben, Michael Runningwater stands beside this proud symbol of his native culture and talks to the crowd about the unity of Man and the

Creator. It is a heartfelt and moving message that seems to bring the gathering into an even closer communion. As the applause dies down, the Maori woman moves to the edge of the inner circle, faces the ocean and begins to sing. Her voice, rich and powerful, soars into the air and out over the water. At first, the crowd seems stunned by the sheer splendor of the voice that rises from their midst, but gradually the sense of unity returns and the gathering begins to sway to its deep and subtle rhythms. The crowd demands an encore, followed by another.

Now there is a moment of silence. People seem to be waiting for the next event to occur but nobody moves to take the initiative. From one sector by the hot tubs comes the ripple of Chinese voices chattering in some form of discussion, the distinctive melody of their voices drawing attention from all sides. Silence again. Suddenly the voices are back, this time in unison, singing a song from their homeland. People sit down to listen; the spontaneous oriental choir remains standing. More applause. A smaller group, Canadians this time, delivers a hesitant rendition of "Four Strong Winds" that grows stronger with each verse. Still more applause. And so it goes on.

It is dark now, but the lights from the Lodge are sufficient to spread a gentle warmth over the company. People are still making music, singing folk songs from around the world. A group of Chinese people stand in a circle, holding hands, moving to the pounding rhythms of a frantic guitarist from Chicago. Two young Caucasian girls, one aged about five the other seven, stand close by, keeping their distance yet watching intently as the oriental dancers struggle to create steps appropriate to the music. They are laughing. A woman in the circle releases her hand from the man to her right and turns, inviting the girls to join them. The elder one puts a finger to her mouth and takes a small step back. Her younger sister hesitates for a moment and then moves to take the woman's hand. Before the circle has time to reconnect, the elder girl rushes forward, grasps the woman's other hand, and reaches out to the unattached man at the end. The circle closes and the dance goes on.

EPILOGUE

We live alone, each striving to keep Heaven and Hell apart, yet always knowing they are one. Once, huddled together and cowering from nature's fury, we stood on guard against the savagery of our neighbors in the forest. Now, cloaked in the regalia of our races, nations, religions and beliefs, we have armed ourselves against the hostile forces of the cosmos, and those that rage within our own hearts. In the name of love, we demand to know that we will not be left abandoned in this godforsaken place. But still, the stuff of our aloneness continues to seep up through the cracks.

We die alone. However scented and sanitized our fortresses, the stench of death is always in our nostrils. However much we flex our muscles over this fragile planet, the earth will reclaim our flesh and our souls will cry out for the gods to take us safely home. Once, the saviors were many. They filled our bellies and stood beside us in the darkness, and it served us to know them well. Then, entranced by our own ascendancy, we cast them in our image, corralled them on a mountain, and negotiated their favors with our accomplishments. But our imaginations eclipsed their magic and, taking their earth-bound powers for ourselves, we placed our restless souls before an even mightier God—one who would take us beyond the grave and into the everlasting light. Only in the service of such a God would we wear the shroud of humility. And to this indivisible God, we handed over our terror and held our humanness in cold storage until, in the inevitable moment of our aloneness, He would walk at our side. And we remained as lost children, calling upon our appointed priests to keep our God of "love" aware of the arrangement and urging our heroes to show us the way.

Now the splendor of our accomplishments has changed the face of this God also and the priests have moved to the laboratory. They tell us of the human genome, but nothing of what lies within our hearts. And while they reach out to measure the distances among the stars, the distance between one human being and another remains a mystery. The institutions and rituals designed to foster our illusions of identity, purpose and belonging are becoming obsolete and empty. Our leaders scramble to satisfy our insatiable demands for security while our medical experts, with their cures and opiates, can do nothing to heal the pain that lies deep within, or the fear that haunts us from cradle to grave. And, at the very core of it all, we find that even our most primary relationships have been pressed into the service of our boundless insecurity. So we, and the planet that sustains us, sink further into dis-ease and, as the illusions pale and tarnish, we wonder what will be left to keep our troubled species together.

At the other end of the spectrum, when we step out into the vast silence of space, we return, not as gods or conquerors, but as humble spectators. For, in truth, there is nowhere for us to go. Though we may dream of a new life elsewhere, we find ourselves as alone in the universe as we are in the diminishing orbits of our individual lives. Should we find others "out there," we would turn them into gods or slaves, for we have no way of relating as equals to any of nature's creations. Through our wondrous new advances in communications, we can talk to each other across the globe with the push of a button; the irony being that we have nothing new to say. So we repeat the same old utterances, seek the same old assurances, make the same old demands and we remain alone, isolated, and justifiably fearful for the future of our planet and ourselves. And we wonder if the cosmos cares, or is even curious, about how we, the most noble of savages, have become the most ignoble of gods.

Now, the prophets are crying out that something is terribly wrong and that, whatever is broken, must be fixed. We call upon our leaders to take charge, our scientists to find the answers and our distant God to intervene. Reactionaries demand a return to what was—small communities, agrarian lifestyles, family values—but, even if such reversals were possible, we surely would be destined to repeat our history and return to the same place. Meanwhile, behind it all, the shadow of the Grim Reaper continues to beckon each life to its inescapable end. Desperate selves call for a renewed commitment to a God who will assure their souls of ascension. Others carve out their pathways to Nirvana by transcending the mundane, to seek harmony within the pristine gardens of serenity. Both are committed to the belief that we must leave the earthly slagheap to find purification somewhere among the stars.

But what if nothing is wrong, nothing needs to be fixed? What if each and every moment of our evolving life contains an infinite storehouse of possibilities through which we might find ourselves within the life and spirit of the cosmos? Perhaps, we are that life and that spirit, all that we fear and that we embrace, our health and our sickness, our aloneness and our relatedness, our life and our death, our Heaven and our Hell?

If this were so, then we would discover a reality that promises no cure for our ailments and urges us to take responsibility for the reclamation of our own souls. But who, in his or her right mind, would give up all hope of salvation, to take the light from the hands of God and strip Satan of his dominion over the darkness? Only some strange inversion of the human psyche would urge us to depose the masters who claim our obedience as the price of their protection. Our journey is short. Better that we leave such matters to the philosophers and the insane, while we walk toward the sepulcher with our eyes closed and our hearts in bondage.

Yet those curious or desperate souls who have peered into the unknown continue to talk of a strange and paradoxical realm. They tell stories of a blissful relatedness to be found at the centre of unbearable aloneness. They speak of a life set free through the unqualified acceptance of death. With words that stun the mind and stir the heart, they describe a universe contained within a grain of sand and a single moment that stretches out into eternity. Prophets or psychotics? Heroes or heretics?

If we had the courage to stand for a while in such a moment, what would we say to ourselves and each other about our humanity? If we could cast aside our telescopes, cosmic charts and scriptures to see our lives in relation to all things, what transformations might take place? If we could come to know the living presence of the God that we have pushed out into the heavens, whose voice would speak to our souls?

And, should we be curious about these things, where would we go to find that place of revelation? If it lies somewhere within us and among us, then surely it will present itself whenever two people stand face-to-face, with no other agenda than the simple quest to see and be seen. For the only external reference for one human life is contained within another human life. And, if there is any pathway to immortality, it must take a direct route through the shadows that stand in our way. But the courage we will need is not that of doing battle with a hostile universe. As Paul Tillich has so eloquently reminded us, we are concerned here with "the courage to Be."